Populism in the Civil Sphere

Populism in the Civil Sphere

Edited by

Jeffrey C. Alexander, Peter Kivisto,
and Giuseppe Sciortino

polity

First published in 2021 by Polity Press

Polity Press
65 Bridge Street
Cambridge CB2 1UR, UK

Polity Press
101 Station Landing
Suite 300
Medford, MA 02155, USA

ISBN-13: 978-1-5095-4473-8
ISBN-13: 978-1-5095-4474-5 (pb)

A catalogue record for this book is available from the British Library.

Typeset in 10.5 on 12 pt Sabon by
Servis Filmsetting Ltd, Stockport, Cheshire
Printed and bound in Great Britain by CPI Group (UK) Ltd, Croydon

The publisher has used its best endeavours to ensure that the URLs for external websites referred to in this book are correct and active at the time of going to press. However, the publisher has no responsibility for the websites and can make no guarantee that a site will remain live or that the content is or will remain appropriate.

Every effort has been made to trace all copyright holders, but if any have been overlooked the publisher will be pleased to include any necessary credits in any subsequent reprint or edition.

For further information on Polity, visit our website:
politybooks.com

Contents

CONTENTS

Notes on the Contributors

Jeffrey C. Alexander is Lillian Chavenson Saden Professor of Sociology at Yale University and the founder and codirector of Yale's Center for Cultural Sociology. Among his recent writings are *What Makes a Social Crisis? The Societalization of Social Problems* (2019) and *The Drama of Social Life* (2017).

Ateş Altınordu is assistant professor of sociology at Sabancı University, Istanbul. His work focuses on religion and politics, secularization and secularism, science and society, and the cultural analysis of contemporary Turkish politics. His articles have been published in the *Annual Review of Sociology*, *Politics and Society*, *Kölner Zeitschrift für Soziologie und Sozialpyschologie*, and *Qualitative Sociology*.

Nelson Arteaga Botello is research professor of sociology at the Facultad Latinoamericana de Ciencias Sociales México and Faculty Fellow at the Center for Cultural Sociology at Yale University. His research interest is focused on violence and culture. His publications include "It was the state: The trauma of the enforced disappearance of students in Mexico," *International Journal of Politics, Culture, and Society* (2018) and *Sociedad, cultura y la esfera civil* (edited with Carlo Tognato, 2019).

Werner Binder is assistant professor of sociology at Masaryk University. After studies in Mannheim, Potsdam, and Berlin, he earned his PhD at the University of Konstanz with a thesis on the Abu Ghraib Scandal. He is author of *Abu Ghraib und die Folgen* (2013), coauthor of *Ungefähres* (with Bernhard Giesen, Marco Gerster, and Kim-Claude Meyer, 2014), and coeditor of *Kippfiguren* (with Kay Junge, Kim-Claude Meyer, and

Marco Gerster, 2013). His fields of interest include sociological theory, cultural sociology, and textual and visual methods of interpretation.

Henrik Enroth is associate professor in the Department of Political Science at Linnaeus University. He has a broad interest in social, cultural, and political theory. His recent work has appeared in journals such as *International Political Sociology*, *European Journal of Social Theory*, and *American Journal of Cultural Sociology*, and in *The Nordic Civil Sphere* (edited by Jeffrey C. Alexander, Anna Lund, and Andrea Voyer, 2019).

Bernadette Nadya Jaworsky is associate professor of sociology at Masaryk University. Her books include *The Boundaries of Belonging: Online Work of Immigration-Related Social Movement Organizations* (2016) and *The Courage for Civil Repair: Narrating the Righteous in International Migration* (edited with Carlo Tognato and Jeffrey C. Alexander, 2020). Her current research focuses on media coverage of refugees, border narratives, and the migration–populism nexus.

Andrew Junker, PhD, teaches sociology at the Chinese University of Hong Kong and is Hong Kong Director for the Yale-China Association. His research interests include social movements, Chinese society, and social theory. He is the author of *Becoming Activists in Global China: Social Movements in the Chinese Diaspora* (2019). Andrew's work has also appeared in journals such as *Sociology of Religion Quarterly*, *Mobilization*, *American Journal of Cultural Sociology*, and *Modern China*, and in *The Civil Sphere in East Asia* (edited by Jeffrey C. Alexander, David A. Palmer, Sunwoong Park, and Agnes Shuk-mei Ku, 2019).

Peter Kivisto is the Richard A. Swanson Professor of Social Thought at Augustana College and Recurring Visiting Professor at the University of Helsinki and the University of Trento. Recent books include *The Trump Phenomenon: How the Politics of Populism Won in 2016* (2017) and *Solidarity, Justice, and Incorporation: Thinking through The Civil Sphere* (edited with Giuseppe Sciortino, 2015). He is the editor of the forthcoming two-volume *Cambridge Handbook of Social Theory*.

Małgorzata Kolankowska received her PhD from the University of Wrocław. She has published the book *Czerwony i Czarny: Polski spór medialny o Chile (Red and Black: Polish Media Discourse on Chile)* (2013) and various papers on Spanish and Polish media and culture. She is interested in the interdisciplinary study of the relations between media, culture, and cultural and collective memory.

María Luengo is associate professor at Universidad Carlos III de Madrid. Her work focuses on journalism and the civil sphere. Recent book publications include *The Crisis of Journalism Reconsidered: Democratic Culture, Professional Codes, Digital Future* (coedited with Jeffrey C. Alexander and Elizabeth Butler Breese, 2016). Her research has appeared in *European Journal of Communication, Media, Culture & Society, Journalism,* and *Journalism Studies,* among others.

Jason L. Mast is research fellow at the Normative Orders Research Center at Goethe University Frankfurt. He researches politics, culture, and cognition. He is coeditor of *Politics of Meaning/Meaning of Politics: Cultural Sociology of the 2016 US Presidential Election* (with Jeffrey C. Alexander, 2019) and the author of *The Performative Presidency: Crisis and Resurrection During the Clinton Years* (2013).

Marcus Morgan is a sociologist at the University of Bristol. His research spans social theory, cultural sociology, and political sociology. He is the author of *Pragmatic Humanism: On the Nature and Value of Sociological Knowledge* (2016) and coauthor of *Conflict in the Academy: A Study in the Sociology of Intellectuals* (with Patrick Baert, 2015). His recent article about movement intellectuals is published in *The Sociological Review* (2020).

Giuseppe Sciortino teaches sociology at the University of Trento. His interests include social theory, migration studies, and cultural sociology. Among his latest publications are *Solidarity, Justice, and Incorporation: Thinking through The Civil Sphere* (edited with Peter Kivisto, 2015) and *The Cultural Trauma of Decolonization: Colonial Returnees in the National Imagination* (edited with Ron Eyerman, 2020).

Carlo Tognato is visiting scholar at the Center for the Study of Social Change, Institutions and Policy by the Schar School of Policy and Government at George Mason University and faculty fellow at the Center for Cultural Sociology at Yale University. His research focuses on civil reconstruction in conflict and postconflict societies, deradicalization, counterradicalization, depolarization, civil courage, and civil intervention.

Celso M. Villegas is associate professor of sociology at Kenyon College. He has published on middle-class formation in populist politics in the

Philippines, South Korea, Venezuela, and Ecuador. He recently published "The middle class as a cultural structure: Rethinking middle-class formation and democracy through the civil sphere," in the *American Journal of Cultural Sociology* (2019) and is working on a book project on the middle class and democracy in the developing world.

Preface and Acknowledgments

This volume is the fifth in an ongoing series of works whose aim is to elaborate, revise, and globalize civil sphere theory (CST), a sociological perspective on solidarity and democracy developed by Alexander, his collaborators, and students over the last three decades. Prior volumes have examined Latin America, East Asia, and the Nordic nations. There are volumes in preparation devoted to India and Canada. A parallel line of development is thematic: beside populism, another volume has explored the implications of CST for the analysis of radical action; another will soon deal with the connection between CST and the notion of cultural trauma.

The contributors to this project convened for two days of intensive conversation in New Haven in June 2019. The gathering was sponsored by the Edward J. and Dorothy Clarke Kempf Memorial Fund established by Yale University's Macmillan Center for International and Area Studies, as well as by the International Migration Laboratory of the University of Trento.

Alexander and Sciortino have collaborated on matters of theory, culture, and politics since the mid-1980s; two decades later, Kivisto joined with them to work on theorizing the civil sphere. As a Yale doctoral student, Anne Marie Champagne has played a pivotal role in organizing these civil sphere projects, and her role in the present collaboration has been indispensable. Nadine Amalfi, Program Coordinator for Yale's Center for Cultural Sociology, admirably administered and organized the June 2019 New Haven conference. Bernadette Nadya Jaworsky, a contributor to this volume, also served, and not for the first time, as a highly professional editor.

We wish to record our gratitude to the contributors to this volume, whose perseverance, political engagement, and theoretical curiosity have made our collaboration not only intellectually exciting but also personally pleasurable. We also wish publicly to express our appreciation to John Thompson, editor and publisher at Polity, for his steady support.

Jeffrey C. Alexander
New Haven, Connecticut

Peter Kivisto
Rock Island, Illinois

Giuseppe Sciortino
Trento, Italy

April 2020

Introduction

The Populist Continuum from Within the Civil Sphere to Outside It

Jeffrey C. Alexander

A specter is haunting our contemporary societies. Its name is "populism," in quotation marks, because scholars can't agree about what it is. Except for one thing: populism is a deviation from democracy, the source of the precarious position so many Western and Eastern, Northern and Southern societies find themselves in today. This volume aims to break the Gordian knot of "populism" by bringing to bear a new social theory, and, in doing so, suggest that the normative judgment about this misunderstood social and political tendency needs reconsidering as well. Populism is not a democratic deviation, but a naturally occurring dimension of everyday democracy. In moral terms, it can be good *or* bad, a force for democratic civil repair *or* a force that undermines its very possibility. As the contributions to this volume demonstrate, populism is a continuum stretching from the political left to the right, fatal to democracy only on the extremes.

The effort to properly understand populism depends on better comprehending contemporary democratic societies and their discontents. Sociologists have rarely been interested in theorizing democracy, and when they have done so, they have had great difficulty (e.g., Bourdieu 1996) understanding the cultural-cum-institutional complexities that can sustain and destroy it. Like the extremist populists who are the civil sphere's enemies, sociologists have reduced democracy to material interest (Lipset 1981 [1960]); to the masses against the elites (Schumpeter 1942; Mills 1956; Michels 1962 [1911]); to the battle of less privileged over more privileged classes (Moore 1966; Wright 2015); to the flourishing of grassroots associations against institutions and states (Putnam 1996; Skocpol 2003); to the triumph of public altruism over private greed (Habermas 1989 [1963]).

This volume offers an alternative. Civil sphere theory (CST) is a

1

sociological model of democracy that incorporates the cultural turn that began transforming the social sciences four decades ago (Alexander 2006). Contributors to *Populism in the Civil Sphere* bring this new theoretical light to bear on the dark political and cultural forces that menace democracies around the world today.

Since democratic political theory first emerged 2,500 years ago, it has rested upon the Socratic notion that virtues like rationality, honesty, altruism, cooperation, autonomy, and liberty are the fundaments of democratic life (Skinner 1978). CST sees such qualities, by contrast, not as existential virtues upon which democratic governments can be built, but as cultural structures central to democratic discourse. Powerful signifying references, they have to be instantiated in social life via symbolic performances and communicative and regulative institutions. CST does not conceptualize democracy only as governmental structure, but rather, in Dewey's (1966 [1916]) words, as a way of life. Democratic life depends less on voting procedures and legal rights – in and of themselves – than on the social existence of a performatively compelling, emotionally vital, and morally universalizing sphere of solidarity, one in which feelings for others whom one will never meet fuels moral recognition and emotional compassion. It is only upon the base of such a moral-cum-emotional form of civil community that the all-important communicative and regulative institutions of democracy can be sustained.

Political democracy depends on feelings of mutual regard, on experiencing a shared solidarity despite deep antipathies of interest and ideology. There must be some historically specific vision of a shared universalism that transcends the particularisms of class, race, gender, sex, region, and nationality. Because populism is highly polarizing, it has the phenomenological effect of stoking anxiety that civil solidarity is breaking apart. Left populists often feel as if civil solidarity is an illusion, that democratic discourse is a fig leaf for private interests, and that the social and cultural differentiation that vouchsafes the independence of the civil sphere merely reflects the hegemony of narrow professional interests or those of a ruling class. Right populists often share the same distrust of, even repulsion for, the civil sphere. What seems civil to the center and left, like affirmative action or open immigration, they call out as particularistic; honored civil icons, such as Holocaust memorials, they trash. Can the sense of a vital civil center survive such criticism and censure from populism on the left and on the right (Schlesinger 1949; Alexander 2016b; Kivisto 2019; Luengo and Ihlebæk 2020)? Only if civil solidarity can regulate ideal and material conflict in such a manner that enemies become frenemies, that sharp antagonism is moderated such that agonism thrives (Mouffe 2000).

Populist rhetoric on both the left and the right is inflammatory in tone and demagogic in style, but is it actually antidemocratic, as social scientific students of populism so often have claimed (Arditi 2005; Moffitt 2016; Müller 2016)? Populists rail against fake news and vested interests that hide the truth, describing only their own side as rational, independent, and honest. Populists call opponents enemies and liars. They attack their opponents as selfish, and brag relentlessly about their own generosity. Populists claim to expose secret conspiracies against "the people," portraying themselves, their parties, and their governments as transparent and responsive, as open for all to see. Populists attack elites and privilege, dividing society into us and them; aligning themselves with the people, they vow to drastically change what they see as the biased and polarizing rules of the social and political game.

While these snapshots of democratic drama can be decidedly alarming normatively, empirically they are part and parcel of every civil sphere. What we see and hear is the binary discourse that has, from the beginning, dynamized and polarized, enabled and constrained, actually existing civil spheres (Alexander 2010; Alexander and Jaworsky 2014; Kivisto 2017; Morgan this volume, Chapter 1). Throughout the history of modern democracies, and ancient ones as well, populist leaders, on both right and left, have "worked the binaries" to suggest that their opponents are civilly incapable, that only they themselves are willing and able to act on behalf of the people's side, to be rational, autonomous, open, cooperative, and altruistic, thus allowing solidarity and liberty to be maintained or restored (Kazin 2006; Judis 2016).

The clear and present danger that extreme, radically populist movements pose to contemporary democracies does not emerge from rhetoric that pits the putatively civil against the uncivil. It comes, rather, when such simplistic yet inveterate binarism is employed to constrain the autonomy of the civil sphere institutions that sustain democratic life. The making and unmaking of civil solidarity, its upgrading and downgrading, depends on connecting the sacred-democratic and profane-authoritarian sides of democratic discourse to ongoing events and struggles in particular times and places. This is the work of civil institutions. The binary discourse of the civil sphere makes democracy broadly meaningful; what communicative and regulative institutions do is to articulate this abstract language in the here and now. Public opinion polls, associations, and journalism (Alexander 2016a) are media of civil communication. They specify democratic values and discourses on behalf of civil solidarity, issuing highly public judgments about the civil and uncivil character of interests, groups, movements, and events, judgments that are, in principle, independent of popular leaders and parties who claim to speak for the people directly. The other filtering mechanisms of civil spheres are regulative, the institutions of voting and electoral competition, the impersonal structures of office, and the precedent-bound and rights-based matrices of law.

The elites who organize and represent these communicative and regulative institutions are civil sphere agents. In principle, their ideal and material interests coincide with the defense of the civil sphere's autonomy. Civil sphere agents (Alexander 2018) mediate the charismatic claims of populist leaders and movements, intertwining interpretation and coercion, producing universalizing, quasi-factual evidence that can symbolically pollute, arrest, and sometimes even incarcerate those who are deemed the civil sphere's antidemocratic enemies. Investigative journalists and crusading attorneys are ambitious for glory, but of a democratic kind. Their hopes to become civil heroes can be stymied by populist demagogues, whether of the right or left, who believe that only they themselves can speak for the people – in immediate rather than mediate ways, as vessels rather than instruments of civil power, as the only true representative of the general will. When the representational process at the heart of modern struggles for power comes to be centered in a single man or woman rather than in relatively independent communicative institutions, you have Caesarism (Weber 1978). When symbolic power is less civil than plebiscitarian, it becomes a modern Prince (Gramsci 1959), a vanguard political party that crystallizes the voice of the people via *their* media, *their* associations, *their* constructions of polls, *their* judges and courts. Buoyed by their presumption to speak for the people, radically populist demagogues seek not only to monopolize the communicative power of symbolic representation, but also to destroy the organizational autonomy of regulative institutions. Radical populists cannot tolerate independent courts interpreting and applying civil discourse. They cannot allow independent media elites to decide who and what is more rational, more honest, and more true, on the one hand, and more secretive, more hidden, and more threatening on the other. The ethical, universalizing regulation of office is deeply compromised, power becomes personal and familial, and corruption becomes quotidian, not deviance but everyday life. Patrimonial domination (Arteaga Botello and Arzuaga Magnoni 2018; Tognato 2018), the culture of deference (Choi 2019), and the fusion of the leader's mystical and earthly bodies (Reed 2020) are alternatives to civil power, to constitutionally regulated office, and the kind of critical, independent communicative and regulative mediation that underpins an ethic of responsibility (Weber 1946 [1922]). Elections become more like spectacles than moral performances, empty showcases for staging dramaturgic

4

authority instead of occasions for agonistic displays of binding democratic discourse.

Under such conditions of discursive constriction and institutional fusion, the presuppositions of a universalizing solidarity become severely constrained. Civil spheres shrink, reflecting the primordial qualities of the leader and party who have grabbed representational power. The civil sphere loses its dialectical dynamism. Rather than moving back and forth across the ideological continuum, populism stops at the far-left or the far-right side. Instead of continuously shifting moments in the pendulum swing of social and cultural history, populism becomes a punctum (Barthes 1981), a point that halts the movement and threatens to break the marvelously subtle, powerful but flexible, finely tuned but always precarious democratic machine.

The centrality of affectual and moral solidarity to CST can give the misleading impression that the theory is idealistic in the empirical sense of "what is," not only in the normative sense of "what should be." This is not the case. Civil solidarity is established in real time and place, in a territory from which others are excluded and by founders and successors who view their own primordial qualities as essential to the demonstration of civil capacity. The sacred "discourse of liberty" that defines democratic motives, relations, and institutions is binary. Its values are relational, contrasted to and intertwined with a "discourse of repression" that lays out the anticivil profane. The individuals, groups, and institutions associated with such polluting qualities must be excluded if civil societies are to survive. Tension between the sacred light that inspires liberty and the polluted darkness that triggers repression lies at the very heart of the civil sphere, which means real existing civil spheres are far from realizing the civil-democratic ideal of normative theory. Amidst the anticivil fragmentations and complexities of modern times, the independent power of civil spheres is always contested and compromised. In political theory, the antidemocratic tradition is portrayed as the antirepublican backlash initiated by such thinkers as Hobbes (Skinner 2018), leavened with counter-Enlightenment thought (Berlin 1979; Alexander 2019a), giving birth to the war against liberty celebrated by Carl Schmitt (1996 [1932]), which continues to animate modern life today. CST projects the same historical struggle, but conceptualizes liberty and repression as the linked binaries of a single discourse, one that continuously forms the backdrop of struggles for democracy and against it.

The paradox that animates CST is that universalizing solidarity and the civil power drawn from it are always and everywhere compromised by modern society's centrifugal parts. The civil sphere promises and helps produce solidarity and democratic integration, yet the noncivil institutions surrounding it, and the internal strains generated by the contradictions of space, time, and function, make the expansion of civil solidarity equivocal and the achievement of civil power precarious. Inclusionary, civil solidarity moves on tracks that cross those along which more exclusionary and primordial solidarities run. The expansion of democratic justice invariably also intertwines with restrictions produced by classes, regions, religions, ethnicities, genders, sexualities, and races. As a normative ideal, the civil sphere is peaceful; as a sociological phenomenon, the civil sphere is contradictory, tense, tumultuous, and contentious. It is still possible, nonetheless, to sustain the reality of a vital center. The more democratic the society, the more heightened and passionate the arguments over who is civil and who is not, who is deserving of incorporation and who isn't. The empirical operation of actually existing civil spheres is never at one with the normative code of democratic solidarity, yet it can still strongly reinforce it.

Populism is triggered by contradictions at the heart of actually existing civil spheres. The historical founders of democratic regimes form elite status groups that seek to restrict civil qualities to certain kinds (their own) of ethnicity, race, religion, gender, sexuality, and class (Alexander 2006: Chapter 8). The institutions and values that abut civil spheres, controlled by elites whose ideal and material interests are noncivil, often intrude into civil spheres, reconstructing the binary codes so they align with their own (Alexander 2018). These structures of civil exclusion and anticivil domination are continuously challenged by populist movements seeking to enlarge incorporation and strengthen civil power (Laclau 2005). Left populist movements call out elites; demand more civil and democratic distributions of economic wealth; and attack racial, religious, ethnic, and regional barriers. They work to purify the compromised civil sphere, to overcome fragmentation and polarization in the name of a more civil cohesion and a more virtuous people. Rather than being dangerous to democracy, such left populist movements reflect nothing more, and nothing less, than the everyday processes of actually existing civil spheres. Dividing the virtuous people from corrupt elites can be a powerfully restorative discourse, despite the often-overweening simplifications and sanctimonious rhetoric of some progressive groups.

As Marcus Morgan and Celso Villegas suggest (Chapters 1 and 2), left populist movements have been at the heart of social liberalism and social democracy (Marshall 1965), making liberal government into a more democratic way of life. The dangers associated with left populism – which have so often allowed it to be conflated with populism on the radical right – have to do with how fast and how far it goes. Demands for repairs in the name of the people – what Swedish social democracy calls "the people's home" (Engelstad and Larsen 2019; Enroth and Henriksson 2019; Enroth this volume, Chapter 8) – can become dangerously impatient, increasingly intolerant of those who defend the material and ideal interests of groups ensconced in the status quo. Progressive populist leaders can become hungry not only for civil power, but also for their own. Left populist parties can come to consider themselves a virtuous vanguard. In the name of righteously progressive reform, they attack the independence of the civil sphere's communicative and regulative institutions, squirming under the pressure of independent criticism and opposing political and legal claims. In this way, populism moves from supporting expanded democracy to supporting repression; the class or ethnic or religious communities left populists once represented as deserving of civil incorporation become new elites who define exclusionary boundaries in their own name. In Chapter 3, Ateş Altınordu analyzes just such a populist inversion in Turkey. Originally representing the excluded and disempowered Sunni religious majority, the seemingly democratic and civilly oriented AKP promised civil repair and incorporation, its leader, Recep Tayyip Erdoğan, hailed as a heroic figure of democratic emancipation. Even as it achieved power and initiated reforms, however, this left populism moved to make Sunni Islam the new core group, primordializing national solidarity in an anticivil way, repressing civil associations, and putting once independent communicative and regulative civil institutions under control of the party state. Nelson Arteaga Botello, in Chapter 4, investigates a similar, if decidedly more secular, process in Mexico. In the name of civil repair, Manuel Lopez Obrador had for decades organized populist challenges to Mexico's crippling economic inequality, patriarchal politics, and ethnic and racial pollution. After he assumed power in 2018, however, Obrador set about undermining the culture and institutions of Mexico's civil sphere, restraining independent associations, challenging critical journalism, and instituting controversial social policies that sidestepped electoral institutions. In Chapter 10, Jason Mast demonstrates that it was not only racial othering but a populist challenge to economic inequality and corrupt elites that fueled Donald Trump's presidential triumph in 2016 (cf. Berezin 2019). After his election, however, Trump deployed his civil capital in the service of harshly anticivil rhetoric, supporting increasingly authoritarian policies. Left populists lead movements that begin as demands for expanding democracy, but once in power, they can consolidate regimes and shape their discourses in ways that constrict and endanger it. This has almost always been the case when left populism equates civil repair with social revolution, as the repeated declension of twentieth-century communism into dictatorship tragically showed (Pérez

2018). As Andrew Junker demonstrates in Chapter 9, moreover, it is also the story of the left populist movements that often continue to convulse revolutionary governments after the dictatorship of the proletariat has been achieved.

Reformist movements that initiate policies to enlarge civil capacity can be understood as "frontlash" movements, occupying a position in social life akin to the role of avant-gardes in art.[1] Leftward social change upends traditional ways of life: the primordial qualities and lifestyles within which civil qualities are experienced and understood; the status elites to whom deference had heretofore been extended; the institutional elites whose competence had guaranteed power and respect. It is along these strained and fearful fault lines that backlash forms. The dialectic of frontlash/backlash is endemic to civil repair and democratic life: Reformation/Counter-Reformation; Enlightenment/anti-Enlightenment; communism/fascism; secularism/fundamentalism; NAACP/Ku Klux Klan. Radically right populist leaders attack the anomie, corruption, and emptiness of modern society, promising to restore solidarity and "the community we have lost" (Enroth, Chapter 8). Nativist, primordial solidarity pushes back against recently incorporated out-groups, such as nonwhites, non-Christians, and nonnationals. Frontlash populism produces backlash populism, whose aim is to constrain, restrict, or roll back the expansions of the civil sphere.

Backlash against progressive changes permeates real existing civil spheres. Conservatism is the rightward movement of a social pendulum that seems, to many, to be swinging dangerously to the left. *Civil* conservatism often has, in fact, the unintended effect of rebalancing a civil sphere, restoring confidence in the existence of a vital center such that frontlash movements live to fight another day. Conservative theorists from Burke (2009 [1790]) to Oakeshott (1975) cautioned against the dangers of radical social change in favor of more incremental and measured forms of civil repair, but such concerns for maintaining a vital center are not exclusive to the right. In the middle of the frontlash whirlwind of the 1960s, the rock 'n' roll group Buffalo Springfield warned in a hit song against "battle lines being drawn," singing "nobody's right if everybody's wrong." Describing "a thousand people in the street, singing songs and carrying signs, [who] mostly say, hooray for our side," the rockers cautioned radical protestors, "it's time we stop, children, what's that sound, everybody look what's going down" ("For What It's Worth," 1967). Another immensely popular act, Simon & Garfunkel, cautioned "slow down, you move too fast" ("Feelin' Groovy," 1966). Two tumultuous years later, the Beatles sang, "you say you want a revolution, well, you know, we all want to change the world. . . . You

8

say you got a real solution, well, you know ... we're doing the best we can," concluding, "all I can tell you is brother you'll have to wait" ("Revolution," 1968).

For right populism as for left, it is a question of how far, how fast? Backlash populism can become determinately anticivil, moving not just to the right but far to the right, reducing civil standing to core group status, polluting those who until recently were outsiders, inciting street violence, and establishing authoritarian regimes that do not just modulate but undermine civil values and institutions. In Chapter 8, Henrik Enroth describes the movement from a "slow down, you move too fast" conservative response to Swedish social democracy, which seemingly endorsed civil values even while redefining them, to a more virulently anti-immigrant, nationalistic, and racist movement that aims to undermine the bounds of Swedish democracy itself. In Chapter 7, Werner Binder shows that the Alternative for Germany (AfD) started as an economically conservative Euroskeptic party, only later becoming transformed into a radical right populist movement that is stridently nationalist, pollutes immigrants, attacks cosmopolitan elites, issues coded anti-Semitic messages ("dog whistles"), and harkens back to Nazi times. In Chapter 5, María Luengo and Małgorzata Kolankowska show how conservative reaction against the Polish Solidarity movement, and the secular, cosmopolitan democracy it created, became an aggressively divisive, radically anticivil force. Acting in the name of the "real Polish people," the PiS has attacked the founding elites of the postcommunist regime, reduced civil solidarity by equating it with primordial bonds of Catholicism and nationalism, and sharply restricted the autonomy of Poland's communicative and regulative institutions. In Chapter 6, Bernadette Nadya Jaworsky describes the Czech Republic as yet another postcommunist European nation that has become engulfed in backlash against civil repair and democratic transformation. Less explicitly racist and more secular than other radical right movements, Czech "center populists" foment an engulfing fear of immigrants in a nation that has actually received scarcely any, a reaction Jaworsky describes as "nativism without immigration."

Endemic to the structure and process of civil spheres, Luengo and Kolankowska suggest (Chapter 5), is a "continuum that stretches from a civil conservative moment to anticivil authoritarian populism." The same continuum stretches to the left as well, from civil progressivism to antidemocratic populism (see Figure 0.1). It is not populism in and of itself but impatience, radicalism, and extremism – and deeply structured blockages to more democratic pathways of repair – that push populist movements to the left and right sides of this continuum, inverting the

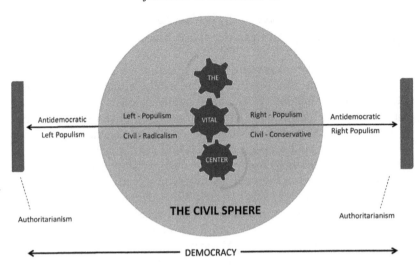

Figure 0.1 *The populist continuum*

sacred and profane sides of the binary discourse of civil society, repressing the autonomy of civil institutions, and endangering the vital center that civil spheres must sustain.

If the chapters that follow delineate the grounding of populism in the contradictions of civil spheres, they also have a great deal to say about the how of populism, not only the what and why. How do the populist performances of protest gain cultural and political success? Nothing is determined; structural change is the emergent result of skillful performances by populist political and cultural actors on the public stage of history. What primes citizen-audiences to welcome antidemocratic performances? What makes them receptive to the inversion of democratic forms?

One reason is the almost entirely neglected phenomenon of transgression (Altınordu, Chapter 3). Influenced by Nietzsche, Georges Bataille (1990 [1957]) argued that breaking free from the restrictive confines of the sacred represents an ever-lurking social temptation (cf. Alexander 2003). As Freud (1961 [1930]) explained, civilization produces deep discontent. Pornography and violence are standards of popular culture. Extremist populism provides an opportunity for audiences to experience the thrill of evil, to "get beyond" what seems to many the boring and routine banality of the everyday.

Another social force that primes citizen-audiences to welcome extreme populism is cultural trauma (Alexander 2011; Eyerman 2019). While frontlash and backlash movements create powerful and embittering experiences of loss, symbolic and material, crucial questions remain: What exactly is the danger? Who are the perpetrators? Who are the victims? Populist movements, their leaders and intellectuals, can be understood as engaging in "trauma work" that addresses such questions in fateful ways. As Luengo and Kolankowska point out in Chapter 5, Polish people experienced severe destabilization in the century and a half after 1795, when Prussia, Russia, and Austria appropriated and partitioned their national territory. After a brief period of independent flourishing in the early twentieth century, the Polish nation was snuffed out once again, first by the Nazis and then by the Soviets. In 1940, the Soviets secretly engineered the mass murder of 22,000 Polish military officers and intelligentsia, a devastating cultural trauma that came to be known as "Katyń" (Bartmanski and Eyerman 2019). Then, only a few years after the rise of Solidarity and the collapse of the USSR allowed the unexpected restoration of Polish independence, the Smolensk air tragedy killed dozens of leading national figures and conservative politicians, including Poland's president. In the midst of these highly destabilizing events, Luengo and Kolankowska suggest, the fallen president's twin brother, co-leader of the conservative populist party, organized a cultural-cum-political process that blamed progressive and secular democrats for the trauma, threatening civil institutions, and pushing the government toward the extreme right.

One widely ramifying effect of such trauma work is the inversion of collective memories. As Werner Binder shows (Chapter 7), West Germany's post-1960s civil sphere had been rooted in memory structures that narrate Nazism as evil, condemn racism, and mandate a radically more democratic government and inclusive solidarity. Portraying Eastern Germans as victims of first Soviet then West German colonization, AfD leaders have performed new memory structures that sacralize the earlier, pre-unification period that Binder calls "pre-postcommunism," reducing Nazism to the trivial and mundane, a mere blip in the otherwise long and great history of the German nation.

These investigations into populist process are not simple renditions of path dependency. They represent contributions to a cultural sociological model of historical explanation.

Grand theorizing about modernity has been skeptical about the discourse and practice of liberty, viewing it not only as merely formal and empty of moral substance, but also as fueling repressive organizational structures like capitalism and bureaucracy. Reification, commodification, rationalization, egoism and anomie, disciplinary power – such interpretations have been organized around what Ricoeur (1970) described as "the hermeneutics of suspicion." In some part, this dark narrative accurately reflects the tragic history of Europe, during which civil spheres, deeply scarred and fragmented, rarely were able to sustain civil control over communicative and regulative institutions. In some other part, however, this narrative reflects a failure of theoretical and normative imagination, a dearth that has, albeit in a very different manner, extended to Anglo-American social theorizing as well. In the United States and the United Kingdom, where democratic life has proved much more durable than in Europe, macrosocial theories about this antirepressive line of modern development are not that easy to find. Pragmatist, microsociological, and mezzo-level institutional theories have not been able to translate the social experience of these democratic societies into persuasive theoretical form.

To effect such translation has been the ambition of CST, inspired by the democratic spirit of pragmatism, informed by European macro-theory, and following the path of the cultural turn. After the Holocaust had transformed genocide into a universal evil, after black civil rights movements in the United States and South Africa had mounted mammoth mobilizations against racial domination, after second-wave feminism had laid down the challenge to patriarchy, CST emerged in the wake of "1989," as a wave of democratic optimism swept the world. The over-throw of state communism in Central and Eastern Europe and the Soviet Union, and of right-wing authoritarianism in Latin America, offered an object lesson in liberty. If not the end of history, a new golden age of democracy had surely begun.

But history is cunning, and that new age of equipoise (Burn 1964) proved short-lived. Over the course of the last decade, the third after the magical one launched in 1989, there has been growing moral unease, emotional anxiety, and social instability. Feeding off this combustible bile, antidemocratic movements have flourished, newly liberal govern-ments have become "illiberal democracies," and, in even the most stabile democratic capitalist and social democratic nations, liberty has become threatened.

Civil spheres can be "populized" into antidemocracies, but such transformative destruction does not happen in the blink of an eye. As right-wing and sometimes left-wing forces push backward (or forward) to demagoguery, activists draw from the sustaining cultural and institu-tional powers of civil spheres and push back. Protecting the vital center, protestors and elites alike defend the autonomy of critical discourse; the right for journalists and legal authorities to make independent interpreta-tions; and the need for civil power, via voting and office, to maintain control over the coercive power of the state. Such resistance is not the principal focus of these essays, but neither is it neglected. Luengo and Kolankowska (Chapter 5) analyze how, in Poland, a powerful trauma of democratic regeneration was triggered by the political assassination of the liberal, antipopulist mayor of Gdansk. Arteaga Botello (Chapter 4) reconstructs the antipopulist narrations of Mexico's centrist and conservative newspapers facing the rise of Obrador. Villegas (Chapter 2) documents how the Philippine middle class has become a carrier for civil authority and has vigorously resisted both right and left populism in recent decades. Binder (Chapter 7) shows that German support for radical right populism has mostly been confined to the traumatized, disgruntled, mostly Eastern minority. Portraying Tony Blair's New Labour as a neoliberal backlash movement against civil incorporation, Morgan (Chapter 1) shows how, in the 2017 UK national elections, Jeremy Corbyn's felicitous performance of left populism made a surprisingly successful case for civil repair.

Engaging in social performances to expose the defects of contemporary civil spheres is what populism is all about. The danger is that such protests against injustice will become concentrated in a single leader and party. The representation of civil capacity must be disbursed among the communicative and regulative institutions that filter, pluralize, and agonistically specify the principles that allow incorporation and exclusion. For, as John Dewey (1966 [1916]: 87) argued over a century ago, "more than a form of government," democracy is "primarily a mode of associational living, of conjoint communicated experience."

Note

1   Here and elsewhere in this Introduction, I draw from Alexander (2019b).

References

Alexander, J. C. (2003) A cultural sociology of evil. In: J. C. Alexander, *The Meanings of Social Life: A Cultural Sociology*. New York: Oxford University Press.

Alexander, J. C. (2006) *The Civil Sphere*. New York: Oxford University Press.

Alexander, J. C. (2010) *The Performance of Politics: Obama's Victory and the Democratic Struggle for Power*. Oxford: Oxford University Press.

Alexander, J. C. (2011) *Trauma: A Social Theory*. Cambridge: Polity.

Alexander, J. C. (2016a) Introduction: Journalism, democratic culture, and creative reconstruction. In: J. C. Alexander, E. B. Breese, and M. Luengo (eds.) *The Crisis of Journalism Reconsidered: Democratic Culture, Professional Codes, Digital Future*. New York: Cambridge University Press.

Alexander, J. C. (2016b) Progress and disillusion: Civil repair and its discontents. *Thesis Eleven* 137(1): 72–82.

Alexander, J. C. (2018) The societalization of social problems: Church pedophilia, phone hacking, and the financial crisis. *American Sociological Review* 83(6): 1049–78.

Alexander, J. C. (2019a) Raging against the Enlightenment: The ideology of Steven Bannon. In: J. L. Mast and J. C. Alexander (eds.) *Politics of Meaning/Meaning of Politics: Cultural Sociology of the 2016 US Presidential Election.* London: Palgrave Macmillan.

Alexander, J. C. (2019b) Frontlash/backlash: The crisis of solidarity and the threat to civil institutions. *Contemporary Sociology* 48(1): 5–11.

Alexander, J. C. and B. N. Jaworsky. (2014) *Obama Power.* Cambridge: Polity.

Arditi, B. (2005) Populism as an internal periphery of democratic politics. In: F. Panizza (ed.) *Populism and the Mirror of Democracy.* London: Verso.

Arteaga Botello, N. and J. Arzuaga Magnoni. (2018) The civil sphere in Mexico: Between democracy and authoritarianism. In: J. C. Alexander and C. Tognato (eds.) *The Civil Sphere in Latin America.* Cambridge: Cambridge University Press.

Barthes, R. (1981) *Camera Lucida: Reflections on Photography.* New York: Hill & Wang.

Bartmanski, D. and R. Eyerman. (2019) The worst was the silence: The unfinished drama of the Katyn massacre. In: R. Eyerman (ed.) *Memory, Trauma, and Identity.* New York: Palgrave.

Bataille, G. (1990 [1957]) *Literature and Evil.* London: Boyars.

Berezin, M. (2019) On the construction sites of history: Where did Donald Trump come from? In: J. L. Mast and J. C. Alexander (eds.) *Politics of Meaning/Meaning of Politics: Cultural Sociology of the 2016 US Presidential Election.* London: Palgrave Macmillan.

Berlin, I. (1979) The counter-Enlightenment. In: I. Berlin, *Against the Current.* Princeton: Princeton University Press.

Bourdieu, P. (1996) *The State Nobility.* Cambridge: Polity.

Burke, E. (2009 [1790]) *Reflections on the Revolution in France.* New York: Oxford University Press.

Burn, W. L. (1964) *The Age of Equipoise: A Study of the Mid-Victorian Generation.* London: Allen & Unwin.

Choi, J. (2019) South Korea's presidential scandal and civil repair. In: J. C. Alexander, D. A. Palmer, S. Park, and A. S.-M. Ku (eds.) *The Civil Sphere in East Asia.* New York: Cambridge University Press.

Dewey, J. (1966 [1916]) *Democracy and Education.* New York: Free Press.

Engelstadt, F. and H. Larsen. (2019) "Nordic civil spheres and pro-civil states. In: J. C. Alexander, A. Lund, and A. Voyer (eds.) *The Nordic Civil Sphere.* Cambridge: Polity.

Enroth, H. and M. Henriksson. (2019) The civil sphere and the welfare state. In: J. C. Alexander, A. Lund, and A. Voyer (eds.) *The Nordic Civil Sphere.* Cambridge: Polity.

Eyerman, R. (ed.) (2019) *Memory, Trauma, and Identity.* New York: Palgrave.

Freud, S. (1961 [1930]) *Civilization and Its Discontents.* New York: Norton.

Gramsci, A. (1959) *The Modern Prince and Other Writings.* New York: International Publishers.

Habermas, J. (1989 [1963]) *The Structural Transformation of the Public Sphere: An Inquiry into a Category of Bourgeois Society.* Cambridge, MA: MIT Press.
Judis, J. B. (2016) *The Populist Explosion: How the Great Recession Transformed American and European Politics.* New York: Columbia Global Reports.
Kazin, M. (2006) *A Godly Hero: William Jennings Bryan.* New York: Random House.
Kivisto, P. (2017) *The Trump Phenomenon: How the Politics of Populism Won in 2016.* Bingley: Emerald Publishers.
Kivisto, P. (2019) Populism's efforts to delegitimize the vital center and the implications for liberal democracy. In: J. L. Mast and J. C. Alexander (eds.) *Politics of Meaning/Meaning of Politics: Cultural Sociology of the 2016 US Presidential Election.* London: Palgrave Macmillan.
Laclau, E. (2005) *On Populist Reason.* London: Verso.
Lipset, S. M. (1981 [1960]) Elections: The expression of the democratic class struggle. In: S. M. Lipset (ed.) *Political Man: The Social Bases of Politics.* Baltimore: Johns Hopkins University Press.
Luengo, M. and K. A. Ihlebæk. (2020) Restaging a vital center within radicalized civil societies: The media, performativity, and the *Charlie Hebdo* attack. In: J. C. Alexander, T. Stack, and F. Khosrokhavar (eds.) *Breaching the Civil Order: Radicalism and the Civil Sphere.* New York: Cambridge University Press.
Marshall, T. H. (1965) *Class, Citizenship, and Social Development.* New York: Free Press.
Michels, R. (1962 [1911]) *Political Parties: A Sociological Study of the Oligarchical Tendencies of Modern Democracy.* New York: Free Press.
Mills, C. W. (1956) *The Power Elite.* New York: Oxford University Press.
Moffitt, B. (2016) *The Global Rise of Populism: Performance, Political Style, and Representation.* Stanford: Stanford University Press.
Moore, B., Jr. (1966) *The Social Origins of Dictatorship and Democracy: Lord and Peasant in the Making of the Modern World.* Boston: Beacon.
Mouffe, C. (2000) *The Democratic Paradox.* London: Verso.
Müller, J.-W. (2016) *What Is Populism?* Philadelphia: University of Pennsylvania Press.
Oakeshott, M. (1975) *On Human Conduct.* Oxford: Oxford University Press.
Pérez, L. M. (2018) *La Joven Cuba*: Confrontation, conciliation, and the quest for the civil through blogging. In: J. C. Alexander and C. Tognato (eds.) *The Civil Sphere in Latin America.* Cambridge: Cambridge University Press.
Putnam, R. D. (2001) The strange disappearance of civic America. *American Prospect* 7: 24.
Reed, I. A. (2020) *Power in Modernity: Agency Relations and the Creative Destruction of the King's Two Bodies.* Chicago: University of Chicago Press.
Ricoeur, P. (1970) *Freud and Philosophy: An Essay on Interpretation.* New Haven: Yale University Press.
Schlesinger, A. M. (1949) *The Vital Center: The Politics of Freedom.* New York: Houghton Mifflin.
Schmitt, C. (1996 [1932]) *The Concept of the Political.* Chicago: University of Chicago Press.
Schumpeter, J. A. (1942) *Capitalism, Socialism, and Democracy.* New York: Harper and Brothers.
Skinner, Q. (1978) *The Foundations of Modern Political Thought*, Volumes 1 & 2. Cambridge: Cambridge University Press.

Skinner, Q. (2018) *From Humanism to Hobbes: Studies in Rhetoric and Politics.* Cambridge: Cambridge University Press.

Skocpol, T. (2003) *Diminished Democracy: From Membership to Management in American Civic Life.* Norman: University of Oklahoma Press.

Tognato, C. (2018) The civil life of the university: Enacting dissent and resistance on a Colombian campus. In: J. C. Alexander and C. Tognato (eds.) *The Civil Sphere in Latin America.* Cambridge: Cambridge University Press.

Weber, M. (1946 [1922]) Politics as a vocation. In: H. H. Gerth and C. Wright Mills (eds.) *From Max Weber.* New York: Oxford University Press.

Weber, M. (1978) Appendix II: Parliament and government in a reconstructed Germany. In: M. Weber (ed.) *Economy and Society,* Vol. 2. Berkeley: University of California Press.

Wright, E. O. (2015) *Understanding Class.* London: Verso.

1

Populism's Cultural and Civil Dynamics
Marcus Morgan

This chapter interrogates dominant definitions of "populism" found in the social sciences, focusing on the term's conceptual utility in understanding recent changes in Western polities. Though populism is typically treated as a deviant form of politics, this chapter finds that it in fact holds remarkable continuities with conventional politics, and indeed culture more generally. It argues that these more general cultural processes can be illuminated by cultural sociology, just as the more specific but still routine political processes can be illuminated by civil sphere theory (CST). The chapter goes on to argue that when populism is understood as a formal mode of public signification, rather than a substantive ideology, the substance it signifies becomes crucial to determining its civility. It suggests that while populism can certainly have anticivil effects, there is nothing inherent in it that precludes it from also acting to promote civil repair.

Populism: Politics as Usual

One way of characterizing "culture" is as an ever-evolving repository of efforts toward meaning-making. Meaning-making reduces complexity so that communication – and, if successful, understanding – can take place. Politics likewise aims toward reducing complexity so as to legitimate efforts to shift, or maintain, power relations. This chapter will suggest that what has been called "populism" may exaggerate these processes but does not break from them. CST teaches us how this reduction of complexity typically takes place on the basis of organizing meaning around a binary structure of motives, relationships, and institutions (Alexander 2006: 53–67). This chapter will argue that populism is unique only in its accentuation of these binaries; its drawing of an explicit frontier between a construction of the "people" – in progressive populism one that is inclusively defined, in regressive populism exclusively so (Judis 2016) – and an "elite" (Laclau 2005; Mouffe and Errejón 2016; Mouffe 2018); its development of polarization; its provocation to an audience to decide on which side of the boundary it chooses to stand; and its invitation toward this audience to actively participate in the unfolding political drama, typically through direct, rather than representative, democratic mechanisms.

While the chapter agrees that useful definitions exclude as much as possible to increase their conceptual grasp, it argues that the difficulty of coming up with a tight, restrictive definition of "populism" is that it is not as tight, restrictive, or discrete a phenomenon as most academic or journalistic accounts present it as being. Rather, populism is best understood as an intensification of routine political dynamics, which are themselves part and parcel of more generalized cultural mechanisms through which social signification takes place; group identities are forged in relation to those they oppose; and collective agency is mobilized in the process. Populism can therefore be understood within CST, which can itself be understood as following the structures and dynamics of meaning-making illuminated by cultural sociology. From this perspective, different examples of political behavior come to be seen as more or less populist by degree, rather than populist or not by categorization.

The chapter reviews five key features shared across dominant definitions: populism's binary logic, its ideological nature, its moralism, its antirationalism, and its antipluralism. It both critiques each feature's definitional centrality and stresses each feature's continuities with "conventional" politics, demonstrating how populism functions in ways that CST, and cultural sociology, would expect it to. The chapter concludes that populism is compatible with both progressive and regressive political programs, and indeed suggests that if certain criteria are met, there is nothing precluding it from playing a similar role to the social movements described in Part III of *The Civil Sphere* (Alexander 2006) in translating restricted political grievances into more universal civil issues, in the process initiating civil repair. Overall, the chapter argues against the independence not only of populism, but also of politics more generally, from culture. It suggests that beyond violence and coercion, though frequently even within these, power, and the struggles that take place over it, must be seen as operating always and everywhere through culture.

Populism as a Binary

Attempts to define populism have a long, fraught, and inconclusive history (e.g., Berlin et al. 1968; Ionescu and Gellner 1969). So much so that many sociologists have deemed it wisest to set the ill-defined term aside (e.g., Jansen 2011). Events over the past few years have, however, predictably propelled the concept back into academic and public prominence. Though the phenomenon is arguably ancient, the term itself was first used to describe two political movements that appeared at the end of the nineteenth century: in Tsarist Russia, a largely unsuccessful effort at mobilizing peasants against feudal exploitation, and in the United States, the movement of mainly farmworkers who rose up to challenge, via the People's Party, what they conceived of as an elite of bankers, railway owners, and the two-party system of government. In a similar sequence of events to that witnessed with the term more recently, it was first used as a pejorative in the US context, but was then quickly reappropriated by those it was intended to deride. Although some prominent observers argue that the movement around the American People's Party fails the test of a genuine populism (e.g., Müller 2016: 88), there is fairly broad consensus that one feature it illustrates – a politics built around a dualistic opposition between an "elite" and some conception of a "people," with whom legitimate democratic power belongs – is the basis on which a minimal definition might be agreed upon (e.g., Kriesi 2014; Bonikowski and Gidron 2016; Mudde and Kaltwasser 2017; Eatwell and Goodwin 2018).

However, while the basic notion that "the binary structure of populist claims is largely invariant" (Bonikowski and Gidron 2016: 7) may apply to left-wing populisms, it is not so clear that it holds for right-wing variants. Judis describes how while left-wing populism conforms to dominant definitions in its "dyadic" structure, consisting of "a vertical politics of the bottom and middle arrayed against the top," right-wing populism, by contrast, is "triadic," in that such "populists champion the people against an elite that they accuse of coddling a third group" (2016: 15).[1] This third group is typically a minority, often an immigrant group or some other relatively powerless scapegoat, revealing an exclusivist – i.e. nonuniversalizing and therefore noncivil – deployment of the "people" in such types of populism.

Definitions based upon the binary criterion also assume there is such a thing as a large-scale politics attempting to win the electoral consent of a polity that does not rely upon some construction of the "people." This assumption is questionable. Democracy is, after all, supposed to be a system in which a people rule (*demos-kratos*), and even in nondemocratic or "formally democratic" systems, lip service is usually paid to this idea to ensure legitimation (Habermas 1976: 36–7). To operate effectively, such a system must therefore presumably decide who this "people" are. Laclau (2005, 2006) has famously argued that constructing a people constitutes the essence of what politics is. Others have suggested that state-formation itself was only possible through determining a "people" (Skinner 2009: 328; Peel 2018). In republics, "the people" is typically so central to grounding democracy that it becomes the cornerstone of constitutions, as in "we, the people." In exclusionary right-wing manifestations, "naming the people" is also used, but in this instance, as a means of excluding the "third group" that Judis identifies, justifying the conviction that this group, which is not part of the essentialized "people," is therefore undeserving of political representation. In technocracies, the "people" are also implicitly constructed, but in this iteration, often as in need of the enlightened guidance of experts, on the assumption that the people are unqualified to govern themselves.

Liberal politics is hardly immune, although it typically conceives itself as being so. This can be illustrated by the recent calls for a "People's Vote" on Brexit in the United Kingdom. The use of the term "people" here, as in the slogan of the largest march – "Put it to the People" – and in the frequent reference to the number of people on street demonstrations, is unmistakably populist. However, it is arguably a populism against populism; a populism that emerged when a mechanism of direct democracy – a people's referendum on leaving the European Union (EU) – failed to go the way that liberal antipopulists, who generally defend a more representative notion of democracy, had proposed, a matter that was in part blamed on the populist mold in which organized Euroskepticism took shape. More direct democracy was the liberal answer to direct democracy gone awry: we need to listen more to the people – another referendum is required to establish what the people *really* think.

Whether or not there is a paradoxical tension between democracy and populism, as some theorists claim (e.g., Urbinati 2017), there is perhaps a simple cultural reason why it is so hard to imagine a politics that does not construct a people. This is that political life, like cultural life more generally, tends to organize itself around either/or distinctions, which, when it comes to issues of large-scale group identity, translate into distinguishing between an "us" and a "them." In democratic systems (or, as mentioned above, often in nondemocratic ones too), since the "people" is the chief democratic category, who is and who is not part of the people becomes paramount. Awareness of the social organization of the cosmos around binaries, the corresponding poles of which can be aligned with one another through analogy, metaphor, and allusion, has been a mainstay of cultural analysis in the social sciences (de Saussure 1966 [1893]; Lévi-Strauss 1967: 29–54; Barthes 1977; Durkheim 1995 [1912]: 33–9), and one that has been productively developed in *The Civil Sphere* (Alexander 2006: 53–67). One need not advocate a Schmittian account of radical friend–enemy divisions (Schmitt 2007 [1932]) to acknowledge that the discourse of civil society cleaves the world into who or what "is" and who or what "is not."[2] These binaries are of course a simplification of the way things really are, but this does not make them any less present within, or functional for, political or other group identity processes.

Populism as an Ideology

There has long been a social scientific perspective that considers populism to be an ideology (e.g., MacRae 1969), providing an overarching normative worldview. Recent mainstream definitions, however, have watered down this position by tending to agree with Mudde's (2004) view of it being only a "thin-centred" ideology, which contrasts with "thick-centred" ideologies (such as liberalism, socialism, or fascism) in that it has "a restricted morphology, which necessarily appears attached to – and sometimes even assimilated into – other ideologies" (Mudde and Kaltwasser 2017: 6; see also Albertazzi and McDonnell 2007; Stanley 2008; Ruzza and Fella 2009).

This conception can serve a functional role for those who see themselves as occupying an antipopulist center-ground in allowing them to critique both an insurgent left and an insurgent right simultaneously, encouraging a horseshoe theory of politics in which the further one travels in either direction on the political spectrum, the more the two extremes begin to resemble one another. As well as damning the left by association, an effect of this has been allowing movements on the far right to cloak themselves in a more respectable vocabulary than might otherwise have been attached to them, since despite "its ambiguous connotations, the word populism has always been more acceptable than labels like racist or extreme right" (Jäger 2018). However, not only does this lend such tendencies a legitimacy they typically do not deserve, but in defining it as an ideology, populism is asked to carry a weight it cannot bear, resulting in formulations – analyzing the substance of Fidesz's politics alongside Syriza's; Trump's alongside Corbyn's (e.g., Wolf 2017) – that obscure far more than they illuminate. Surely the most salient ideological feature of a politician like Marine Le Pen is her nativism and authoritarianism, not her populism, just as the most significant attribute of a politician like Bernie Sanders is his democratic socialism. If populism is just a byword for being against the status quo, then it functions to permit groups to frame themselves as defenders of antipopulism rather than defenders of the status quo. Conceiving populism as an ideology forfeits its analytic utility by failing to mark out anything useful.

These kinds of difficulties have led some to jettison entirely the notion of populism as ideology – be it thin- or thick-centered – and argue that it is not an "actor-level" phenomenon, but a "speech-level" one, revealing how "politicians often rely on populist language selectively, presenting the same political claims in either populist or nonpopulist terms depending on the audience and broader social context" (Bonikowski 2016: 13). Whether this involves arguing that populism is more akin to a "discourse" (Aslanidis 2016), a "rhetorical strategy" (Bonikowski 2016), a "style" (Ekström et al. 2018), a "stylistic repertoire" (Brubaker 2017), or a "frame" (Aslanidis 2018), this alternative perspective recognizes that populism refers more to the form through which politics is done than to any specific ideological content. Seeing populism in this way ties it to appearance, impression, aesthetics, and, importantly, performance (Moffitt 2016). Adopting this alternative understanding is therefore attractive to a cultural sociological approach, for it allows populism to be set free from debates over substantial content, and yoked instead to the symbolic struggles of civil spheres, and the metadiscourse of civil society through which they occur.

When we understand populism in this performance-based way, we again detect it in places that are unexpected by those who use the term as simply a shorthand for politics they disagree with. Tony Blair (2017), for instance, whose Institute claims to work to push back against the threat from a rising "tide of populism," relied extensively on populist signification while leader of the Labour Party, to the extent that one initially enthusiastic (though quickly critical) cultural theorist, Stuart Hall, came to recognize him as epitomizing populism (1998: 13). The following flourishes from Blair's 1999 Conference Speech might be given as typical examples:

> The future is people. . . . The national creative genius of the British people. But wasted. The country run for far too long on the talents of the few, when the genius of the many lies uncared for, and ignored. . . . The old elites, establishments that have run our professions and our country too long. . . . [T]he elite have held us back for too long. . . . New Labour . . . can modernise the nation, sweep away those forces of conservatism to set the people free. (Blair 1999)

22

The eminently populist slogan "For the Many, Not the Few," now associated with Corbyn's "populist rebranding" of the Labour Party (Stewart and Elgot 2016), found its initial airing during Blair's controversial redrafting of Clause IV (the clause in the Labour Party Constitution that prior to Blair's amendments referred explicitly to the socialistic aim of securing "common ownership of the means of production").[3]

Barack Obama likewise deployed populist language in his various campaigns, and on occasion explicitly identified himself with the term (Obama 2016). The "We" in the slogan "Yes, We Can," for instance, evoked a constructively ambiguous "people." Originally a slogan of Cesar Chavez's United Farm Workers ("*Sí, se puede*"), the phrase was most famously used by Obama in the rousing 2008 speech he delivered in Chicago's Grant Park upon winning the presidency. After telling the assembled crowd that this is "your victory," he concluded his rhetorical tour de force by making the connection explicit: "[W]here we are met with cynicism and doubts and those who tell us that we can't, we will respond with that timeless creed that sums up the spirit of a people: *Yes, we can.*" Eight years later, the phrase provided the name for the archetypal left populist party that grew out of the *indignados* movement in Spain, Podemos.

Mudde and Kaltwasser at moments recognize such continuities between the public performances of populist and (apparently) nonpopulist leaders, but since their understanding of populism is rooted in a substantial conception of ideology, they dismiss them as simply attempts by non-populists "to set themselves apart from other mainstream politicians and (try to) look authentic" (2017: 76). From a cultural sociological perspective, in which politics in mass societies *is* performance (Alexander 2010, 2011; Mast 2012), this distinction makes little sense. Viewing populism as a mode of public signification rather than a thin-centered ideology not only reveals its continuity with other forms of politics but also allows us to see populism as a form of cultural work, a way of narrating "brute facts" and making them meaningful. Its efficacy (or lack thereof) can then be explained through its success in mobilizing the binaries of the civil sphere, attempting to align its own motivations, relationships, and institutions with the positive poles of civil codes and polluting those of its adversaries.

Populism as Moral

A third common theme in recent influential definitions has been to emphasize morality as existing at the core of populism. Mudde and

Kaltwasser claim that "the key distinction in populism is moral" (2017: 35), Bonikowski argues that "populism is based on a rudimentary moral logic" (2016: 12), and Müller suggests that the term should only be used to identify "a particular moralistic imagination of politics" in which the "people" are conceived as morally untainted, whereas the "elites" are understood as morally corrupt (2016: 20). In this manner, populism's tendency to divide the world into "good" and "evil" is deemed to be both reductive, in that it eschews nuance in favor of Manichaeism, and dangerous, in that it excites collective anxieties and resentments rather than providing discursive space for dispassionate assessments of competing courses of action, meaning that "the likelihood of productive dialogue and compromise is reduced" (Bonikowski 2016: 22).

From a cultural sociological perspective, however, using morality as populism's *differentia specifica* is again unsatisfactory. This is because not only are moral ideas themselves seen to be always and everywhere culturally formed (Geertz 1968; Durkheim 1973; Douglas 1983; Morgan 2014), but morals are also recognized as animating almost all other instances of social classification (Durkheim and Mauss 2009 [1903]: 48–52). Processes of moral idealization are, as Stavrakakis and Jäger (2018: 559) point out, "present in nearly all identifications, in all passionate attachments, from love to religion and from cultural taste (distinction) to football"; therefore, they ask, "How could power relations be exempt? Especially since identity and difference, love and hate, play such a significant role in all political identification?" While this point is occasionally acknowledged (e.g., Müller 2016: 38), its consequences fail to be. Political philosophy, including most of the classical cannon – Plato, Aristotle, Kant, Mill, etc. – has long been characterized by an extension of moral philosophy into the public sphere, since both ultimately deal with normative matters of "what should be" rather than "what is." There is no need to agree with Crick's interest-based account of politics (Alexander 2006: 111) to accept his contention that "conflicts, when personal, create the activity we call 'ethics' . . . and such conflicts, when public, create political activity" (Crick 1962: 20).

This continuity between individual, social, and political life, of which populism is a part, can be made sense of through the resources offered by a social science that places symbolism at its center. Once contemporary societies are recognized as alive with the sacred (Durkheim 1995 [1912]: 418–48; Lynch 2012), processes of public symbolization can no longer be presented as supplying flat cognitive maps of the world – a mere semiotic metaphysics – but must instead be seen as "suffused with an aura of deep moral seriousness" (Geertz 1957: 421). Populism's attempt to associate the sacred with a construction of "the people," in which democratic

24

legitimacy rests, and the profane with a construction of "the elite," of course reduces the complexity of the actual world, but the "nuance and ambiguity of empirical actions does not often make an appearance in the public language of civil society" (Alexander 2010: 10–11). Civil society's dichotomies not only organize meaning made elsewhere, but through their relative autonomy as culture structures in fact partially generate this meaning (Alexander and Smith 1993). The struggles that take place around identifying good and evil, and the arraying of events, issues, and figures on either side of this binary, constitute much of what goes on in the civil sphere, and just as populism is said to connect an idealization of the "people" to a vilification of the "elite," so *The Civil Sphere* (Alexander 2006: 193–209) shows how the discourse of liberty and the production of civic virtue are internally connected to the discourse of repression and the production of civic vice. Since this is an empirical and not a normative claim, it is also resistant to the charge that it falls victim to the fallacy of the excluded middle: the question of whether or not binary moral distinctions are nuanced or correct is irrelevant to the recognition that they hold social force.

Indeed, it is clear that the symbolic work involved in the very attribution of "populism" to certain forms of politics, and not to others, is typically itself accompanied by a heavy dose of moralism (Taguieff 1995), to the extent that we may wish to ask "whether or not having become an accusation, it can remain an analytic concept" (Geertz 1973: 194). There is more than a little truth in Fukuyama's (2016) claim that "populism is the label that political elites attach to policies supported by ordinary citizens that they don't like." Others have gone further, arguing that liberal antipopulism in fact hinges upon a substitution of broader political discourse for a narrower moral one. Mouffe (2002: 1), for instance, in an extension of Schmitt's argument that liberalism rests upon an impossible attempt to evacuate the category of the "political," has argued that such approaches mean that ethical deliberation is asked to fill the role of political struggle: "[W]e are now urged to think not in terms of right and left, but of right and wrong."

There are also good reasons why morality in political affairs ought to be welcomed. First, the notion that collective moral resentments are automatically unacceptable in political life, and that reaching a compromise that is prewritten into institutions that already exist is desirable, rules out many of the most valuable political advances – including those discussed at length at the end of *The Civil Sphere* (2006) – as beyond the pale. It threatens to imply the notion that "politics as usual" should form the horizon of politics in general. In apartheid South Africa, rational dialogue with an unjust system was impotent at tackling the predicament that Blacks faced. Legitimation of collective moral grievances with domestic and international audiences, the association of the state with evil, and the association of the freedom struggle with good was far more crucial to winning civil incorporation than processes of public deliberation (Morgan 2018).

Second, politics without a moral element risks transmuting into managerialism, and it is in fact the insistence upon this failed conception of what politics involves – what Sandel (2018) calls "technocratic liberalism" – that helps in part explain the collapse of so many liberal democratic parties in recent years at the expense of populism. Sandel argues that after years of a predominantly neoliberal form of globalization – in which moral and cultural injustices, tied to economic inequalities, have been typically experienced by political subjects as a denial of social esteem – it is important that a clear and progressive moral voice returns to political life. Indeed, he sees such a return as doubly necessary, in that strident moral voices already exist in right-authoritarian populist movements, the seductions of which can only be countered by an equally robust account of the moral imperative of progressive politics. Denying this imperative in the name of a fictitious liberal neutrality not only, by default, cedes moral questions to the sphere of private deliberation, but also feeds the very forces it claims to oppose.

Once again, a feature purported to be unique to populism turns out to in fact be characteristic of politics more broadly conceived, revealing more universal features of the civil sphere, and in fact cultural life more generally. Not only is morality inadequate as a distinguishing feature of populism, but its conscious reintroduction back into politics might also be treated as a welcome development.

Populism as Irrational

Classical social theory was preoccupied with the shift from traditional to modern societies, accompanied by a corresponding shift from myth to reason as the predominant organizational principle of social life. Whether through a movement away from the "theological" through the "metaphysical" toward the "positive" stage, or through processes of "disenchantment" or "bureaucratization," or even "the rational development of productive forces," the classical progressivist assumption was that modernity was defined by a process that – albeit typically with internal contradictions – unleashed and expressed rationality. Although Durkheim (1984 [1893]) was not himself immune to this assumption, as can be seen especially in his early doctoral dissertation on the shifts in

26

the division of labor in society, he nevertheless came to recognize, and especially so in his late work, that "there is something eternal in religion," and that "common sentiments" conveyed through symbols, and sustained through rituals, infused modern life far more profoundly than the modernization stories had allowed for (Durkheim 1995 [1912]: 429).

As the previous section argued, categorical symbolization is rarely a neutral process, and the terms "rational" and "irrational" typically carry moral evaluations. Establishing the irrationality of those with whom one disagrees has proven a time-honored means of pollution. From Arnold's (1993 [1869]: 79) description of the "anarchy" of the "raw and unkindled masses" or Le Bon's (2006 [1896]: 10) account of the crowd as characterized by "impulsiveness, irritability, incapacity to reason, absence of judgement and critical spirit, and exaggeration of the sentiments," which he noted were "almost always observed in beings belonging to inferior forms of evolution – in women, savages, and children," the charge of irrationality has long functioned as a powerful means of exclusion (Foucault 1988).

Perhaps unsurprisingly, therefore, populism is often described as an irrational tempest in the calm waters of rational politics (Goodhart 2017: 57). In the United Kingdom, the Brexit vote was widely treated as an accidental outburst of xenophobic irrationalism, just as Corbyn's initial support was initially explained away as "summer madness" (Toynbee 2015), and later diagnosed as "Corbynmania." As Müller (2016: 1) notes, typically "populists are 'angry'; their voters are 'frustrated' or suffer from 'resentment.'" While Müller (2016: 101) himself avoids such associations, other influential accounts oppose the populist idea of a "general will" to the more "rational process" of political deliberation "constructed via the public sphere" (Mudde and Kaltwasser 2017: 18), characterize populists as specializing "in action" but "rarely attempting deep thought" (Canovan 1999: 15), or else locate the dangers of populism in its tendency "to encourage politics based on fear and resentment rather than informed policy debate" (Bonikowski 2016: 22; see also Rico et al. 2017). Even cultural sociological accounts have located populist motivation in the "allure" of the "irrational" (Wagner-Pacifici and Tavory 2017: 319), though others have correctly recognized that we need not agree with the reasons behind populism to acknowledge that such reasons exist (Gorski 2017: 348).

Relying as it does upon the civil structure that sacralizes reason and profanes its opposites (Alexander 2006: 57), othering populists as irrational helps simultaneously reassure antipopulists of their own reasonability. It also helps avoid uncomfortable questions concerning the links between antipopulist politics and the recent rise of passionate populism they so fear. The discourse of "populism," when used in this undeniably moral way, likely entails the unintended consequence of encouraging the very phenomenon it condemns, since populist sentiments rely upon an image of a distant elite, always ready to counter reports of lived experience with carefully reasoned arguments. We therefore see a "working of the binaries" (Alexander 2010: 89–110) in the very identification of populism as irrational: "Liberal-democratic capitalism has imposed itself as the only rational solution to the problem of organizing modern societies; its legitimacy could be put into question only by 'unreasonable' elements" (Mouffe 1999: 3).

The apparently less-excitable politics with which populism is typically contrasted features in political theory in the contention that fundamental questions and antagonisms can be rationally answered and overcome by public reasoning. This approach is associated most famously with Kant, and was later developed in different ways by Rawls and Habermas. It is also an approach that is critiqued in *The Civil Sphere* (Alexander 2006: 13–17). Turner defends against this critique, contrasting a broken American political sphere in which "politics as performance have so far blocked the emergence of a rational policy of economic and financial reform" with a more rationalistic British one, in which the emotivism of Thatcher is presented as an aberration – "the only example of a recent British prime minister who walked the boundaries and talked the binaries" (Turner 2015: 69). Churchill, who we are told was "undoubtedly the twentieth-century hero of British political life," was apparently "not inclined to conduct domestic political elections on the basis of a moral binary" (Turner 2015: 70). Turner neglects to mention Churchill's record in domestic elections, never having won the national popular vote, and having been promptly voted out of office at the end of World War II – which, with its deeply polarized and emotionally charged atmosphere, Turner (2015: 70) concedes ought to be seen "as a titanic struggle between the noble virtues of liberalism and the craven values of fascism." Since not long after Turner's piece was published, and certainly since the European Union referendum, it has become almost a cliché to suggest that British parliamentary and extraparliamentary politics have become increasingly emotional. Commentaries on the rise of populism in the United Kingdom typically point out the deepening and sharpening of the binaries of political life, the failure of "phlegmatic" and "lugubrious" characters, and the rise of charisma and emotion as core to political success. As Will Davies (2019: 15) puts it in a recent book on the phenomenon: "Democracies are being transformed by the power of feeling in ways that cannot be ignored or reversed." Increasingly, social scientific studies have identified the impossibility of an emotionless politics, whatever one's substantive political orientation (Loseke 1993; Marcus 2000; Weber 2012).

By drawing on Durkheim's insights, one opportunity that CST offers in making sense of the debate over whether populism ought to be characterized as rational or emotional is a way to transcend the opposition itself. It does this through a focus on symbolism, ritual, and performance. Sign systems are rationally ordered in structured ways that depend upon distinction, difference, and opposition to generate meaning. What society decides to make sacred, for instance, it does so by ensuring that it is "set apart" from the profane (Durkheim 1995 [1912]: 44). In generating such meaning, these categories move beyond being merely analytic codes, and begin to acquire moral and emotionally laden social significance. While others have convincingly demonstrated how emotion and reason are almost always mutually embedded within the "alchemies of the mind" (Firth 1958: 150–83; Elster 1998; Goodwin et al. 2001), focusing upon symbolism, and the ritual processes that take place around it, has the added advantage of again revealing the continuities between apparently highly variable cultural practices. In this case, it allows us to see populism as consistent with other forms of politics, and indeed public culture more generally, since all are compelled to operate through the same symbolic channels.

The Civil Sphere (Alexander 2006) stands in opposition to two influential political models: interest-based and deliberative democratic. In place of these models, it offers an approach in which successful performance is capable of redrawing the boundaries of solidarity and moral cohesion. Performance trumps realism and ontology, since it is the performed appearance of sound judgment, fairness, integrity, or truth that matters, not the ontological presence or absence of such things.[4] Politics, like culture more generally, works through persuasion, not rational accomplishment, enlightened revelation, or the realist resolution of some conjunctural balance of forces.[5] While symbolization (the medium of performance) takes place within a rationally ordered (and therefore rationally accessible) set of binaries, these binaries do not remain mere cold logical distinctions. Moreover, the claims that are made for where particular events, relationships, or figures are to fit within this logical structure succeed or fail on the basis of their appeal to an audience's feelings. This means that the same rules of performative success apply whether one's cause is in fact worthy or not. Since political struggle is, at its heart, "moral and emotional" (Alexander 2010: xii), this chapter will later argue that suppressing these elements in an effort to achieve some pristine reasonability simply yields these potent motivational resources to whatever other political forces are prepared to use them.

29

Populism as Antipluralist

A final definitional criterion that dominant accounts of populism tend to reach consensus around is the notion that populism is a way of conducting politics that is by its nature "anti-pluralist" (Galston 2018). Although it speaks "the language of democracy," populism, so we are told, is in fact "always *antipluralist*," and therefore offers a "degraded form of democracy" (Müller 2016: 3, 6; see also Mounk 2018).[6] This is apparently linked to its Rousseauian claim to represent the "will of the people," but doing so in a noninstitutionalized manner that treats the categories of the "elite" and the "people" as "homogeneous" (Müller 2016: 6; see also 7, 12, 18). This nonempirical "claim to exclusive representation" (Müller 2016: 6) is said to lead to a second danger with populism: an inability to recognize the legitimacy of its opponents (Bonikowski 2016: 22). This section will address these connected claims in turn, arguing that while they may provide an accurate account of certain varieties of populism, they by no means apply to all instances, and therefore once again fall short as definitional criteria.

Populists, we are told, consider "society to be ultimately separated into two homogeneous and antagonistic groups" (Mudde 2004: 543; see also Müller 2016: 6, 18). This is said to derive from their sharing an understanding of "the political" with Schmitt, who believed that "the existence of a homogeneous people is essential for the foundation of a democratic order," and in listening to what Rousseau called the "general will" of this homogeneous group, "those who do not belong to the demos . . . consequently, are not treated as equals" (Mudde and Kaltwasser 2017: 18). Populism is therefore said to be irredeemably antipluralist in its rejection of an image of "society as a heterogeneous collection of groups and individuals with often fundamentally different views and wishes" (Mudde 2004: 543–4).

Such charges may apply to nativist populisms, but there are good reasons to assume that it is the nativism, not the populism, that produces them. While inspired by Schmitt (Mouffe 1999), left populist theory departs from his thinking at various significant junctures. One such juncture is that neither the "elite" nor the "people" are considered homogeneous wholes. Drawing on Gramsci, theorists of left populism have instead argued for the importance of articulating the fundamentally heterogeneous interests of segmented groups into a "people." Gramsci (1971: 191) had argued that successful leaders and parties could articulate disconnected groups, transforming them "from turbulent chaos into an organically prepared political army." If the "people" in left populism were conceived as a pre-existing homogeneous unit, as the mainstream definitions suggest, such hegemonic articulation would clearly be unnecessary: articulation is required precisely because heterogeneity is acknowledged. Constructing salient shared distinctions by drawing a political frontier is very different to claiming homogeneity. The very power of the concept of "the people" to mobilize – which, if the arguments above are accepted, it must be acknowledged is a power it holds over liberal democracy as much as the radical democracy advocated by left populism – is its capacity to act as an "empty signifier" to be filled with whatever content political agents determine (Laclau 1996). This is also, of course, what allows it to lend itself to both right- and left-wing invocations (Badiou et al. 2016).

Owing to its moralistic nature, populism is also charged with being "typically based on a fundamental rejection of the political legitimacy of one's opponent," so that "the likelihood of productive dialogue and compromise is reduced" (Bonikowski 2016: 22).[7] While this charge no doubt applies to certain forms of what Hall (1979) called "authoritarian populism," it again sits uneasily with theories of left populism, which have been at pains to stress that while politics will never be able to eradicate antagonism entirely, such conflicts can, and should, be transformed into "agonistic" relationships (Mouffe 2013). Whereas Schmitt (2007 [1932]: 26) saw politics as in essence defined by an antagonistic, and ultimately lethal, struggle of friends against enemies, Mouffe (2013) not only critiques the opposite rational-liberal view that a nonantagonistic consensus lies hidden, awaiting discovery through reasoned debate, but also argues that antagonism can be transformed into agonism through appropriate democratic institutions; the very institutions that mainstream accounts would have it that populists undermine. Whereas the Schmittian image is a war against enemies, the left populist image represents a struggle against adversaries in which the viewpoints of one's opponents are taken as authentic. The adversary becomes "a legitimate enemy with whom there exists a common ground," and while adversaries might "fight against each other," they nevertheless – in stark contrast to what populism's critics charge – "share a common allegiance to the ethico-political principles of liberal democracy" (Mouffe 1999: 4).

This transformation of enemies into adversaries, antagonism into agonism, opens up the possibility of a civil populist politics, in other words, a populism conducted within a broader shared civil solidarity, which makes reference to the same civil metalanguage as that of its opponents. It is presumably for this reason that Alexander quotes Mouffe's work appreciatively in *The Civil Sphere*, in its insistence that "'the novelty of democratic politics is not the overcoming of this us/

them opposition.' The challenge, rather, 'is to establish this us/them discrimination in a way that is compatible with pluralist democracy' ... which 'consists in domesticating hostility'" (Alexander 2006: 124). What Mouffe (2018: 91–2) describes as the "conflictual consensus that constitutes the basis of a pluralist democracy," Alexander would, I suspect, simply call the routine struggles that occur with reference to the shared "discourse of civil society," in which neither the possibility of consensus nor that of progress is assumed, but the legitimacy of one's opponent certainly is.

Interestingly, even within varieties of national populism (Eatwell and Goodwin 2018) that endanger but fail to break civil autonomy, these conditions can hold to the extent that "enemies" can be refashioned into "frenemies" (Alexander 2019: 6). What is threatening about such forms of populism, typified in figures like Trump, is less their delegitimizing of opposition and more their direct assault upon civil institutions (the judiciary, the media, etc.) that ensure the autonomous functioning of the civil sphere (Alexander 2019: 8; Kivisto 2017). These conditions clearly do not hold, however, in the more extreme expressions of exclusionary populism that Trump routinely flirts with. These expressions of populism bar and expel on the primordial bases of blood or soil and in so doing attack the foundation of the shared togetherness that defines membership in the civil sphere. In such cases, what Victor Serge called "respect for the man in the enemy" (2012 [1951]: 375) is indeed lost. However, this loss is a function not of populism but of nativist essentialism and the quest for purity – political tendencies that appear both in the presence and in the absence of populist signification.

Populism as Civil Repair?

The focus of dominant definitions of populism has typically been upon its dangers, distortions, and reductions. The one consistent virtue identified in such accounts is its capacity to act as a canary in the coal mine for social grievances (Bonikowski 2016: 23; Mudde and Kaltwasser 2017: 40). Here, I would like to argue that just as it can function as a threat to civil solidarity, populism also holds the potential to act as an agent of civil repair.

There are at least two ways of telling the story of the recent rise of populism. One is that healthy, responsive, and pluralist liberal democratic systems were unexpectedly rocked by the eruption of irrational forces. This story posits populism as the cause of Western polities' current ills. There is, however, an alternative story, which casts populism as an effect as much as a cause, and which can be told by drawing upon the ideal types of the civil sphere.

This story begins by decentering populism and instead bringing into focus the democracies in which it has arisen. Although the civil sphere is analytically independent, actual civil spheres are "always deeply inter-penetrated by the rest of society" (Alexander 2006: 194; 2013: 123–4). Noncivil spheres constantly edge into the civil sphere, threatening to distort its priorities. Such spheres aim toward more restrictive goals, employ variant standards of justice, and exchange information through alternative media. The economic sphere poses a particular threat to civil imperatives in its pursuit of profit above justice, efficiency above solidarity, and its communication through the reductive medium of price rather than the rich symbolism of performance. While Alexander (2006: 206–8) recounts the beneficial inputs of the economic into the civil sphere, he also notes the obvious risks it poses to the solidarities of civil life.

The alternative story of the rise of populism identifies how, from the late 1970s onward, Western liberal democracies progressively submitted to a narrow set of economic priorities, allowing the market to structure sectors – education, utilities, healthcare, social care, transportation, etc. – in which civil imperatives had previously governed during the postwar consensus period. Many of the Western leaders who rose to power in the wake of this Reagan/Thatcher revolution not only continued to wel-come market forces into the civil domain but also attempted to evacuate not only antagonism but also agonism from politics. Through political triangulation, the arbitration of competing demands, and the technical administration of the economy, initially highly popular leaders such as Blair, Schröder, and Clinton attempted to forge a consensus politics "beyond left and right" (Giddens 1994) in which "debate on the sensible givens of a situation" (Rancière 2003: 4) became stifled. This did not of course mean that fundamental social conflict disappeared – social movements in the Global North blossomed during this period – but this conflict struggled to find adequate expression in institutionalized democratic channels. While all the traditional institutions of democracy remained intact, an increasing proportion of the imperatives driving decision-making became outsourced to experts (Crouch 2004), and the role of the *demos*, upon which democracy apparently rested, became more and more circumscribed (Rancière 1998). When democratic processes were required, marketing and public relations mechanisms – such as focus groups and professional communications strategies – increasingly stepped in to devise or defend "policy" in a manner that fundamen-tally divorced it from "politics" (Schmidt 2006). Governance began to resemble management, the revolving doors between political assemblies and elite private sector organizations began to spin ever faster, apathy increased, party membership and voter turnout dropped (Mair 2013), and democratic societies entered their "postdemocratic" phase (Crouch 2000, 2004).

At no time was this more apparent than following the 2007–8 economic crisis. A global event caused by elite economic mismanagement was met with a political response that protected this elite, on their own advice, at the expense of broader populations. The choice to pursue austerity policies of course had material effects, but these effects were also experienced symbolically, in ways that solidified public distrust in politico-economic elites. Across Europe, but especially so in Southern European countries like Spain and Greece, "necessary" economic imperatives further colonized areas in which civil solidarity had once held sway.

Social democratic parties founded in the nineteenth or early twentieth century in an attempt to provide representation to workers and offer institutional barricades against the anticivil incursions of the economic sphere detached themselves from their traditional electoral base by failing to shield them against swingeing public service cuts, or even pioneering their implementation. Such parties are now paying the electoral price (Bickerton 2018). While center-right parties had long been comfortable with market priorities driving public policy, this unholy pact between social democratic organs and the market, combined with the associated evacuation of agonism from politics, provides an alternative account of where the populist "backlash" (Alexander 2019), in both its regressive and progressive manifestations, originated.

All this is not to say that the recent wave of what has been labelled "populism" can be reduced to an epiphenomenal effect of a postdemocratic political culture meeting its postcrisis moment. The evident success of populism as a mode of doing politics has led to it becoming an effective and autonomous culture structure in its own right, and one that has been self-consciously drawn upon and implemented by politicians eager to win votes. Moreover, cultural work invariably mediates between the reality and the perception of public issues, and the populisms that have sprung from this neoliberal postpolitical landscape have worked away at making these material and political realities meaningful. It is hardly a great surprise that anti-elitism has characterized many of them. Some have made austerity meaningful through a focus on ethnically or racially marked "enemies within," whom they identify as really to blame for the lack of opportunities and declining public services, and in the process have degraded civil solidarity even further.

Other populisms, however, have kept open the possibility, though by no means the guarantee, of civil repair. This is especially the case where populist signification has been combined with substantive policy to address those grievances – both moral and material – that nativist populism feeds upon. Such populisms promise a return of the political by drawing excluded groups into the democratic orbit in ways that can "translate" their sectoral grievances into universal civil issues of concern to societies at large (Alexander 2006: 231–2). Populism, conceived in the weak, formal manner argued for in this chapter, has not been the primary cause of the current crisis of Western politics, though certain of its expressions can no doubt be seen to have hastened it. One challenge for progressives is to resist treating populism as some easy solution. Nevertheless, drawing upon the preceding discussion, we might identify certain conditions that would enhance its viability, when combined with appropriate substantive policy, to act in the interests of civil repair.

First, in the discussion of the binary feature of populist politics and the critique of the tendency to treat populism as an ideology, it was argued that we need to challenge the notion that contention is alien to democracy and that the solution to populism is a return to a consensus style of public administration. Friend–enemy, us–them, and pure–polluted distinctions, which are often presented as unique to populism, are, cultural sociology teaches us, in fact expressions of more universal culture structures, which, when evoked in an agonistic manner, can be understood as homologous with the binaries that compose the "discourse of civil society." As the three examples that form Part III of *The Civil Sphere* illustrate, it has been precisely the construction of political frontiers around pressing issues that has historically led to civil expansion.[8] If movements had not convincingly used the discourse of civil society to simplify reality into good and evil, coding those forces pushing for civil repair as pure and those acting against it as polluted, the success of these movements would have been far less certain. However, if populism is understood as a formal mode of political signification, rather than a substantive ideology, the substance with which it works is clearly critical. Polarization needs to occur around the right issues, and issues that social movements have brought to the fore in recent years, and populist politics may be well placed to carry forward, include those around inequality and climate degradation. Compelling arguments exist that such issues deserve to be made subject to the binary treatment of the discourse of civil society, since they have been inadequately addressed by the routine functioning of civil sphere institutions, especially under the distorting influence of market-oriented imperatives.

Since civil repair will emphatically not be brought about by a triadic populism that scapegoats relatively powerless and defenseless communities for social ills, it is also key that such frontiers be open and inclusive. This inclusivity must involve a willingness to hear the grievances of those seduced by exclusivist populism, and a preparedness to invest in the cultural work necessary to reframe their concerns in universalizing, civil terms. Whether it comes from the left or the right, any populism that defines the frontiers of political life in essentialized, closed, and primordial terms is, by its very nature, nonuniversalizing and anticivil.

Second, it was suggested that treating morality and emotion as automatic threats to democratic politics is likewise problematic. Not only does this position too often fall back upon the flawed alternative assumption that political contention is settled only through ratiocinative modes of public discourse, drained of values or feelings, but it also cedes these powerful motivating forces to those anticivil tendencies currently using them to such great effect. Just like civil restriction, the success of civil translation depends upon its appeal to feelings, beliefs, and ideals as much as cognition. Neglecting moral language and emotive performance in the public signification of politics is not only foolhardy in an environment in which anticivil forces readily make use of it, it can also be experienced as an affront by groups whose exclusion is experienced in moral terms, and whose anger at such exclusion is felt in visceral ways. A populism capable of civil repair would therefore need to be culturally creative and dramatically astute in its telling of moral tales, its harnessing of public feeling, and its constructing of shared affect. This would involve engaging not only in the statics but also in the dynamics of the civil sphere (Alexander 2006: 60–2), fashioning compelling narratives capable of supplanting those of restrictive, anticivil populism. Feelings mustered in support of civil restriction will be conquered not simply by reasoned arguments, but by evoking more powerful feelings in support of civil expansion. Compelling exclusionary narratives will be displaced not simply by a presentation of facts, but by crafting even more compelling universalizing stories.[9]

Third, populism must be both agonistic and pluralistic if it is to function as a force for civil repair. Working within the shared semantic coding of the civil sphere and elaborating dynamic narratives capable of inspiring hearts as well as minds, such a populism would need to treat its opponents as adversaries to be struggled with and ultimately persuaded, rather than enemies to be silenced and ultimately eradicated. Its pluralism would derive from its creation of a "people" composed of coalitions articulated across difference. Such difference would need to be conceived not as a problem to be overcome, as in *völkisch* conceptions of a "people," but as a resource to be celebrated or a productive tension capable of promoting civility by occasionally testing it. Such articulations will fail if they are conceived as rooted within the spontaneous alignment of predetermined "interests." Instead, they must be understood as the outcome of ongoing cultural work aimed at tying together segmented grievances into hegemonic civil solidarities. In this sense, a progressive appeal to the "people" would need to be seen as a forever unfinished project.

Conclusion

The preceding section has suggested that like the social movements described in the final part of *The Civil Sphere* (Alexander 2006), populism can promote civil repair by translating restricted sectoral grievances into universal civil concerns, with the goal of incorporating previously excluded groups into the fold of social solidarity. Such processes are neither guaranteed nor often complete, however. Populisms can either fail in their efforts at representation, faltering in their capacity to successfully mobilize the metalanguage of civil society, or they can push – consciously or not – in the opposite direction, asserting particularistic claims and promoting forms of civil exclusion rather than incorporation.

These qualifications stem from the weaker, nonsubstantive definition of populism that this chapter has proposed: if populism is taken to be a formal mode of doing politics, rather than a substantive set of political ideas, whether it promotes civil restriction or repair, or both, is not something that can be settled in the abstract. The main purpose of this chapter has been to suggest that many of populism's formal dynamics can be connected, via CST, to what is usually considered to be nonpopulist politics, and, via cultural sociology, to the routine ways in which culture operates in most other spheres of social life.

Just as routine processes of group identity formation structure their meaning around either/or oppositions, so too does populism work the binaries of the civil sphere, cementing unity with those it defines as a "people," and breaking ties with those it does not. Understanding populism as a mode of public signification rather than an ideology (thin-centered or otherwise) allows us to recognize it as a form of cultural work that codes its own motivations, relationships, and institutions in civil terms, and those of its adversaries in terms of the opposite. Just as in other spheres of cultural distinction, moral judgments of good and evil animate these classifications, so that populism's efficacy is determined at least as much by its persuasive power in appealing to an audience's values and feelings as by its ability to rationally demonstrate its propositions.

Finally, this chapter has defended against the view that populism is inherently antipluralist, suggesting that populist signification can, and often does, operate within a broader acknowledgment of civil togetherness.

Since politics – and populism as a specific mode of doing politics – is obligated to operate through culture, effective social scientific tools for analyzing culture are, unsurprisingly, also effective tools for analyzing populism. Moreover, populism paints boldly what more routine politics tends to sketch more faintly: its categorizations are clear-cut, its public significations sharp, its binaries transparent, and its moral and emotional resonances distinct. Within it, we can discern clearly the structured ways in which culture reduces complexity, allowing information to be conveyed and meaning organized. Focusing our attention on such pronounced modes of political expression promises therefore to strengthen our understanding of the civil sphere.

Notes

This chapter was originally prepared for, and presented at, the New Haven conference that took place in the summer of 2019, where this present volume was developed. It benefited greatly from the input of the organizers and participants of that meeting. With the permission of the editors of this volume, it was subsequently published in slightly revised form as "A cultural sociology of populism" in the *International Journal of Politics, Culture, and Society*.

1 Making the same point in a slightly different way, Brubaker (2017: 362) describes this in terms of a "*vertical* opposition between 'the people' and 'the elite,'" as distinct from a "*horizontal* opposition between 'the people' and outside groups and forces."
2 This explains why civil incorporation, for instance, is not a process that comes about spontaneously, but is hard won through symbolically oriented political struggle (Alexander 2006: 425–57).
3 Corbyn explicitly connected the theme in various public rallies to the final line of Shelley's famous poem on passive resistance during the Peterloo Massacre, "The Masque of Anarchy" (1819): "Rise like Lions after slumber, In unvanquishable number – Shake your chains to earth like dew, Which in sleep had fallen on you – Ye are many – they are few."
4 This account of politics resonates with humanistic accounts of knowledge, in which "truth" is a compliment we ascribe to knowledge that seems to be "paying its way" or managing to convince a relevant community on the basis of that community's standards of justification (James 1981 [1907]; Rorty 1982: xxv; Morgan 2016).
5 This point has been forcefully made in an astute study of social movement success by Woodly (2015), in which she argues that political victory depends upon "political acceptance," which is distinct from "political agreement." Whereas the latter involves acceptance of a movement's policy goals, the former is simply an acceptance of the cultural relevance of a movement's concerns to public discourse.

6 It should be noted that Mudde's position, which draws upon Canovan's earlier arguments (1999), is more nuanced, arguing that populism is in many ways more democratic (yet less liberal) than liberal democracy, which is characterized as "a complex compromise of popular democracy and liberal elitism, which is therefore only partly democratic" (Mudde 2004: 561). Alexander (2010: 278–9) also touches on this point in his discussion of how the democratic resonances of the Preamble to the US Constitution's reference to "We, the people" were tempered by the more liberal specifications of the Bill of Rights amendments.

7 As argued in the section before last, an irony that is too often lost in such claims is that the moralizing rhetoric of liberal antipopulism can itself come across as antipluralist, not only through the ease with which it shades into elitism, but in its rejection of the legitimacy of what it conceives as populist voices by labelling them such.

8 It is worth noting how many of the new populist parties and their leaders have emerged from what *The Civil Sphere* identifies as the primary agents of civil repair: social movements.

9 For an illustration of the fundamental inadequacies of fact-based politics in shaping perceptions, feelings, and motivations, see Smith and Howe's (2015) analysis of climate consciousness.

References

Albertazzi, D. and D. McDonnell (eds.). (2007) *Twenty-First Century Populism: The Spectre of Western European Democracy.* Basingstoke: Palgrave Macmillan.

Alexander, J. C. (2006) *The Civil Sphere.* New York: Oxford University Press.

Alexander, J. C. (2010) *The Performance of Politics: Obama's Victory and the Democratic Struggle for Power.* Oxford: Oxford University Press.

Alexander, J. C. (2011) *Performative Revolution in Egypt: An Essay in Cultural Power.* London and New York: Bloomsbury Academic.

Alexander, J. C. (2013) De-civilizing the civil sphere. In: J. C. Alexander (ed.) *The Dark Side of Modernity.* Cambridge: Polity.

Alexander, J. C. (2019) Frontlash/backlash: The crisis of solidarity and the threat to civil institutions. *Contemporary Sociology: A Journal of Reviews* 48(1): 5–11.

Alexander, J. C. and P. Smith. (1993) The discourse of American civil society: A new proposal for cultural studies. *Theory and Society* 22(2): 151–207.

Arnold, M. (1993 [1869]) *Culture & Anarchy and Other Writings.* Cambridge: Cambridge University Press.

Aslanidis, P. (2016) Is populism an ideology? A refutation and a new perspective. *Political Studies* 64(1): 88–104.

Aslanidis, P. (2018) Populism as a collective action master frame for transnational mobilization. *Sociological Forum* 33(2): 443–64.

Badiou, A., P. Bourdieu, J. Butler, G. Didi-Huberman, S. Khiari, and J. Rancière. (2016) *What Is a People?* New York: Columbia University Press.

Barthes, R. (1977) Introduction to the structural analysis of narratives. In: R. Barthes, *Image Music Text.* Glasgow: Fontana Press.

Berlin, I., R. Hofstadter, D. MacRae, L. Schapiro, H. Seton-Watson, A. Touraine, F. Venturi, A. Walicki, and P. Worsley. (1968) To define populism. *Government and Opposition* 3(2): 137–79.

Bickerton, C. (2018) The collapse of Europe's mainstream centre left. *New Statesman*, May 1. https://www.newstatesman.com/world/europe/2018/05/collapse-europe-s-mainstream-centre-left.

Blair, T. (1999) Full speech to Labour Conference. *The Guardian*, September 28. https://www.theguardian.com/politics/1999/sep/28/labourconference.labour14.

Blair, T. (2017) Renewing the centre. Tony Blair Institute for Global Change, March 17. https://institute.global/tony-blair/renewing-centre.

Bonikowski, B. (2016) Three lessons of contemporary populism in Europe and the United States. *Brown Journal of World Affairs* 23(1): 9–24.

Bonikowski, B. and N. Gidron. (2016) Multiple traditions in populism research: Toward a theoretical synthesis. *APSA Comparative Politics Newsletter* 26(12): 7–14.

Brubaker, R. (2017) Why populism? *Theory and Society* 46(5): 357–85.

Canovan, M. (1999) Trust the people! Populism and the two faces of democracy. *Political Studies* 47(1): 2–16.

Crick, B. (1962) *In Defence of Politics*. London: Bloomsbury.

Crouch, C. (2000) *Coping with Post-democracy*. London: Fabian Society.

Crouch, C. (2004) *Post-democracy*. Cambridge: Polity.

Davies, W. (2019) *Nervous States: How Feeling Took Over the World*. London: Jonathan Cape.

de Saussure, F. (1966 [1893]) *Course in General Linguistics*. London: McGraw-Hill.

Douglas, M. (1983) Morality and culture. *Ethics* 93(4): 786–91.

Durkheim, É. (1973) *On Morality and Society*. Chicago: University of Chicago Press.

Durkheim, É. (1984 [1893]) *The Division of Labour in Society*. London: Palgrave Macmillan.

Durkheim, É. (1995 [1912]) *The Elementary Forms of the Religious Life*. London: The Free Press.

Durkheim, É. and M. Mauss. (2009 [1903]) *Primitive Classification*. London: Routledge.

Eatwell, R. and M. Goodwin. (2018) *National Populism: The Revolt Against Liberal Democracy*. London: Penguin.

Ekström, M., M. Patrona, and J. Thornborrow. (2018) Right-wing populism and the dynamics of style: A discourse-analytic perspective on mediated political performances. *Palgrave Communications* 4(1): 122–47.

Elster, J. (1998) *Alchemies of the Mind*. Cambridge: Cambridge University Press.

Firth, R. (1958) Reason and unreason in human belief. In: R. Firth, *Human Types*. London: Thomas Nelson.

Foucault, M. (1988) *Madness and Civilization: A History of Insanity in an Age of Reason*. London: Vintage Books.

Fukuyama, F. (2016) American political decay or renewal? The meaning of the 2016 election. *Foreign Affairs*, July/August. https://www.foreignaffairs.com/articles/united-states/2016-06-13/american-political-decay-or-renewal.

Galston, W. A. (2018) *Anti-Pluralism: The Populist Threat to Liberal Democracy*. New Haven: Yale University Press.

Geertz, C. (1957) Ethos, world-view and the analysis of sacred symbols. *The Antioch Review* 17(4): 421–37.

Geertz, C. (1968) Thinking as a moral act: Ethical dimensions of anthropological fieldwork in the new states. *The Antioch Review* 28(2): 139–58.

Geertz, C. (1973) *The Interpretation of Cultures*. New York: Basic Books.

Giddens, A. (1994) *Beyond Left and Right*. Cambridge: Polity.

Goodhart, D. (2017) *The Road to Somewhere: The Populist Revolt and the Future of Politics*. Oxford: Oxford University Press.

Goodwin, J., J. M. Jasper, and F. Polletta (eds.). (2001) *Passionate Politics*. Chicago: University of Chicago Press.

Gorski, P. (2017) Why evangelicals voted for Trump: A critical cultural sociology. *American Journal of Cultural Sociology* 5(3): 338–54.

Gramsci, A. (1971) *Selections from the Prison Notebooks*. London: Lawrence & Wishart.

Habermas, J. (1976) *Legitimation Crisis*. London: Heinemann Educational.

Hall, S. (1979) The great moving right show. *Marxism Today*, January: 14–20.

Hall, S. (1998) The great moving nowhere show. *Marxism Today*, November/December: 9–14.

Ionescu, G. and E. Gellner (eds.). (1969) *Populism: Its Meanings and National Characteristics*. Letchworth: Garden City Press.

Jäger, A. (2018) The myth of "populism." *Jacobin*, January 3.

James, W. (1981 [1907]) *Pragmatism*. Cambridge, MA: Hackett Publishing Company.

Jansen, R. S. (2011) Populist mobilization: A new theoretical approach to populism. *Sociological Theory* 29(2): 75–96.

Judis, J. B. (2016) *The Populist Explosion: How the Great Recession Transformed American and European Politics*. New York: Columbia Global Reports.

Kivisto, P. (2017) *The Trump Phenomenon: How the Politics of Populism Won in 2016*. Bingley: Emerald Publishers.

Kriesi, H. (2014) The populist challenge. *West European Politics* 37(2): 361–78.

Laclau, E. (1996) Why do empty signifiers matter to politics? In: E. Laclau, *Emancipation(s)*. London: Verso.

Laclau, E. (2005) *On Populist Reason*. London: Verso.

Laclau, E. (2006) Why constructing a people is the main task of radical politics. *Critical Inquiry* 32(4): 646–80.

Le Bon, G. (2006 [1896]) *The Crowd: A Study of the Popular Mind*. New York: Cosimo.

Lévi-Strauss, C. (1967) *Structural Anthropology*. New York: Anchor Books.

Loseke, D. (1993) *Constructing Conditions, People, Morality, and Emotion: Expanding the Agenda of Constructionism*. New York: Routledge.

Lynch, G. (2012) *The Sacred in the Modern World: A Cultural Sociological Approach*. Oxford: Oxford University Press.

MacRae, D. (1969) Populism as an ideology. In: G. Ionescu and E. Gellner (eds.) *Populism: Its Meanings and National Characteristics*. Letchworth: Garden City Press.

Mair, P. (2013) *Ruling the Void: The Hollowing-out of Western Democracy*. London: Verso.

Marcus, G. (2000) Emotions in politics. *Annual Review of Political Science* 3(1): 221–50.

Mast, J. L. (2012) *The Performative Presidency: Crisis and Resurrection during the Clinton Years*. Cambridge: Cambridge University Press.

Moffitt, B. (2016) *The Global Rise of Populism: Performance, Political Style, and Representation*. Stanford: Stanford University Press.

Morgan, M. (2014) The poverty of (moral) philosophy: Towards an empirical and pragmatic ethics. *European Journal of Social Theory* 17(2): 129–46.

Morgan, M. (2016) Humanising sociological knowledge. *Social Epistemology* 30(5–6): 555–71.

Morgan, M. (2018) Performance and power in social movements: Biko's role as a witness in the SASO/BPC Trial. *Cultural Sociology* 12(4): 457–77.

Mouffe, C. (1999) Introduction: Schmitt's challenge. In: C. Mouffe (ed.) *The Challenge of Carl Schmitt*. London: Verso.

Mouffe, C. (2002) *Politics and Passions: The Stakes of Democracy*. London: Centre for the Study of Democracy.

Mouffe, C. (2013) *Agonistics: Thinking the World Politically*. London: Verso.

Mouffe, C. (2018) *For a Left Populism*. London: Verso.

Mouffe, C. and Í Errejón. (2016) *Podemos: In the Name of the People*. London: Lawrence & Wishart Ltd.

Mounk, Y. (2018) *The People vs. Democracy*. Cambridge, MA: Harvard University Press.

Mudde, C. (2004) The populist zeitgeist. *Government and Opposition* 39(4): 541–63.

Mudde, C. and C. R. Kaltwasser. (2017) *Populism: A Very Short Introduction*. Oxford: Oxford University Press.

Müller, J.-W. (2016) *What Is Populism?* Philadelphia: University of Pennsylvania Press.

Obama, B. (2016) I'm the real populist, not Trump. *Politico*, June 29. https://www.politico.com/video/2016/06/obama-im-the-real-populist-not-trump-059801.

Peel, P. (2018) The populist theory of the state in early American political thought. *Political Research Quarterly* 71(1): 115–26.

Rancière, J. (1998) *Disagreement*. Minneapolis: University of Minnesota Press.

Rancière, J. (2003) Comment and responses. *Theory & Event* 6(4). https://muse.jhu.edu/article/44787.

Rico, G., M. Guinjoan, and E. Anduiza. (2017) The emotional underpinnings of populism: How anger and fear affect populist attitudes. *Swiss Political Science Review* 23(4): 444–61.

Rorty, R. (1982) *Consequences of Pragmatism*. Minneapolis: University of Minnesota Press.

Ruzza, C. and S. Fella. (2009) *Re-inventing the Italian Right: Territorial Politics, Populism and "Post-Fascism."* New York: Routledge.

Sandel, M. J. (2018) Populism, liberalism, and democracy. *Philosophy & Social Criticism* 44(4): 353–9.

Schmidt, V. A. (2006) *Democracy in Europe: The EU and National Polities*. Oxford: Oxford University Press.

Schmitt, C. (2007 [1932]) *The Concept of the Political*. Chicago: University of Chicago Press.

Serge, V. (2012 [1951]) *Memoirs of a Revolutionary*. New York: New York Review of Books Classics.

Skinner, Q. (2009) A genealogy of the modern state. *Proceedings of the British Academy* 162: 352–70.

Smith, P. and N. Howe. (2015) *Climate Change as Social Drama: Global Warming in the Public Sphere*. Cambridge: Cambridge University Press.

Stanley, B. (2008) The thin ideology of populism. *Journal of Political Ideologies* 13(1): 95–110.

Stavrakakis, Y. and A. Jäger. (2018) Accomplishments and limitations of the "new" mainstream in contemporary populism studies. *European Journal of Social Theory* 21(4): 547–65.

Stewart, H. and J. Elgot. (2016) Labour plans Jeremy Corbyn relaunch to ride anti-establishment wave. *The Guardian*, December 15. https://www.theguardian.com/politics/2016/dec/15/labour-plans-jeremy-corbyn-relaunch-as-a-leftwing-populist.

Taguieff, P. A. (1995) Political science confronts populism: From conceptual mirage to a real problem. *Telos* 103: 9–43.

Toynbee, P. (2015) This was the week the Labour leadership contest turned nasty. *The Guardian*, July 23. https://www.theguardian.com/commentisfree/2015/jul/23/labour-leadership-contest-jeremy-corbyn.

Turner, B. S. (2015) Civil sphere and political performance: Critical reflections on Alexander's cultural sociology. In: P. Kivisto and G. Sciortino (eds.) *Solidarity, Justice, and Incorporation: Thinking through The Civil Sphere*. Oxford: Oxford University Press.

Urbinati, N. (2017) Populism and the principle of majority. In: C. R. Kaltwasser, P. Taggart, P. O. Espejo, and P. Ostiguy (eds.) *The Oxford Handbook of Populism*. Oxford: Oxford University Press.

Wagner-Pacifici, R. and I. Tavory. (2017) Politics as a vacation. *American Journal of Cultural Sociology* 5(3): 307–21.

Weber, C. (2012) Emotions, campaigns, and political participation. *Political Research Quarterly* 66(2): 414–28.

Wolf, M. (2017) The economic consequences of Jeremy Corbyn. *Financial Times,* October 5. https://www.ft.com/content/0e956c1e-a8e5-11e7-93c5-648314d2c72c.

Woodly, D. R. (2015) *The Politics of Common Sense: How Social Movements Use Public Discourse to Change Politics and Win Acceptance*. Oxford: Oxford University Press.

2

#Disente and Duterte

The Cultural Bases of Antipopulism in the Philippines, 2001–2019

Celso M. Villegas

This chapter analyzes two ways in which the Philippine civil sphere has challenged populism in the past twenty years: the "successful" 2001 protests that removed President Joseph Estrada; and the "failure" to prevent the rise of President Rodrigo Duterte in 2016. Using a close reading of print media, digital media, and secondary sources from 2000 to 2019, this chapter makes two broad arguments. First, it argues that the several attempts to remove, forestall, or otherwise counteract populist politics in the Philippines follow the civil sphere's logic of frontlash and backlash (Alexander 2018, 2019). Specifically, these two instances of antipopulism were oriented toward defending the frontlash advances of the country's dramatic democratic transition in 1986: the People Power Revolution.

Second, this chapter argues that such defenses of frontlash have relied on and have transformed the cultural understandings of the middle class. Civil sphere actors in 2001 creatively reacted to foreign criticism and domestic unrest by constructing a symbolically pure, democratic, middle-class subject: the harbinger of modernity, united by its enlightened education and rationality. In 2016, presidential candidate Mar Roxas attempted to deploy the civil code against Duterte, using the tacit middle-class code *disente* (decent) to characterize himself and his supporters. That maneuver was countered by Duterte's brash counterperformances and by media-savvy pro-Duterte critics. Turning "*disente*" into an ironic hashtag, pro-Duterte bloggers threw the logic of the civil sphere back against Roxas and eventually against regime opponents. In the welter of that debate about decency and democracy, there came a heightened sense of the political importance of the middle class, but in a negative way: as defectors from the democratic frontlash of 1986 and now fundamentally antidemocratic. Without a democratic middle class at its symbolic core, the resistance to Duterte has stalled.

Populism and the Civil Sphere

There is a fruitful conversation to be had between recent theoretical work on global populism and recent innovations in civil sphere theory (hereafter CST). In the past twenty years, scholars have expanded the conceptual and empirical breadth of populism. They have pushed past its classical definition as an "irrational" form of mobilization tied to dependent economic development and have redefined it as a normative component of democracy (e.g., Canovan 1999; Laclau 2005), a political strategy (e.g., Weyland 2001), a thin ideology (e.g., Mudde and Kaltwasser 2013), a form of pragmatic political action (e.g., Jansen 2016), or a form of political performance (e.g., Moffitt 2016). Empirically, scholarship has moved past a focus on populist leaders and followers to populism's Manichean discourse pitting the pure "people" against the impure elite (e.g., de La Torre 2010), as well as populism's right- and left-wing variants across regions (e.g., Mudde and Kaltwasser 2013). Social movements and massive protests like Occupy Wall Street and Tahrir Square have also been characterized as populist (e.g., Arditi 2015).

However, with breadth there comes a lack of depth and integration. Scholars have not avoided Kurt Weyland's (2001) concerns about conceptual stretching as empirical cases of populism multiply, resulting in "deflationary" approaches to the concept (Molyneux and Osborne 2017) and attempts to put political, ideological, and structural definitions in conversation with one another (Gidron and Bonikowski 2013). But what hamstrings populism studies is a lack of an integrative *theoretical* perspective. Indeed, for the study of populism to be "truly cumulative, . . . [it has] to be based upon one theoretical framework, even if it is relatively minimal" (Mudde 2015: 446).

CST offers a framework that can unify the discursive, institutional, performative, and normative strands of populism studies. Situating populism inside the civil sphere, we can understand the pure people/polluted elite distinctions as binary oppositions linked to the discourses of liberty and repression. If populist leaders and movements are at least aware of the horizons of the civil sphere, then they communicate the contradictions of real-existing civil spheres – of space, time, and function (Alexander 2006: 196–209) – in what Laclau (2005) describes as discursive "logics of equivalency" (cf. Alexander 2019: 9). "The people" condenses the various destructive intrusions of noncivil spheres, unresolved national integration, and gaps in collective narration in opposition to the "elites" who would otherwise ignore these contradictions. Thus, in a more productive and expansionary form, populism within the horizon of the civil sphere can be a "societalizing" form of "frontlash" that overcomes marginalization (Alexander 2018: 1068–9). This is where Obama, Occupy, and Tahrir Square would find their common civil-populist qualities (Alexander 2013).

In contrast to the expansionary possibilities of populism in the civil sphere, CST also theorizes a darker, ideal-typical form of populism – a reactive "backlash" that (1) amplifies polarization and (2) attacks the autonomy of the civil sphere's communicative and regulative institutions. In deeply divided societies, "social indignation can become refracted in a manner that fails to engage the full horizon of common concern," with the "paradoxical result" of a "deepening polarization that can lead to the weakening, and sometimes even destruction, of the civil sphere" (Alexander 2018: 1068). Here Obama's "[gestures] to a post-imperial foreign policy [and a] post-white, multicultural American ethnicity . . . were experienced as frighteningly frontlash by the status quo ante" (Alexander 2019: 6). The Trumpian backlash to Obama was oriented against the mediating power of communicative institutions (polling, civil associations, journalism) and state-access guarding regulatory institutions (voting, office, parties, and law). As Alexander (2019: 8) puts it, "Under such conditions of discursive constriction and institutional fusion, the presuppositions of a universalizing solidarity become severely constrained" and "civil spheres shrink."

CST also insists on the importance of pragmatic, contingent cultural performances in generating the populist "mood" (see Canovan 1999: 6–7). The contentious populist speech (Gauna 2016) and the populist rally (Karakaya 2018) are central ways in which leader-performers engage with follower-audiences. CST argues that successful performances help audiences *associate* emotions with their cognitive assessments of events (Karakaya 2018). These performances are not *just* pragmatic (cf. Jansen 2016), but also require a savvy understanding of background representations and scripts (Alexander 2011), and, in the modern era, support teams of scriptwriters, event producers, and digital media influencers. Furthermore, if populist charisma is social performance, then we should also take seriously the range of charismatic counterroles that act as foils for the populist leader: supplicating "devoted followers," incompetent "unworthy challengers," and referential "colossal players" (Joosse 2018) fill out populism's performative ecosystem. In cultural sociological terms, populist charisma is a contingent experience of complex performative fusion. And as such, society-wide, polarizing, extraordinary populist moods are a function of the dramatic tension between carrier-performers of frontlash and backlash, their agents and foils, and the emotional release of audiences watching for (and expecting) both success and failure.

In summary, CST offers a single framework that takes into account the deep binary tensions in the background of populist moments, the institutional advances and breakdowns possible in frontlash and backlash, as well as the dramatic quality of populism-as-performance. Based on that, approaching populism from the civil sphere offers these normative suggestions: "Substantively, the contemporary resistance is a fight to maintain what frontlash has gained," and it "proceeds by defending the structure and culture of the civil sphere" (Alexander 2019: 9). This means ensuring that the civil code "cannot be allowed to become concentrated in the representational capacities of a leader and party" (Alexander 2019: 9). Resisting backlash therefore requires an integrated approach: populist performance and moods are situated against the background of binary codes and operate within the institutional dynamics of frontlash/ backlash.

Returning to Class in Populism Studies through the Civil Sphere

In this new global populist mood, populism studies have begun to pay positive attention to the ethics, mass movements, and organizational strategies of "the resistance," especially in the Global North (e.g., Snyder 2017; Meyer and Tarrow 2018; Fisher 2019). Here social class appears, albeit in intersectional form – "white working class," "middle-class white women," and other classed categories put finer points on polarized distinctions of "the people" vs. "elites." Two decades ago, a populist wave began to pass across Asia and Latin America, prompting a distinctly different sentiment about civil society opposing populism: a negative one. Democratically elected populist leaders were removed from power following massive protests, including Joseph Estrada in the Philippines. The "civil society coup" (see esp. Encarnación 2002; Kurlantzick 2013) was jointly the result of over-optimism about civil society after the democratic transitions of the 1980s and 1990s, and the rising anxieties of the developing world middle class against populists and the urban poor.

The irony is that despite abandoning political economy as the theoretical foundation for studying populist politics, class formation never truly went away as explanans and explanandum. The classic studies of populism in Latin America (e.g., di Tella 1965; Germani 1978) were essentially studies of aborted or interrupted class formation, with populist leaders like Perón redirecting materially felt inequalities irrationally toward his leadership. Even as Weyland (1996) devised the concept of "neopopulism" to explain neoliberal populists like Peru's Alberto Fujimori and Argentina's Carlos Menem, one dimension of his analysis revealed how the urban poor came to vote for economic policies that would hurt them. The shift to strategy and ideology (e.g., Mudde and Kaltwasser 2013) was intended to solve the left vs. right populism debate – and thus follow empirical trends in both Latin America and Europe – but in doing so it reduced the expression of social class in politics to parties and discourse-as-strategy (see Bonikowski and Gidron 2015). Even Ernesto Laclau's (2005) vaunted poststructuralist take on populism essentially imagines populist politics as a heightened form of class formation, where "the people" *sui generis* approvingly takes the place of "class." In a fundamental way, populism studies still reckon with a deviancy model of class formation: classes *should* have their own interests derived from their location in the economy, but instead populism interrupts, redirects, or substitutes for them (see Somers 1992). What classes *mean* both analytically and empirically is assumed to be something other than what they say or represent during populist moments.[1]

Fortunately, CST does not come with this theoretical baggage and thus offers a way back to a meaningful engagement with social class and populism. Its core claims may have been developed in contradistinction with neo-Marxian arguments that rooted civil society in class interests (see Alexander 2006: 26–9), but CST is nurtured by strong social democratic roots. "Though not all societies are simply class societies" (Alexander 2007: 14), Karl Polanyi and T. H. Marshall strongly inform CST's logic of civil incorporation (Alexander 2006: 19, 26, 32–3, 44, 198). In short, "the collective obligations" that make up class solidarity are to be found in the "noneconomic, religious, and political-cultural" features of the civil sphere (Alexander 2006: 559fn39). This tracks with a raft of historical studies of class discourse which argue that political language cannot be decoded "to reach a primal and material expression of interest since it is the discursive structure of political language which conceives and defines interest in the first place" (Jones 1983: 21–2; see also Wahrman 1995; Parker 1998).[2]

The core political languages are the discourses of liberty and repression, built up from the sacred and profane codes of the civil sphere (Alexander 2006: 53–67). These languages are supplemented by the noneconomic, religious, and political-cultural languages offered up by other social spheres in boundary relation with the civil sphere. When functional, spatial, and temporal contradictions coalesce in societalizing frontlash or regressive backlash, new collective representations of class are the product (Alexander 2006: 203–5). The civil sphere's dynamics propel class formation; populist moments should therefore be understood as fundamentally class-formative not class-degenerative. Even profane, negative assessments of classes serve as cultural reference points for the state of the populist moment and the potentialities of political alliances.

Though the people/elite binary rises to master status, CST suggests that populist moments transform codes and promote performances that key in to culturally deep collective representations of class. We need to know about these deep representations to understand the culturally structured logic of a populist moment; we cannot do that with a populism rooted in a deviancy model of class formation.

Successful Antipopulism in the Philippines and the Sacred Representation of the Middle Class, 2001

To recap, viewing populism as embedded in the civil sphere integrates several analytical threads in populism studies. The People represent condensed contradictions of the civil sphere against a hitherto distant Elite. Such a form of code-switch not only societalizes multiple social problems, but also offers the possibility of expanding and repairing the civil sphere. Reactive forms of populism, however, damage the institutional autonomy of the civil sphere and weaken it. These frontlash and backlash forms of populism transform the *dramatis personae* of politics, as populist agents for frontlash and backlash spar with heightened audience expectations. And because the incorporative logic of the civil sphere drives the logic of class formation, new meanings for social classes emerge as populism prompts new cultural-structural formations.

Now, we turn to the Philippines to illustrate these claims. In 1998, vice-president and former movie star Joseph "Erap" Estrada won a three-way race for the Philippine presidency with 39.86 percent of the vote. Building on the underdog persona of his movie roles to personally identify with the urban poor, Estrada's election was a "populist rupture" (Laclau 2005) that wrested the presidency away from dynastic families (Anderson 1988; Case 2003). His electoral vehicle/political party, *Pwersa ng Masa Pilipino* (Power of the Philippines Masses), redefined the derogatory term *masa* (as in "unwashed masses") as a point of pride, much like Perón's *descamisados* did in Argentina. His consistent performances of sincerity with the urban poor endeared him to millions who had not felt like the Philippine president cared about or represented them, while simultaneously provoking the ire of the middle class and upper classes for disrupting the predictable social boundaries of urban life (Garrido 2008, 2018). Left-leaning intellectuals joined Estrada's cabinet as an opportunity to enact pro-poor policies, despite increasing evidence of personal and governmental corruption (e.g., Constantino-David 2001).

However, Estrada's presidency created what Paul Joose calls "incredulous onlookers" (2018: 938) in the media and among the old political elite who were baffled by Estrada's continued popular support, despite his gaffes with the English language and administrative incompetence (Hedman 2001). No small part of this criticism was derived from Estrada's coziness with business leaders and politicians who had been close to former dictator Ferdinand Marcos, ousted in the 1986 People Power Revolution. Estrada's presidential campaign was bankrolled by Marcos's widow Imelda and by one of Marcos's business partners, Edward "Danding" Cojuanco: "Estrada's inauguration in June 1998 brought many old Marcos friends and followers back to the center of power for the first time in 12 years" (Landé 2001: 90). Insofar as Estrada's pro-poor populism gathered momentum for frontlash both discursively and to a certain degree institutionally, the return of politically impure Marcos cronies made his populism seem like a return to the past. This is the axis on which resistance would revolve.

In October 2000, Ilocos Sur Governor Luis "Chavit" Singson implicated Estrada in a complex gambling and money laundering scheme involving an illegal numbers game called *jueteng*. In November, on the force of that accusation, Estrada was impeached for graft, betraying the public trust, and defying the constitution. Anti-Estrada protestors gathered at the Senate and millions of Filipinos watched the trial on television or heard it on the radio. The day-to-day social drama involved watching or hearing pro- and anti-Estrada senators clash and probe witnesses during testimony, amplified through a daily news cycle dedicated to interpreting the trial's latest events. Though Estrada's movie star lifestyle in the presidency had previously led to seamy, tabloid-style rumors about multiple mistresses and bacchanalia in the presidential palace, the impeachment trial was an institutionalized social drama with sordid details about pseudonyms and secret payoffs balanced against procedural points of order and senatorial grandstanding. This was the social drama of populism, focused and fused in a society-wide way.

With corruption on everybody's mind, in an October 27 column titled "What About Us Middle Class?" lifestyle writer Thelma Sioson San Juan wondered out loud about the state of the middle class in the Philippines "in the midst of things," not least of which was the "induced class war between rich and poor" (San Juan 2000). "Who's thinking of and speaking for the middle class that is so easy to crush now more than ever before?" she queried. San Juan argues that the middle class suffers for its honesty:

> It's the salary-earning middle class that dutifully pays taxes, that wants to earn from its education and profession, that doesn't want to be profligately nouveau, that wants to raise its children as productive citizens – that wants to stay in this country.

"The middle class' decent way of earning money in a corrupt country," she continues, "is getting to be a lost art." And she wonders if elite Catholic education is inculcating its students with "a strong value system" as effectively as it did when she attended school. Thus, in the midst of the "induced class war" that Estrada had perpetrated upon them, the middle class has been forgotten and its way of life is being threatened. The poor, on the other hand, "are heard, as token" but "forcibly wooed" (San Juan 2000): that is to say, used by Estrada to fuel his corrupt ambitions.

On January 21, 2001, the curtain fell on Estrada. Four days earlier, the Senate voted 11–10 to leave unopened a sealed envelope containing bank documents, possibly tying Estrada to the *jueteng* payoff. For a population that had been watching or listening to Estrada's impeachment proceedings for the past few months, the news that the most damning evidence against him was not admissible was akin to having the country's most popular soap opera end before it had come to its climax. As the prosecution walked out in disgust, and the Senate president resigned in protest, the hundreds of thousands of people camped outside the Senate and at the shrine commemorating the first EDSA People Power[3] clamored for Estrada to step down. The recognizable faces of the first EDSA Revolution – former presidents Corazón Aquino and Fidel Ramos, and Manila Archbishop Jaime Cardinal Sin, among others – stirred up the crowd, calling upon Estrada to resign, as was his moral obligation in the face of this new "People Power 2," or "EDSA 2." As the protests continued to both swell and grow more fervent over the course of the next few days, the military removed its support from his government. Estrada left the presidential palace. Chief Justice of the Supreme Court Hilario Davide declared the presidency "vacant," allowing Vice-President Gloria Macapagal Arroyo to assume the remainder of Estrada's term.

This EDSA 2 – the "sequel" to the first EDSA Revolution – marked for some the restoration of the Philippines' democratic path and its civil sphere against the institutional backlash of the Estrada administration. For foreign audiences, however, EDSA 2 was an exercise in "rich people's power." While participants and sympathizers celebrated the fall of Estrada, foreign observers began to question the validity of EDSA 2 as a democratic event and lamented its effects on the political stability of the Philippines. One piece that would be a lightning rod for criticism, Anthony Spaeth's article in *Time* entitled "Oops, We Did it Again" (2001), speculated that it was a conspiracy of "Manila's business aristocracy," the "landed gentry" as typified by Corazón Aquino and the Catholic Church:

51

In the mid-'80s, the Elite and the Church banded together to help organize Manila's masses against Marcos, a moment of triumph they have never forgotten. The fact that a high percentage of Filipinos loved Estrada was exasperating. Even more inconvenient was his grip on the Senate, which seemed to ensure that he would stay in power. The solution: to bring hundreds of thousands of Filipinos onto Manila's streets.

"People Power," he concluded, "has become an acceptable term for a troubling phenomenon: one that used to be known as mob rule." Jim Mann (2001) of the *Los Angeles Times* contrasted EDSA 2 with previous forms of People Power around the world: "Now, by contrast, we are witnessing the use of people power against a leader who was the winner of a legitimate democratic election"; he continues, "No matter how understandable it was, this outbreak of people power doesn't seem like an advance for the cause of democracy; quite the opposite." And William Overholt (2001) stated, "It is either being called mob rule or mob rule as a cover for a well-planned coup . . . but either way, it's not democracy."[4]

But EDSA 2 faced criticism not only from abroad, but domestically as well: on May 1, 2001 a counterrevolt featuring personages loyal to Estrada – Senator Miriam Defensor-Santiago, Estrada's spiritual advisor and head of the charismatic El Shaddai movement Mike Velarde, and former coup leader Gregorio Honasan – as well as hundreds of thousands of Estrada's lower-class supporters who had been the bulk of his electoral support in his various stabs at public office, took to the streets. These estimated 500,000 protestors also gathered at the EDSA Shrine; they claimed that the Arroyo presidency was illegitimate, but most consequentially, 50,000 of them stormed the presidential palace and had to be subdued by military force. EDSA 3, as it would be called, made violently apparent the great class disparity between its participants and those of EDSA 2. It continued to affirm many foreign observations that ousting Estrada was really "rich People's Power," that is to say, an elite-driven backlash against the civil institutions of voting and office.

To disarm both foreign and domestic critics, pundits, scholars, and activists alike drew on the civil code to specify the middle-class basis of the EDSA 2 protests. In doing so, they defined a new collective representation of the middle class. Pundits and scholars claimed three things: that (1) the revolt was the Filipino moral majority speaking out – regular citizens forming and mobilizing an organized civil society; that (2) civil disobedience for a common good is an inherent and inexplicable trait of Filipinos; and that (3) it represented a revolutionary break with the past – the end of unaccountable politics and hijacked democracy – but also was the inevitable heritage of the first People Power movement in 1986 and the destiny of the middle class. All of these claims stake out a resistance position vis-à-vis the backlash experienced in Estrada's corruption and cronyism: a defense of the democratic frontlash first impelled by the People Power movement.

One claim was that EDSA 2 was a natural outcome of Philippine democracy, and, if anything, it represented the deepening of the democratic process. In CST terms, EDSA 2 was experienced as resistance to an antidemocratic backlash inherent in Estrada's presidency. Columnist Paul Rodrigo encapsulated the feelings of many of the participants, supporters, and promoters of EDSA 2 when the international press bore down on them:

> People Power is not a club to be wielded by the elite or by any faction. It is a mysterious, unpredictable outpouring of collective energy that seems to arrive when we most need it. That last sentence will seem like mysticism to most foreigners, but a Filipino will know it is true. (Rodrigo as cited in Mydans 2001)

For Rodrigo, this ineffable quality of EDSA 2 is distinctly national and it is distinctly autonomous from the mundane machinations of politics. Indeed, his explanation of EDSA 2's "unpredictable outpouring of collective energy" hews closely to the civil sphere's capacity for civil repair through a remaking of feelings of solidarity. But more importantly, when taken in the context of opposing Estrada's populism, Rodrigo's claims make clear that Philippine democracy is capable of self-correction in ways that exceed the Global North's limited procedural vision of democracy. In that sense, People Power is understood as the redemptory face of democracy given situated cultural form. As Seth Mydans (2001) observes, the responses of those who would justify the revolt vis-à-vis democratic practices gravitated toward one point: "Democratic institutions in the Philippines are not functioning as they should, they said, requiring periodic course corrections from a vigilant public." In other words, public intellectuals moved to defend EDSA 2 as not only sincerely and authentically performed, but also deeply representative of already-existing but fragile codes and narratives of Philippine democracy. When asked if there would be another People Power-type protest in the future, former President Corazón Aquino responded, "With two political revolutions in just 15 years, is Philippine democracy sustainable? My answer is, more than ever because we had those two revolutions in just 15 years" (Mydans 2001), suggesting that periodic renewal of the EDSA 2 type was actually an institutional feature of Philippine democracy. In other words, EDSA protests were understood as culturally specific, regularized forms of frontlash.

Still, a mere frontlash-populist framing of EDSA 2 would not be enough. If EDSA 2 could be scrutinized as simply elite-led, then it would be framed not as the peak of a second wave of frontlash, but rather as the return of elites to power against populist rule. The "Rich People's Power" labelling of the event needed to be disarmed, and in doing so, scholars, pundits, and activists created a new collective representation of the middle class. "In pitting the Insulares and Peninsulares[5] . . . against the masses," Ranier Ibaña (2003: 19) wrote, "Mr. Estrada's rhetoric failed to take cognizance of the middle classes which eventually turned the tide against his feudal interpretation of society." Taking issue with foreign and domestic criticism of EDSA 2, several public intellectuals and key participants in EDSA 2 contributed to *Between Fires* (2001), a volume of essays attempting to answer "questions . . . among Filipinos and foreign observers alike, over whether the Filipinos have unlocked and harnessed the powers of mass political mobilization" (Doronila 2001b: vii). In the lead piece in the volume, Cynthia Bautista (2001) summarizes the available poll data from two weeks after the event. In response to the claim that EDSA 2 was an elite coup, Bautista presents data that 47 percent of the respondents who participated at EDSA were from Class C, or the middle class based on dwelling and consumer goods in the home. However,

> The estimated proportion of Metro Manila-based middle-class participants in People Power 2 could be higher if the D rallyists with at least some college education and those in middle class occupations were added to the C group. Doing this would result in slightly more than half of the EDSA rallyists (56%) falling under the middle class category. (Bautista 2001: 8, fn. iv)

What is interesting is that Bautista reclassifies D-class respondents by education – diminishing the size of the poor, in effect – and leaves untouched the A and B classes, who are much more likely to be college-educated than those in the D class, and who are usually grouped with C in public opinion surveys. Education is important because it allows for a "modern sensibility imbibed through humanist education, attained formally through schools and universities or achieved in the practice of ideologically motivated social movements and religious organizations" (Bautista 2001: 13). Educated, enlightened, and modern, and politically active, the middle-class protestors at EDSA centrally disarm the rich people's power claim.

As such, middle-class protestors could be claimed to have a moral and intellectual perspective that allowed them to see the big picture of Philippine democracy. Public intellectual Randy David (2004: 242) tentatively defined People Power as an unarmed political gathering, sustained in a symbolic place, characterized by spontaneous organization and solidarity. However, he added:

In addition, one might say, based on the Philippine experience, that people power is best associated with the *middle classes* and the relatively better-educated sectors of society. There is of course nothing intrinsically middle class about people power, except maybe its reliance on the most modern means of communication to mobilize and keep its participants informed and connected. (David 2004: 243, emphasis in original)

This claim of technological modernity assisted in making a moral claim – "it was," in Cecilia Uy-Tioco's assessment, "a revolution by cell phone" (2003: 3), "[facilitating] the communication and cooperation between groups normally located at the ends of the ideological divide" (2003: 11). But Vicente Rafael is highly critical of assessments like Uy-Tioco's. In his analysis, the middle class "believed they could master their relationship to the masses of people with whom they regularly shared Manila's crowded streets and utilize the power of crowds to speak to the state" (Rafael 2003: 399). A communication fetish, the cell phone precipitated "telecommunicative fantasies ... predicated on the putative 'voicelessness' of the masses" (Rafael 2003: 400). "In short," he writes, "the middle class invests the crowd with the power of the cell phone: the power to transmit their wish for a moral community" (Rafael 2003: 412). Seen in contrast to mass "voicelessness," the cell phone served as symbol of distinction between the middle class and its mass opponents. In several ways, the collective representation of a coordinated, educated, and self-directed middle class at EDSA 2 linked it to the civil codes of self-control and rationality – features absent among Estrada's supporters at EDSA 3.

Such civil/anticivil counterpoising did not preclude that, one day, the poor would be able to militate for their own interests. José Abueva (2001: 96) warned that "the nation's legions of poor people, once sufficiently empowered, may finally rise against a society and political system they judge to be hopelessly unjust and oppressive." Ranier Ibaña (2003: 21, 22) noted that the pro-Estrada EDSA 3 "was not a product of deliberate processes of discourse and educational programs" but was the result of "an emotional identification" by the poor "with a folk hero who promised to emancipate them from their wretched situation"; in fact, their "frustration from actually having access to the opportunities of social participation ... led to [EDSA 3]." In addition, Randy David (2004: 178) suggested that EDSA 3 should not be "associated with the underprivileged classes of Philippine society," for "[any] crowd has the potential of being transformed into a mob if subjected to the same rabble-rousing and inflammatory speeches that the EDSA shrine protesters went through." In all these explanations for EDSA 3, the contrasts

Table 2.1 EDSA 2 and EDSA 3 protestors in binary opposition

EDSA 2	EDSA 3
Thinking	Unthinking
Educated	Uneducated
Voluntary	*Hakot* (paid off)
Disciplined and orderly	Spoiling for a fight
Righteously indignant	Frustrated

and the ongoing classification struggle are clear: the half million urban poor were "raw material for the ambitions of cynical politicians and media icons, or warm bodies for military power grabs disguised as people power" (David 2004: 179; see Table 2.1).[6] In short, the anticivil coding of Estrada's poor supporters read like a benighted paternalism. Still, the refined collective representation of the middle class built on binary codes – educated/uneducated, disciplined and orderly/spoiling for a fight, righteously indignant/frustrated – demarcated the middle class from the poor, but did not preclude the poor's future inclusion.

To tie these three themes together – self-regulation, objective majority, moral coding – the role of the middle class was to power the process of ongoing renewal and to continue to expand by spreading its values to the poor. In the Epilogue to the coffee-table book *People Power 2: Lessons and Hopes*, we learn:

> Ironically, the so-called EDSA 3 happened even as the country's intel-ligentsia and upper and middle classes were trying to consolidate the lessons from People Power 2. The poor, their ranks multiplied by worsening poverty, economic disparity, chronic corruption, and bad governance, had opened the wounds of society yet again. ...
> ... But there were some heartening developments: [People Power 2] brought to the fore the potential of civil society for influencing the country's governance; reaffirmed the existence of the middle class and the values it cherishes; raised the hope that disparate classes could come together for the common good. (San Juan 2001: 249)

And, as Ranier Ibaña (2003: 23) argued, it is, in fact, the "critical role" of the middle class to mediate between "the elite and the poorest of the poor," for "[w]ithout the mediation of the middle classes through the institutions of civil society, the tension between our traditional lifeworld and our modernizing social systems are [*sic*] bound to intensify in our daily lives." But, moreover, EDSA 2 was the product of a historically ascendant middle class, one in line with the historical trajectory of Philippine politics from the first EDSA and even earlier:

Those who toppled Mr. Estrada from the office of the presidency are heirs of the great revolutionary tradition of the middle classes at the turn of the 20th century. It was then that the so-called *Illustrados*, children of Filipino middle-class families, were emancipated from the anonymous masses by virtue of their social participation in the processes of European modernization that eventually reached the shores of colonial countries like the Philippines. (Ibaña 2003: 18)

Ibaña (2003: 19) goes on to say, "[A]lthough the Philippine middle classes had a checkered history of collaboration with foreign domination, their revolutionary potentials can be discerned if we take a closer look at our recent history," namely the student protests in 1970 known as the "first quarter storm," People Power in 1986, and EDSA 2. In short, the collective representation of the middle class at EDSA 2 was not only coded but also narrated to be the hero of Philippine democracy against threats both foreign and domestic.

In summary, the populist moment in the Philippines from 1998 to 2001 found its dramatic resolution through the EDSA 2 protests and their critical defense. Drawing on background symbols, already-existing collective representations, and the original EDSA narrative script, supporters of EDSA 2 set the middle class as the best argument for protecting what were considered frontlash gains from the original People Power revolution in 1986 from Estrada's corruption and his irrational followers. Though not following the procedures of electoral democracy, defending the integrity of the presidential office and of the gains in the EDSA revolution were understood as a necessary and indigenous renewal of the political system. In all these ways, the populist mood evoked by the Estrada presidency resolved in an attenuated understanding of the middle class as his ultimate dramatic foil.

Failed Antipopulism and the Profane Middle Class, 2016–2019

If the EDSA legacy had been affirmed in the early 2000s in an extra-institutional way, then it underwent an institutionalized revival with the election of Corazón Aquino's son Benigno "Noynoy" Aquino III to the presidency in 2010. Building on his family's link to the anti-Marcos movement, Aquino proposed a reformist solution to his predecessor Gloria Macapagal Arroyo's corruption. In a contest of "reformist and populist campaign narratives" (Thompson 2010: 163), Aquino leveraged his predecessor Arroyo's unpopularity and corruption for his victory, "[allowing] him to claim that it was Arroyo's poor leadership that was to blame for her failings, not the reformist political order" (Thompson 2016: 43). He ran with reformist slogans like the *Daang Matuwid* ("straight path") and *walang wang-wang* (lit. "no sirens," a reference to special treatment for politicians' cars in traffic), and his victory represented the "return of decency in government" (Villacorta 2011). In CST terms, Aquino positioned his presidency on the side of defending the advances of the democratic frontlash of the EDSA Revolution.

However, Aquino's administration failed on several fronts, from infrastructure, development projects, disaster management, and domestic security. His own family's oligarchic status came under intense scrutiny as his failures suggested not reform but a retrenchment of elite privileges. The reform-versus-populism choice reappeared in the 2016 election campaign, but this time with Rodrigo Duterte. For years the mayor of Davao, a major city in the southern island of Mindanao, Duterte leveraged the administration's failures against itself while touting his tough-on-crime, pro-Mindanao/anti-Manila credentials (Thompson 2016: 56). Duterte's brash, aggressive self-promotion of his law-and-order rule of Davao (Curato 2016) performed well against the four other candidates: Grace Poe, adopted daughter of movie star and one-time presidential candidate Fernando Poe Jr.; Jejomar Binay, mayor of Manila's business district Makati; longtime senator Miriam Defensor Santiago; and Mar Roxas, former senator and Aquino cabinet member. Duterte managed to wrongfoot his rivals, none of whom had counted on him entering the race.

It was not just Duterte's late start and outsider status that characterized the new populist moment. The subsequent, heightened populist mood emerged as he positioned himself as the charismatic aggressor and his opponents as unworthy foils. At the beginning of March 2016, with Election Day just two months away Duterte was behind Poe and ahead of Roxas in major polls (e.g., Santos 2016). Coming into the race last, Duterte benefited from ongoing criticisms of his opponents: Poe, the one-time front-runner, was under intense scrutiny about her Philippine citizenship, and Roxas had to carry the baggage of the incumbent government's failed promises. For his part, Duterte had promised to end the drug trade in three to six months by empowering police and protecting them from prosecution. At the same time, he had made a series of would-be political gaffes up to this point in the election, including calling Pope Francis a "son of a whore" the December prior. Then, at a campaign stop in mid-April 2016, captured on a video that swiftly became viral, he told a "rape joke" about an Australian missionary who was killed in a prison hostage situation in 1989:

When the bodies were brought out, they were wrapped. I looked at her face, son of a bitch, she looked like a beautiful American actress. Son of a bitch, what a waste. What came to mind was [that] they raped her, they lined up. I was angry because she was raped, that's one thing. But she was so beautiful, the mayor should have been first. What a waste. (Ranada 2016a)

Duterte's opponents tried to trap him in a textbook definition of a political gaffe: "an unintentional and/or inappropriate statement or behavior ... bringing into question [a politician's] knowledge, wisdom, and/or politically acceptable attitudes" (Frantzich as adapted by Sheinheit and Bogard 2016: 971). But, unlike US Senate candidate Todd Akin's "legitimate rape" gaffe in 2012, when pressed on his words, Duterte did not claim his "rape joke" was a misstatement, but insisted that in the original context in which he said it, his statements were emotionally appropriate and an affect from his class identity:

I am willing to lose the presidency. Do not make me apologize for something which I did [that was really] ... called for at the moment. . . . [Son of a bitch, that's who I am], do you want me to be courteous all the time? . . . That's the truth. . . . I really speak that way because I came from a poor family. I'm not the son of a rich person. (Ranada 2016b)

He then insisted that having been moved by the woman's beauty in death, he commanded his police forces to "bury" her killers. Thus instead of diminishing his campaign, Duterte came off as authentic, his poll numbers rising over the course of April to place him in front-runner status: "Duterte's shock value – from his rape joke to the cursing of the Pope – became the reliable emotional climax to television news and social media chatter in the election season" (Curato and Ong 2018: 7). In other words, like the Estrada trial, Duterte's shocking speech fused audiences to his performance on a regular basis.

In response to Duterte's rapid rise, the administration's standard-bearer, Mar Roxas, began to articulate a code of decency in his political speeches. As we saw above, "decency" had been deployed during EDSA 2 as a symbolic quality of the democratic middle class. For Roxas, however, being *disente* rose to the position of a symbol with master status, defining his campaign, himself as a person, his supporters, and eventually the entirety of the opposition to Duterte. In CST terms, Roxas sought to play the codes of civility and social class in such a way as to activate the solidarity that they might promise his campaign, the deeper narrative and cultural-structural implications linking him to the legacy of the EDSA Revolution – and as a defense against the backlash implications of a Duterte presidency. In the second presidential debate in March 2016,

Roxas linked decency to the unfinished project of the Benigno Aquino administration, the *Daang Matuwid*, and the promise of economic comfort through moral righteousness:

> In the Philippines, it's hard to be decent. Often decent people are the ones who get caught and have a hard time. .... We must fight for the *Daang Matuwid*. If we don't do what we say, if we're wrong, let's correct it, for we can achieve decency in our country. I invite you: let's bring the Philippines back to decent people. (Inquirer.net 2016)

But more pointedly, Roxas used *disente* aggressively against Duterte, framing the latter's hostile speech and tough-on-crime approach as profanely opposed to decent Filipinos. A campaign press release on April 11 entitled "Roxas kay Duterte: Ang Pangulo Dapat Disente" (Roxas to Duterte: The President Must Be Decent) stated, "According to Roxas, he is confident that citizens will choose a decent Filipino as president because the people's priority is to select the leader as a good example for the youth and give a good impression to the country" (Office of Mar Roxas 2016). After calling Duterte's promises to end the drug trade "empty" in an April 13 statement, Roxas concluded: "The Filipino is polite, the Filipino is humble, the Filipino is hardworking, the Filipino is *disente*. They will not allow a bully to lead them" (Alvarez and Macas 2016). And on April 18, responding directly to Duterte's rape joke, Roxas linked Duterte's flippancy about rape to torture:

> Rape violates one's dignity. Rape is not just a crime of sex. Rape is a crime of control. Rape is a crime of subjugation. What differentiates torture from rape? In torture, you handcuff a person and subject him to things that he dislikes. Rape is the same. So this is a serious matter. (Cupin 2016)

Roxas went on to declare, "That is why, Mayor Duterte, I will be your enemy. I will not allow a dictatorship in our country" (Cupin 2016). In his closing statement in the final presidential debate on April 24, Roxas combined the economic implications of decency with their moral ones, urging voters to vote for him to continue the *Daang Matuwid*:

> Another six years of honest, decent, hardworking governance and we can achieve our dreams. A Philippines that is prosperous and decent. Full of opportunity, free from fear, and free to dream. A prosperous and decent Philippines [where] there is dignity [; where] there is fear of [the] Lord. Pride. This is the Philippines we fight for. .... This is a fight for decency, for honesty, for our future. On May 9, we will prove to the whole of the Philippines and around the world, there are still more decent Filipinos. We still have many good Filipinos. We still have many more righteous Filipinos. (Manila Bulletin Online 2016)

Table 2.2 Mar Roxas: *disente* symbolic code vs. Duterte

Sacred – Roxas	Profane – Duterte
Decent (*disente*)	Indecent
Honest	Liar
Humble	Bully
Moral/righteous (*matuwid*)	Immoral
Hard-working	Lazy
Doer	Talker
Democratic	Dictatorial

In all these selections, it is clear that Roxas seemed to intensify his use of *disente* in the last month of the campaign. He made a consistent case for the sacrality and master status of decency as a symbolic code, inviting voters to see themselves as decent and therefore opposed to Duterte (Table 2.2). Roxas established the moral boundaries between decency and Duterte, positioning himself and his supporters on the pure side of the binary. On the other was Duterte, a potential dictator, misogynist, bully, and liar. If Duterte were to win, then the moral obligations of office would be lost on him – and Roxas conversely would be able to carry the moral weight of the presidency. To be Duterte's enemy, Roxas suggested, would mean to defend the frontlash gains of the Aquino administration, the legacy of People Power, and the decency of the hard-working middle class.

But it was perhaps a consequence of Roxas' mechanical consistency with *disente* and the high standards of the symbolic opposition it implied that he not only failed to stem Duterte's rising support in the last month of the campaign, but also unwittingly gave pro-Duterte bloggers a tool with which to troll him and his supporters. In insisting on continuity with Aquino's *Daang Matuwid*, while having to answer for the regime's failures, Roxas had set a high bar to cross – even if his campaign represented defending the moral and institutional gains of People Power. In the last televised debate on April 24, Duterte and Roxas had a testy exchange over the effectiveness of a government health program in Davao. Roxas concluded by saying, "People are looking at your behavior, Mayor Duterte, and you're not worthy. On May 9th, the winner will be righteous, the winner will be decent, the winner will be worthy, the winner will be Mar Roxas." "*Susmaryosep* [Jesus, Mary, and Joseph]," Duterte replied in frustration, to the delight of the audience. Like Marco Rubio against Donald Trump, Duterte had turned Roxas into an unworthy challenger, bolstering his charismatic stature (see Joose 2018: 929–33). Compared to Duterte, Roxas' invocation of *disente* made him seem robotic, patronizing, and elitist.

At the same time, Roxas opened himself up to criticism that he could not live up to the moral purity necessary to be *disente*. In the words of one columnist,

> With all due respect, please stop this drama about being "disente." Because we always remember your silence or your protection of your partymates accused of graft, corruption, plunder, malversation [*sic*] of public funds, and other crimes. That's not being "disente." That's being a co-conspirator or an enabler of the corrupt. (T. Cruz 2016)

Here, the columnist situates Roxas with the forces of backlash, not front-lash: if Roxas was complicit in abetting the previous administration's corruption, then the moral obligations of office could hardly be met by someone simply *performing* decency.

On social media, Duterte supporters – mocked as "Dutertards" by opponents – found niches in the blogosphere, Twitter, and Facebook (see esp. Sinpeng 2016), launching the trolling of #dilawan (yellow, the color of the Liberal Party), #yellowtard, and #disente supporters of Roxas. "*Disente*" and "*dilawan*" in the ironic mode continued (and continues) to be used in print, online, and on social media to criticize Duterte's opponents. Pro-Duterte bloggers like former girl band member-turned-administration official Mocha Uson were "carrier agents" who, though without traditional media legitimacy, had "know-how, and networks to disseminate the story and keep it alive by posting links, new articles, and interacting with citizen spectators on new media platforms" (Sheinheit and Bogard 2016: 974). These consisted of image macros of public spaces strewn with trash after Liberal Party rallies, videos of politicians and Liberal Party supporters swearing or otherwise acting in *bastos* (indecent) ways. Thus, in cultural sociological terms, Roxas sought to calibrate decent/indecent with the civil sacred/profane, and used a romantic genre to amplify the distance between decent/ Roxas/democracy and indecent/Duterte/dictatorship. Duterte and his supporters countered with irony performed through exasperation. The effect was not to deny the decent/indecent binary opposition, but to diminish its metonymic power and render it a tool to deflate narrative and defuse performance (see Smith 1998, 2005). In terms of frontlash and backlash, the effect was to discount Roxas, the Liberal Party, and those against Duterte as morally incapable of being the leading edge of protecting the advances of frontlash. It was instead Duterte who represented frontlash.

Disente continued to have a life of its own after Duterte's election. Pro-Duterte blog GetRealPhilippines.com user rsutida responded to speculation that Duterte might be impeached or otherwise removed from office just a few months into his term by profaning "The Yellows" using an ironic logic:

> In the Philippines there's a significant number of people comprising a small, but perpetually annoying group that think in terms of *how things should be* rather than adapt and work with what's available because of *how things are*. Lovingly called *The Yellows* – named after the banner color of the Aquino Clan after the 1986 EDSA Revolution – they also branded themselves and their cause *"disente"* (decent) as early as the campaign period as a counterpoint for Mar Roxas against the popular, but foul-mouthed Duterte.
>
> The Yellows, along with a small group of other dissenters who do not necessarily view the Aquinos as patron saints, have taken to the streets to voice their disapproval of controversial initiatives of the administration like the war on drugs and the Marcos burial. Some even matched the president's penchant for hyperbole by declaring the Philippines is in the early stages of the apocalypse.
>
> You don't like Duterte, fine. You hate his mannerisms and policies, fine. You'd rather have pristine, sweet-talking, politically-correct, thieving dipshits endorsed by the equally corrupt CBCP [Catholic Bishops Conference of the Philippines]; that's fine, too. To each his pawn in the never-ending powerplay that is politics.
>
> But kindly drop the "moral" and "decent" bullcrap. We're all Pinoys here, and you're not fooling anyone. (rsutida 2016, emphasis in the original)

What is telling about rsurtida's statement is that it exhibits a postmodern awareness of the narrative tropes (apocalypse) and symbolic codes (*disente*) that they argue animate the opposition. A true Pinoy (Filipino), according to rsurtida, already bears a cynical reading of politics. To harp on decency and morality is not only insincere but also plays right into the manipulative logic of the ruling elite: the People/Elite binary is built here on the decent/indecent binary logic that marked the presidential campaign.

After Duterte's first State of the Union address in 2017, GetRealPhilippines.com webmaster Benign0 also defended the regime from opponents who would end it early:

> It should be no mystery why the way Duterte wears *who he is* on his sleeve today is so refreshing to Filipinos. It is because he introduces *consistency* in what was once a *fake democracy*. I would have liked to have said that not one of the many presidents who sat in Malacañang actually mirrored the Filipino electorate as accurately and that Duterte broke that trend. However, in actual fact, former President Joseph "Erap" Estrada beat Duterte to that title in 1998. But the Erap presidency provides important context to the Duterte administration. Like

Duterte today, Erap was relentlessly demonized by the same camp of *disente* Filipinos (at the time just as presumptuously calling themselves "civil society") and, on the back of that vilification campaign, was successfully removed from office *illegally*. Fast forward to today and it is now easy to see with the benefit of that hindsight that the ouster of Erap is being used as the same model *by the same mob* to end the Duterte government prematurely. (Benign0 2017, emphasis in the original)

In this passage, Benign0 historicizes the *disente/dilawan* opposition. Like rsurtida above, he approaches the opposition cautiously: they are not to be trusted because "the same mob" is planning to oust Duterte just as they ousted Estrada, another president who truly represented the Filipino voter. For the purposes of this chapter, Benign0's statement highlights one of the contrasting conditions for the success of EDSA 2 and the failures of recent years: a self-aware opposition media environment that has proven capable of disarming claims to decency and civility. The defense of frontlash that EDSA 2 represented was now recast as elite backlash.

Indeed, the emerging scholarly consensus is that the Duterte regime marks the end of the political-symbolic dynamics set by the 1986 EDSA Revolution that toppled the dictatorship of Ferdinand Marcos (see, e.g., Curato 2016, 2017; Arguelles 2017; Hayadarian 2017; Teehankee 2017; Webb 2017). Mark Thompson (2016: 58) writes, "It is symbolic of the death of the EDSA . . . political order that Duterte ordered a 'hero's' reburial of Marcos in the Libingan ng mga Bayani cemetery, which took place in mid-November 2016 after Marcos critics failed to convince the Supreme Court to block the internment." In this break with the EDSA legacy, scholars have observed Duterte's new moral (Kusaka 2017), discursive (Teehankee 2017), emotional (Curato 2016) politics that reject a hypocritical, elitist, and Manila-driven civility and replace it with an uncivil, redemptory populism that is at best ambivalent toward authoritarianism (Webb 2017).

But there are clear indications that Duterte's populism is destructive for the civil sphere. His drug war has taken the lives of an estimated 20,000 people through extrajudicial police killings; a process which received laudatory comments from US President Donald Trump: an "unbelievable job on the drug problem" (Savillo 2019). Duterte has arrested political opponents like Senator Lila de Lima and prominent journalist Maria Ressa. These actions clearly shrink the civil sphere.

Still, media commentators have noted Duterte's strong support among the middle class, interpreted as having been frustrated by the Aquino regime's failures and the feeling that the need for stability trumped democracy (see Webb 2017). Randy David, who was quoted above as linking People Power to the middle class, expressed concern that the middle class was now the anchor for what he called "Duterismo." Comparing Duterismo to European fascism, David (2016) notes, "The supreme irony is that the typical bearers of these values – the educated middle classes – found themselves cooperating with, if not actively supporting, the movement." This shift is consequential as David closely associated People Power as a concept to its middle classness; now, education could not bring the kind of enlightenment about democracy that it did fifteen years prior.

Polling data also no longer fit the representation of a democratic middle class. Julio Teehankee commented on polling data showing Duterte's high support among classes ABC (upper, upper-middle, middle): "The Duterte phenomenon is elite-driven. It is not the revolt of the poor. It is the angry protest of the new middle class: BPO [Business process outsourcing] workers, Uber drivers, and OFWs [overseas foreign workers]" (R. G. Cruz 2016). And Narciso Reyes, Jr. (2016) concludes,

> Not surprisingly, [Duterte's] rising support comes not only from the poor and wretched of the earth but also from a big chunk of a frustrated and disenchanted middle class – lodged between the impoverished masses into which it fears sliding and the power elite to which it aspires to belong, with both classes impatiently clamoring for change and reform.

Compare these observations to the work generated to defend EDSA 2 from charges that it was elite-driven. Thinking through CST, we can identify a symbolic break in the collective representation of a democratic middle class. While the middle class at EDSA 2 was in line with the continuity of Philippine self-determination and democracy, this "new" middle class is "frustrated and disenchanted" – characteristics used to describe the urban poor at EDSA 2.

In the words of Imelda Deinla (2017), "The Philippines looms towards authoritarian rule unless the middle class withdraws its support for President Rodrigo Duterte's illiberal policies." Although "the Filipino middle class does not fear Duterte . . . they have been so insecure that they are willing to take a chance on his draconian measures":

> Targeting the drug addicts and the "yellows" or those who opposed administration policies as "enemies of the state" has been the object through which insecurity has been magnified. The middle class are insecure because they are frustrated and disempowered to affect policies and decisions that will fulfil their aspirations to a higher level. They are angry because despite their increasing prosperity, the Filipino middle class suffer from the high cost of living, poor delivery of basic services, and the everyday struggle to stay safe and secure within their homes and properties. (Deinla 2017)

The middle class "are in a fragile state and feel a deep sense of instability" (Deinla 2017). Like the commentators above, Imelda Deinla identifies Duterte's core support among the middle class. In doing so, she attributes this class with insecurity, fragility, and struggle – all characteristics that she suggests lead them toward Duterte's draconian anticivil policies.

In a key contrast, Duterte's economic development plan explicitly targets a growing middle class, addressing security, comfort, and stability:

> The 25-year vision foresees a Philippines that is a "prosperous, predominantly middle-class society where no one is poor." . . . In 2040, we will all enjoy a stable and comfortable lifestyle, secure in the knowledge that we have enough for our daily needs and unexpected expenses, that we can plan and prepare for our own and our children's future. (Rappler.com 2016)

Compared to Deinla's statement, Duterte's development plan emphasizes the symbolic opposites in her claims: stability/instability, stable/fragile, secure/insecure. Thus, we see cultural-structural shifts in the metonymic status of codes that characterize the new debate about the middle class.

Conclusion

This chapter has demonstrated that populism and antipopulism can be understood through the symbolic, institutional, and performative logic of the civil sphere. It has also shown that inasmuch as populism offers the seductive condensation of politics into *masa* vs. the elite, social class remains a fundamental meaningful reference point for civil sphere action. Using a comparison of antipopulist codes, symbols, and performances during EDSA 2 and during the 2016 presidential elections, this chapter has demonstrated that shared binary oppositions drawing on the civil code were fundamental components of Philippine antipopulism. It has shown that social actors understood these codes as impacting their symbolic understanding of social class, particularly the middle class, and that they were the creative results of contingent performative circumstances. For EDSA 2, foreign criticism and counterprotest saw civil society actors construct a democratic and civic middle class capable of defending the advances of frontlash from the first EDSA Revolution. In contrast, in opposing Duterte, civil sphere actors found their code of decency easily deflated by media-savvy and self-aware carrier agents on social media. Safety, security, and stability rose to master status, and the opposition languished on the negative side of those codes in imagining the middle class.

These findings lead to three conclusions. First, locating Philippine antipopulism's CST frontlash/backlash logic is not straightforward. While operating within the symbolic horizon of the civil sphere, EDSA 2 removed a democratically elected president, and thus, by definition, it was extra-institutional. It also precipitated a backlash from Estrada's supporters that required drawing on class distinctions to defend. These features suggest that EDSA 2 was in fact an attack on voting and office with a marginalizing result: anticivil, antipopulist backlash. Contemporary media-savvy carrier agents also understand EDSA 2 as such, the last card of the #disente against Duterte in the light of their electoral defeat. Here, we might register agreement with Anthony Spaeth (2001) and Jim Mann (2001) that mob rule by any other name is still mob rule, and reinforce the arguments of Joshua Kurlantzick (2013) that middle-class protest has deleterious effects on democracy in the long run.

Here CST's frontlash/backlash dynamics must be understood in the context of the symbolic construction of social class and the transnational quality of civil spheres themselves. This chapter reinforces how civil societies symbolically construct their middle classes to describe them as either democratic or antidemocratic. Elsewhere, I have identified a consistent, transhistorical, and translocal symbolic logic that emerges when social actors attempt to relate the middle class to democracy (Villegas 2019). "Decency" appears as a positive, solidaristic marker of the middle classes in cases as far-ranging as nineteenth-century England (Wahrman 1995), nineteenth- and twentieth-century Peru (Parker 1998), and twentieth-century Brazil (Owensby 1998), and we can definitively add twenty-first-century Philippines to that list. I also identify consistent negative symbolic codes applied to the middle class, descriptors that diminish its civil stature and profane it – instability, insecurity, anxiety, among others – which also appear in this chapter as negative descriptors of the middle class in the Philippines. As Roxas' performative failures indicate, the effectiveness of these middle-class codes is subject to their creative deployment. For the study of populism through CST, a symbolic-structural approach to class shows how the civil sphere is relatively autonomous and can help create democratic or antidemocratic class actors, not the other way around.

Finally, this chapter touches on the transnational quality of the civil sphere. For the Philippines, the civil sphere is necessarily inflected with the history of colonialism and American empire (see Go 1999), with Duterte's regionalism as one long-run result of that history. Civil purity and self-determination have a complicated relationship, as evidenced by foreign criticism of EDSA 2 and its defense as both fully Filipino and – by the dint of the middle class – a fully global story of democracy. Latter-day bouts with populism, especially with Duterte being compared to Donald Trump in the United States, to Jair Bolsonaro in Brazil, and to other authoritarian populists, could have the effect of globalizing antipopulist resistance. On the other hand, looking at the Philippines through the gaze of an American concerned with Trump may do more to provincialize the Philippines than to treat it as a case that experiences its populism in *coeval* ways. It is good to remember that Duterte was elected before Trump. For CST, this global populist moment offers an important opportunity to demonstrate the promise of the civil sphere as a collective, global horizon for solidarity.

Notes

1 This is also the fundamental presupposition propping up the "empathy walls" (Hochschild 2017) that stand between Trump supporters and opponents. Asking deviancy-based questions like "what's the matter with Kansas?" or "why did the white working class vote against their own interests?" alienates liberals from conservatives in the United States (cf. Wuthnow 2018).
2 Although in *The Civil Sphere*, Alexander takes on Polanyi's *The Great Transformation* (2001 [1944]) with sustained but measured criticism (e.g., Alexander 2006: 26), he agrees wholeheartedly with the latter's criticism of economic-reductionist notions of class formation, citing these key excerpts: "Once we rid ourselves of the obsession that only sectional, never general, interest can become effective, . . . as well as the twin prejudice of restricting the interests of human groups to their monetary income, the breadth and depth of the protectionist movement lose their mystery" (Polanyi as cited in Alexander 2006: 32). In this sense, we can get at the breadth and depth of populism by making the same moves.
3 I will use both "People Power" and "EDSA" interchangeably. EDSA is the nickname for the Epifiano de los Santos Freeway in Manila, a major north–south thoroughfare linking Manila proper with Quezon City to the north, and the gathering place for protestors in 1986 and 2001. The "2" in EDSA 2 can either be read as *dos* or *two*.
4 See one summary response in Doronila (2001a).
5 "Insulares" and "Peninsulares" refer to the Spanish colonial-era distinction between Spaniards born in the Philippines and Spaniards who had settled in the Philippines, respectively.
6 Or as Ibaña (2003: 22) suggests similarly, "It will not be surprising to find out that the constituencies of political figures that emerged from the military establishment will come from the camp of the inarticulate."

References

Abueva, J. V. (2001) A crisis of political leadership: From "electoral democracy" to "substantive democracy." In: A. Doronila (ed.) *Between Fires: Fifteen Perspectives on the Estrada Crisis.* Pasig: Anvil Publishing.

Alexander, J. C. (2006) *The Civil Sphere*. New York: Oxford University Press.

Alexander, J. C. (2007) Keeping faith with *The Civil Sphere*, and my critics. *Perspectives*, October: 10–15.

Alexander, J. C. (2011) *Performance and Power*. Cambridge: Polity.

Alexander, J. C. (2013) The arc of civil liberation: Obama–Tahrir–Occupy. *Philosophy and Social Criticism* 39(4–5): 341–7.

Alexander, J. C. (2018) The societalization of social problems: Church pedophilia, phone hacking, and the financial crisis. *American Sociological Review* 83(6): 1049–78.

Alexander, J. C. (2019) Frontlash/backlash: The crisis of solidarity and the threat to civil institutions. *Contemporary Sociology* 48(1): 5–11.

Alvarez, K. C. and T. Macas. (2016) Mar Roxas calls Duterte's campaign promises "Ampaw." *GMA News Online*, April 13. https://www.gmanetwork.com/news/news/nation/562545/mar-roxas-calls-duterte-s-campaign-promises-ampaw/story/.

Anderson, B. (1988) Cacique democracy in the Philippines: Origins and dreams. *New Left Review* 169(1): 3–31.

Arditi, B. (2015) The people as re-presentation and event. In: C. de la Torre (ed.) *The Promise and Perils of Populism*. Lexington: University of Kentucky Press.

Arguelles, C. (2017) "We are Rodrigo Duterte": Dimensions of the Philippine populist public. *Asian Politics & Policy* 11(3): 417–37.

Bautista, M. C. R. (2001) The revenge of the elite on the masses? In: A. Doronila (ed.) *Between Fires: Fifteen Perspectives on the Estrada Crisis*. Pasig: Anvil Publishing.

Benign0. (2017) Duterte reminded Filipinos who they REALLY are during his #SONA2017 address. *GetRealPhilippines.com*, July 27. https://www.getrealphilippines.com/2017/07/duterte-reminded-filipinos-who-they-really-are-during-his-sona2017-address/.

Bonikowski, B. and N. Gidron. (2015) The populist style in American politics: Presidential campaign discourse, 1952–1996. *Social Forces* 94(4): 1593–621.

Canovan, M. (1999) Trust the people! Populism and the two faces of democracy. *Political Studies* 47(1): 2–16.

Case, W. (2003) Interlocking elites in Southeast Asia. *Comparative Sociology* 2(1): 249–69.

Constantino-David, K. (2001) Surviving Erap. In: A. Doronila (ed.) *Between Fires: Fifteen Perspectives on the Estrada Crisis*. Pasig: Anvil Publishing.

Cruz, R. G. (2016) Why Duterte is popular among wealthy, middle class voters. *ABS-CBN News Online*, May 1. https://news.abs-cbn.com/halalan2016/focus/04/30/16/why-duterte-is-popular-among-wealthy-middle-class-voters.

Cruz, T. (2016) Dear Mr. Mar Roxas. *Manila Bulletin*, April 16. https://www.pressreader.com/philippines/manila-bulletin/20160416/281848642770870.

Cupin, B. (2016) Roxas to Duterte: I'll be your enemy. *Rappler*, April 18. https://www.rappler.com/nation/politics/elections/2016/129944-mar-roxas-rodrigo-duterte-enemy.

Curato, N. (2016) Politics of anxiety, politics of hope: Penal populism and Duterte's rise to power. *Journal of Current Southeast Asian Affairs* 35(3): 91–109.

Curato, N. (2017) We need to talk about Rhody. In: N. Curato (ed.) *A Duterte Reader*. Manila: Ateneo de Manila University Press.

Curato, N. and J. C. Ong. (2018) Who laughs at a rape joke? Illiberal responsiveness in Rodrigo Duterte's Philippines. In: T. Dreher and A. A. Mondal (eds.) *Ethical Responsiveness and the Politics of Difference*. Cham: Palgrave Macmillan.

David, R. (2004) People power and the legal system. In: R. David, *Reflections on Sociology and Philippine Society*. Quezon City: University of the Philippines Press.

David, R. (2016) Dutertismo. *Philippine Daily Inquirer*, May 1. https://opinion. inquirer.net/94530/dutertismo.

de La Torre, C. (2010) *Populist Seduction in Latin America*. Athens: Ohio University Press.

Deinla, I. (2017) Duterte and the insecurity of the Philippine middle class. *ANU Governance and the Power of Fear Blog Series*. http://regnet.anu.edu.au/news-events/news/7036/duterte-and-insecurity-philippine-middle-class.

di Tella, T. (1965) *Populism and Reform in Latin America*. London: Oxford University Press.

Doronila, A. (2001a) EDSA II worries Western media. *Philippine Daily Inquirer*, January 29.

Doronila, A. (2001b) Introduction. In: A. Doronila (ed.) *Between Fires: Fifteen Perspectives on the Estrada Crisis*. Pasig: Anvil Publishing.

Encarnación, O. G. (2002) Venezuela's "civil society coup." *World Policy Journal*, Summer: 38–48.

Fisher, D. R. (2019) *American Resistance: From the Women's March to the Blue Wave*. New York: Columbia University Press.

Garrido, M. (2008) Civil and uncivil society: Symbolic boundaries and civic exclusion in Metro Manila. *Philippine Studies* 56(4): 443–66.

Garrido, M. (2018) Why the poor support populism: The politics of sincerity in Metro Manila. *American Journal of Sociology* 123(3): 647–85.

Gauna, A. (2016) Populism, heroism, and revolution: Chávez's cultural performances in Venezuela, 1999–2012. *American Journal of Cultural Sociology* 6(1): 37–59.

Germani, G. (1978) *Authoritarianism, Fascism, and National Populism*. New Brunswick: Transaction Publishers.

Gidron, N. and B. Bonikowski. (2013) Varieties of populism: Literature review and research agenda. Weatherhead Center for International Affairs Working Papers Series No. 13-0004. https://scholar.harvard.edu/files/gidron_bon ikowski_populismlitreview_2013.pdf.

Go, J. (1999) Colonial reception and cultural reproduction: Filipino elites and United States tutelary rule. *Journal of Historical Sociology* 12(4): 337–68.

Hayadarian, R. J. (2017) *The Rise of Duterte: A Populist Revolt against Elite Democracy*. London: Palgrave Pivot.

Hedman, E. L. (2001) The spectre of populism in Philippine politics and society. *South East Asia Research* 9(1): 5–44.

Hochschild, A. (2017) *Strangers in Their Own Land: Anger and Mourning on the American Right*. New York: The New Press.

Ibaña, R. R. A. (2003) Lifeworld-systems analysis of People Power 2 and 3. *Kritika Kultura* 3(July): 17–24.

Inquirer.net. (2016) FULL TRANSCRIPT: 2nd #PiliPinas2016 presidential debate in UP Cebu. https://newsinfo.inquirer.net/775643/full-transcript-2nd-pilipinas2016-presidential-debate-in-up-cebu.

Jansen, R. S. (2016) Situated political innovation: Explaining the historical emergence of new modes of political practice. *Theory and Society* 45(4): 319–60.

Jones, G. S. (1983) *Languages of Class: Studies in English Working Class History, 1832–1982*. Cambridge: Cambridge University Press.

Joose, P. (2018) Countering Trump: Toward a theory of charismatic counter-roles. *Social Forces* 97(2): 921–44.

Karakaya, Y. (2018) The conquest of hearts: The central role of Ottoman nostalgia within contemporary Turkish populism. *American Journal of Cultural Sociology*. doi:10.1057/s41290-018-0065-y.

Kurlantzick, J. (2013) *Democracy in Retreat: The Revolt of the Middle Class and the Worldwide Decline of Representative Government*. New Haven: Yale University Press.

Kusaka, W. (2017) Bandit grabbed the state: Duterte's moral politics. *Philippine Sociological Review* 65(S1): 49–75.

Laclau, E. (2005) *On Populist Reason*. London: Verso.

Landé, C. (2001) The return of "People Power" in the Philippines. *Journal of Democracy* 12(2): 88–102.

Manila Bulletin Online. (2016) Mar Roxas' closing statement at #PiliPinasDebates2016. *YouTube*, April 25. https://www.youtube.com/watch?v=y5M66z3DKY0.

Mann, J. (2001) A risky move by Filipinos. *Los Angeles Times*, January 24.

Meyer, D. S. and S. Tarrow (eds.). (2018) *The Resistance: The Dawn of the Anti-Trump Movement*. New York: Oxford University Press.

Moffitt, B. (2016) *The Global Rise of Populism: Performance, Style, and Representation*. Stanford: Stanford University Press.

Molyneux, M. and T. Osborne. (2017) Populism: A deflationary view. *Economy and Society* 46(1): 1–19.

Mudde, C. (2015) Conclusion: Further thoughts on populism. In: C. de la Torre (ed.) *The Promise and Perils of Populism: Global Perspectives*. Lexington: University of Kentucky Press.

Mudde, C. and C. R. Kaltwasser. (2013) Exclusionary vs. inclusionary populism: Comparing contemporary Europe and Latin America. *Government and Opposition* 48(2): 147–74.

Mydans, S. (2001) Expecting praise, Filipinos are criticized for ouster. *New York Times*, February 2. https://archive.nytimes.com/www.nytimes.com/learning/students/pop/010206snaptuesday.html.

Office of Mar Roxas. (2016) Roxas kay Duterte: Ang Pangulo Dapad Disente. https://web.archive.org/web/20170426053807/http://blog.marroxas.com/2016/04/11/roxas-kay-duterte-ang-pangulo-dapat-disente/.

Overholt, W. H. (2001) It's People Power again, but this time without the people. *New York Times*, January 24. https://www.nytimes.com/2001/01/24/opinion/IHT-its-people-power-again-but-this-time-without-the-people.html.

Owensby, B. (1999) *Intimate Ironies: Modernity and the Making of Middle-Class Lives in Brazil*. Stanford: Stanford University Press.

Parker, D. S. (1998) *The Idea of the Middle Class: White-Collar Workers and Peruvian Society, 1900–1950*. University Park: Pennsylvania State University Press.

Pilapil, G. L. (2016) Duterte, democracy and inevitability. *Philippine Daily Inquirer*, May 26. https://opinion.inquirer.net/94912/duterte-democracy-and-inevitability.

Polanyi, K. (2001 [1944]) *The Great Transformation: The Political and Economic Origins of Our Times*. Boston: Beacon Press.

Rafael, V. L. (2003) The cell phone and the crowd: Messianic politics in the contemporary Philippines. *Popular Culture* 15(3): 399–425.

Ranada, P. (2016a) VIRAL: Video of Duterte joking about raped Australian woman. *Rappler*, April 16. https://www.rappler.com/nation/politics/elections/2016/129784-viral-video-duterte-joke-australian-woman-rape.

Ranada, P. (2016b) Duterte: "Not sorry for rape remark, that's how I speak." *Rappler*, April 17. https://www.rappler.com/nation/politics/elections/2016/129844-duterte-reaction-rape-joke-australian-woman.

Rappler.com. (2016) Duterte's Ambisyon Natin 2040: Middle-class society for PH. *Rappler*, October 15. https://www.rappler.com/nation/149252-duterte-ambisyon-natin-2040-ph-development-plan.

Reyes, N., Jr. (2016) In our image: The rise of Duterte. *Philippine Daily Inquirer*, May 4. https://opinion.inquirer.net/94582/image-rise-duterte#ixzz5q6BimEBt.

rsurtida. (2016) The populists and the guardians of "decency." *GetRealPhilippines.com*, December 15. https://www.getrealphilippines.com/2016/12/populists-guardians-decency/.

Ruiz, E. de V. and G. Kabiling. (2019) Gov't gets "very good" performance rating in latest SWS survey. *Manila Bulletin*, March 12. https://news.mb.com.ph/2019/03/12/govt-gets-very-good-performance-rating-in-latest-sws-survey/.

San Juan, T. S. (2000) What about us middle class? *Philippine Daily Inquirer*, October 27.

San Juan, T. S. (2001) Epilogue. In: T. S. San Juan (ed.) *People Power 2: Lessons and Hopes*. Pasig: ABS-CBN Publishing.

Santos, E. P. (2016) Poe slightly ahead of Duterte in New Pulse Asia survey. *CNN Philippines*, March 15. http://nine.cnnphilippines.com/news/2016/03/15/Poe-Duterte-Pulse-Asia-survey.html.

Savillo, L. (2019) Trump phone call to Duterte left White House staff "genuinely horrified." *Vice*, October 16. https://www.vice.com/en_asia/article/3kxj49/trump-duterte-phone-call-drug-war-human-rights.

Sheinheit, I. and C. J. Bogard. (2016) Authenticity and carrier agents: The social construction of political gaffes. *Sociological Forum* 31(4): 970–93.

Sinpeng, A. (2016) How Duterte won the election on Facebook. *New Mandala*, May 12. https://www.newmandala.org/how-duterte-won-the-election-on-facebook/.

Smith, P. (1998) Barbarism and civility in the discourses of fascism, communism, and democracy: Variations on a set of themes. In: J. C. Alexander (ed.) *Real Civil Societies: Dilemmas of Institutionalization*. London: Sage.

Smith, P. (2005) *Why War? The Cultural Logic of Iraq, the Gulf War, and Suez*. Chicago: University of Chicago Press.

Snyder, T. (2017) *On Tyranny: Twenty Lessons from the Twentieth Century*. New York: Tim Duggan Books.

Somers, M. (1992) Narrativity, narrative identity, and social action: Rethinking English working-class formation. *Social Science History* 16(4): 591–630.

Spaeth, A. (2001) Oops, we did it again. *Time*, January 29. http://content.time.com/time/world/article/0,8599,2054385,00.html.

Teehankee, J. (2017) Was Duterte's rise inevitable? In: N. Curato (ed.) *A Duterte Reader*. Manila: Ateneo de Manila University Press.

Thompson, M. (2010) Reformism vs. populism in the Philippines. *Journal of Democracy* 21(4): 154–68.

Thompson, M. (2016) Bloodied democracy: Duterte and the death of liberal reformism in the Philippines. *Journal of Current Southeast Asian Affairs* 35(3): 39–68.

Uy-Tioco, C. A. (2003) The cell phone and Edsa 2: The role of a communication technology in ousting a president. Paper presented at the 4th Critical Themes in Media Studies Conference, New School University, October 11, New York.

Villacorta, W. (2011) *Noynoy: Triumph of a People's Campaign.* Pasig: Anvil Publishing.

Villegas, C. M. (2019) The middle class as a culture structure: Rethinking middle-class formation and democracy through the civil sphere. *American Journal of Cultural Sociology* 7(2): 135–73.

Wahrman, D. (1995) *Imagining the Middle Class: The Political Representation of Class in Britain, c. 1780–1840.* Cambridge: Cambridge University Press.

Webb, A. (2017) Why are the middle-class misbehaving? Exploring democratic ambivalence and authoritarian nostalgia. *Philippine Sociological Review* 65(S1): 77–102.

Weyland, K. (1996) Neopopulism and neoliberalism in Latin America: Unexpected affinities. *Studies in Comparative International Development* 31(3): 3–31.

Weyland, K. (2001) Clarifying a contested concept: Populism in the study of Latin American politics. *Comparative Politics* 34(1): 1–22.

Wuthnow, R. (2018) *The Left Behind: Decline and Rage in Rural America.* Princeton: Princeton University Press.

3

Uncivil Populism in Power

The Case of Erdoğanism

Ateş Altınordu

Populism has become one of the most popular topics in social science since the double shock of Trump's election victory and the Brexit vote in 2016. In response to what seems to be a ubiquitous political trend in Western and Eastern Europe, South and North America, the Middle East, and South Asia, a plethora of conferences and monographs, edited volumes, and journal articles have been devoted to the subject. As a result of this recent surge of work, the literature seems to have reached a certain maturity, with early statements (Ionescu and Gellner 1969; Canovan 1981), classic syntheses (Müller 2016; Mudde and Kaltwasser 2017), exploration of historical waves,[1] classifications of populism's subtypes (left-wing vs. neoliberal, inclusionary vs. exclusionary, democratic vs. authoritarian, insurgent vs. incumbent), and investigations of its relationship to social domains such as the economy (Rodrik 2018), religion (Marzouki et al. 2016), and cultural values (Norris and Inglehart 2019). The emerging need to organize and summarize this exponentially growing literature has led to the publication of two major handbooks on the subject (Kaltwasser et al. 2017a; de la Torre 2019).

With some important exceptions, the field of populism is dominated by political scientists, who "began to take ownership of this topic" as early as the 1980s (Kaltwasser et al. 2017b: 6), and, as a result, by analytical frameworks drawn from political science. The best among these studies combine carefully defined analytical categories with extensive knowledge of the empirical cases and have significantly contributed to our understanding of the phenomenon. Given this explosion of work on the subject – and its frequent repetitiveness – what is, if any, the added value of approaching this topic from a cultural sociological perspective?

In this chapter, I suggest two ways in which cultural sociology can make distinctive contributions to populism studies. The first is through a social performance approach, which would further our understanding of how populism works and help explain why some populist projects succeed while others fail. The second is through sociological theories of democratic civility, which would allow us to investigate populism's institutional and normative relationship to liberal democracy through a coherent analytical framework.

Virtually all writing on the phenomenon notes that populist ideology relies on a moral distinction between a virtuous people and a corrupt elite who oppress them (Müller 2016; Mudde and Kaltwasser 2017). Moreover, while a charismatic, personalistic leader is not a feature of all populisms all of the time, it is central to most populisms most of the time (Moffitt 2016). Social performance theory (Alexander 2004, 2010; Mast 2013) offers distinctive tools for the analysis of populism's cultural texture and political style in a way that goes beyond the political ideology perspective of the "ideational approach" (Mudde 2017) and the mystified notion of charismatic leadership that is often posited rather than explained (cf. Garrido 2017).[2]

Populisms are characterized by blatant contradictions throughout: leaders with questionable personal morality who receive the votes of religious-conservative constituencies (Gorski 2017b); the poor who support parties and leaders that do not serve their material interests (Garrido 2017); privileged ethnic groups that experience a strong sense of existential threat (Fisher and Taub 2019); populations who mobilize on the basis of xenophobic appeals despite not having substantive exposure to refugees or immigrants (Chase 2017; Schaub et al. 2020); and populist leaders who present themselves "as both ordinary and extraordinary" (Moffitt 2016: 38). To these, I will add another in this chapter: populists in government who have consolidated their power in the polity but continue to mobilize supporters based on an antiestablishment message.

The fact that populist leaders "get away with" these blatant contradictions leads civil critics to label their constituencies as irrational: the latter either lack the critical capacity to identify these contradictions or are too mesmerized by the charisma of the populist leader to question their claims. A cultural sociology of populism might instead explain the puzzling success of the populist appeal by offering an account of the "performative operations" (Laclau 2005) populist leaders engage in to transcend these contradictions. Overcoming these contradictions requires skillful meaning work that reconstructs the "virtuous people" vs. "corrupt elite" dichotomy and reasserts the populist leadership's identification with the former in the face of changing background conditions. Social performative analysis would thus significantly contribute to the emergent literature on populism as political style or performance (Moffitt 2016; Garrido 2017; Ostiguy 2017; Karakaya 2018), which focuses on the "how" of populism.

Cultural sociology can also make a distinctive contribution to populism studies by investigating the relationship of this phenomenon to liberal democracy[3] through the framework of democratic civility. While some sociologists and anthropologists have explored this theme in a variety of empirical settings (e.g., Hefner 1998, 2000; Gorski 2017a), the most articulate mid-range sociological theory in this vein is to be found in Jeffrey Alexander's *The Civil Sphere* (2006). A distinctive strength of civil sphere theory (CST) is its understanding of the culture and institutions of liberal democracy in relationship to each other: the regulatory (elections, courts, office) and communicative institutions (journalism, civil associations, public opinion polls) of the civil sphere ultimately refer to the same "code of civil society" that serves to symbolically articulate civil solidarity in the wider society. This complementary understanding of the culture and institutions of liberal democracy based on a shared normative logic allows a parsimonious analysis of the simultaneous threat that many populisms pose to the culture of civil solidarity and the organizational autonomy of democratic institutions.

Populists in Power

While some scholars of populism focus on populists in government (Heinisch 2003; Mudde 2013; Albertazzi and McDonnell 2015; Batory 2016; Kaltwasser and Taggart 2016; Taggart and Kaltwasser 2016), their work has thus far addressed a limited number of questions: Do populist parties lose their electoral support when they join the government? How do members of populist parties evaluate participation in government? Are populists able to achieve their policy goals once in power? What strategies can domestic actors and international institutions employ to protect liberal democratic institutions from populist governments? This chapter will address a key puzzle that has been largely neglected in this literature and is of potential significance for various cases of populism: How can political leaders and parties who stay in power over an extended period maintain their populist credentials?[4]

As some political scientists have observed, when "populists attain power and move from being outsiders to being insiders – and often insiders with real power," this "changes the game fundamentally" (Taggart and Kaltwasser 2016: 346–7). Extended periods in government effectively transform populist actors into the new political establishment. Yet, as Müller (2019) points out, there is much evidence against "the naïve view that once in power, populists have to cease criticizing 'the establishment' (for they themselves are now the establishment)."

The Turkish case provides a striking example of this tendency. During more than seventeen years in government,[5] Recep Tayyip Erdoğan and the Justice and Development Party (AKP) have concentrated political power in their hands to a degree unprecedented in the multi-party Turkish polity. Over the course of this period, they have gradually dismantled existing checks and balances and eventually redesigned the constitutional order according to their preferences. Yet, Erdoğan and his associates have continued to derive political capital from identification with the virtuous people against a culturally alien and morally corrupt elite. The following sections will use the analytical tools of cultural sociology and CST to reconstruct Erdoğan's populist trajectory. Through this case study of incumbent populism in contemporary Turkey, I will explain how populists might maintain their anti-establishment credentials even as they move from opposition to government and stay in power for extended periods.

Populism in Turkey

Erdoğan's political style fits most criteria on the populist leader checklist. Throughout his political career, he has claimed to represent the pious and conservative people, the silent majority from the Anatolian heartland,[6] against a culturally alien and self-serving elite who have monopolized cultural authority, political power, and economic resources. His claim to be "of the people" is made credible not only through his rhetorical skills, but also through his social background. Erdoğan grew up in Kasımpaşa, a poor neighborhood of Istanbul known for its traditional "tough guy" culture. As a youth, he worked as a street vendor to support his education and developed a passion for soccer – and would have pursued a professional career in the sport if it was not for his father's strict opposition (Çakır and Çalmuk 2001: 11–25).

Erdoğan's mental and bodily internalization of these childhood experiences is evident in the expressions he "gives off" (Goffman 1959): in the tone of his speech as well as in his bodily gestures and facial expressions. In interviews, he has often referred to his experience of growing up in a poor conservative neighborhood (Aytaç and Öniş 2014: 45). His love of soccer is well known among the public, and he has often sought to use his government's infrastructural support for soccer teams to gain votes, although not always successfully (Keddie 2018).[7] Erdoğan commonly uses informal interjections to express defiance against the targets of his criticism and mocks his political opponents for being remote from the ways of life of ordinary people.[8]

While populism nominally constituted one of the "six arrows" of the new republic's official Kemalist ideology, this did not go beyond an affirmation of the principle of national sovereignty and a denial of class conflict in Turkish society (Parla and Davison 2004: 80–6). Populism substantively entered Turkish politics with Adnan Menderes, the head of the conservative Democrat Party, who served as prime minister in the 1950s. His relentless critique of bureaucratic elites who putatively sought to suppress "the national will of the people," his promotion of public Islam against the strict secularism of Kemalist founders, his developmentalist policies catering to the rural masses, his charismatic hold over his followers, and his personalized way of exercising power led to his characterization as a populist by many scholars of Turkish politics (Sayarı 2002).[9]

Yet scholars of populism consider Erdoğan as the leader who has perfected this art in Turkish politics. A recent study of populist speech across forty countries found that Erdoğan was "the only non-Latin American leader to warrant a 'very populist' label ... and the only right-wing leader to reach that level of populist discourse" (Lewis et al. 2019). Others who focused on his combination of populist talk with neoliberal policies have classified him as a "neoliberal populist" (Yıldırım 2009), "neopopulist"[10] (Yağcı 2009), or "right-wing populist" (Aytaç and Öniş 2014).

The following two sections examine Erdoğan's populist trajectory through three periods: (1) his rise to prominence within Turkish political Islam and on the national political scene (1989–2001); (2) his first two terms as prime minister (2002–11); and (3) his authoritarian consolidation of power after 2011. These three periods are marked by divergent institutional constellations, transformative events, and performative challenges. In response to this shifting background, Erdoğan's populist strategies have varied across these three periods in terms of their dose, the emphasis on civil solidarity vs. uncivil exclusion, the salience of religious identity, the attitude toward international entities, and the grounds for claims to victimhood.[11] These stages are summarized in Table 3.1.

Table 3.1 The three stages of Erdoğan's populist trajectory

Period	Strategic challenge	Paradigmatic event(s)	Nature of populism	Dose of populism	People vs. elite	Foreign entities	Primary basis of victimhood
1989–2001	Mobilization/ electoral success	The February 28 process (1997–2001)	Uncivil (Islamist)	High	Pious people vs. secularist elite	US & Israel: forces of evil/ EU: Christian Club	Secularist state policies (headscarf ban), discrimination against pious Muslims
2002–2011	Political survival	The presidential election crisis (2007)	Civil	Low until mid-2007, medium after mid-2007	Tutelage by uncivil state institutions/ de-emphasis on religious identity	Pro-EU-accession	Tutelary regime
2012–2019	Authoritarian consolidation of power	Gezi protests (2013)/the failed coup attempt (2016)	Uncivil (authoritarian)	Medium until mid-2013, high after mid-2013	Sunni conservative majority vs. others/ Muslim peoples vs. Western hegemons	The "mastermind"/ international finance lobby	Western-backed attempts to topple the government

Stages I and II: Erdoğan's Rise and Political Survival

The period between 1989 and 2001 saw Erdoğan's rise to prominence within Turkish political Islam and his ascent to the national political stage as the mayor of Istanbul.[12] In this phase of electoral mobilization, Erdoğan employed an unfettered populist rhetoric, drawing on the idioms of Turkish political Islam which he had mastered in the anticommunist National Turkish Students Union (MTTB) and in the youth branch of the National Salvation Party (MSP) (Cagaptay 2017: 49–50). He thus attacked the republican elites for having abandoned Islam, imitating the West, and oppressing the pious people – and advocated a return to Islam as the solution to the country's problems (Çakır and Çalmuk 2001). The Islamist-populist strategy proved immensely successful. Erdoğan built a reputation within the Islamic movement for his inflammatory oratory style, especially for his skill in reciting poetry (Çakır and Çalmuk 2001: 19–30). Although he had been a political outsider unknown on the national stage until then, he was elected as mayor of the country's largest city in 1994 (Aytaç and Öniş 2014: 44). During his mayoral campaign, Erdoğan began to refer to his party as "the voice of the silent masses," a theme he would reiterate in the course of his political career (Al Jazeera Türk 2017).

The same heated rhetoric, however, led in 1998 to Erdoğan's conviction by a State Security Court for "inciting hatred based on religious differences." Erdoğan was stripped of his position as mayor, banned from politics, and sentenced to ten months in prison. While he eventually served only four months of his sentence, his victimization by secularist state institutions significantly contributed to his populist credentials (Aytaç and Öniş 2014: 44; Cagaptay 2017: 4). The political mobilization of Turkish Islamists in this period greatly benefited from the grievances resulting from the headscarf ban in universities and the military-led crackdown on Islamic actors and organizations known as the "February 28 process" (Altınordu 2010).

The second stage, beginning roughly in 2002, posed a new set of institutional and performative challenges. The AKP, the new party founded by Erdoğan and his associates, won a plurality of votes in the general elections that year, and formed the first single-party government in Turkey in more than a decade. Initially banned from running for office, Erdoğan became prime minister in March 2003 following a by-election.

The AKP's primary strategic goal in this period was to avoid repression by secularist state institutions. These fears were not unwarranted: a coalition government led by the Islamic Welfare Party (RP) had been toppled by the military in 1997, and the RP and its successor, the Virtue Party, had been banned by the Constitutional Court in 1998 and 2001, respectively. The military and the Constitutional Court had justified these interventions in the political process with reference to the "reactionary activities" of Islamic politicians against the secular republican regime. In their first two terms in government, Erdoğan and his associates thus de-emphasized the role of religion in the AKP's political identity and refashioned themselves as "conservative democrats." To disperse doubts about the civil orientation of the organization, party officials and programs repeatedly emphasized the AKP's commitment to the secular republic and denounced the political instrumentalization of religion on principle (Altınordu 2016: 162–3).

At the same time, the AKP government undertook a major legislative campaign to confine the military and the high judiciary to their proper boundaries. The Turkish military had periodically intervened in the political process, starting with the coup d'état of 1960 (Cizre 1997), while the Constitutional Court had dissolved more than two dozen political parties – mostly Kurdish and Islamic – since its foundation in 1961 (Celep 2014). Erdoğan and his associates employed the trope of the "tutelary regime" to denote the chronic nature of these uncivil intrusions in the Turkish polity. By claiming guardianship of the polity, AKP politicians argued, the military and the judiciary flouted the democratically formed will of the people.[13] By forcing all state institutions back to their proper jurisdictions, the AKP would deliver the nation from tutelage. The tutelary regime talk was populist in its basic structure, as it pitted the people against arrogant "state elites," identified Erdoğan and the AKP with the former, and sought to remove institutional obstacles to popular sovereignty. It represented, however, a civil form of populism, as it defined "the people" broadly and demanded the reordering of the polity in accordance with the criteria of the civil sphere.

Turkey's official candidacy for the European Union offered a crucial anchor for this project of civil reform. A series of "harmonization packages" passed in 2003 and 2004 in accordance with the EU's Copenhagen Criteria significantly curtailed the political power of the military, while strengthening the freedoms of expression, association, assembly, religion, and minority rights (Hale and Özbudun 2010: 57–62). The constitutional amendments of 2010 provided the High Council of Judges and Prosecutors – the body deciding on the appointments, promotions, and dismissals of judges and prosecutors – with a more pluralist structure (Özbudun 2015: 45).

While different political camps in Turkish society evaluated these structural reforms in divergent ways, both sides employed the civil code to assert the validity of their own interpretation (Alexander 2006: 53–67). Many AKP supporters and political liberals celebrated the reforms as removing the structural bases of uncivil intrusion by state institutions, and as a move toward a rule-regulated, inclusive polity. Others, most notably Kemalist nationalists but also some on the left, were highly suspicious of the government's intentions. While the AKP government justified these reforms with reference to civil values, they argued, its real aim was to remove all checks and balances in the political system in order to then freely implement its uncivil Islamist project. In other words, Erdoğan and his associates were acting in a deceitful, calculating, and conspiratorial manner (Altınordu 2016).

The presidential election of 2007 proved to be a turning point in Erdoğan's populist trajectory. Following the presidential nomination of Abdullah Gül – a politician with an Islamist pedigree whose wife wore a headscarf – the AKP faced a strong backlash from secularist actors. The military issued a warning on its website, followed by a controversial decision by the Constitutional Court annulling the first-round vote in the parliament. In response, the Erdoğan government called not only for early general elections but also for constitutional amendments that would institute direct elections for the presidency (Altınordu 2016: 164). This was a quintessentially populist move in that it directly appealed to popular will in the face of obstruction by countermajoritarian institutions.

Having decided to fight back against the secularist bloc, Erdoğan adopted an unabashedly populist discourse that framed members of the Constitutional Court and the military as arrogant elites who disrespected the popular will (Dinçşahin 2012). Through the Constitutional Court's decision, he argued, "the will of the majority [was] imprisoned by the minority" (quoted in Dinçşahin 2012: 632). Erdoğan criticized the opposition of the Republican People's Party (CHP) to direct elections for the presidency in similar terms: "We're now going to the people, but they are running away from the people. The CHP is scared of the people. It is not the people's party but the elite's party" (quoted in Dinçşahin 2012: 632–3). Drawing parallels to the Democrat Party tradition of the 1950s, Erdoğan depicted the struggle between tutelary elites, on the one hand, and conservative leaders representing the people, on the other, as the underlying theme of Turkish political history:

> They could not put up with the national will, with the nation having the last word. When multi-party politics was first introduced, those [the Democrat Party] who said "enough, the nation has the last word," came to power with huge support. ... [N]ow we say, "enough, the nation will make the decision" and that is how we will proceed. We will

go to the nation . . . both for general elections and for the presidential elections. (Quoted in Dinçşahin 2012: 634)

This populist discourse projecting Erdoğan, his party, and the nation itself as the victims of a self-serving elite proved very effective. The AKP increased its votes by more than 12 percent in the parliamentary elections in July, Gül was installed as president in August, and the constitutional amendments proposed by the government were adopted in a referendum in October. While the country's chief prosecutor filed a case with the Constitutional Court the following year, asking it to shut down the AKP owing to its antisecular activities, the court decided against outlawing the party (Constitutional Court Decision, E. 2008/1, K. 2008/2).

The immensely successful outcome of Erdoğan's response to the presidential crisis proved to him that populism could serve as his most reliable instrument at critical political junctures. In the lead-up to the 2010 referendum on judicial reform, he asserted that "the elite, who rely on the status quo, oppose a 'yes' vote" and called the opponents of the proposed amendments "coup-lovers," associating them with the ultimate act of disrespect for the popular will (Dinçşahin 2012: 637–8). As will be discussed in the next section, Erdoğan's populist discourse would take an increasingly uncivil turn as he faced the dilemma of populism in power to a greater extent.

Stage III: The Dilemma of Populism in Power

In June 2011, the AKP commenced its third consecutive term in government. Nearly nine years of bureaucratic appointments, major structural reforms in the judiciary, and two controversial trials charging hundreds of officers with conspiracy against the government had significantly weakened the secularist opposition against the AKP within the state. Moreover, the presidency, which held significant veto power, was now occupied by a close associate of Erdoğan. A political scientist thus observed, "The 2011 elections certified the end of bureaucratic guardianship as a major source of opposition to the AKP" (Tezcür 2012: 129).

While this new institutional constellation provided Erdoğan with considerable freedom of action, it also meant that he would now have to face up to the dilemma of populism in power. As already discussed, the critique of the tutelary regime had been a central pillar of his populist discourse, and Islamic politicians' claims to victimhood – as when Erdoğan was sent to prison in 1999 and Gül's election to presidency was blocked in 2007 by the Constitutional Court – had boosted their populist appeal.

Now that the secularist institutions of guardianship had been dismantled, the trope of advancing the unhampered implementation of the popular will against obstructive state elites lost its resonance.

Another way in which Erdoğan and other AKP politicians accumulated populist capital was through previous struggles with secularist actors over the public presence of Islam, framed in terms of an opposition between the pious people and the secular elite. Grievances resulting from controversies such as the headscarf ban in universities, the status of religious public schools known as the *imam hatips*, and the aborted plans for the construction of a mosque in Istanbul's Taksim Square played a crucial role in the electoral rise of Islamic parties from the mid-1980s on (Altınordu 2010). As a rising figure in political Islam throughout this period, Erdoğan – who himself attended an *imam hatip* and whose wife and daughters wore headscarves – received his share of populist credentials from religious defense. While AKP politicians de-emphasized the religious identity of their party and toned down their criticism of Kemalist *laïcité* to avoid a secularist crackdown, they still benefited from their publicly known stances on these issues.

The AKP's policy success in this area ironically reduced the relevance of these credentials. Through legislation and administrative regulations, AKP governments lifted the ban on wearing the headscarf in universities (2010), civil service (2013), high schools (2014), the judiciary (2015), the police force (2016), and, finally, the military (2017) (Agence France-Presse in Istanbul 2017). A 2019 decision of the government-controlled Higher Education Council provided *imam hatip* graduates with an equal opportunity to enter university. Three years later, the government reopened the middle schools of *imam hatips* that had been shut down in the course of the February 28 process. Moreover, the religious public school system has expanded significantly under the AKP governments (Butler 2018). Construction on the Taksim Mosque, anticipated for decades by the religious-conservative constituency, began in February 2017 (*Hürriyet* 2017). Finally, during the AKP's tenure in government, the budget and size of the Directorate of Religious Affairs, the state agency providing for Sunni religious infrastructure and personnel, has grown exponentially (Doğan 2019). Given the satisfactory resolution of religious citizens' grievances and the increasing hegemony of a state-backed Sunni Islam in the public realm, religious defense lost its once crucial role as a pillar of Erdoğan's populist mobilization.

The Gezi events of 2013 posed the most serious threat theretofore to Erdoğan's populist credentials. The antigovernment protests, the largest in the history of the Turkish republic, showed that social discontent against the AKP government had reached a critical threshold. The brutal response of the police to the demonstrators dramatized the extent to which the Erdoğan government was now for many citizens associated with the establishment. The dilemma of populism in power had reached a critical stage.

Erdoğan responded to this challenge in three ways. First, he increased the dose of uncivil themes in his populist discourse, redefining the people in primordial terms and framing his opponents as enemies rather than adversaries. Second, he encroached on the organizational autonomy of civil sphere institutions in order to curtail dissent. Finally, he projected his populist discourse to an international scale, positing a series of global conspiracies against his government, on the one hand, and claiming the leadership of Muslim peoples against Western hegemons, on the other.

Erdoğan portrayed the protests as the work of a secular minority who, he argued, sought to overthrow his government representing the religious-conservative majority (Altınordu 2013). He thus characterized large numbers of mostly young people demonstrating in the parks and streets as elites, compared the street protests to military interventions against elected politicians, and glossed over the participation of some religious organizations and citizens in the antigovernment demonstrations: "We and people like us have been oppressed in this country for a long time. . . . Now this group has won 50% of the vote. But . . . some people still want to oppress it" (quoted in Altınordu 2013).

In his public pronouncements during the protests, Erdoğan repeatedly referred to two events of doubtful authenticity in order to fuel polarization between religious and secular citizens. The first story concerned a headscarved woman with a baby, who was violently assaulted by Gezi protestors in the central Istanbul neighborhood of Kabataş. Nine months after what became known as the "Kabataş incident," security footage leaked to a television station revealed the fictitious nature of this account (Aslangül 2015). Erdoğan also asserted that Gezi protestors – who had taken shelter from tear gas fired by the riot police – had desecrated the Dolmabahçe Mosque by consuming alcohol in this historic place of worship. The *muezzin* of the mosque, who denied this claim, was eventually removed from his post by the Directorate of Religious Affairs (Bayer 2013).

During the Gezi protests, Erdoğanists also disseminated a myth about an alleged plot to execute their leader, evoking the theme of his imminent martyrdom. Adnan Menderes, the populist prime minister of the 1950s, had become a martyr figure for Turkish conservatives following his execution by the military junta in the aftermath of the 1960 coup. While Turgut Özal – another conservative leader – died in office from a heart attack in 1993, the belief that he had been poisoned gained traction over time in Turkey's conservative circles. Erdoğan's supporters now claimed that the organizers of the Gezi protests and their foreign backers conspired to execute him.[14]

Erdoğan's efforts during the Gezi events to consolidate his religious-conservative base by designating them as "the people" and other citizens as its enemies was symptomatic of the larger uncivil turn his populism had taken after 2011. In his third term as prime minister, he began to use the word "atheist" as an epithet, equating lack of religious belief with immorality (Altınordu forthcoming). In 2012, in response to criticism for his remarks that his government wants to "raise a religious youth," Erdoğan asked rhetorically: "do you expect us to raise an atheist genera-tion?" (*Cumhuriyet* 2012). In another speech two years later, Erdoğan juxtaposed a variety of identities anathema to his religious-conservative constituency to rail against university students who had protested against him during an opening: "I conducted an opening in Ankara on Monday. ... Despite whom? Despite those leftists! Despite those atheists! These are atheists, these are terrorists!" (*Cumhuriyet* 2014). Erdoğan also occasionally resorted to sectarian appeals when he believed that these would translate into electoral gains. In his election campaign in 2011, he recurrently underlined that Kılıçdaroğlu, the head of the opposition party CHP, was an Alevi, sending uncivil signals of primordial solidarity to the majority Sunni community (Altınordu 2013). Despite protests, in 2016 the government named a new bridge over the Bosphorus after Yavuz Sultan Selim, an Ottoman sultan who is anathema to Turkey's Alevis because of the massacre he carried out against their ancestors in the sixteenth century (Tekin 2016).

These instances demonstrate that in response to rising social discontent against his government, Erdoğan sought to renew his populist credentials by increasing the dose of uncivil elements in his political discourse. The civil populism that marked the AKP's first two terms in government had focused on defending the autonomy of the civil sphere against uncivil intrusions by secularist actors and the legitimacy of a religious presence in the public sphere. Erdoğan now clearly abandoned this orientation for an uncivil populism which defined the people in primordial terms – pious Sunni conservatives – and excluded other citizens – unbelievers, Alevis, people with nontraditional lifestyles, leftists, political liberals, and members of the Kurdish movement – from the boundaries of the national community. The latter groups, Erdoğan argued, posed constant threats to the "real" people.

Within the same period as Erdoğan increasingly injected uncivil themes into his populist discourse, his administration also attacked the organizational autonomy of the communicative and regulative institutions of the civil sphere. The government brought virtually all media of mass communication under its control by engineering the purchase of newspapers and television channels by cronies and persecuting critical journalists (Yeşil 2016). In the aftermath of the 2016 coup attempt, the government summarily shut down and seized the assets of nearly 150 media outlets. International monitors of press freedom observed these developments with serious concern: Freedom House demoted Turkey's press freedom status from "partly free" to "not free" in 2014, while the Committee to Protect Journalists has ranked the country as "the world's worst jailer of journalists" every year since 2016 (Freedom House 2019).

Civil associations and activists were similarly subject to intrusions by the increasingly authoritarian Erdoğanist regime. Under the state of emergency following the aborted putsch, more than 1,500 foundations and associations were shut down by government decree, while prominent civil society actors were arrested on charges related to terrorism (Freedom House 2019). In January 2016, Erdoğan targeted "Academics for Peace," more than a thousand academics who had signed a petition condemning the Turkish government's violations of human rights in the course of its armed struggle with Kurdish guerrillas. Erdoğan characterized the petition as "treachery by the so-called intellectuals" and called upon all public institutions to punish the signatories, who "come out against the integrity of the country and unity of the nation" (Hürriyet 2016). Many university administrations soon launched disciplinary investigations, while public prosecutors filed antiterrorism lawsuits against 739 of the signatories. In the following three-and-a-half years, many signatories were fired from their academic posts and convicted by the courts, before a Constitutional Court decision in July 2019 paved the way for their acquittal (Bianet 2019).

The AKP government's uncivil intrusions also extended to the regulative institutions of courts, electoral competition, and voting. With a series of laws passed in 2014 and mass purges of judges and public prosecutors following the coup attempt of 2016, the AKP has brought the country's court system under government control (Özbudun 2015; Zeller et al. 2017). Members of parliament from the pro-Kurdish Peoples' Democratic Party (HDP), including the two co-chairs of the party, were arrested in November 2016, while nearly a hundred elected mayors were replaced by government appointees (Freedom House 2019). With the transition to an authoritarian presidential regime in the spring of 2017, political power was further concentrated in the hands of Erdoğan (Esen and Gumuscu 2018). Finally, the controversial decisions of the High Election Council during the constitutional referendum of April 2017 and after the local elections of March 2019 compromised electoral integrity (Gumrukcu and Coskun 2019).

Erdoğan's final strategy for regenerating his populist credentials was to project his populist narratives to the international level. Erdoğan and the progovernment press claimed that global powers were the real agents behind the Gezi protests of 2013 and the failed coup attempt of 2016 (Cagaptay and Aktas 2017). Erdoğan has referred to these conspiratorial foreign powers alternatively as the "mastermind" or the "interest-rate lobby" (Akyol 2016). The latter term – with thinly veiled anti-Semitic connotations – suggested that dark forces fueled political instability in Turkey to topple Erdoğan's government, as his economic policies defied the interests of global finance. These narratives of foreign conspiracy against Turkey not only cast Erdoğan as the bold defender of national interests against sinister global elites but also justified the centralization of power in his person (Cagaptay and Aktas 2017).

Having witnessed his rising popularity in the Middle East following an altercation with Israel's prime minister Shimon Peres in 2009, Erdoğan adopted a populist discourse on the international level, which cast him as the voice of downtrodden Muslim peoples against Western powers and Israel. This discourse, which "blends post-colonialist theory with anti-Westernism" (Cagaptay and Aktas 2017), was evident in Erdoğan's heated speech to the Organization of Islamic Cooperation in 2014:

> Those who come to the Islamic geography from outside like its oil, gold, diamonds. They like its cheap labor force, conflicts, fights, disagreements. Believe me, they do not like us. . . . They like the corpses of our children. How much longer are we going to sit back and watch? (Comcec.org 2015)

In his speeches abroad, Erdoğan has also criticized the veto power of the permanent members of the UN Security Council and advocated reform with his catchphrase, "the world is larger than five."[15] Erdoğan's claim to the leadership of the Muslim peoples against Western hegemons does not only target Muslims outside of Turkey, it also feeds into the neo-Ottoman fantasies of grandeur at home, which represent a longing for the restoration of Turkey as a major regional power under Erdoğan's leadership (Cagaptay 2019).

Conclusion

The trajectory of Erdoğanist populism presented in this chapter is supported by a major study which examined populist discourse in forty countries across the globe over the last two decades (Lewis et al. 2019). According to Team Populism's political speech analysis, when Erdoğan first came to power as prime minister in 2003, he did not qualify as a populist. Starting in 2007 – when, I argued, the presidential election crisis led him to change course – his public speeches put him in the "somewhat populist category." From 2014 on – in the aftermath of the Gezi events – he came to be classified as "very populist," his score well exceeding those of Viktor Orbán (2010–18), Silvio Berlusconi (2001–6), and Donald Trump (2016–18). The researchers interpreted this as "a sign of how much the Turkish leader has changed during his 16 years at the helm of his country's political system" (Lewis et al. 2019). In this chapter, I have explained these changes in the dose and nature of Erdoğan's populism with reference to the institutional and performative challenges he has faced in the course of his political trajectory.

In the earlier stages of his political career, Erdoğan employed a religious-populist discourse, which helped him rise within the Islamic political movement and ascend to the national political stage as the mayor of Istanbul. In his first two terms as prime minister, political survival vis-à-vis secularist state institutions was a strategic priority. Erdoğan thus adopted a civil form of populism, which de-emphasized religion as a political identity and defined the people broadly. At the same time, his government took a critical stance toward the military and judiciary intrusions into the civil sphere and undertook structural reforms to dismantle the "tutelary regime."

Having eliminated the bases of secularist opposition in state institutions, in their third term in government, Erdoğan and the AKP faced a major performative challenge that I have referred to as the dilemma of populism in power: how to credibly claim the representation of the people against the establishment when they had become the establishment itself. Erdoğan responded to this challenge by adopting an uncivil form of populism to consolidate his base, attacking the organizational autonomy of civil sphere institutions to curtail dissent, and reproducing his political narratives at a global level to renew his populist credentials.

When Erdoğan alludes to the Alevi identity of an opposition leader to dismiss him, equates leftists and atheists with terrorists, or refers to the Academics for Peace as "the so-called intellectuals . . . whose names are ours but whose mentality is foreign to us" (*Hürriyet* 2016), he deliberately engages in uncivil exclusion, setting the boundaries of communal solidarity in ascriptive terms.[16] While one can undoubtedly detect some continuities in populism with democratic politics as usual (Alexander 2018), uncivil populists such as Orbán, Trump, and Erdoğan not only attack the autonomy of democratic institutions but also significantly threaten the values of the civil sphere on which liberal democracies must rely.

Notes

1 These historical waves include early examples of the Russian *Narodniki* and the US People's Party in the late nineteenth century, classical Latin American populisms of the mid-twentieth century, the rise of "neopopulism" in Latin America and right-wing anti-immigrant populism in Europe in the 1990s, leftist Latin American populisms in the first decade of the twenty-first century, and, finally, the global surge of populism in the aftermath of the Great Recession.

2 The political science literature contains important exceptions that pay attention to the performative aspects of populist performance, such as Moffitt (2016). Yet overall, only about 1 percent of articles on populism in selected political science journals exemplify the cultural approach, compared to 28 percent that adopt an ideological perspective and 13 percent that approach populism as a political strategy (Kaltwasser et al. 2017b: 12).

3 For an overview of the literature on populism and liberal democracy, see Rummens (2017).

4 Among contemporary populisms, the same question is raised by the cases of Venezuela, where Hugo Chávez was president from 1999 to 2013, Ecuador, where Rafael Correa was president from 2007 to 2017, and Hungary, where Viktor Orbán has been back in power since 2010.

5 At the time of writing in April 2020.

6 The centrality of the notion of a heartland to populist discourse has been noted by Taggart (2000).

7 In a stadium opening in 2014, Erdoğan participated in a celebrity match, where he received praise for the three goals he scored. Another political leader whose populist credentials have benefited from a "passion for playing soccer" is Abdalá Bucaram of Ecuador (de la Torre 2010: 91).

8 An interjection Erdoğan commonly uses to address the targets of his criticism – international organizations, opposition politicians, the country's intellectuals – is "*ey.*" This trademark expression is relished by his followers and parodied by his critics. He often refers to opposition politicians with forms of address associated with European culture, such as "Bay Kemal" (Mr. Kemal) or "*monşer*" (a word derived from the French "*mon cher,*" which, according to the dictionary of the Turkish Language Institute, refers to "someone who emulates the West in their behavior").

9 As in the case of Erdoğan half a century later, Menderes shifted from a civil to a noncivil form of populism in the mid-1950s, moving from an advocacy for individual rights, political pluralism, and press freedom to increasingly illiberal discourses and practices (Sayarı 2002).

10 These authors place Erdoğan in the same category as the Latin American neopopulists such as Carlos Menem in Argentina, Fernando Collor in Brazil, and Alberto Fujimori in Peru (Weyland 1996).

11 This argument is in line with recent work which conceives of populism as a matter of degree rather than a binary category (Jagers and Walgrave

2007; Deegan-Krause and Haughton 2009; Rooduijn and Akkerman 2017) and recognizes that "the degree of populism that a given political actor employs may vary across contexts and over time" (Gidron and Bonikowski 2013: 9).

12 In 1989, Erdoğan ran for mayor of Istanbul's Beyoğlu district. While he lost the election, in the course of this campaign he established himself as "the face of the rising generation in the RP [Welfare Party]" (Cagaptay 2017: 63).

13 For a classic discussion of guardianship, see Dahl (1980). For a discussion of the historical role of the institutions of guardianship in the Turkish polity, see Tezcür (2010).

14 The purported victim of the "Kabataş incident" thus asserted that her attackers had cried, "We will hang Erdoğan, do you get it?" (Aslangül 2015). During the height of the protests, widely circulated social media posts featured Menderes's, Özal's, and Erdoğan's pictures side by side with the caption, "You hung Menderes; you poisoned Özal; we will not let you have Erdoğan" (*Türkiye* 2013). Similar posters were soon placed on billboards in Ankara (Çimen 2013).

15 Erdoğan obtained the commercial patent for this phrase in March 2019 (Yılmaz 2019).

16 Mudde and Kaltwasser's (2013) category of "exclusionary populism," to the extent it focuses on the symbolic exclusion of specific groups from "an ethnicized people," is similar to uncivil populism as defined in this chapter.

References

Agence France-Presse in Istanbul. (2017) Turkey lifts military ban on Islamic headscarf. *The Guardian*, February 22. https://www.theguardian.com/world/2017/feb/22/turkey-lifts-military-ban-on-islamic-headscarf.

Akyol, M. (2016) Erdoğanism [noun]. *Foreign Policy*, June 21. https://foreignpolicy.com/2016/06/21/erdoganism-noun-erdogan-turkey-islam-akp/.

Al Jazeera Türk. (2014) Erdoğan'dan 'monşer' çıkışı. *Al Jazeera Türk*, July 6. http://www.aljazeera.com.tr/haber/erdogandan-monser-cikisi.

Al Jazeera Türk. (2017) Portre: Recep Tayyip Erdoğan. *Al Jazeera Türk*, April 17. http://www.aljazeera.com.tr/portre/portre-recep-tayyip-erdogan.

Albertazzi, D. and D. McDonnell. (2015) *Populists in Power*. Abingdon and New York: Routledge.

Alexander, J. C. (2004) Cultural pragmatics: Social performance between ritual and strategy. *Sociological Theory* 22(4): 527–73.

Alexander, J. C. (2006) *The Civil Sphere*. New York: Oxford University Press.

Alexander, J. C. (2010) *The Performance of Politics: Obama's Victory and the Democratic Struggle for Power*. New York: Oxford University Press.

Alexander, J. C. (2018) Frontlash/backlash: The crisis of solidarity and the threat to civil institutions. *Contemporary Sociology* 48(1): 5–11.

Altınordu, A. (2010) The politicization of religion: Political Catholicism and political Islam in comparative perspective. *Politics & Society* 38(4): 517–51.

Altınordu, A. (2013) Occupy Gezi, beyond the religious–secular cleavage. *The Immanent Frame*, June 10. https://tif.ssrc.org/2013/06/10/occupy-gezi-beyond-the-religious-secular-cleavage/.

Altınordu, A. (2016) The political incorporation of anti-system religious parties: The case of Turkish Islam (1994–2011). *Qualitative Sociology* 39(2): 147–71.

Altınordu, A. (Forthcoming) Is Turkey a postsecular society? Secular differentiation, committed pluralism, and complementary learning in contemporary Turkey. In: K. Barkey, S. Kaviraj, and V. Naresh (eds.) *Negotiating Democracy and Religious Pluralism: India, Pakistan, and Turkey*. Oxford: Oxford University Press.

Aslangül, A. (2015) Kabataş'ta yalan kesin, rivayet muhtelif; işte emniyetten Elif Çakır'a 'Zehra gelin' metinleri. *T24*, March 12. https://t24.com.tr/haber/kabatasta-yalan-kesin-rivayet-muhtelif-iste-emniyetten-elif-cakira-zehra-gelin-metinleri,290216.

Aytaç, S. E. and Z. Öniş. (2014) Varieties of populism in a changing global context: The divergent paths of Erdoğan and Kirchnerismo. *Comparative Politics* 47(1): 41–59.

Batory, A. (2016) Populists in government? Hungary's "system of national cooperation." *Democratization* 23(2): 283–303.

Bayer, Y. (2013) Dolmabahçe Camisi'nin imam ve müezzini gitti. *Hürriyet*, September 21. http://www.hurriyet.com.tr/gundem/dolmabahce-camisinin-imam-ve-muezzini-gitti-24756039.

Bianet. (2019) AYM, Barış Akademisyenleri için 'hak ihlali' kararı verdi. *Bianet*, July 26. http://bianet.org/bianet/ifade-ozgurlugu/210902-aym-baris-akademisyenleri-icin-hak-ihlali-karari-verdi.

Butler, D. (2018) With more Islamic schooling, Erdoğan aims to reshape Turkey. *Reuters.com*, January 25. https://www.reuters.com/investigates/special-report/turkey-erdogan-education/.

Cagaptay, S. (2017) *The New Sultan: Erdoğan and the Crisis of Modern Turkey*. London: I. B. Tauris.

Cagaptay, S. (2019) *Erdoğan's Empire: Turkey and the Politics of the Middle East*. London: I. B. Tauris.

Cagaptay, S. and O. R. Aktas. (2017) How Erdoğanism is killing Turkish democracy: The end of political opposition. *Foreign Affairs*, July 7. https://www.foreignaffairs.com/articles/turkey/2017-07-07/how-erdoganism-killing-turkish-democracy.

Çakır, R. and F. Çalmuk. (2001) *Recep Tayyip Erdoğan: Bir Dönüşüm Öyküsü*. Istanbul: Metis Yayınları.

Canovan, M. (1981) *Populism*. New York: Harcourt Brace.

Celep, Ö. (2014) The political causes of party closures in Turkey. *Parliamentary Affairs* 67(2): 371–90.

Chase, J. (2017) AfD populists milk anti-refugee anger in German region with few asylum seekers. *DW.com*, August 16. https://www.dw.com/en/afd-populists-milk-anti-refugee-anger-in-german-region-with-few-asylum-seekers/a-39876990.

Çimen, M. (2013) Erdoğan Ankara'da gövde gösterisiyle karşılanacak. *Radikal*, June 9. http://www.radikal.com.tr/turkiye/erdogan-ankarada-govde-gosterisiyle-karsilanacak-1136882/.

Cizre, Ü. (1997) The anatomy of the Turkish military's political autonomy. *Comparative Politics* 29(2): 151–66.

Comcec.org. (2015) Sayın Cumhurbaşkanımızın otuzuncu İSEDAK toplantısında yapacakları konuşma (İstanbul, 27 Kasım 2014). http://www.comcec.org/wp-content/uploads/2015/08/30IS-SP-1-tr.pdf.

Cumhuriyet. (2012) Ateist mi yetiştirecektik. *Cumhuriyet,* February 2.

Cumhuriyet. (2014) Yine "nefret dili'ni kullandı. *Cumhuriyet,* February 28.

Dahl, R. A. (1980) The Moscow discourse: Fundamental rights in a democratic order. *Government and Opposition* 15(1): 3–30.

de la Torre, C. (2010) *Populist Seduction in Latin America.* Athens: Ohio University Research in International Studies.

de la Torre, C. (ed.). (2019) *Routledge Handbook of Global Populism.* London and New York: Routledge.

Deegan-Krause, K. and T. Haughton. (2009) Toward a more useful conceptualization of populism: Types and degrees of populist appeals in the case of Slovakia. *Politics & Policy* 37(4): 821–41.

Dinçşahin, Ş. (2012) A symptomatic analysis of the Justice and Development Party's populism in Turkey, 2007–2010. *Government and Opposition* 47(4): 618–40.

Doğan, R. (2019) Diyanet'in önlenemez yükselişi. *Artı Gerçek,* September 16. https://www.artigercek.com/haberler/diyanet-in-onlenemez-yukselisi.

Esen, B. and S. Gumuscu. (2018) The perils of "Turkish presidentialism." *Review of Middle East Studies* 52(1): 43–53.

Fisher, M. and A. Taub. (2019) "Overrun," "outbred," "replaced": Why ethnic majorities lash out over false fears. *The New York Times,* May 1. https://www.nytimes.com/2019/04/30/world/asia/sri-lanka-populism-ethnic-tensions.html.

Freedom House. (2019) Country Report on Turkey – 2018. https://freedomhouse.org/country/turkey/freedom-world/2019.

Garrido, M. (2017) Why the poor support populism: The politics of sincerity in Metro Manila. *American Journal of Sociology* 123(3): 647–85.

Gidron, N. and B. Bonikowski. (2013) Varieties of populism: Literature review and research agenda. Working Paper Series No. 13-0004. https://scholar.harvard.edu/files/gidron_bonikowski_populismlitreview_2013.pdf.

Goffman, E. (1959) *The Presentation of Self in Everyday Life.* New York: Anchor Books.

Gorski, P. (2017a) *American Covenant: A History of Religion from the Puritans to the Present.* Princeton: Princeton University Press.

Gorski, P. (2017b) Why evangelicals voted for Trump: A critical cultural sociology. *American Journal of Cultural Sociology* 5(3): 338–54.

Gumrukcu, T. and O. Coskun. (2019) Turkey's election board under pressure to explain Istanbul vote annulment. *Reuters,* May 16. https://www.reuters.com/article/uk-turkey-election/turkeys-election-board-under-pressure-to-explain-istanbul-vote-annulment-idUKKCN1SM1SD.

Hale, W. and E. Özbudun. (2010) *Islamism, Democracy and Liberalism in Turkey: The Case of the AKP.* Abingdon and New York: Routledge.

Hefner, R. W. (ed.). (1998) *Democratic Civility: The History and Cross-Cultural Possibility of a Modern Political Ideal.* New Brunswick: Transaction Publishers.

Hefner, R. W. (2000) *Civil Islam: Muslims and Democratization in Indonesia.* Princeton: Princeton University Press.

Heinisch, R. (2003) Success in opposition – failure in government: Explaining the performance of right-wing populist parties in public office. *West European Politics* 26(3): 91–130.

Hürriyet. (2016) Cumhurbaşkanı Erdoğan: "Suriye kökenli bir canlı bomba saldırısı." *Hürriyet,* January 12. http://www.hurriyet.com.tr/gundem/cumhur baskani-erdogan-suriye-kokenli-bir-canli-bomba-saldirisi-40039427.

Hürriyet. (2017) Taksim Camii'nin temeli atıldı. *Hürriyet*, February 17. http://www.hurriyet.com.tr/gundem/taksim-camiinin-temeli-atildi-40368952.

Ionescu, G. and E. Gellner (eds.). (1969) *Populism: Its Meaning and National Characteristics*. London: Weidenfeld & Nicolson.

Jagers, J. and S. Walgrave. (2007) Populism as political communication style: An empirical study of political parties' discourse in Belgium. *European Journal of Political Research* 46(3): 319–45.

Kaltwasser, C. R. and P. Taggart. (2016) Dealing with populists in government: A framework for analysis. *Democratization* 23(2): 201–20.

Kaltwasser, C., P. Taggart, P. O. Espejo, and P. Ostiguy (eds.). (2017a) *The Oxford Handbook of Populism*. Oxford: Oxford University Press.

Kaltwasser, C., P. Taggart, P. O. Espejo, and P. Ostiguy. (2017b) Populism: An overview of the concept and the state of the art. In: C. R. Kaltwasser, P. Taggart, P. O. Espejo, and P. Ostiguy (eds.) *The Oxford Handbook of Populism*. Oxford: Oxford University Press.

Karakaya, Y. (2018) The conquest of hearts: The central role of Ottoman nostalgia within contemporary Turkish populism. *American Journal of Cultural Sociology*. doi:10.1057/s41290-018-0065-y.

Keddie, P. (2018) Understanding authoritarianism through soccer. *The New Republic*, May 7. https://newrepublic.com/article/148313/understanding-authoritarianism-soccer.

Laclau, E. (2005) *On Populist Reason*. London: Verso.

Lewis, P., C. Barr, S. Clarke, A. Voce, C. Levett, and P. Gutiérrez. (2019) Revealed: The rise and rise of populist rhetoric. *The Guardian*, March 6. https://www.theguardian.com/world/ng-interactive/2019/mar/06/revealed-the-rise-and-rise-of-populist-rhetoric.

Marzouki, N., D. McDonnell, and O. Roy (eds.). (2016) *Saving the People: How Populists Hijack Religion*. Oxford: Oxford University Press.

Mast, J. L. (2013) *The Performative Presidency: Crisis and Resurrection during the Clinton Years*. Cambridge: Cambridge University Press.

Moffitt, B. (2016) *The Global Rise of Populism: Performance, Political Style, and Representation*. Stanford: Stanford University Press.

Mudde, C. (2013) Three decades of populist radical right parties in Western Europe: So what? *European Journal of Political Research* 52(1): 1–19.

Mudde, C. (2017) Populism: An ideational approach. In: C. R. Kaltwasser, P. Taggart, P. O. Espejo, and P. Ostiguy (eds.) *The Oxford Handbook of Populism*. Oxford: Oxford University Press.

Mudde, C. and C. R. Kaltwasser. (2013) Exclusionary vs. inclusionary populism: Comparing contemporary Europe and Latin America. *Government and Opposition* 48(2): 147–74.

Mudde, C. and C. R. Kaltwasser. (2017) *Populism: A Very Short Introduction*. Oxford: Oxford University Press.

Müller, J.-W. (2016) *What Is Populism?* Philadelphia: University of Pennsylvania Press.

Müller, J.-W. (2019) Populists don't lose elections. *The New York Times*, May 8. https://www.nytimes.com/2019/05/08/opinion/populists-dont-lose-elections.html.

Norris, P. and R. Inglehart. (2019) *Cultural Backlash: Trump, Brexit, and Authoritarian Populism*. Cambridge and New York: Cambridge University Press.

Ostiguy, P. (2017) Populism: A socio-cultural approach. In: C. R. Kaltwasser, P. Taggart, P. O. Espejo, and P. Ostiguy (eds.) *The Oxford Handbook of Populism*. Oxford: Oxford University Press.

Özbudun, E. (2015) Turkey's judiciary and the drift toward competitive authoritarianism. *The International Spectator* 50(2): 42–55.

Parla, T. and A. Davison. (2004) *Corporatist Ideology in Kemalist Turkey: Progress or Order?* Syracuse, NY: Syracuse University Press.

Rodrik, D. (2018) Populism and the economics of globalization. *Journal of International Business Policy* 1: 12–33.

Rooduijn, M. and T. Akkerman. (2017) Flank attacks: Populism and left–right radicalism in Western Europe. *Party Politics* 23(3): 193–204.

Rummens, S. (2017) Populism as a threat to liberal democracy. In: C. R. Kaltwasser, P. Taggart, P. O. Espejo, and P. Ostiguy (eds.) *The Oxford Handbook of Populism*. Oxford: Oxford University Press.

Sayarı, S. (2002) Adnan Menderes: Between democratic and authoritarian populism. In: M. Heper and S. Sayarı (eds.) *Political Leaders and Democracy in Turkey*. Lanham, MD, and Oxford: Lexington Books.

Schaub, M., J. Gereke, and D. Baldassarri. (2020) Strangers in hostile lands: Exposure to refugees and right-wing support. Under review.

Taggart, P. (2000) *Populism*. Buckingham: Open University Press.

Taggart, P. and C. R. Kaltwasser. (2016) Dealing with populists in government: Some comparative conclusions. *Democratization* 23(2): 345–65.

Tekin, A. (2016) Aleviler Yavuz Sultan Selim'e neden itiraz ediyor? *Gazete Duvar*, August 26. https://www.gazeteduvar.com.tr/gundem/2016/08/26/aleviler-yavuz-sultan-selime-neden-itiraz-ediyor/.

Tezcür, G. M. (2010) *Muslim Reformers in Iran and Turkey: The Paradox of Moderation*. Austin: University of Texas Press.

Tezcür, G. M. (2012) Trends and characteristics of the Turkish party system in light of the 2011 elections. *Turkish Studies* 13(2): 117–34.

Türkiye. (2013) Menderes'i astınız, Özal'ı zehirlediniz, Erdoğan'ı yedirmeyiz." *Türkiye*, June 3. https://www.turkiyegazetesi.com.tr/gundem/42775.aspx.

Weyland, K. (1996) Neopopulism and neoliberalism in Latin America: Unexpected affinities. *Studies in Comparative International Development* 31(3): 3–31.

Yağcı, A. (2009) *Packaging Neoliberalism: Neopopulism and the Case of Justice and Development Party*. M.A. thesis. Institute for Graduate Studies in the Social Sciences, Boğaziçi University.

Yeşil, B. (2016) *Media in New Turkey: The Origins of an Authoritarian Neoliberal State*. Urbana, Chicago, and Springfield: University of Illinois Press.

Yıldırım, D. (2009) AKP ve neoliberal popülizm. In: İ. Uzgel and B. Duru (eds.) *AKP Kitabı: Bir Dönüşümün Bilançosu*. Istanbul: Phoenix Yayınevi.

Yılmaz, Ö. (2019) Dünya 5'ten büyük artık tescilli! *Milliyet*, March 25. http://www.milliyet.com.tr/siyaset/dunya-5-ten-buyuk-artik-tescilli-2847729.

Zeller, E., J. I. Matos, T. Trotman, and G. Michelini. (2017) Situation of Turkish judiciary – platform report. https://www.medelnet.eu/images/2018/Situation-of-Turkish-Judiciary-Platform-Report.pdf.

4

The Populist Transition and the Civil Sphere in Mexico

Nelson Arteaga Botello

On July 1, 2018, Andrés Manuel López Obrador won Mexico's presidential elections following two failed attempts at the presidential seat. The party that nominated him, the *Movimiento de Renovación Nacional* (*Morena*), or Movement of National Renovation, obtained a majority in Congress.[1] Throughout the presidential campaigns he participated in, López Obrador displayed a populist discourse, where he presented himself as the legitimate, indisputable leader of the will of the people – the "real people," "common people," or "men in the street." His definition of "the people" has always included the impoverished sectors of the urban and rural areas, the impoverished middle classes, the students and the unemployed, as well as any other social group that has suffered the effects of neoliberalism: the elderly, children, small entrepreneurs, indigenous people and women, as well as people from diverse sexual orientations. This discourse brought the "people" back to the political scene, after a long, thirty-five-year absence (Leal 2014). López Obrador once said, "If it is populist to support the poor, the elderly and the young, I want to be on the list; if it is messianic to fight corruption, I also want to be on that list" (García 2017).

Since his first presidential campaign in 2006, López Obrador has highlighted his apparent connection to the wisdom and virtues of the people. In his view, this connection gives him the legitimacy to lead the so-called Fourth Transformation of the country, which constitutes a revolutionary change similar to the Independence War (1810–21), the Reform War (1858–61), and the Mexican Revolution (1910–21). This transformation aims at ending the political and economic elites – "the mafia of power" – as well as at solving the problems of violence, corruption, and social inequality. López Obrador's proposal is part of the tradition of "left-wing populisms" that make significant efforts at satisfying the needs of marginalized groups, workers, and peasants while expanding the mechanisms of direct democracy and assembly. On the other hand, as far as the exercise of power is concerned, they undermine the communicative and regulatory institutions within the civil sphere (Alexander and Tognato 2018a). Such populism has been deployed within the Mexican revolutionary regime itself, on several occasions.

Upon becoming president-elect, López Obrador promoted a populist transition toward the beginning of his government (August 8), prolonging it until his inauguration as constitutional president (December 1). First, he undermined "civil service regulatory institutions" (Alexander 2006: 138). He urged his congressional majority to defend the election mechanism that allowed him to have an attorney general for his political group and to reduce the salaries of federal bureaucrats, forcing many civil servants to resign and be replaced by supporters of the Fourth Transformation. Second, he altered the concept of voting as an institution of the civil regulation of state power (Alexander 2006: 107) by promoting several popular consultations to support and justify executive decisions taken beforehand. Finally, in judging that the opinions and behavior of all civil and political actors are governed exclusively by private and selfish interests, López Obrador announced the drafting of a Moral Constitution to act as a code of civic virtue.

The goal of this chapter is to show how, during the populist transition period, López Obrador polarized society, in some cases undermining the autonomy of the regulatory institutions of the civil sphere. Populists polarize society by demonstrating the existence of a polluted and corrupt elite constantly victimizing the people, who are judged as essentially pure (Mudde 2004; Müller 2016; Spillman 2019). This implies that populists also dispute the legitimacy of the rules by which the elites play (Kivisto 2019). Following civil sphere theory (CST), it could be said that López Obrador's populism generated pressure on the legitimacy of civil power by restoring it to a framework of legitimacy and nondemocratic membership discourses, which competed with each other (Alexander and Tognato 2018b; Kivisto and Sciortino 2018). Both López Obrador and his supporters and detractors used symbolic codes derived from the Mexican civil and patrimonial sphere in semantic innovations concerning the significance of the figure of the president, the democratic institutions, and attributions of the civil and noncivil character of social and political actors. The analysis in this chapter aims to increase the complexity of CST in empirical and analytical terms. Alexander (2015) has stressed that inside partial civil spheres, conflicting interests can undermine the development of democratic institutions because the conflict between purity and impurity is structured differently than that of the civil discourse.

When López Obrador assumes himself to be a leader who embodies the wisdom and purity of the people, he attains enough legitimacy to question – as he deems fit – institutions and democratic discourses as anticivil, thereby activating consuetudinary codes and institutions, which allow the regulation of social and power relations based on client and corporate negotiations. Insofar as López Obrador divides social life into friends and enemies, he activates the relationships of reciprocity and trust based on the deference that characterizes the patrimonial regime as positive. This enables understanding of how a real and partial civil sphere works in a populist context, in which the center of rational competition between left and right is lost (Alexander 2016; Kivisto and Sciortino 2018), favoring the polarization of political and social positions, thereby undermining the independence of the civil sphere.

Thus, López Obrador's discourse and actions constructed the idea that society was caught in a struggle between forces of good and evil, within the framework of contaminated institutions. In this sense, he activated powerful binary codes during the transition: we/them, people/elites, pure/corrupt, disinterest/profit, austerity/misuse, change/status quo, reliable/unreliable, moral/immoral, and tradition/modernity. He maintained and reinforced these binary codes during the first hundred days of his government.

The end of the transition undoubtedly yielded positive numbers for the new president. Public opinion polls showed that between 55 and 67 percent of the population supported his decisions (Carretto 2018). Mexican society perceived that the president-elect was truly breaking with the power of the elites and the political establishment, generating civil reparation processes, and broadening the sense of democracy. The question is whether that populist discourse by the left will push toward a divisive, antagonistic, antisolidary, and, therefore, undemocratic direction, which would destroy the autonomy of the civil sphere by fusing it with the patrimonial character of the state.

This chapter is a case study that allows us to account for the efforts of the communicative institutions in the civil sphere (particularly by the liberal media), in order to activate the regulatory institution of the presidency and demand that the president limit his actions to the norms and laws regulating civil life in the republic. It also shows how some conservative and leftist media supported López Obrador's efforts to restore the symbolic strength of the presidency. However, while the conservative media considered López Obrador's actions as a means to return the presidential figure to its central position in national political life, guaranteeing a set of changes without risking the unity and order of the nation, the left assumed that the patrimonialist presidential role occupied by López

Obrador acquired the strength of a noncivil input, which would expand and strengthen democracy.

Patrimonialism, Democracy, and Populism

To interpret the weight of populism in the formation of the current democracy in Mexico, and considering CST, we must account for "a world of values and institutions, which generates the capacity for social criticism and democratic integration at the same time" (Alexander 2006: 4). In the specific case of Mexico, one must recognize the way democratic and patrimonial codes confront each other. The coexistence and competition between civil and noncivil discourses characterizes the political experience of several countries. As Baiocchi (2006) shows in the case of Brazil, civil discourse is confronted by that of corporate sphere, which perceives dependence, tutelage, and clientelism as positive relationships between political power and citizens. Tognato (2011, 2018) suggests that in Colombia, democratic discourse competes with that of the *hacienda* (the large estate), which positively values the harmonic relations between the *patrón* and the subordinate, *peón*.

The Mexican patrimonial code was derived from the presence of institutions and political leadership with ample autonomy for negotiation and caused the bureaucracy to perceive the administration of the state as an instrument for personal gain (Falcón 2015: 590). This allows political leaders to perpetrate corrupt acts with a certain legal immunity, using their power authoritatively and discretionally, and cultivating patronage relationships. This does not signify a complete absence of rules. The patrimonialist regime in Mexico operates on principles based on tradition, but within a legal order characterized by a complex fabric of laws, a highly differentiated bureaucratic system, and specialized political leaders. This favors large degrees of autonomy, but political leaders recognize the existence of a legal framework they cannot violate.

The patrimonial norm can be discredited in the eyes of the governed if political leaders do not recognize the legal and customary limits that must ensue before this discretionary norm. This has effects on their honor and integrity, and contaminates the positions they occupy. When political leaders cannot contain their passions or desires, and lose their sense of existing limits on the discretionary action that they must observe, they may show themselves incapable of governing, or, even worse, lose their sense of political order. In a patrimonial regime, unbridled behavior is negatively perceived compared to self-control and sobriety. An excessive, even open, display of social relations can also be seen as polluting, in contrast with a low-key, reserved, and modest profile. The inability to distinguish between legal and customary rules is still overlooked when their difference is positively assessed. In Mexico's case, the president of the republic is the key political figure who condenses the patrimonial power of the political system, and symbolically, indisputably embodies the center of Mexican politics (Meyer 1976: 243).

Mexican patrimonialism takes its background from Porfirio Díaz's dictatorship regime (1880–1910), which established clear consuetudinary rules that allowed for the first political system of a national nature with a clientelist and corporate negotiating network (Falcón 2015). This was eroded at the beginning of the twentieth century by the increasing demand for land by an impoverished peasantry, by demands for better working conditions for laborers in the incipient national industry, and as a result of the lack of democratic representation mechanisms (Zapata 2004). The 1910 Revolution articulated these demands, and they ultimately were incorporated, along with other social and political rights, in the 1917 Constitution.

This new constitutional framework was not enough to regulate the power strife among revolutionary leaders, or to handle the political demands made by the postrevolutionary society (Langston 2017). As Aguilar (1993) suggests, it took the leaders of the Revolution more than twenty years to implement an institutionalized political apparatus that updated and innovated, within an emerging democracy, the political structures and the patrimonial Porfirist culture.

During the government of General Lázaro Cárdenas (1936–40), the regime framed and organized the peasant and worker sectors and extensively linked them to the state through the PRI (*Partido Revolucionario Institucional*/Institutional Revolutionary Party). Cárdenas consolidated social and economic reforms to the benefit of broad sectors of the population (Magrini 2019). He laid the foundations for the operation of the patrimonial regime as he consolidated the civil demands of the Revolution, through an informal contract between society and government (Zabludovsky 1989). The hyper-presidentialist regime met the minimum number of social claims through the PRI, and guaranteed a restricted civil sphere. The mass politics of Cardenism was a version of similar processes experienced in Brazil, Argentina, and Ecuador (Mudde and Kaltwasser 2017).

Unlike every other populist experience in Latin America, though, Cardenism institutionalized the transmission of power among political and corporate groups inside the PRI. In the 1960s and 1970s, the mobilization of peasants, unions, and students, along with the middle class, pushed the state to meet the accumulated social demands while challenging the foundations of the Mexican political regime. The latter's response was violent repression, while the regime endeavored to reactivate the alignment between presidential power and the needs of Mexican society. Thus, a discourse was frequently pursued that exalted the supposed virtues of "the people," constituting an attempt to renew the values and principles of the Mexican Revolution. Political parties interpreted governmental action as populist. Critics, meanwhile, accused populism of creating a personality cult around the person occupying the position of president, to the detriment of the office itself.

The presidential patrimonial system lost its legitimacy toward the end of last century. Civil discourse gained ground and the value of the rule of law in democratic life was affirmed over arbitrary political conduct. Political discourse changed; the "people" were no longer used. The government and political parties referred, instead, to "society," "civil society," and its "citizens," which highlighted the autonomous individual, thereby questioning the forms of belonging associated with the authoritarian past and the language of class struggle (Contreras 2014).

In 2000, the National Action Party (*Partido Acción Nacional*, or PAN) snatched the presidency from the PRI in a historic election. However, in the years of the PAN administration (between 2000 and 2012), several governance issues emerged. The conflict among the cabinet members paralyzed the exercise of government and the lack of experience facing government management issues was obvious. The PAN disregarded republican rituals, which it considered to be relics of the authoritarian regime. Consequently, there arose a questioning of not only the PAN as a government, but also the president himself as the material and symbolic center of national political life. Pleas for a return to the former power of the president increased significantly.

In the 2012 presidential election, the PRI platform promised the restoration of the mythical and sacred aura that had characterized the postrevolutionary presidency (Arteaga and Arzuaga 2018). In the first two years of his presidency, Enrique Peña Nieto reached several agreements with unions, political parties, and the media, as well as business and association leaders, thereby imitating the traditional practices of the PRI, projecting the restoration of the centrality of presidential power. However, after his second year in office, Peña Nieto faced a series of corruption scandals involving his closest collaborators and governors linked to his party. For many, this revealed that the return of the old presidential aura also meant the reactivation of its vices. During the 2018 election, López Obrador regularly insisted on the fact that these problems had a moral substratum. Thus, he defended his political proposal as a personal ethical position. He exalted his disdain for property and economic gain,

101

which allowed him to ensure "charismatic leadership" with a "gift of grace" (Weber 1978). López Obrador considered that this gave him sufficient legitimacy to restore the magical, sacred capacities of the presidency, while combating its vices and corruption.

I focus on explaining this process with classifications, judgments, and categorizations from debates conducted in five main newspapers in Mexico: El Universal, Excélsior, Milenio, Reforma, and La Jornada. The first three are conservative media, while the fourth and fifth take liberal and left-wing positions, respectively. The media construction of the binary narratives used to classify and typify motifs, social relations, and institutions, which permits the formation of a moral space that distinguishes pure from impure, will be observed.

As for civil discourse, free and autonomous action is contrasted with dependent and manipulated action. Open, critical, and honest relationships contrast with opaque, discretionary, and strategic relationships. Finally, institutions subject to inclusive and impersonal rules are contrasted with discretionary, exclusionist, and personalized institutions. Regarding the patrimonialist discourse, authority, self-control, and sobriety are positively valued, while action driven exclusively by law, desire, passion, and frivolity is seen as contaminated. The relationships must be regulated by principles of reciprocity, trust, deference, discretion, and a measured style, not by unilateralism, criticism, rudeness, and excess. Finally, institutions regulated by common law are positively valued, in contrast to institutions governed by the personality and arbitrariness of the individuals in power. Regarding populist discourse, action by the charismatic leader that is subject to the motives of the people is positively valued, in contrast with action that is subject to elite groups. Similarly, establishing direct relations with the people is positively evaluated, and may occur through plebiscites, consultations, and assemblies in which the institutions are susceptible to manipulation, to serve the interests of the masses, as opposed to indirect forms of representative democracy.

When López Obrador states that he embodies the will of the people and that he possesses the moral purity to lead the country, his populism becomes intertwined with the Mexican patrimonialist field, given that the latter positively judges that the leaders controlling their desires and passions maintain their political relations in a low profile, and use customary norms rather than the law when their wisdom dictates that they favor the people. The "charismatic revolutionary ends" of the populist leader also authorize him to use his qualities and attributes to transform or dismantle customary norms and rules, and the institutions of the civil sphere, all intended to free the people from corrupt and authoritarian political and bureaucratic elites.

102

The Rise to Power

During Peña Nieto's government, the PRD (*Partido de la Revolución Democrática*/Party of the Democratic Revolution) gradually moved away from its social discourse and the symbols of the left to occupy positions more aligned with those of the PAN and the PRI. The main founders and moral leaders of the PRD resigned, arguing that it had distanced itself from the ideals that initially gave rise to it. López Obrador led one of the main groups that opted out of the PRD to found the Morena party in 2014. In 2018, Morena nominated him as its candidate. López Obrador proposed confronting insecurity and violence, and combating corruption. In particular, he pledged to cancel the construction of the New Mexico City International Airport (NAICM), in his view a symbol of the corruption of the previous government. He promised to reduce the salaries of the president and all government officials. He also offered to cancel lifelong pensions received by former presidents. With the savings that would follow, he asserted that it would be possible to support the poor with social programs. He proposed the revocation of the mandate after three years in office and the elimination of the president's immunity to impeachment as well as the cancellation of the legislative reforms approved by Enrique Peña's government.

José Antonio Meade, the PRI's candidate for the "All for Mexico" coalition (along with the Green Ecologist Party and the New Alliance Party), and Ricardo Anaya, the PAN's candidate for the "For Mexico, at the Front" coalition with the PRD and the Citizen Movement, focused their campaigns on attempting to contaminate the proposals by López Obrador. He was branded as a populist wanting to impose the PRI's former approach to government and portrayed as a warlord without an appreciation for democratic institutions. López Obrador nevertheless won the presidential race, receiving 53 percent of the votes, 31 percentage points more than the PAN candidate and 37 points more than the PRI candidate. When the National Electoral Institute announced the results in the evening of election day, López Obrador called for national reconciliation and affirmed that with his triumph, the state would stop being a committee at the service of minorities, but instead would represent all Mexicans, rich and poor, rural and urban dwellers, migrants, believers and nonbelievers, human beings of all streams of thought and sexual preferences.

Between the election date and his inauguration by the Federal Electoral Tribunal, López Obrador maintained a low profile and took few political positions in the media. In his postinaugural speech, he declared that his triumph was a consequence of the mandate given to him by the poor, and broad sectors of the middle class and the wealthy, to put an end to the prevailing arrogance, influence, dishonesty, inefficiency, corruption, and impunity. He made a commitment to respect the division of power and the work of judges, legislators, and autonomous bodies. Finally, he warned: "We have the public support. The people have commanded me to conduct the Fourth Transformation of the country" (*Aristegui Noticias* 2018a).

López Obrador's speech was inclusive and antipopulist in tone, making it explicit that he represented all Mexicans, although in making the remark that he represented particularly the poor, he connected with his religious and left-wing inheritance (*Aristegui Noticias* 2018a). As Krauze (2006) has shown, López Obrador has declared himself an evangelical. Nevertheless, his bond with the goals of the people bears the spiritual influence of poet Carlos Pellicer. It seems that this influence ultimately characterized López Obrador's religious bias.

The Populist Transition

The actions taken by López Obrador during the transition had an impact on the regulatory institutions of the Mexican civil sphere. On the one hand, he maintained the mechanism for appointing the attorney general, despite his party having a majority in Congress, and tried to dismantle the bureaucracy (which was decried as elitist and corrupt) by reducing the salaries of civil servants. In so doing, he dealt a severe blow to the civil service as a regulatory institution that enables control over, as Alexander (2006) suggests, the instrumental force of political power, which can frequently serve personal, partisan, and group interests. On the other hand, by promoting "popular consultations" (referendums) that were manipulated to support and justify decisions taken beforehand, the vote adopted a different meaning as an institution of civil regulation of the state's power (Alexander 2006). Finally, López Obrador's conviction that the country was experiencing a crisis of individualism, selfishness, and petty interests led him to propose the drafting of a mechanism for moral regulation of civil and political relations. For five months, he tried to establish a "leadership democracy" (Weber 1978), a charismatic domination, the legitimacy of which derived from the will of the dominated.

Civil Service

When López Obrador announced that he would not alter the mechanism whereby the next attorney general of the republic would be elected, a competition was opened between civil and patrimonialist fields regarding the interpretation of this decision. The newspaper *Reforma* (liberal) and some conservative newspaper columnists, particularly from *Excélsior*, *Milénio*, and *El Universal*, took a critical stance toward the president's decision, affirming that it reproduced the authoritarian practices of the PRI's political regime. They argued that with support from his legislative majority, this action would allow the president-elect to ensure the appointment of not only a prosecutor who was linked to his political project, but also a "comrade auditor" providing immunity and impunity for his administration. They noted that López Obrador reproduced the same patterns regarding the prosecution of justice, as well as the protection of possible criminal acts by the president and his closest allies (Alexander 2018; Puig 2018; Zuckerman 2018b). The president was presented with a proposal to modify the mechanism through which a prosecutor would be appointed, which would allow civil society to collaborate in the appointment process (Alanís 2018a; Bartolomé 2018).

Two positions were deployed within the patrimonialist field. The first, which comprised conservative media columnists from *Excélsior* and *El Universal*, supported López Obrador's decision, arguing that he would be able to operate within the traditional rules that allowed the president some control over the attorney general. They noted that questioning the designation mechanism made no sense, as this was the traditional way of organizing the justice system in Mexico; regardless, it would be necessary to focus on its operational design (Cabeza de Vaca 2018; López Ayllón 2018; Magaloni Kerpel 2018; Ríos 2018). It was argued that civil society organizations did not guarantee the appointment of impartial and autonomous prosecutors. It was also asserted that civil society organizations had not been elected in any electoral process and therefore do not represent anyone and have no legitimate intervention powers in the appointment of the new prosecutor (Fernández 2018; Marín 2018a). The second patrimonialist position, supported by left-wing columnists, specifically from the newspaper *La Jornada*, indicated that the charismatic leadership of the new president, his team's honesty, and the purity of his project were sufficient to ensure that the mechanism for appointing the prosecutor would operate properly. It was argued that it was necessary for the future president to have a close relationship with the prosecutor in order to shield the permanence and continuity of the Fourth Transformation, exempting the head of state from accusations by the power elite of some nonexistent crime, as was the case in Brazil with Lula da Silva and Dilma Rousseff, or in Argentina, with Cristina Kirchner (Hernández López 2018). In this sense, the positive assessments of the Mexican patrimonial regime were activated in stressing that the election of the prosecutor was adequate, for it allowed López Obrador to appoint someone he trusted entirely, an old friend, ensuring the relationships of reciprocity, camaraderie, and deference by the prosecutor of the republic toward him as president as he embarked on the radical transformation of the country.

The president's proposal through his bench in Congress to reduce his monthly salary to $5,000 and establish a regulation that would prevent federal officials from having a salary similar to or higher than that of the president was also included in this debate. According to López Obrador, this initiative demonstrated a commitment to the people, because a salary reduction would allow the generation of savings for social programs. When legislators passed the Federal Public Servants Compensation Act, the measure was well received by the public because it was interpreted as real action against officials with excessive shameful salaries in a country with over 50 million poor people (Barbosa 2018; Beteta 2018a; Galván Ochoa 2018; Sesma Suárez 2018). Thus, in *La Jornada*, for example, the alignment of López Obrador's measure with the nineteenth-century precedent of the "feelings of the nation" letter was warmly welcomed.[2] The president's decrease in salary was positively valued within the patrimonial code for it displayed the authority and capabilities of self-restraint, self-mastery in the face of the concentration of economic resources, as well as the wisdom to restrain desires for personal enrichment and to avoid the frivolity characteristic of those preceding him in that office.

From the civil field, the conservative and liberal newspapers accused the president of forcing the resignation of trained officials to replace them with mediocre employees loyal to his political project (Berruga 2018; Buendía 2018a; Huchim 2018). This action was criticized on two levels. On the one hand, it sought the creation of a bureaucracy comprised of faithful followers, accusing the dismissed public officials of operating in the interest of the power elites (Valdés Ugalde 2018a; Zamora 2018). On the other hand, it was untrue that the savings from the wage cut would be enough to finance the social programs for the Fourth Transformation (Raphael 2018; Sarmiento 2018a; Vargas 2018). Facing these arguments, columnists from *La Jornada* argued, from the patrimonial field of the left, that members of the current bureaucracy would be forced to resign their posts because they did not identify with the Fourth Transformation; they also challenged the assertion that the civil service was staffed by well-trained specialists. As one columnist declared, "[T]he current bureaucracy keeps the country inside a hole" (Fernández-Vega 2018). Thus, the left appealed to the need for the president to institute a bureaucratic apparatus of the faithful, and to dismiss public officials disengaged from a commitment to his political project.

From the conservative patrimonialist field, these interventions in the public function by the president-elect were evaluated as positive, guaranteeing the purification of the public administration. For the left-wing patrimonialist camp, López Obrador strengthened his revolutionary political project with these actions, and also endowed the poorest people with resources. For the civil sector, these proposals were classified as populist: destined to dismantle the independence of the public function in the name of well-being for the "Mexican people"; perhaps more serious was the fact that they allowed the concentration of administrative power with the new president. In other words, populist interventions were described as a mechanism for cultivating patronage relations and for the personal use of the public administration. Thus, López Obrador's populist intervention maintained, and in some cases legitimized, the executive's control over the civil service.

Popular Consultations

Between the end of September and November 2018, López Obrador announced the release of a series of public consultations. First, a vote was to be held on the cancellation of construction work on the NAICM, begun during the previous administration. The argument was that the construction violated a nature reserve, and was the crystallization of corruption and the peddling of influence between economic elites and political power. López Obrador noted it was to be the first of a series of public consultations to be conducted, and that those "who are against the consultation oppose it because they are accustomed to authoritarianism and imposition" (El Sol de México 2018). The Business Coordinating Council, the country's most important economic power group, indicated that the president could not promote this type of exercise, which lacked legal and technical validity and was not legally binding. They called on López Obrador to rethink and refrain from affecting economic development on account of his political whims (Oblea 2018). The opposing political parties also warned that if the referendum took place, the country would suffer losses because business owners would have no trust to invest in the future (Político Mx 2018).

In the civil field, it was argued that public consultations were not subject to the mechanisms of institutional regulation (Aparicio 2018; Valadés 2018). Mostly, the liberal and conservative media warned that

107

López Obrador was promoting an illegal action in order to fulfill his populist campaign promise, canceling a work viewed as synonymous with the corruption of the previous government (Cueva 2018). However, they also noted that with this plebiscite, López Obrador was seeking to strike a moral blow to the business owners who had benefited from the NAICM contracts. This opened the door for a group of business owners deemed as morally pure and closer to the Fourth Transformation to receive government contracts (Marín 2018b; Rodríguez Cortés 2018). The design and application of the consultation was also criticized. It was noted that the ballots were placed only in Morena's electoral strongholds, the ballot gathering system allowed people to vote more than once, and the staff operating the ballot boxes openly supported López Obrador (Jáuregui 2018; Zuckerman 2018c). It was therefore considered that the consultation only acted to legitimize a decision already made by the president (Zambrano 2018b). When the results were released, and 80 percent of the votes supported the cancellation of the NAICM project, the idea that it had all been a farce was proven in the eyes of these members of the media (Berrueto 2018; Valdés Ugalde 2018b).

The left-wing patrimonialist camp defended public consultations as a way to broaden the bases of representative democracy, which had long concentrated the decision-making regarding any project in a group of supposedly select experts who actually were merely people close to the president in office. Ostensibly, such experts or technocrats always moved, at least in this case, in accordance with interests contrary to those of the nation's citizens, who were considered ignorant and incapable (Calderón 2018a; Gómez 2018). Through consultations, López Obrador demonstrated that he was a leader capable of listening to the people, comprehending their will, and taking their wisdom and values into account.

The NAICM consultation opened up a discussion on the role and function of plebiscites in a representative democracy. From the civil field, particularly among conservative and liberal media, it was argued that popular consultations were a populist measure to demonstrate that López Obrador knew and embodied the voice of the people (Sarmiento 2018c). It was noted that plebiscites were a subterfuge by the new president, through which he could show himself as the recipient of the will of the people, although his aim was actually to concentrate more power in his own hands (Aziz 2018). For these media, this expressed a clear strategy that threatened the constitutional principles of representative democracy (Beteta 2018b; Islas 2018).

The former director of the National Electoral Institute, meanwhile, warned that consultations could motivate citizen participation, but only when institutional frameworks were respected (Rivas 2018; Woldenberg 2018). In this sense, López Obrador was accused of ignoring the limits of discretionary action and the political patrimonial order. As José Buendía (2018b) pointed out, "Citizen participation to define policies and public works that transcend a six-year period is positive for democracy, but badly done if it is distorted and generates distrust in the state and its capacity to resolve conflicts, as symbolized by the history of the new airport." In this sense, certain voices in the conservative media called on the president-elect to improve the plebiscitary mechanisms; this way, he would reinforce his leadership.

The debate continued when López Obrador announced that he would submit a set of social and ecological programs for consultation: a universal pension for senior citizens; scholarships for young people who did not study or work; scholarships for students; pensions for people with disabilities; medical care for people without access to health services; free Internet coverage; and the planting of fruit and timber trees in different areas of the country.

From the civil camp, it was argued that it was unlikely that anyone would oppose giving resources to the country's most disadvantaged population groups (Heath 2018; Sarmiento 2018b). However, it was pointed out that, like the NAICM consultation, López Obrador's decision regarding social programs had already been made, so the new consultation exercise merely served to legitimize what was already planned and budgeted. The consultations were evaluated as a means of projecting the image that the new president had in-depth knowledge related to the will of the people, and was able to intuit their desires (Casar 2018; Etcheverry 2018; Guarneros Saavedra 2018; Rojas 2018). The civil camp expressed criticisms asserting that the design and implementation of the consultation did not enable it to be conducted with the minimum legal and technical requirements, in addition to accusations that the ballot boxes were once again located in Morena's electoral strongholds (Dresser 2018; López-Doriga 2018; Peredo 2018).

By contrast, from the patrimonialist field on the left, the relevance of the consultation was highlighted because it showed the president's connection to the people, and that he was establishing mechanisms of participative democracy that challenged the country's stagnant and corrupt representative democracy. However, it was pointed out that this change would require learning and willingness by all: "Participatory democracy constitutes, without a doubt, the best possible form of government, but it requires citizens to be aware of what this change implies and means" (Calderón 2018b; see also Meyer 2018). In this sense, López Obrador was considered a leader who returned democracy and its institutions to their popular origin, although the people lacked the education and conscience to make it their own. The consultations were a means that allowed the patrimonial discourse to question laws and institutions judged as elitist and antidemocratic, placing the will of the people before them. Patrimonialists positively valued the consultations when it considered that the president acknowledged the need to disrupt the law, if the values and norms they considered to emanate from the people were thereby ensured. López Obrador's populist consultations weakened the vote as an institution for the civil regulation of state power, becoming a means to reproduce the patrimonial institutions. As such, the criticism of the populism that had characterized the 1970s was also reactivated. López Obrador was accused of exalting the cult of personality to the detriment of the office of president.

A Moral Constitution for the Country

In late 2018, as a campaign proposal, López Obrador called for the drafting of a Moral Constitution for Mexico that would become a guide for public life and political and social coexistence. According to him, the dissolution of the family, individualism, the thirst for consumption, neoliberal culture, competition, and material success had profoundly eroded moral frameworks. For the elected candidate, the country needed a moral guide similar to that written in 1944 by the poet Alfonso Reyes, who was asked by the government during the years in which the postrevolutionary regime was consolidated to write a Moral Primer that would serve as a foundation for respect and civility among citizens. To inspire the Moral Constitution, López Obrador announced the government's reprinting of the booklet written by Reyes. According to the president-elect, the latter would serve as a "guide to values that will become a collective pact to begin a new stage, adopt new practices, rescue values dear to our people, and encourage behavioral patterns." The issues that this constitution would take into consideration included respect for the family, society, homeland, and nature, because "Moving forward, as a nation, requires strengthening values and rescuing our identity and our roots" (*Animal Político* 2018a).

Although the presidential proposal emphasized that the Moral Constitution would not have an obligatory legal status, but was instead intended to provide guidelines for coexistence condensed into one single document, a critical response emanated from the patrimonial and civil fields. Voices in the conservative, left-wing, and liberal media highlighted the risks involved in drafting a moral "constitution," suggesting that it would have the rank of a mandatory law (Hernández Navarro 2018;

110

Homs 2018b; Lozada León 2018). There was concern regarding the type of sanctions that could be derived from faults committed against the "constitution," as well as whether it would affect the diversity of moral and ethical perspectives existing in Mexican society (Morales Lechuga 2018). It was argued that the Moral Constitution would not be an effective instrument in the elimination of corruption, the reduction of violence, and the pacification of the country (Morera 2018; Zambrano 2018a).

It was pointed out that democratic governments do not have the power to legislate moral matters, since the imposition of a particular morality defined by the state would limit individual freedoms (Patán 2018). Some commentators from the liberal milieu warned that the Moral Constitution was a risk for the secular state and the exercise of liberal rights; they asserted that its wording represented an anteroom for religious leaders to establish moral decrees with the support of state institutions (Silva-Herzog Márquez 2018; Turrent 2018). The conservative media, particularly *El Universal* and *Excélsior*, stressed the existence of a contradiction in the president's appeal, on the one hand, to forgive corrupt figures and delinquents of the past and, on the other, to write a Moral Constitution (Alanís 2018b; Musacchio 2018). Thus, López Obrador's proposal was interpreted as yet another effort to concentrate more power in his own hands, which would now be derived from the moral sphere (Beltri 2018b; Zuckerman 2018a). His aim was apparently to establish a moral framework to justify his dictatorial decisions, as other authoritarian states have done before (Bartra 2018; Beltri 2018a; Pérez Gay 2018).

The Moral Constitution had support from among some in the conservative and left-wing patrimonial field as it was considered a good indication of the president's will to improve public life in Mexico. They justified their stands on the grounds that a measure of this nature was understandable, given the deep degree of corruption resulting from the outgoing government. They warned that the Constitution would not be binding or result in any punishment, because it would only aim to improve coexistence among the people and "strengthen the moral structures" of society (Crespo 2018; Miguel 2018; Peralta Saucedo 2018; Valdés 2018). They claimed that such a proposal revealed the true moral conviction of the incoming government to fight corruption and the excesses of the political class that still enjoyed the benefits of power (Homs 2018a).

Nevertheless, some columnists from the left and conservative patrimonial field considered that while they did not doubt the good will of the president to recover certain social values, they also believed that it was still best to maintain faith in the functioning of the legal system and the administration of justice (Garza 2018). As one writer stated: "To make the coexistence between government and citizenship and among citizens more viable, it is enough to enforce the Political Constitution of the United Mexican States and the laws that emanate from it" (Martínez García 2018). In this sense, they called on the president to avoid transgressing the customary and political limits of the patrimonial regime.

In the face of corrupt elites, López Obrador's populist proposal to represent and embody the country's moral virtue also encompassed his characterization of the way in which social elements are interlinked. The proposal for a Moral Constitution to serve as a mechanism for regulating civil and political relations was positively received by the conservative and left-wing patrimonial camp, as a means of solving the country's problems. What is patrimonial about the Moral Constitution discourse is the idea that a society works better if people learn to restrain themselves, master themselves, and maintain sobriety, along with a measured attitude. According to López Obrador, if society can restrain itself, if it is considered within the bounds of the Moral Constitution project, it will be possible for relationships of reciprocity, trust, deference, and discretion to be established.

From the civil camp, conservative, liberal, and left-wing columnists stressed the impossibility of imposing a set of rules based on a moral imperative beyond the legal and democratic normative order. Thus, López Obrador's proposal was characterized as a radical attempt to transform the country's life for the better, even in its moral sphere. For others, he expressed an attempt, similar to that of the postrevolutionary regime in the 1940s and the populism of the 1970s, to revive the set of values and moral principles of the past. In this way, for some, the populism of the new president reactivated the positive pretensions of the patrimonial regime toward becoming a positive input that regulated the moral life of society; meanwhile, for others, it confirmed López Obrador's intentions to transform the presidency into a form of noncivil regulation that governed the country's social life as a whole.

The disputes between the civil codes and the noncivil codes of patrimonialism have characterized the debate before and after the democratic transition. The positions that endorsed the civil codes – particularly from liberals and leftists – opposed those who wielded arguments favoring the patrimonial code – the conservative groups. The consolidation of the discourse and López Obrador's populist actions has provoked reactions within the institutions of the civil sphere. Some have accused the president of wanting to restore presidential *authoritarianism*, while others believe he seeks to update the president's *authority*. In the eyes of their critics, López Obrador and his followers suggest a civil reparation of the democratic institutions and the use of the patrimonial regime to that effect as a noncivil input in order to radicalize democracy. These standpoints have substantially transformed liberal, left-wing, and conservative orientations. As we have seen here, the liberal wing and a part of the conservative wing call upon López Obrador to adhere to the civil codes and to keep a distance from populism and authoritarianism, while the left-wing and others on the conservative side encourage and defend the decision of the president to activate the noncivil input of the patrimonial system.

After the Transition

In January 2019, the president introduced the drafting board of the Moral Constitution and called for a national convention. Alejandro Gertz was appointed Attorney General of the Nation for the next nine years. The new prosecutor was an old friend and advisor to López Obrador; thus the opposition parties did not hesitate to assert that the president had proposed a "comrade auditor" to protect him during his administration, which would last for three more years (Martínez Huerta 2019). As such, with the support of his party in Congress, the president was able to implement control mechanisms in one of the main areas of public service. However, the proposed Federal Law of Remuneration of Public Servants, which was approved by Congress during the transition period, suffered a setback just seven days after López Obrador was inaugurated. The Supreme Court of Justice of the Nation (SCJN) suspended the law to prevent irreparable and unjustified damage to those with an employment contract with the federal government. The president warned that the SCJN had made a mistake: "Because it is not understanding the new reality that there can be no rich government with poor people, and forgetting Juárez [leader of the Second Transformation], who said that the civil servant had to learn to live within his just means [that is to say, without luxuries and riches, but not in poverty]" (*Animal Político* 2018b).

López Obrador launched other populist actions, thereby tending to reproduce and generate the binary codes of us/them, people/elites, pure/corrupt, disinterest/profit, austerity/waste, change/status quo, reliable/unreliable, moral/immoral, and tradition/modernity. To distinguish himself from the previous government and its elitism, corruption, profit, and waste, he announced that he would live in the *Palacio Nacional* and transform the official residence of *Los Pinos* into a museum. Likewise, he decreed the sale of the presidential airplane, as well as the vehicles reserved for the sole use of the president. He also decreed the dissolution of the Presidential General Staff, the president's security guard, and its subsequent replacement by a small security group composed only of women.

López Obrador issued a presidential decree suspending the pension of former presidents and any type of support teams. He announced that every morning he would hold a press conference. In these conferences, the president answers journalists' questions, sets the agenda of the government, and establishes social programs and horizons for transformation. This allows him to project the idea that his government is open, close to the people, and transparent to public opinion, whereas the conferences in fact provide a vantage point from which he identifies his enemies and his allies. To emphasize that his government is rejecting the status quo and stands for the restoration of trust and morality, López Obrador has decided to close programs or cancel economic resources when he suspects the existence of inadequate resource management. For example, he closed the program of children's homes and shelters that care for women who are victims of violence. He also stopped transferring funds to civil society organizations, accusing them of having an agenda that was unresponsive to aiding the poor.

López Obrador has cut the budgets of regulative institutions of the civil sphere that he accuses of being corrupt and elitist, such as the SCJN, the National Institute of Statistics and Geography, the National Electoral Institute, the National Institute of Access to Information, and the Energy Regulation Commission, as well as the Institute of Educational Evaluation and the Electoral Tribunal of the Judiciary of the Federation. Each of these institutions has responded to the president critically, noting that it is necessary that he respects the institutions which have had a key role in the construction of the country's democratic scaffolding.

López Obrador has been quite critical toward the press. His attacks have been directed toward journalists, whom he has accused of defending standpoints opposing his administration owing to the fact that they supposedly received benefits and bribery from previous governments. In May 2019, he accused thirty-six journalists of receiving illegal money from the previous administration, which was denied by every one of them, presenting proof of the legality of the resources received, amounts, allocation of resources, and corresponding tax payments. The journalists blamed López Obrador for the environment of intolerance and bad faith under the new government. The group of accused journalists works for mass media with liberal and conservative views. The president attacks the press in a general fashion for its criticism of his political standpoint. Nevertheless, it is clear that a particular attack exists against *Reforma*, especially when this newspaper showed that homicide rates had increased a hundred days after his takeover.

López Obrador attacked *Reforma* when it released a letter sent by the government of the republic to Philip VI, King of Spain, and to Pope Francis, demanding that they publicly apologize for the genocide led by the Kingdom of Spain and the Vatican against the indigenous peoples of Mexico during the *Conquista*. The president demanded that *Reforma* reveal the source who had provided it with the letter. The newspaper said that this demand violated the ethics of journalism. López Obrador, in turn, accused *Reforma* of supporting the reactionaries and conservatives, of seeking to incite a plot against his government, and gave the following warning: "If you go beyond the limits, you know what will happen." This statement was condemned by international and national bodies in defense of journalists because it was interpreted as a threat against freedom of the press in Mexico by the president. The Internal Revenue Service has also called upon *Reforma* to clarify its tax situation more than once, which has been interpreted as a direct infringement of freedom of the press.

At the end of his first hundred days in office, the president achieved a 67–86 percent approval rating in the polls for his performance. Public opinion highlights his efforts to put an end to corruption, as reflected in the approval of the reduction of salaries and dismissals of civil servants, and to reduce poverty, particularly through the promotion of social programs and the allocation of resources to the poor that had previously been destined for other areas of the government. The exercise of popular consultations has also been labeled successful (Moreno 2019). The poll results are so favorable for the president because the questions have focused on the transformative nature of his administration, particularly in his effort to engage in civil repair of the country's politics. In this case, the polls reproduce – as Alexander (2006) suggests – the categories of purity and impurity already provided by the civil discourse; therefore, opinions of the president end up reflecting the situation that has been defined in accordance with the binary categories compromised by the discourses of the president himself and the mass media.

López Obrador has sought to restore, on the one hand, the identification of presidential power with the needs of Mexican society, and, on the other, the noncivil face of the patrimonial nature of state power. Faced with these noncivil restorations of patrimonial order, social mobilizations have been generated. The president has been urged to limit his actions to the civil normative character of the office, in accordance with the cries of "No to dictatorship," and "No to messianism." Among these demands, the president has been called upon to cease his populist discourse, which

115

polarizes the country. The executive has been called upon to make civil reparations to those in disagreement, thereby restoring the universal character of legal norms and citizenship under the slogan "Respect the law and govern for all." It was also requested that the government prevent plebiscites in the future, because they are a form of corruption that allows the president to legitimize his authoritarian decisions. The aim was to vindicate the vote as an institution for the civil regulation of state power. In this sense, civil resistance to López Obrador's populism may be observed. Social movements, the liberal press, as well as people from the artistic world, have come out to defend freedom of expression and criticize the president's actions. There is also questioning of the president by regulatory institutions. In the future, there might very well be delegitimization scandals and crises, which will allow these critiques to take on some depth and reactivate the civil nature of the democratic codes and institutions before the patrimonial regime.

Conclusion

López Obrador's leftist populism is a civil reparation project responding to the accumulation of grievances against those who have held political power and the processes of social exclusion that have accompanied the Mexican democratic transition. The actions that López Obrador has conducted have been aimed toward re-establishing the machinery of social solidarity through social politics and attempting to show the popular face of presidential power. His project has sought to radicalize the democratization process of the country with an anti-elitist, anti-institutional, anti-neoliberal discourse opting for community, for horizontal relations, and for plebiscitary expressions of what is popular. This effort has brought back the "noncivil" code of patrimonialism, with its ways of restricted solidarity, membership, and inclusion. López Obrador's leftist populism is an answer to the right-wing authoritarian governments that dominated the country for years, but it has also turned to judging the failure of democratic institutions without any kind of filter. Intending to radicalize democracy through a leftist populism that at the same time activates noncivil codes and practices expresses the paradox of wanting to expand democratic and civil universals using particularistic forms of political and social inclusion.

López Obrador regards himself as a populist who thwarts authoritarian institutions which are disguised as democratic – with elites and power groups wearing the mask of the citizenry – but awaken dark forces of Mexican politics. This allows him to articulate his discourse within the consistent framework of liberal and democratic demands that expand the civil sphere. Thus his government presents itself as morally convincing despite its appeal to particularistic codes of a patrimonial nature, in contrast with the universalist aspirations of the civil sphere. Therefore the critiques of his government are interpreted as a questioning of the civil effort being made to repair the debts left by the transition process and democratic alternation. He turns the agonizing actors of the national political scene into antagonists, polarizing society and blurring, little by little, the center of rational competition of democratic political order.

As suggested by Alexander (2006), the real civil sphere is always under pressure, limited, and interpenetrated in its boundaries by the relationships it establishes with other, noncivil, spheres. In the case of Mexico, in the past few years, the communicative and regulatory institutions of the civil sphere have been able to expand before noncivil codes of a patrimonial nature. Progress has especially been made in the regulations over the presidency. However, López Obrador's populism is not helping to hold back noncivil expressions regarding the presidency; rather, it has triggered the response of the civil sphere's institutions to demand that the president adhere to the civil limits of the office. In this respect, the discursive and, in many cases, legal dispute aroused by López Obrador's populism must also be interpreted as part of the increasing power of the civil sphere in Mexico.

Notes

1 Morena led a broader coalition of parties to support López Obrador's candidacy called "Together We'll Make History." The parties included in the coalition were *Partido del Trabajo* (PT), or Labor Party, and *Partido Encuentro Social* (PES), or Social Encounter Party.
2 The letter was promulgated in 1813 during the War of Independence (Mexico's First Transformation), establishing that civil servants' salaries should not allow them access to superfluous goods (de la Torre 2018).

References

Aguilar, H. (1993) La invención de México: Notas sobre nacionalismo e identidad nacional. *Nexos* 187(4): 49–61. https://www.nexos.com.mx/?p=6803.
Alanís, E. (2018a) ¿Tendremos #FiscalíaQueSirva y #SeguridadSinGuerra? *El Universal*, September 11. https://www.eluniversal.com.mx/columna/elisa-alanis/nacion/tendremos-fiscaliaquesirva-y-seguridadsinguerra.

Alanís, E. (2018b) La Cuarta Transformación Militarizada. *El Universal*, November 16. https://www.eluniversal.com.mx/columna/elisa-alanis/nacion/la-cuarta-transformacion-militarizada.

Alexander, J. C. (2006) *The Civil Sphere*. New York: Oxford University Press.

Alexander, J. C. (2015) Nine theses on *The Civil Sphere*. In: P. Kivisto and G. Sciortino (eds.) *Solidarity, Justice, and Incorporation: Thinking through The Civil Sphere*. Oxford: Oxford University Press.

Alexander, J. C. (2016) Progress and disillusion: Civil repair and its discontents. *Thesis Eleven* 137(1): 172–82.

Alexander, J. C. and C. Tognato. (2018a) Introduction: For democracy in Latin America. In: J. C. Alexander and C. Tognato (eds.) *The Civil Sphere in Latin America*. Cambridge: Cambridge University Press.

Alexander, J. C. and C. Tognato (eds.). (2018b) *The Civil Sphere in Latin America*. Cambridge: Cambridge University Press.

Alexander, R. (2018) Fiscalía a modo. *Excélsior*, September 8. https://www.excelsior.com.mx/opinion/columnista-invitado-nacional/fiscalia-a-modo/1263681.

Animal Político. (2018a) Qué es la constitución moral y cuál es su objetivo según AMLO. *Animal Político*, November 26. https://www.animalpolitico.com/2018/11/que-es-constitucion-moral-amlo/.

Animal Político. (2018b) AMLO critica a la Corte por frenar la ley de reducción de salarios; es una ofensa para el pueblo, dice. *Animal Político*, December 8. https://www.animalpolitico.com/2018/12/amlo-corte-salarios-ofensa/.

Aparicio, J. (2018) Consulta sesgada. *Excélsior*, October 25. https://www.excelsior.com.mx/opinion/javier-aparicio/consulta-sesgada/1274017.

Aristegui Noticias. (2018a) Este fue el discurso de AMLO tras recibir constancia de presidente electo. *Aristegui Noticias*, August 8. https://aristeguinoticias.com/0808/mexico/este-fue-el-discurso-de-amlo-tras-recibir-constancia-de-presidente-electo-video/.

Aristegui Noticias. (2018b) AMLO define el concepto "fifi." *Aristegui Noticias*, November 21. https://aristeguinoticias.com/2111/mexico/amloenaristeguinoticias-define-el-concepto-fifi-enterate/.

Arteaga, N. and J. Arzuaga. (2018) The civil sphere in Mexico: Between democracy and authoritarianism. In: J. C. Alexander and C. Tognato (eds.) *The Civil Sphere in Latin America*. Cambridge: Cambridge University Press.

Aziz, A. (2018) AMLO: ¿Solo o con el Estado? *El Universal*, November 6. https://www.eluniversal.com.mx/articulo/alberto-aziz-nassif/nacion/amlo-solo-o-con-el-estado.

Baiocchi, G. (2006) The civilizing force of social movements: Corporate and liberal codes in Brazil's public sphere. *Sociological Theory* 24(4): 285–311.

Barbosa, M. (2018) Ley de Salarios Máximos. *Milenio*, September 14. https://www.milenio.com/opinion/miguel-barbosa/la-causa-lo-causado/ley-de-salarios-maximos.

Bartolomé, F. (2018) Templo Mayor. *Reforma*, August 2. https://www.reforma.com/aplicaciones/editoriales/editorial.aspx?id=139457.

Bartra, R. (2018) Equivalentes morales. *Reforma*, August 21. https://www.reforma.com/aplicaciones/editoriales/editorial.aspx?__rval=1&id=140558.

Beltri, V. (2018a) El próximo error de diciembre. *Excélsior*, September 3. https://www.excelsior.com.mx/opinion/victor-beltri/el-proximo-error-de-diciembre/1262502.

Beltri, V. (2018b) Se vale disentir. *Excélsior*, November 19. https://www.excel
sior.com.mx/opinion/victor-beltri/se-vale-disentir/1279243.

Berrueto, F. (2018) La consulta. *Milenio*, August 19. https://www.milenio.com/
opinion/federico-berrueto/juego-de-espejos/la-consulta.

Berruga, E. (2018) La diplomacia mexicana. *El Universal*, July 26. https://www.
eluniversal.com.mx/articulo/enrique-berruga-filloy/nacion/la-diplomacia-mexi
cana.

Beteta, O. (2018a) De la oligarquía a la democracia. *El Universal*, July 27.
https://www.eluniversal.com.mx/columna/oscar-mario-beteta/nacion/de-la-
oligarquia-la-democracia.

Beteta, O. (2018b) ¿Democracia participativa . . . o autoritarismo? *El Universal*,
November 2. https://www.eluniversal.com.mx/columna/oscar-mario-beteta/
nacion/democracia-participativa-o-autoritarismo.

Buendía, J. (2018a) ¿Cuál es la agenda del próximo gobierno? *Excélsior*, July
19. https://www.excelsior.com.mx/opinion/jose-buendia-hegewisch/cual-es-la-
agenda-del-proximo-gobierno/1253263.

Buendía, J. (2018b) Costos, AMLO y consulta NAIM. *Excélsior*, October 25.
https://www.excelsior.com.mx/opinion/jose-buendia-hegewisch/costos-amlo-
y-consulta-naim/1274016.

Cabeza de Vaca, D. (2018) Claves para la Fiscalía autónoma. *El Universal*,
July 25. https://www.eluniversal.com.mx/articulo/daniel-cabeza-de-vaca-hern
andez/nacion/claves-para-la-fiscalia-autonoma.

Calderón, E. (2018a) Consulta NAIM, educación y olvido. *La Jornada*, October
13. https://www.jornada.com.mx/2018/10/13/opinion/020a1pol.

Calderón, E. (2018b) La importancia de la segunda consulta. *La Jornada*,
November 24. https://www.jornada.com.mx/2018/11/24/opinion/020a1pol.

Carretto, B. (2018) AMLO asumirá la presidencia con una aprobación superior a
50%, según encuestas. *ADN Político*, November 26. https://adnpolitico.com/
presidencia/2018/11/26/amlo-llega-con-aprobacion-de-mas-de-la-mitad.

Casar, M. (2018) ¿Por qué? *Excélsior*, November 21. https://www.excelsior.
com.mx/opinion/maria-amparo-casar/por-que/1279704.

Contreras, J. (2014) *La experiencia de la democracia: Cambio político y conceptual en el México contemporáneo*. Mexico City: El Colegio de San Luis.

Crespo, J. (2018) Bancarrota nacional y promesas de campana. *El Universal*,
September 24. https://www.eluniversal.com.mx/articulo/jose-antonio-crespo/
nacion/bancarrota-nacional-y-promesas-de-campana.

Cueva, A. (2018) El aeropuerto maldito. *Milenio*, August 19. https://www.mile
nio.com/opinion/alvaro-cueva/ojo-por-ojo/el-aeropuerto-maldito.

de la Torre, J. (2018) 22,570 empleados con salarios arriba de $108,000.
Milenio, July 20. https://www.milenio.com/opinion/jesus-de-la-torre-pbro/
areopago/22-570-empleados-salarios-108-000.

Dresser, D. (2018) Volando bajo. *Reforma*, November 5. https://www.reforma.
com/aplicaciones/editoriales/editorial.aspx?id=145137.

El Sol de México. (2018) AMLO da "segunda llamada" para participar en la
consulta del NAIM. *El Sol de México*, October 23. https://www.elsoldemexico.
com.mx/mexico/politica/amlo-da-segunda-llamada-para-participar-en-la-con
sulta-del-naim-2266692.html.

Etcheverry, A. (2018) En tiempos de consultas y grandes obras. *Excélsior*,
November 25. https://www.excelsior.com.mx/opinion/columnista-invitado-
nacional/en-tiempos-de-consultas-y-grandes-obras/1280567.

Falcón, R. (2015) *El jefe político: Un dominio negociado en el mundo rural del Estado de México*. Mexico City: El Colegio de México.

Fernández, J. (2018) La sociedad civil no designa fiscal. *Excélsior*, July 10. https://www.excelsior.com.mx/opinion/jorge-fernandez-menendez/la-sociedad-civil-no-designa-fiscal/1251312.

Fernández-Vega, C. (2018) México SA. *La Jornada*, July 19. https://www.jornada.com.mx/2018/07/19/opinion/020o1eco.

Galván Ochoa, E. (2018) Dinero. *La Jornada*, July 12. https://www.jornada.com.mx/2018/07/12/opinion/006o1eco.

García, C. (2017) "Mesiánico y populista si es por los pobres": AMLO. *El Universal*, May 16. https://www.eluniversal.com.mx/articulo/nacion/politica/2017/05/16/mesianico-y-populista-si-es-por-los-pobres-amlo.

Garza, R. (2018) Moral vs. ley. *Milenio*, August 28. https://www.milenio.com/opinion/roberta-garza/articulo-mortis/moral-vs-ley.

Gómez, L. (2018) NAIM, entre la consulta y la encuesta. *Milenio*, October 16. https://www.milenio.com/opinion/leopoldo-gomez/tercer-grado/naim-entre-la-consulta-y-la-encuesta.

Guarneros Saavedra, F. (2018) Transición. *Excélsior*, November 25. https://www.excelsior.com.mx/opinion/fabiola-guarneros-saavedra/transicion/1280557.

Heath, J. (2018) Cuadrando números. *Reforma*, July 25. https://www.reforma.com/aplicaciones/editoriales/editorial.aspx?id=139001.

Hernández López, L. (2018) Fiscalía, ¿solidaria o distante? *La Jornada*, November 6. https://www.jornada.com.mx/2018/11/06/opinion/016o1pol.

Hernández Navarro, L. (2018) La constitución moral. *La Jornada*, August 28. https://www.jornada.com.mx/2018/08/28/opinion/021a1pol.

Homs, R. (2018a) ¿Quién es realmente Andrés Manuel? *El Universal*, August 4. https://www.eluniversal.com.mx/articulo/ricardo-homs/nacion/quien-es-realmente-andres-manuel.

Homs, R. (2018b) Constitución moral para el bienestar del alma. *El Universal*, September 6. https://www.eluniversal.com.mx/columna/ricardo-homs/constitucion-moral-para-el-bienestar-del-alma.

Huchim, E. (2018) Delegados, salarios, arcoíris. *Reforma*, July 18. https://www.reforma.com/aplicaciones/editoriales/editorial.aspx?__rval=1&id=138548.

Islas, J. (2018) Consultar al pueblo. *El Universal*, November 4. https://www.eluniversal.com.mx/articulo/jorge-islas/nacion/consultar-al-pueblo.

Jáuregui, M. (2018) Muy enojado. *Reforma*, October 26. https://www.reforma.com/aplicaciones/editoriales/editorial.aspx?__rval=1&id=144554.

Kivisto, P. (2019) Populism's efforts to de-legitimize the vital center and the implications for liberal democracy. In: J. L. Mast and J. C. Alexander (eds.) *Politics of Meaning/Meaning of Politics: Cultural Sociology of the 2016 US Presidential Election*. London: Palgrave Macmillan.

Kivisto, P. and G. Sciortino. (2018) Conclusion: Democracy and the civil sphere in Latin America. In: J. C. Alexander and C. Tognato (eds.) *The Civil Sphere in Latin America*. Cambridge: Cambridge University Press.

Krauze, E. (2006) El mesías tropical. *Letras Libres*, June 30. https://www.letraslibres.com/espana-mexico/revista/el-mesias-tropical.

Langston, J. (2017) *Democratization and Authoritarian Party Survival*. Oxford: Oxford University Press.

Lealí, A. (2014) De pueblo a sociedad civil: El discurso político después del sismo de 1985. *Revista Mexicana de Sociología* 76(3): 441–69.

López Ayllón, S. (2018) Hacia una fiscalía que sirva. *Milenio*, August 22. https://www.milenio.com/opinion/sergio-lopez-ayllon/entresijos-del-derecho/hacia-una-fiscalia-que-sirva.

López-Doriga, J. (2018) ¡Vaya con el Tren Maya ... ! *Milenio*, October 4. https://www.milenio.com/opinion/joaquin-lopez-doriga/en-privado/vaya-con-el-tren-maya.

Lozada León, L. (2018) La Constitución Moral o Silabario de los Valores. *Milenio*, September 2. https://www.milenio.com/opinion/luis-lozada-leon/opinion/la-constitucion-moral-o-silabario-de-los-valores.

Magaloni Kerpel, A. (2018) Peña, AMLO y la FGR. *Reforma*, August 4. https://www.reforma.com/aplicacioneslibre/editoriales/editorial.aspx?id=139583&md5=eec059526980891cb3d9d2bc800b2c4b&ta=0dfdbac11765226904c16cb9ad1b2efe&lcmd5=f80a3346614c2aabe9a3891f923301a2.

Magrini, A. (2019) Populismo y revolución en México: Reflexiones en torno a los lenguajes políticos durante los años setenta. *Revista Historia Autónoma* 14(1): 195–212.

Marín, C. (2018a) La disputa por la fiscalía general. *Milenio*, July 11. https://www.milenio.com/opinion/carlos-marin/el-asalto-la-razon/la-disputa-por-la-fiscalia-general.

Marín, C. (2018b) Dónde el aeropuerto ya es lo de menos. *Milenio*, October 26. https://www.milenio.com/opinion/carlos-marin/el-asalto-la-razon/donde-el-aeropuerto-ya-es-lo-de-menos.

Martínez García, C. (2018) ¿Consenso moral? *La Jornada*, November 21. https://www.jornada.com.mx/2018/11/21/opinion/018a1pol.

Martínez Huerta, D. (2019) Alejandro Gertz (colaborador de AMLO) se convierte en el primer fiscal general. *ADN Político*, January 18. https://adnpolitico.com/congreso/2019/01/18/alejandro-gertz-colaborador-de-amlo-se-convierte-en-el-primer-fiscal-general.

Meyer, L. (1976) La encrucijada. In: D. Cosio Villegas, F. Calderón, L. González, C. Villegas, and M. Navarro (eds.) *Historia General de México*, Vol. 4. Mexico City: El Colegio de México.

Meyer, R. (2018) Proyecto nacional, el camino del Tren Maya. *Milenio*, November 24. https://www.milenio.com/opinion/roman-meyer/la-columna-roman-meyer/proyecto-nacional-el-camino-del-tren-maya.

Miguel, P. (2018) Regeneración moral. *La Jornada*, September 21. https://www.jornada.com.mx/2018/09/21/opinion/026a2pol.

Morales Lechuga, I. (2018) ¿México necesita fiscal moral? *El Universal*, August 8. https://www.eluniversal.com.mx/articulo/ignacio-morales-lechuga/nacion/mexico-necesita-fiscal-moral.

Moreno, A. (2019) A 100 días, AMLO tiene 78% de aprobación. *El Financiero*, March 4. https://www.elfinanciero.com.mx/nacional/a-100-dias-amlo-tiene-78-de-aprobacion.

Morera, M. (2018) Proyecto ominoso y mucha demagogia. *El Universal*, November 15. https://www.eluniversal.com.mx/articulo/maria-elena-morera/nacion/proyecto-ominoso-y-mucha-demagogia.

Mudde, C. (2004) The populist zeitgeist. *Government and Opposition* 39(4): 541–63.

Mudde, C. and C. R. Kaltwasser. (2017) *Populism: A Very Short Introduction*. Oxford: Oxford University Press.

Müller, J.-W. (2016) *What Is Populism?* Philadelphia: University of Pennsylvania Press.

Musacchio, H. (2018) ¿Impunidad a los corruptos? *Excélsior*, November 22. https://www.excelsior.com.mx/opinion/humberto-musacchio/impunidad-a-los-corruptos/1279983.

Oblea, M. (2018) Los empresarios otra vez contra AMLO, ahora por la consulta sobre NAICM. *La Silla Rota*, October 23. https://lasillarota.com/empresarios-contra-consulta-amlo-naicm/253702.

Patán, J. (2018) Constitución moral. *Milenio*, August 7. https://www.milenio.com/opinion/julio-patan/malos-modos/constitucion-moral.

Peralta Saucedo, R. (2018) La Paz de Westfalia y la Constitución Moral. *Excélsior*, August 27. https://www.excelsior.com.mx/opinion/ricardo-peralta-saucedo/la-paz-de-westfalia-y-la-constitucion-moral/1261033.

Peredo, X. (2018) No hubo luna de miel. *Reforma*, November 23. https://www.reforma.com/aplicaciones/editoriales/editorial.aspx?id=146244.

Pérez Gay, R. (2018) Contra las grandes verdades. *Milenio*, August 8. https://www.milenio.com/opinion/rafael-perez-gay/practicas-indecibles/contra-las-grandes-verdades.

Político Mx. (2018) México es el gran perdedor tras consulta sobre NAICM: PAN. *Político Mx*, October 29. https://politico.mx/minuta-politica/minuta-politica-partidos-politicos/m%C3%A9xico-es-el-gran-perdedor-tras-consulta-sobre-naicm-pan/.

Puig, C. (2018) Una nueva fiscalía que ¿olerá a viejo? *Milenio*, September 12. https://www.milenio.com/opinion/carlos-puig/duda-razonable/una-nueva-fiscalia-que-olera-a-viejo.

Raphael, R. (2018) AMLO ganará más de lo que se dice. *El Universal*, November 19. https://www.eluniversal.com.mx/columna/ricardo-raphael/nacion/amlo-ganara-mas-de-lo-que-se-dice.

Ríos, V. (2018) #FiscalQueSirva no es suficiente. *Excélsior*, August 26. https://www.excelsior.com.mx/opinion/viridiana-rios/fiscalquesirva-no-es-suficiente/1260897.

Rivas, F. (2018) ¿Cuándo nos van a consultar? *El Universal*, October 30. https://www.eluniversal.com.mx/articulo/francisco-rivas/nacion/cuando-nos-van-consultar.

Rodríguez Cortés, R. (2018) Santa Lucía: ¿Quiere AMLO iniciar con inestabilidad económica? *El Universal*, October 24. https://www.eluniversal.com.mx/columna/raul-rodriguez-cortes/nacion/santa-lucia-quiere-amlo-iniciar-con-inestabilidad-economica.

Rojas, P. (2018) ¿Consultar o ratificar? *El Universal*, November 19. https://www.eluniversal.com.mx/columna/paola-rojas/nacion/consultar-o-ratificar.

Sarmiento, S. (2018a) Wall Street y AMLO. *Reforma*, July 11. https://www.reforma.com/aplicaciones/editoriales/editorial.aspx?__rval=1&id=138137.

Sarmiento, S. (2018b) Cuadrar las cifras. *Reforma*, September 13. https://www.reforma.com/aplicaciones/editoriales/editorial.aspx?id=142013.

Sarmiento, S. (2018c) El pueblo manda. *Reforma*, November 2. https://www.reforma.com/aplicaciones/editoriales/editorial.aspx?__rval=1&id=144981.

Sesma Suárez, J. (2018) El cambio, una oportunidad para mejorar. *Excélsior*, July 26. https://www.excelsior.com.mx/opinion/opinion-del-experto-nacional/el-cambio-una-oportunidad-para-mejorar/1254722.

Silva-Herzog Márquez, J. (2018) Arrogancia en la Victoria. *Reforma*, August 6. https://www.reforma.com/aplicaciones/editoriales/editorial.aspx?__rval=1&id =139661.

Spillman, Lyn (2019) Landscapes, fields, and stages. In: J. L. Mast and J. C. Alexander (eds.) *Politics of Meaning/Meaning of Politics: Cultural Sociology of the 2016 US Presidential Election*. London: Palgrave Macmillan.

Tognato, C. (2011) Extending trauma across cultural divides: On kidnapping and solidarity in Colombia. In: R. Eyerman, J. C. Alexander, and E. Butler Breese (eds.) *Narrating Trauma: Studies in the Contingent Impact of Collective Suffering*. Boulder, CO: Paradigm Publishers.

Tognato, C. (2018) The civil life of the university: Enacting dissent and resistance on a Colombian campus. In: J. C. Alexander and C. Tognato (eds.) *The Civil Sphere in Latin America*. Cambridge: Cambridge University Press.

Turrent, I. (2018) Las caras de López Obrador. *Reforma,* August 5. https://www. reforma.com/aplicaciones/editoriales/editorial.aspx?id=139612.

Valadés, D. (2018) Consulta constitucional. *Reforma*, September 25. https://www. reforma.com/aplicaciones/editoriales/editorial.aspx?__rval=1&id=142715.

Valdés, M. (2018) ¿Constitución moral? *Milenio*, November 28. https:// www.milenio.com/opinion/mauricio-valdes/comentario-debate/constitucion-moral.

Valdés Ugalde, F. (2018a) ¿Qué Estado queremos tener? *El Universal*, August 19. https://www.eluniversal.com.mx/articulo/francisco-valdes-ugalde/nacion/ que-estado-queremos-tener.

Valdés Ugalde, F. (2018b) Una consulta por encima de la Constitución. *El Universal*, October 28. https://www.eluniversal.com.mx/articulo/francisco-valdes-ugalde/nacion/una-consulta-por-encima-de-la-constitucion.

Vargas, E. (2018) De bolsillos rotos. *Milenio*, August 5. https://www.milenio. com/opinion/erik-vargas/el-desmenuzadero/de-bolsillos-rotos.

Weber, M. (1978) *Economy and Society: An Outline of Interpretive Sociology*. Berkeley: University of California Press.

Woldenberg, J. (2018) Debería suspenderse. *El Universal*, October 23. https:// www.eluniversal.com.mx/articulo/jose-woldenberg/nacion/deberia-suspend-erse.

Zabludovsky, G. (1989) The reception and utility of Max Weber's concept of patrimonialism in Latin America. *International Sociology* 4(1): 51–66.

Zambrano, J. (2018a) Necesaria una izquierda social y democrática. *El Universal,* October 11. https://www.eluniversal.com.mx/articulo/jesus-zambrano/nacion/ necesaria-una-izquierda-social-y-democratica.

Zambrano, J. (2018b) Construir contrapesos. *El Universal*, November 22. https://www.eluniversal.com.mx/articulo/jesus-zambrano/nacion/construir-contrapesos.

Zamora, A. (2018) Ignorancia y concentración del poder. *Excélsior*, November 27. https://www.excelsior.com.mx/opinion/arturo-zamora/ignorancia-y-con centracion-del-poder/1280912.

Zapata, F. (2004) ¿Democratización o rearticulación del corporativismo? El caso de México. *Política* 42: 13–40.

Zuckerman, L. (2018a) Atisbos del estilo personal de gobernar de AMLO. *Excélsior*, August 27. https://www.excelsior.com.mx/opinion/leo-zuckermann/ atisbos-del-estilo-personal-de-gobernar-de-amlo/1261035.

Zuckerman, L. (2018b) Tanta vuelta para que AMLO tenga a su "fiscal carnal." *El Universal*, September 11. https://www.excelsior.com.mx/opinion/leo-zuck ermann/tanta-vuelta-para-que-amlo-tenga-a-su-fiscal-carnal/1258997.

Zuckerman, L. (2018c) Morena y AMLO sí hacen fraude: Aquí los números. *Excélsior*, November 28. https://www.excelsior.com.mx/opinion/leo-zucker mann/morena-y-amlo-si-hacen-fraude-aqui-los-numeros/1281210.

5

Far-Right Populism in Poland and the Construction of a Pseudocivil Sphere

María Luengo and Małgorzata Kolankowska

Therefore, twenty-five years after August '80, I repeat to myself what the inimitable Antoni Słonimski[1] taught me: Poland is a country of miraculous and unexpected events; in the Polish pot, both the devil and the angel are cooking.

Anything is possible in Poland – even changes for the better.

Adam Michnik, *In Search of Lost Meaning* (2011: 36)[2]

Populism, Nativism, and the Development of a Polish Pseudocivil Sphere

Populism has shifted toward institutionalized authoritarianism in Poland. Since the far-right PiS party (*Prawo i Sprawiedliwość*/Law and Justice) swept the October 2015 elections, the rule of law and independent journalism have been under attack. State media outlets were taken over a few months after PiS came into office, when the ruling party approved a new law that allowed the treasury minister to appoint and fire senior figures from Poland's public TV and radio stations, Telewizja Polska and Polskie Radio. The National Broadcasting Council had previously been the body responsible for making such decisions. Furthermore, in 2018, a controversial judicial reform threatened to put the courts under political control by changing the Constitutional Court and the status of prosecutors so that they would have to report directly to the justice minister. Since communicative and regulative institutions represent the organizational power of the civil sphere's moral community (Alexander 2006), the weakening of media and legal power means abuse of power and uncivil incursion into the civil sphere. In fact, these measures have triggered social conflict and opposing responses from civil society, independent lawyers and judges, and European institutions.

Since the 1990s, conservative, anticommunist, and right-wing liberal[3] movements have been active in Poland's political sphere. However, far-right leaders and ideologies have operated within the confines of a democratic political spectrum whose poles were a socialist left dominated by the SLD (*Sojusz Lewicy Demokratycznej*/Democratic Left Alliance) and a liberal center right dominated by the UW (*Unia Wolności*/Freedom Union). Following the collapse of Poland's communist regime in 1989, both Solidarity and the communist coalition fragmented into factions. Political atomization resulted in party mergers and regroupings during the parliamentary elections that took place between 1991 and 1997, which gave rise to short-term coalition governments. Although these were volatile, they operated within the rules of the democratic game. The victory of Solidarity and its Catholic leader Lech Wałęsa did not automatically lead to the establishment of a Polish Republic of "Christian values," as many might have expected (Davies 2005). On the contrary, democratic equality was present in the way in which UW and the SLD organized themselves within a relative equilibrium that kept the religious hierarchy off the political playing field.

In recent decades, Polish populism has emerged over three different phases (Matyja 2018). The first phase was the ascent to power of two new parties: the conservative nationalist LPR party (*Liga Polskich Rodzin*/League of Polish Families) and the left nationalist SRP (*Samoobrona Rzeczpospolitej Polskiej*/Self-Defense of the Republic of Poland), founded respectively in 2001 and 1992. Both parties shared an antagonistic stance toward Poland's entry into the European Union and suspicions of the country's economic elite. These populist attitudes were accompanied by the discursive shift undertaken by the liberal center-right PO party (*Platforma Obywatelska*/Civic Platform) in its 2001 electoral campaign. This shift was characterized on a rhetorical level by the party's antiestablishment sentiments and demands to replace the country's proportional electoral system, which favored political minorities, with one based on single-member constituencies. It also called for other political reforms such as the establishment of a limit on the number of parliamentarians and the elimination of the Senate. The electoral battle between the Law and Justice and the Civic Platform parties in 2005 aroused a second phase of impassioned populism, in which PiS's populist rhetoric started to coalesce around a discursive struggle between "solidary Poland" and "liberal Poland" (Matyja 2018). PiS ultimately won the elections, thanks to the conversion of both the League of Polish Families and Self-Defense of the Republic of Poland to the "solidary Poland" bloc. The third phase was the return of the PiS party to government after the 2015 presidential and parliamentarian elections. That year the party ran an anti-Semitic and antimigrant campaign, warning of diseases allegedly carried by the asylum seekers Poland agreed to take in and accusing its main competitor, Civic Platform, of letting Poland become a puppet of Germany within the EU.

PiS's exclusionary discourse shapes what we propose to call a Polish *pseudocivil sphere* that equates the PiS movement with the "will of the Polish people," based on a nativist perception of Polish society. Poland's 2015 elections also, and more importantly, revealed the exclusionary ways in which PiS associates its opponents – both the center-right PO and the center-left and left-wing parties – with a "late postcommunism."[4] In particular, PO's political project, led by former prime minister Donald Tusk, was identified as "the Tusk system," which, according to PiS, was part of a profoundly corrupt postcommunist and anti-Polish elite that seized control of the country (Szczerbiak 2016). Today, PiS leaders still taint their opponents – for example, they defame the image of Lech Wałęsa and Solidarity – and spread counternarratives on communist agents that bring past *proof* into the present in order to delegitimize current public figures and push them away from the political scene. Another discursive practice consists of *de-communization* – that is, the clearing out of institutions, street names, and other bastions of communism's heritage. In parallel, the ruling party has tried to gain legitimacy in the civil sphere. The PiS leaders and their actions are "filtered" through discourses of "Polishness," "our nation first," and "an independent Poland." This purifying discursive process entails, among other features, the denial of certain "falsehoods" concerning the role of Poland in World War II, especially in relation to Auschwitz. The PiS discourses also emphasize, in a way that uses Wałęsa as a negative counterpoint, the heroic role played by Lech Kaczyński, former president of Poland, and his twin brother Jarosław, who is currently the head of PiS.

Recent sociological studies have characterized instances of new far-right populism as unusual or fringe reactions, or as deviations from the normal functioning of liberal democracies. But, in our view, an explanation of this phenomenon can be found within the dynamics of democratic societies themselves. By taking a broader civil sphere perspective and zooming in on the Polish case, we argue that the creation of PiS's pseudocivil solidarity in Poland intimately links far-right populism to the cultural and institutional dynamics of current civil societies, and that its discursive formation rests deeply within existing polarities of the discourse of Poland's civil sphere. In order for populist logic to empirically "materialize" in leaders, groups, and political parties and ultimately reach state institutions, it first has to be intertwined – and then remain – with the civil sphere's discourses of the pure and impure, the sacred and the profane (Alexander 2006). And in order for far-right attitudes and ideologies to be institutionalized, they must "work" within the very subjective dimension of the civil sphere by using symbolic codes to pollute enemies and opponents through uncivil characterizations. The populist discourse thus needs to metamorphose in the overarching discursive framework of the civil sphere to successfully spread across society. In the Polish case, civil and uncivil codes have been activated by PiS both before and after its rise to power in 2015. These latent codes make it possible to explain the rebirth of the far right's overt expression of its attitudes and feelings and its move from Poland's political fringes to the mainstream. Such codes can be deciphered in relation to different national narratives and symbols that appeal to Polish people.

Theorizing the civil sphere as the nesting ground of far-right populist movements raises at least two significant questions that we would like to bring into focus in our empirical examination. First, when does a particular far-right ideology, intertwining with the discourse of the civil sphere, develop a populist justification for solidarity that, paradoxically, is structured in an uncivil particularistic and primordial way that actually undermines civil solidarity itself: that is, the autonomy of the civil sphere that allows universalism, pluralism, or critique (Alexander 2006)? Second, once far-right populist parties achieve power, when and why might they evolve into an institutionalized authoritarianism? This chapter responds to these questions by looking at one socially divisive contemporary event that took place before PiS came to power and one that occurred after its entry into government: respectively, the Smolensk air crash (April 10, 2010) and the killing of the mayor of Gdańsk (January 14, 2019). We present these two cases as tipping points in PiS's evolving populism. The Smolensk air crash triggered an exclusionary discourse that, at the level of the symbolic structures of the civil sphere, first targeted opponents as postcommunists and anti-Polish and then, progressively, took aim at individuals and groups that do not have a reductive conservative and nativist conception of Poland. The case of Gdańsk's mayor, meanwhile, illustrates how this anticivil exclusionary attitude manifested itself empirically at the civil sphere's institutional level through undemocratic practices in relation to civil institutions. Media and civil reactions against the control of the media were particularly visible and contested in this second case.

We reviewed media opinion articles and editorials, scholarly works, and other intellectual works produced by Poland's media and intellectual elites on these two cases. We looked at specific issues raised by these cases that significantly polarized society, and we examined a diverse set of discourses published in media outlets that ranged from the pro-PiS and progovernment Telewizja Polska (TVP), the far-right *Nasz Dziennik* daily, and the conservative weekly magazine *Gazeta Polska* to ideologically opposing outlets such as *Gazeta Wyborcza*, *Polityka*, *Newsweek Polska*, and the TVN television channel. We focused on the specific narratives used by these media and academic elites regarding particular actors – for example, former president Lech Kaczyński or Gdańsk's mayor Paweł Adamowicz – and on the contentious issues raised by the two cases.

In this chapter, we bring forward critical theoretical arguments on the far right's breakthrough, its institutionalization, and its ongoing hold on political power, as well as on the civil sphere's responses to it. First, through analysis of pro- and anti-PiS discourses on the 2010 Smolensk air crash, we explore how recent European far-right populist movements such as Poland's Law and Justice party have gained prominence in the political arena. By a form of accretion and osmosis, populist rhetoric and ideology are nourished, shared, handed down, and crafted within and from particular national civil ideals. Second, populist movements use symbols and mythical stories that bring them into conflict with their own rhetoric. We will show the civil reaction to PiS's populism by bringing to light the symbolic codes that help to describe and explain critical responses. We do so in particular by focusing on discourses arising from the case of Gdańsk's mayor. Finally, by comparing the different public discourses on both cases, we will conclude that, in order to develop, establish, and maintain a sort of pseudocivil sphere, populist ideologies appeal to powerful symbols of the sacred and the profane and of good and evil, whose power has arisen and grown through their deep embeddedness in the value systems of national civil spheres. In the Polish case, the cult of PiS's leaders and the party's polarizing and exclusionary ideology borrow myths and symbols that strongly resonate in Poland's society and culture. At some point, as we noted at the beginning of this chapter, the PiS movement moved from populism toward institutionalized authoritarianism. The creation of a particularistic pseudocivil sphere allowed the party to uncivilly exclude others by representing them as traitors, personalizing public media, and eroding judicial independence. Understanding these tipping points may help not only in differentiating between conservative ideologies and far-right populism but also in describing the continuum that stretches from a civil conservative movement to anticivil authoritarian populism.

The Discursive Formation and Transformation of PiS: The Smolensk Air Crash

The ability of PiS leaders to spread their ideology across society is rooted in the way in which they unify an audience through common meaningful events in which symbolic codes of the Polish civil sphere are at stake. The Smolensk air crash case illustrates this quite well. The crash, which killed the former Polish president Lech Kaczyński and another ninety-five leading Poles in 2010, has become a memorable and mobilizing event that sharply polarized Polish society. More significantly, the case shows how PiS manages to appeal to universal narratives of trauma, suffering, and redemption that, in a manner closely related to Polish national identity, serve as core symbolic structures for the construction of a *pseudocivil* sphere, whose *civil* values are supported by a part of Polish society. It is "pseudo," as we will show, mainly in the sense that PiS discourse leaves out those whom the movement sees as postcommunists. And, within the national scripts of post-1989 Poland, to characterize people or movements as postcommunist is to denounce them as standing for illegitimate, foreign, and uncivil occupation.

On April 10, 2010, the plane carrying Lech Kaczyński crashed as it was landing in the city of Smolensk in western Russia. Among the passengers killed were the wife of the president, Maria Kaczyńska, the former president of Poland in exile Ryszard Kaczorowski, the chief of the Polish General Staff, senior Polish military officers, the president of the National Bank of Poland, Polish government officials, eighteen members of the Polish parliament, and members of the Polish clergy. The Polish delegation was on its way to a commemoration for the twenty-two thousand Polish officers and intellectuals who were murdered in the Katyń Forest in 1940. Initiated by the Soviet government officer Lavrenti Beria and approved by Joseph Stalin and the Politburo of the Soviet Communist Party, the Katyń massacre was denied and covered up by the Soviet government and Polish People's Republic after World War II.

President Lech Kaczyński's undelivered speech was prepared in the same spirit of recovering the true history of Katyń as "the Golgotha of the East."[5] The event put in motion a range of symbolic actions that ended up with the erection, on April 15, 2010, of the Smolensk Cross in Krakowskie Przedmieście, in front of the presidential palace in Warsaw. The cross was initially understood as an expression of solidarity with the victims and particularly with the deceased president. However, it became the subject of a political struggle. The Katyń cover-up, meanwhile, was presented in pro-PiS discourses as a direct accusation against the left-wing government of the Polish People's Republic (*Polska Rzeczpospolita Ludowa*, PRL). In the words of a *Gazeta Polska* article (April 14, 2010), "Hiding the truth about Katyń . . . had become one of the bases of communist politics in Poland after World War II. . . . [It was] the founding lie of the PRL."

As a traumatic national event, the Smolensk crash triggered shared feelings of solidarity with the victims, but also, particularly among Lech Kaczyński's followers, sentiments of fear and "estrangement," of being abandoned. These feelings morphed into private, public, and sacred encounters. Polish sociologist and political scientist Tomasz Żukowski, a former advisor to President Lech Kaczyński, compared the aftermath of the crash to the death of John Paul II in 2005. Żukowski (2011: 115) pointed out that in both cases "a whole national community based on religion and faith was formed around the loss of its country's head."

The president was praised as a father for the Poles. The parallel with the pope went a step further. The sacralization of Lech Kaczyński manifested itself during his funeral and the place in which he and his wife were buried. Kaczyński's burial took place in the crypt of Wawel Cathedral in Kraków, a place reserved for kings and heroes. It is the resting place of, among other figures, Józef Piłsudski, the architect of Polish independence in 1918.

Piotr Gliński and Jacek Wasilewski present the emotional shock produced by the event as the initiation of an institutional change in Polish society. They suggest that the change was cultural at first and implied the restoration of crucial national and civil values such as "responsibility to the Polish community," "patriotism," "solidarity," "devotion," and "self-determination." However, in order to introduce a "great change," Gliński and Wasilewski (2011: 10) explain, it was necessary to modify the system on the basis of five principles: "new quality of politics, transformation of the media world, reinforcement of civil society's power, qualitative change of the functioning of public institutions, and, finally, new standards for the education system."

Civil justice, solidarity, loyalty, Christian values, and autonomy ("an independent Poland") were integrated into contemporary mythical narratives on Polish national culture. These myths reinforce the "Polak–Katolic equation"; they take the form of stories about "an eternally and primordially Catholic Polish nation," as sociologist Geneviève Zubrzycki (2006: 204) puts it, and they are reflected in public discourses. Significant places, actions, and figures – the city of Smolensk; President Lech Kaczyński; the state funeral of the president and his wife in Kraków's Wawel Cathedral; the cross commemorating the crash that was erected outside the presidential palace in the days of mourning; Russian political actors; and Donald

Tusk (the prime minister of Poland when the crash happened) – acted as *signs* that oriented the main lines of narrative construction.

Defining Boundaries:
Smolensk and Katyń as Symbolic Scenarios of National Identity

The accident scene represented a place of suffering. The plane crash overlapped with the never-ending story of the Katyń massacre. Smolensk was associated with Katyń, and both places acted as distinctive signs of Poland as a martyr that sacrificed itself for Europe. Media discourse produced examples from Polish literature to connect the Smolensk case with the national myth of Poland's martyrdom. The tragedy of the air crash revived the rooted idea of a suffering nation that was selected by God in order to undertake a messianic mission. The concept of Polish messianism was created in the nineteenth century, when Poland did not exist on European maps. The effect of three partitions (1772, 1793, and 1795) was the division of the Polish–Lithuanian Commonwealth among three empires: Habsburg Austria, the Kingdom of Prussia, and the Russian Empire. Poland was reduced from a powerful state to nonexistence. The fragmentation had crucial consequences for the spirit and culture of Poland. The nation's suffering was expressed by Polish romanticist poet Adam Mickiewicz and echoed by all forms of culture, especially literature, poetry, and music. The year 1939 is often treated as a fourth partition, because Poland was attacked by both Germany and Russia, while the communist era is considered a time of slavery.

In an opinion article in the far-right daily *Nasz Dziennik* (April 22, 2010), the priest Czesław Bartnik described the suffering of the "banished." He used a biblical analogy, the psalm of Rachel, wife of patriarch Jacob, weeping for her children. The evocation of her weeping in a biblical psalm of great lyrical power in the Book of Jeremiah (31:15) represents the pain of the banished children of Israel. Bartnik's text reads, "Today Rachel is Mother Poland, which is mourning her children. ... [They were] terribly murdered in Katyń and so many other places in the ex-Soviet Union. ... [She] is bemoaning the victims of the horrible catastrophe near Smolensk, because neither the first [children/victims] nor the second [children/victims] ones are present."

In a similar fashion, the conservative weekly magazine *Gazeta Polska* characterized Smolensk as Poland's place of suffering on the first page of its special edition on April 12, 2010. The main headline read, "Katyń Has Killed Again." This special issue included articles that linked the tragedy of Smolensk to the Katyń massacre. The Smolensk air crash unified Poles, but it also brought out Poland's so-called "white spots," a metaphor used to refer to tragic events in the history of Russian–Polish relations that have come to be surrounded by the silence (Rotfeld and Torkunov 2015) of Polish–Russian history and conspiracy theories. In another column within *Gazeta Polska*'s special issue, journalist and writer Marcin Wolski referred to the "condemned symbolism of history" to argue that there were parallels between different events within Poland's history.

Wolski's article offers a vision of a growing danger in relation to the opposition parties, which Wolski held responsible for the recent events. A *Gazeta Polska* article by Polish-German linguist Józef Darski accused the Civic Platform party of double-dealing and mendacity. Darski evoked another historical event: the death in 1922 of Poland's first constitutional president, Gabriel Narutowicz, who was assassinated by Eligiusz Niewiadomski five days after taking office.[6] Darski leveled accusations directly at PO's representatives, pointing out that they had assumed masks of sorrow when in fact they were happy because their dreams had come true: the president was dead. Darski described Polish society as divided between, on the one hand, those who had not accepted the presidency of Lech Kaczyński and had rejected national identity and forgotten the past and, on the other, those who had followed the president. He wrote:

> There are two Polands. One is built on common history and the other one is built on lies and villainy. And there is no possibility of there being unity between us so you can more easily destroy what is left of freedom of expression, historical truth, memory, national identity, and everything that is precious for us and hateful for you. Being united with you means being a servant for someone else.

Writer and journalist Rafał A. Ziemkiewicz shared Darski's opinion. In a *Gazeta Polska* article entitled, "The End of the Right in Poland" (April 15, 2010), he suggested that what had been lost was not only the president but also the moment for change, as the people (Civic Platform) in office did not deserve to hold it.

On the other side of the political spectrum, *Gazeta Wyborcza* exemplified the way in which anti-PiS discourse gave meanings to the site of the air crash. A feature published on April 11, 2010, reported on a mass for the victims. Under the headline "We Can't Say This Is Katyń Vol. 2," the article focused on statements made by Archbishop Józef Życiński, who warned against a return to political struggle: "We mustn't talk about a Katyń volume 2, because it is illogical and unfair. This is a different world of different Russians who can express their solidarity with us." *Gazeta Wyborcza* journalist Marcin Wojciechowski wrote, "Thank you, Russian brothers" (April 12, 2010), and he described how he was deeply touched by the kindness and compassion of the Russian authorities and ordinary people. He asserted that the Smolensk tragedy could paradoxically be a step toward reconciliation between the two nations. The daily focused on presenting different places in Poland where meetings and prayers expressed solidarity with the victims.

Deploying a discourse that was more powerful than that of its opponents, however, PiS articulated a meaningful equivalence between Katyń and Smolensk to construct the latter as a national symbol of Polish suffering. Both settings allowed PiS to demarcate symbolic boundaries between, on the one hand, "true" Poles, represented by supporters of the dead president Lech Kaczyński and his PiS party, and, on the other hand, PiS's opponents. Opposition groups were located outside of these symbolic scenarios and associated with "villainy," "falsehood," and "complacency" (about the political threat posed by Russia). As we will discuss later, the Smolensk–Katyń narrative continuum effectively kept the liberal left and right out of the kind of "*civil* primordiality" (Alexander 2006) that shaped the public discourse on the occasion of the Smolensk air crash.

The Revival of Polish National Messianism and the Sacred Figure of the President

In the pro-PiS media, the Catholic faith was articulated at the heart of Poland's nationhood, and Smolensk was symbolically linked to the Polish nation's messianic mission. As had occurred at other times in history, God had allowed Poland's suffering for a holy purpose. The conflation of the Christian values of sacrifice and the mysticism of romantic suffering was highlighted by journalist Tomasz P. Terlikowski in his *Gazeta Polska* column through the expression "Battle for Souls" (April 14, 2010). Terlikowski stated that the tragedy "should be analyzed from the perspective of religion" and viewed as a "mission" of suffering akin to that experienced by Christ. He observed that first "neither the place nor the time were holy." Smolensk "had been sanctified by the blood of Polish patriots" and the moment had a liturgical poignancy: "The victims sacrificed their lives on Divine Mercy Sunday Eve." Terlikowski observed that revelations of God's mercy – the three partitions, the insurrections, World War II, Katyń, the Warsaw Uprising, and communism – were the proof of Poland's being "selected" or "called to participate in suffering" as a whole nation. He concluded that the tragedy was part of a mission to be understood and fulfilled and that Poles would be judged upon it on the Day of the Lord. That particular mission was to bring about Europe's return to its Christian roots.

Commenting on the loss of Lech Kaczyński, a *Gazeta Polska* editorial (April 14, 2010) read, "They took the heart of Poland from us." It associated Kaczyński with Polish society's sacred messianic mission. In his opinion article mentioned above, journalist and *Gazeta Polska* editor-in-chief Tomasz Sakiewicz argued that the Smolensk tragedy brought an end to the responsibility that Kaczyński had taken over from John Paul. The pope's death marked the end of an era and the beginning of changes "that had not been possible earlier." The president was sacralized in pro-PiS discourse, but this sacralization was contested by opposition media and intellectuals. In an article entitled "Carnival of Sorrow," cultural anthropologist Joanna Tokarska-Bakir (*Gazeta Wyborcza*, April 4, 2010) uses Victor Turner's terminology to describe the national mourning in the aftermath of the plane crash. She distinguishes three stages of the rite of mourning: "exclusion," "liminality," and "inclusion." According to her explanation, Polish society was suddenly excluded from its normal reality. It entered into the phase of liminality, a threshold of silence, suspension of reason, and uncertainty, which paved the way for unity and communion. In the Polish case, Tokarska-Bakir explained, an immanent element to the mourning ritual was the sacrifice of martyrs. She quoted remarks that were made by the former PiS deputy Zbigniew Girzyński and show the sacred role of the president as subject of the social ritual. She added that, according to Polish scholar of literary romanticism Maria Janion, "Poland is a nation that is not able to admit defeat. . . . The deaths of Poles have to be sacrificial or heroic, because human death humiliates them." This was the reason the nation looked for examples from the past in an attempt to somehow explain this traumatic situation, she concluded.

In left-wing magazine *Krytyka Polityczna* (April 16, 2010), the philosopher Agata Bielik-Robson wrote an opinion article in which she put forward the same argument regarding mourning as a martyrdom ceremony. She argued that the event was not a carnival, but, in the words of the article's title, a "Polish triumph of Thanatos." For her, the president's death was the culmination of his *thanatopolitics*, which had been based on his attitude of sacrifice. He became a hero just because he died. The death itself was the basis of his sacred figure. Bielik-Robson points out, "*Consummatum est*: Lech Kaczyński's death here, similarly to the crucifixion of Jesus, [acts] as a sign of truth that gives a new meaning to all activity during his life." According to her, Kaczyński became "an incarnation of the totemic Father," and at the same time a symbol of the past that Polish people had decided to eliminate in order to finally participate in the life of Western civilization. The father represents the archaic type of sovereign power. To emancipate themselves, the sons have to kill the father. However, a sense of guilt remains. In Bielik-Robson's words, "[The majority of Poles] actually 'killed the father' who did not let them live. Let the dead bury the dead – the Poles have chosen life." According to the sociologist Maja Drzazga-Lech (2011), the situation of trauma supported the symbolic mechanism for creating myths or accepting existing ones. In this sense, PiS had narrated the death of the president in a way that turned it into a myth that fitted the historical context of the Katyń murders.

Signs of Polarization: The State Funeral and the Smolensk Cross

On April 18, 2010, the president's state funeral was held in Kraków. After the ceremony, Kaczyński and his wife were buried among Poland's kings and heroes in a crypt in the city's Wawel Cathedral. The act contributed to both the sacralization of the president and the further polarization of Polish society. Divisions arose between, on the one hand, the many Poles who felt the burial location was inappropriate for a divisive and combative figure and, on the other, those who saw Kaczyński as heroic because he had died in the line of duty. Reports on the event showed polarizing discourses on the matter. Discourses in favor of the president represented the funeral as a patriotic and religious ritual centered on a significant figure who, according to Drzazga-Lech (2011: 223), truly personified the values of "patriotism," "historical truth," "solidarity," and "courage," among others.

Meanwhile, a bitter controversy emerged because of a large cross that was erected by a group of Polish scouts in front of the presidential palace in Warsaw to commemorate the victims of the air crash. Pro-PiS media presented the cross erected in response to the Smolensk crash as a symbol recalling the Polish nation's past, associated with Polish martyrdom and resilience. During the three partitions, the Christian faith had been the sign of Polish identity, and this situation had repeated itself during the communist regime, when the Church supported the opposition. The cross was a clear signal of fighting against the regime. Through the cross, the Polish nation identified itself with the messianic mission of Christ. It symbolized suffering, love, and victory over evil. The cross erected outside the palace therefore brought about this intimate intertwining of Polish national identity, politics, and religion, but it did so in a postcommunist Poland where the symbol conveyed polysemic and contested meanings in public spaces. The controversy generated further questions about the presence of religious symbols in Poland's public life. What was initially merely a commemorative sign that aimed to honor the victims of the tragedy inspired defenders of and protestors against it to come out in force. Over the month that followed, people whom pro-PiS and right-wing media discourses described as "true Poles" went there to pray, sing patriotic hymns, and hold their hands aloft in response to the cross's detractors in a manner that recalled the freedom and diversity movement in communist Poland. Religious images of Pope John Paul II, saints, and Our Lady of Częstochowa were displayed alongside photos of Kaczyński. The political leader was depicted as a quasi-religious hero in the same way as he had been in the symbolic acts of the state funeral.

This meaning of the cross was contested by media opposed to PiS. A *Newsweek* feature entitled "Polish Crusades" and written by journalists Dariusz Koźlenko and Andrzej Stankiewicz (August 18, 2010) reconstructed the radicalized atmosphere that the cross generated. In their view, the cross was not supposed to cause a contentious debate; it represented a fight, a "crusade." They described how defenders of the cross had met opposing forces that mobilized in rallies calling for its removal. The people of Poland were engaged in a fight in which it was mandatory to take sides. It was not enough to approach the setting, pray, and pay tribute to the victims. The *Newsweek* article was accompanied by a photograph that showed people holding rosaries in their hands and, at the same time, tussling with police officers. The Smolensk cross was ultimately transferred to St. Anne's Church in Warsaw in the middle of September 2010.

The opposing discourses on the state funeral and the Smolensk cross revealed the split within Polish society regarding the place of religion in Poland's public life. They echoed reactions to other controversial events involving the presence of religious symbols in the public sphere: for example, the "crosses of Auschwitz" case. In 1998, fringe groups from the far right, self-defined as "Catholic Poles," erected some three hundred crosses near the concentration camp in reaction to the rumor that the papal cross that was erected in 1979 to commemorate John Paul II's historical mass in 1979 in Poland and that still remains outside Auschwitz was going to be removed. Sociologist Geneviève Zubrzycki (2006: 219) has noted how the event manifested the way in which core symbols of a "sacred–secular religious nationalism," which were first secularized and *resacralized* as national, are being contested and "secularized again" in a postcommunist Poland. First, they are being contested by liberal, civic, and secular actors and groups from both the left and right to whom national religious symbols represent an imposition and stand for intolerance toward others and for a traditionalist view of Poland that excludes those who do not share it. Second, they are being "secularized again" after having been sacralized as national symbols. Contrary to the usual understanding of secularism as the decline of religion, Zubrzycki forcefully argues that, in the Polish case, secularism represents a complex cultural and social struggle that takes place not only between secular liberals and ethnonationalist religious conservatives but also between opposing camps within Catholicism. One of these camps represents "open Catholics" and "purists" who advocate depoliticizing religion and purifying it to restore its deepest spiritual meaning, and the other comprises "traditionalists" and "integrists" who argue in favor of maintaining a link between Catholicism, Polishness, and the Polish nation (Zubrzycki 2006: 221). Despite its critics, this traditionalist discourse, which was championed by the pro-PiS media and impressively intertwined with the potent symbols of Polish suffering and messianism, proved most powerful in the aftermath of the Smolensk air crash and ultimately prevailed as the dominant interpretation of the event.

The Characterization of Those Outside PiS's Pseudocivil Sphere

On May 12, 2010, Paweł Paliwoda, a journalist at the right-wing *Gazeta Polska*, wrote an opinion article on the current situation of Poland on the occasion of the air crash. The text was accompanied by an image depicting a map in which Poland is split in two, with the initials of the Civic Platform party appearing in the breach between the two parts of the territory. The heading read, "The State of Civic Platform is not mine." The text added that this political organization had divided Poland. This image allegorically parallels PiS's discourse on PO's connection to the air crash. PO was the principal political force in the country when the accident happened: it was the largest party in Poland's coalition government from 2007 to 2015, and its leader, Donald Tusk, was prime minister from 2007 to 2014. A few days later, the front page of *Gazeta Polska* (May 19, 2010) displayed a doctored photo of Donald Tusk and Bronisław Komorowski[7] in which their mouths were sewn shut with a length of thread whose end drew the communist symbols of the hammer and sickle. This time, the heading read, "The Government Hides the Truth: The Fog over Smolensk." The two PO politicians were accused of being responsible for the accident. In the following days, a photo that showed Putin expressing his condolences to Tusk was used to editorialize about a conspiracy behind the Smolensk air crash. This apparent plot would be recalled on several occasions by the future prime minister Antoni Macierewicz when PiS came to power after the 2015 elections, and it defined one of the main lines of PiS discourse on Smolensk: Russia as the perpetrator of a conspiracy against the Polish government; Donald Tusk as a figure involved in that conspiracy; and his political force, PO, as traitors. This characterization of PiS's main opponents as traitors crystallized in the high confrontational style of the PiS campaign during the 2015 elections. However, as shown by these texts and images published by *Gazeta Polska* in the aftermath of the plane crash, an anticommunist sentiment was present long before. Such sentiment became uncivil to the extent it was used as a referential value to exclude others from a reductive conception of Polish society.

Media discourses on the controversial monthly celebrations and marches commemorating the Smolensk accident, and on the corresponding countermarches, demonstrate the discursive formation and re-creation, which persists to this day, of opponents of PiS ideology as antipatriotic and anti-Catholic foreigners. Following an incident during one of these marches in June 2017, the right-wing newspaper *Nasz Dziennik* (June 13, 2017) published an opinion article by PiS senator Stanisław Kogut entitled "Great Amnesia of The Third Republic's Elite." Kogut described political opponents and some members of the clergy as "instigators" who represent "the forces of evil." The article read:

> I wonder what it is about the monthly marches that makes Satan hate them so much. Whenever the 10th of each month approaches, strange forces are activated. The cross in Krakowskie Przedmieście was painful; the Rosary is also painful. They prevent Jarosław Kaczyński from praying at the graves of his neighbors. Is this the freedom for which liberals fight? The Poland of their dreams is the country where there is no place for God. I cannot agree with such a reality. Poland is beautiful and great because it's Catholic.

The Reaction: Cultural Desecration on the Fringe of the Public Arena

The symbolic acts of sacralization were met with counteracts of desecration. The latter, however, were not performed as effectively as the former. The sociologist Agnieszka Mościcka-Bogacz (2011) emphasizes, for example, the activities at this time of Polish filmmaker Andrzej Wajda (one of the key directors of the Polish transition, whose works include the 2007 movie *Katyń*), criticism of the funeral at Wawel Cathedral, and theories that identified the president as being responsible for the air crash. In the context of the funeral, sharp criticism against Lech Kaczyński came from national and international media outlets. On April 23, 2010, journalist Piotr Smolar interviewed Wajda. During the interview, Wajda warned of the consequences of placing the president in Wawel, and he suggested that the disaster might have been the president's fault. Wajda's critical opinion of the president's burial was also published as a letter in *Gazeta Wyborcza* (February 14, 2010). He stated that "President Lech Kaczyński was a good, humble person, but there are no reasons for

139

burying him in Wawel among the Kings of Poland and close to Marshal Piłsudski." In the process of demythologizing the president, media articles and other public statements attributed him with antivalues such as provincialism, traditionalism, obscurantism, anti-Catholicism, and refusal to compromise, as Mościcka-Bogacz has pointed out (2011: 242). In a *Gazeta Wyborcza* column, Polish journalist and political commentator Rafał Kalukin (April 11, 2010) described the deceased president as "a man obsessed with the past, filled with spirits, or more precisely with devils from Poland's bloody history . . . ; this obsession constituted the basis of his many claims toward more powerful neighbors."

The left-wing weekly *Polityka* published an article ("Human Man") by Jacek Żakowski, a journalist and critic of PiS (April 17, 2010), that highlighted the profane side of the president. Żakowski underlined that it was not easy to deal with him and that the main problem was his personal dichotomy: "He was not radical, but he led a radical party. . . . He was moderate, emphatic, and warm, but the party's members were not merciful."

Żakowski affirmed that treating individuals with opposing political views in this manner was Lech Kaczyński's general rule, though when he lost against his opponents in elections, he became tough, "but not brutal." Żakowski shared *Gazeta Wyborcza* journalist Kalukin's opinion on the relationship between the twin brothers: although Lech was not independent from his brother, he distanced himself from PiS's more radical branch. Żakowski depicted Lech Kaczyński as one of the more tragic characters of Polish politics. He argued that on the one hand, he was loyal to Piłsudski's ideas on independence, but, on the other hand, "he had to sign alliances and accept political measures that he rejected. . . . Because of this, it was possible to open a new path for debate based on pluralism." He concluded that "the president died just when he was close to being able to have an influence on politics. This proves that we have lost an important person." This article exemplifies the way in which some discourses tended to moderate emotions and to rationally describe the merits and flaws of Kaczyński's presidency.

The Mobilization of Civil Codes against Authoritarian Populism: The Killing of the Mayor of Gdańsk

Nine years after the Smolensk tragedy, Poland mourned Paweł Adamowicz, the mayor of the Polish city of Gdańsk. On January 14, 2019, Adamowicz was stabbed on stage in front of thousands of people during a charity concert.[8] Adamowicz had served as mayor of the city since 1998. He represented the powerful PO's liberal voice in Poland, and he supported minority groups, refugees, and migrants in the face of antimigrant sentiment within the country. The attack took place a few minutes before the traditional "Light to Heaven," a symbolic moment that closed the event with fireworks. Just before the attack the mayor had said, "Gdańsk is generous, Gdańsk shares good, Gdańsk wants to be a city of solidarity." The perpetrator was Stefan W., an ex-convict from Gdańsk who shouted his desire for revenge against PO. The high-profile, traumatic event of Adamowicz's death was another blow to Polish society.

By focusing on significant signs such as Paweł Adamowicz himself, the city of Gdańsk, and the culprit, it is possible to highlight several parallels between this event and the Smolensk air crash. Both cases are related to the death of a president: the president of the country and the president of a city (the Polish term for "mayor" is literally "city president"). Both died while carrying out their work. In both cases, the deaths were tragic and unexpected; they had a high impact on the media and they sharply polarized society. Both triggered talks on the need for social change. The two events brought about the search for a culprit. In the Smolensk case, the right-wing PiS accused Donald Tusk of having conspired with Russia to organize the alleged attack. In the second case, pro-PiS and progovernment media outlets were accused of having induced the perpetrator to commit the crime through their criticisms of Adamowicz. Finally, both cases sparked debates that sought parallels with Poland's past. However, this time the strong PiS's accusations against a beloved mayor, the solidary atmosphere that surrounded his death, and other symbolic aspects presented in what follows caused an intense civil reaction against the ruling PiS party. On this occasion, the belief in a crucial need for social change came from opposing ideological forces.

The Civil Consecration of Adamowicz

The sacralization process of Paweł Adamowicz began on the day of his death. As in the case of Smolensk, the emotional impact of his death was associated with the place: Gdańsk, an extraordinarily meaningful city for Poles, which had given birth to Lech Wałęsa and the Solidarity movement, and which, since the early 1980s, has been a symbol of the fight for freedom. That Adamowicz was participating in a charity event and had just made some remarks on goodness when he was assassinated only heightened the impact of his death. Generosity, integrity, and decency became the leitmotif of his civil consecration. As we will see later, his friendly attitude contrasted with the antagonistic atmosphere – described as "hatred" by the anti-PiS media – created by the Law and Justice party's discourse on him. As in the case of Lech Kaczyński's death, the culprit was sought among the opposing political camp. In this case, PiS was accused of continually attacking Adamowicz. Contrary to pro-PiS public TVP, TVN, a private channel, enhanced his figure in a fervent and moving segment broadcast on March 2, 2019 on the TV channel's show *Dzień dobry TVN*. The title of the segment – "The Amazing Gdańsk of Adamowicz"– suggested that, thanks to Adamowicz, the city had become an exceptional place. He was described as a good person. His employees underlined his loyalty, punctuality, and sensibility toward others. His brother highlighted his clandestine activity during the communist era. And one of his friends stressed that he had an "inner strength," remembering his election as leader of the 1988 strike. Politician and journalist Aleksander Hall argued that Adamowicz kept Gdańsk "a city of freedom and solidarity." One of his employees observed that the mayor openly greeted everyone at the town hall every day. Adamowicz's driver, Czesław Główczewski, revealed that he was often given money by the mayor to donate it to seven of the most deprived families in the area.

The liberal media discourse highlighted the need for change. This sense of political change was accentuated because of the release of *Newsweek* editor-in-chief Tomasz Lis's book entitled *Dying for Gdańsk* in April 2019. Through different interviews with public figures, the book ritualized Adamowicz's assassination by transforming a narrative of "martyrdom" into one of a hero who left his message of goodness with his last breath. In the introduction to the book, Lis underlines Adamowicz's "open," "multicultural," and "tolerant" view of the city (2019: 10). Donald Tusk appears as one of the interviewees in the book. He describes Adamowicz as "belonging to the group of those who believed deeply in the sense of a synthesis between a balanced Polish conservative Catholicism and liberalism" (2019: 23).

The Attempt to Demonize PO's Leader: Storytelling in Pro-PiS Media

The top stories on *Wiadomości*, the main news program of the pro-government channel TVP, indicate that Gdańsk's mayor had constantly been the object of criticism from PiS. For example, news headlines used expressions such as "The Mysteries of Gdańsk's Mayor" (June 20, 2017) to suggest that Adamowicz was implicated in the Amber Gold scandal (a pyramid-scheme fraud that involved the sale of gold); and "New Problems for Gdańsk's Mayor" (July 13, 2018) to report on the verdict from Adamowicz's trial on a charge of attacking a member of All-Polish Youth (*Młodzież Wszechpolska*), a far-right organization. The TVP news stories presented Adamowicz as a dishonest figure who was not transparent about his finances and who disrespected history.

In the aftermath of the murder, pro-PiS media narratives of Adamowicz's death were constructed through the same elements: the date of the funeral to be held in Gdańsk's Bazylika Mariacka (an important and symbolic site), the farewell ceremony, the perpetrator, and the causes of the attack. News stories from the progovernment TVP focused on factual details. For example, one story mentioned that the perpetrator was detained by a technical assistant instead of a security guard. This fact highlighted that the event did not have enough security. Similarly, TVP news stories underlined the mass nature of the concert, another indicator that security measures were not adequate, and they dwelt on aspects that they used to place blame on Jerzy Owsiak (the organizer of the concert where the assassination took place) and his organization, whose ideological orientation is at odds with that of PiS. Overall, Adamowicz's lengthy career of service was scarcely recognized.

The pro-PiS news media accused its opposing media outlets of nationally and internationally presenting the Gdańsk mayor's death as a political murder committed by a mentally ill, right-wing criminal who was inspired by a hate campaign allegedly led against Adamowicz by the ruling right-wing party and progovernment media. Opinion articles presented the opposition media's performance as taking advantage of the tragedy to attack the ruling party and distorting the facts and the real role that Adamowicz played in Polish politics. His murder was presented in the context of Polish local politics and the battle within Civic Platform for the position of mayor of Gdańsk – Donald Tusk's bastion – and against Adamowicz. This battle was caused by Adamowicz's involvement in many scandals, tax-fraud accusations, and questionable public policies, as well as by the way in which he distanced himself from Tusk and Civic Platform. Thus, the murder was seen as a blessing for the opposition and an occasion for the opposition party to stir up the masses through a new martyr. The context in which the atrocious murder took place in Gdańsk – that is, in broad daylight and in front of TV cameras – reinforced its powerful symbolism. The narrative connected the tragic event to the Smolensk air crash, which was suggested to have been orchestrated in some way and not simply a tragic accident. This left an unspoken accusation hanging in the air: both events were linked to the same people, who had the malign goals of falsely blaming the ruling PiS party and seeking domination in Europe. The narrative held that the questioning of TVP's media ethics was simply a smoke screen to hide this agenda.

The Energizing of Civil/Anticivil Codes Brought About by Independent Media

TVP's main news program was openly criticized by different media outlets. A *Rzeczpospolita* headline (January 15, 2019) read, "TVP's *Wiadomości*: A Record of Blundering." The article quoted comments from media representatives from both the right and the left. Even far-right journalist Rafał Ziemkiewicz disapproved of the TVP news program on his Twitter account. Civic Platform politician Marcin Kierwiński said, "Was it so difficult to respect Mayor Adamowicz's death? Was this hate festival necessary?" *Rzeczpospolita* vice-editor-in-chief Michał Szułdrzyński wrote in his column (January 15, 2019), "The two political camps have noticed the symbolic strength of Mayor Adamowicz and turned to partisan logic." Szułdrzyński recognized gestures of solidarity from members of the government. However, he argued that these gestures were removed from TVP's afternoon broadcast. He made a reference to *Dziennik Telewizyjny*, the TV news program during the communist era:

> How can one believe in PiS's honesty of intentions if the program controlled by the ruling party can produce one of the most disgusting pieces in the history of Polish media? Talking about hate speech, TVP's employees curiously were just able to remember PO's aggressive comments, but there was no word about the way in which their PiS opponents expressed themselves. The TV news program has not really helped PiS. If anything can influence the outcome of the elections, it is precisely such hypocrisy: on the one hand, there are those reflective faces of Andrzeja Dudy and Mateusza Morawiecki in Warsaw Cathedral and, on the other hand, there is blasphemy on TVP. PiS legitimizes TVP's questionable performance. Partisan logic has won.

Four weeks later, *Newsweek* (February 12, 2019) reported on an ethics inquiry that had focused on TVP's reporting on the Gdańsk mayor throughout 2018. The research had been conducted by the Polish Media Ethics Council (*Rada Etyki Mediów*). The Council's report stated that Adamowicz "has been the subject of calumny on TVP" and that "the public has a right to the truth." Accusations against TVP were based on Twitter posts made by journalist Krzysztof Leski, who had been studying the propagandistic nature of TVP's news production. Leski was challenged by right-wing political activist Piotr Lisiewicz in a *Gazeta Polska* column entitled, "I Do Not Like You So I'll Call You a Murderer: The Shower of Lies About TVP is an Offense to Common Sense" (January 30, 2019). Lisiewicz criticized attacks against TVP arguing that the murderer had fed on TVP's hate messages. He emphasized Adamowicz's lack of transparency regarding financial issues and the other accusations of fraud made against him. By inverting terms and accusations, Lisiewicz criticized the way in which a *Newsweek* journalist reported on the Gdańsk tragedy, and he accused this journalist of hate speech. Opposition politicians who appeared in the media accused the PiS ruling party of not being capable of preventing aggression and acts of violence such as the burning of photos of Lech Wałęsa by the nationalist organization All-Polish Youth.

In an interview for the German daily *Die Welt*, Aleksandra Dulkiewicz, a former spokesperson for Paweł Adamowicz who was appointed mayor of Gdańsk following Adamowicz's death, pointed out that "since 2010 PiS had been deepening divisions among Poles." She added that PiS blamed PO for the Smolensk air crash and that "this prevents people from a common mourning. . . . This is a moment when the analogy between the two tragedies can be perceived and the intensification of conflict is increasing."

Discourse from opposition media organizations such as *Polityka* and TVN described Gdańsk's mayor as a trustworthy person who was intent on carrying out his mission. For example, a *Polityka* article published on January 14, 2019, read, "Gdańsk was his mission and the passion of his life." The article highlighted that Adamowicz could not be pigeonholed in conservatism, as he supported women's empowerment, migrant rights, and the fight against discrimination. In an interview with *Newsweek*'s Tomasz Lis (January 27, 2019), Paweł Adamowicz's wife, Magdalena, reaffirmed how her family had been hounded by TVP journalists and rejected by people after the mayor had become the subject of public scrutiny. Lis asked about her husband's response. She answered by sharing some anecdotes about the couple's everyday life: "When attending mass, at the moment of exchanging the greeting of peace, there were people who turned their backs and did not want to shake hands. . . . I was very nervous in such situations. . . . My husband smiled and said to those people: 'I wish you a good Sunday!'"

The case of Gdańsk's mayor has revealed the way in which PiS is provoking a civil reaction that is increasingly spreading across the Polish population. In a *Newsweek* editorial entitled "Counterrevolution" (July 11, 2016), Tomasz Lis accused PiS of "communism bloated with holy water." Arguing that Jarosław Kaczyński's government was increasingly becoming the People's Republic of Poland, in which the opposition was considered to be betraying the mother country, Lis wrote that

the state, as in the communist era, is imposing its own version of culture and history on society. Its own version of culture is a revival of "national form and socialist content." Its version of history erases

145

some historical chapters, gets rid of Poland's heroes, and creates new ones; and this confirms a truth that has already been known since the communist regime: the most difficult thing to predict is the past.

In a column entitled "How Martyrdom Has Killed the Third Polish Republic," the journalist Cezary Michalski (*Newsweek*, November 1, 2017) criticized PiS's reviving of the romantic myth of Poland as a nation of martyrs who fight and suffer for their mother country. By the same token, in an article published by the center-left weekly magazine *Polityka* (February 14, 2017), sociologist and journalist Sławomir Sierakowski described PiS's populism through an alternative discursive axis: one of "solidarity" instead of "neoliberalism"; of "order" instead of "chaos," at the cost of media pluralism and judicial independence; of "authoritarianism" instead of "liberal democracy"; and of "power" instead of "truth."

Conclusion: From Populist Rhetoric to Authoritarian Politics

On January 19, 2019, the funeral mass of Paweł Adamowicz was held at Gdańsk's vast Gothic St. Mary's Basilica. At the event, Polish politicians from both PiS and PO sat side by side as they joined Adamowicz's widow, two daughters, and other family members. During the mass, Dominican priest Ludwik Wiśniewski made a dramatic appeal to the gathered multitude for unity. Wiśniewski asserted firmly, "You have to end hate. You have to end hate speech. You have to end contempt. You have to end unjust accusations made about others. We will no longer be indifferent to the spreading of poison" (*TVN 24*, January 19, 2019). Wiśniewski's speech echoed the letter that he had sent to Poland's papal nuncio Celestino Migliore in December 2010, the year in which the Smolensk air crash took place. The letter denounced the "embarrassing division" within the Polish episcopate and clergy. This "shameful division," he stated, was reflected in the support of "formally" Catholic initiatives that split society and the Church (*wPolityce.pl*, December 14, 2010). He directly referred to bishops who had collaborated with the priest Tadeusz Rydzyk's right-wing newspaper *Nasz Dziennik*. The letter triggered criticism from actors in the Church hierarchy as well as from Catholic media. The controversy reflected the ongoing divide between the so-called "Toruń Church," associated with the city where Father Rydzyk's *Radio Maryja* is based, and "the Łagiewniki Church." The expression "Łagiewniki Church" was first used by Jan Rokita, a prominent center-right politician and PO's former president, in a speech at the

Sanctuary of Divine Mercy in Łagiewniki (near Kraków). Rokita coined the term to identify Catholics opposed to Rydzyk. Survey data show that only a small minority of Poland's population listens to *Radio Maryja* or reads *Nasz Dziennik*. However, as Brian Porter-Szűcs has noted, when one shifts focus from the general Catholic population to the most devout Catholics, support for "the Toruń Church" increases steadily. According to Porter-Szűcs (2011: 393), "It is hard to deny that [Father] Rydzyk embodies several trends with deep roots in Polish Catholicism." And it was precisely the religious symbols of Roman Catholicism, closely intertwined with a particularistic nationalism, that characterized PiS's discursive formation and transformation, as the cases of the Smolensk air crash and the assassination of Paweł Adamowicz show.

Media discourses on the Smolensk air crash first recalled an ethos that had been present in Poland's postcommunist era: honesty, courage, solidarity, and selfless work performed for others. These moral principles had been highlighted by those who witnessed the historical changes of August 1980 ("The Polish Revolution") and those who produced historical narratives about them (Garton Ash 1983; Davies 2001; Lukowski and Zawadzki 2001). These codes were in some respects embedded in the main signs carried in the public discourses on this case. However, particular religious signs, such as the cross, were then overlaid with further opposite meanings, romanticism, passions, and reductive interpretations. Yet this set of values and its corresponding set of countervalues – dishonesty, fear, antagonism, and greed – remained in public descriptions of actors and actions. They came into play in discourses on the murder of Gdańsk's mayor. The city of Gdańsk is loaded with symbolism. The 1980 Gdańsk shipyard strike, supported by Polish intellectuals and the Catholic Church, resulted in the realistic and peaceful agreements that restored Poland's independence. Solidarity had managed to mobilize Polish society by uniting people around the movement's signs of identity: nationalism, Catholicism, workers' demands and aspirations, and democratic values. The barbaric assassination of Gdańsk's mayor happened in the middle of a solidary event. However, as Adam Michnik (2011) has subtly expressed, Solidarity's unifying forces were no longer complementary but divisive and conflicting.

Pro-PiS and official discourses on both events coded opponents and their actions within narratives of conspiracy, allies vs. enemies, and "genuine" Poles vs. "fake" ones. Polish national values of "faith," "patriotism," or "fatherland" were used as symbolic scaffolding in the construction of such narratives. Regarding "faith," one relevant point was the way in which the pro-PiS discourses saw the party as an incarnation of Catholicism: anyone who did not identify with the party's view was an enemy of God. In this sense, the liberal center-right PO, PiS's main opposing force, was presented as a continuation of communism, whereas the left was not even included in the discursive struggle. Reforms were conceived as a step forward to establish a new order based on traditional conservative values. Paradoxically mixed with elements of right-wing extremism, xenophobia, solidarity, and nationalism, civil values were – and are still – subverted to provide scripts to political leaders and their ruling party to sustain the PiS's pseudocivil sphere.

Discourse on the murder of Gdańsk's mayor showed how PiS's populism has been contested by its critics, who accuse the ruling party and its leaders of anticivil religiosity, illiberalism, and authoritarianism. Drawing on anti-PiS discourses, we have demonstrated the extent to which far-right populism has also developed anticivil codes in relation to its opponents, with these codes being capable of articulating counterdiscourses in order to mobilize counterpublics for the purposes of resistance and civil repair. This case shows how anticivil codes were strongly activated when populism developed into a rigid control of public media that molded news on the murder to fit the official narrative of the ruling party.

Social polarization and division among Catholics and other sociodemographic constituencies – PiS's supporters come from smaller towns and rural areas (CBOS 2017) – were present in the most recent parliamentary elections, which took place on October 10, 2019. The polls resulted in another victory for the ruling Law and Justice party, which won a narrow majority in the parliament. While the party won just under 44 percent of the vote for the lower house (the Sejm) – it won 38 percent in 2015 – it secured only 235 seats out of a possible 460. The rest of the seats were distributed between the main opposition party, Civic Coalition (27.4 percent); a grouping of left-wing parties (12.56 percent); the conservative Polish Coalition (8.6 percent); and a new far-right party, Confederation (6.8 percent).

The PiS 2019 electoral campaign resulted in an effective fusion of solidarity (the generous welfare program Family 500+, which aims to provide financial support to families, has radically changed the perception of state family policy: CBOS 2016) and ethnonational Catholicism. PiS's populist rhetoric successfully coexists with an authoritarian politics that is capable of sustaining a pseudocivil sphere that mainly comprises an ideological framework – one that operates at both the discursive and institutional levels – of an idealistic national religious community. The ideological framework sets the discursive boundaries between friends and enemies. At the institutional level, PiS's controversial judicial reforms aimed at dismantling a "corrupt" legal system that is "subservient" to "postcommunist elites" have caused alarm nationally and internation-

FAR-RIGHT POPULISM IN POLAND

ally. National reactions from the Polish judges' association *Iustitia* and from citizens have reached the rest of Europe. On September 17, 2018, the European Network of Councils for the Judiciary (ENCJ) suspended the membership of the Polish National Judicial Council (KRS) after it reached the conclusion that "the KRS is no longer the guardian of the independence of the judiciary in Poland. It seems instead to be an instrument of the executive."[9] Although these institutional actions are beyond the scope of this chapter's discourse analysis, they seem to open up paths toward civil repair.

Notes

1 Antoni Słonimski (1895–1976) was a poet, dramatist, and journalist known for his critical attitude toward communism.
2 Adam Michnik (1946–) is the former leader of Poland's dissident movement, as well as the founder and editor-in-chief of *Gazeta Wyborcza*.
3 In this chapter, we use "liberal" in the European sense rather than in the American one.
4 PiS's leaders currently use the term "late postcommunism" to describe their opponents, and it has been included within the party's program for the last parliamentary elections on October 13, 2019.
5 The term "Golgotha of the East" was first used by the priest Zdzisław Paszkowski, who was a chaplain to the Katyń families. In 1995, the International Year of Katyń, he organized an event named "Golgotha of the East: Poland Remembers." The act aimed to engage fifty-five churches in Poland in installing a cross bearing the inscription "Golgotha of the East." A painting/bas-relief titled *Holy Mother of Katyń* was made in 1999 to commemorate the victims. It depicts the analogy between Katyń and Golgotha: the Virgin Mary embraces a dead body with a head wound (an alleged victim of the Katyń massacre), and a caption reads, "Help to forgive."
6 Niewiadomski was a fanatic within the right-wing National Democratic Party. Interestingly, he was treated as a hero by a right-wing faction of this political force.
7 Politician Bronisław Komorowski won the presidential election on July 4, 2010, after the death of Lech Kaczyński. After his activist militance in Solidarity and other political parties, he ended up in Civic Platform. His fight for Poland's presidency against Jarosław Kaczyński, the twin brother of the dead president, confronted the two main political forces that prevail in today's Poland: the pro-European liberal right-center PO party and the nationalistic and Euroskeptic conservative right PiS party.
8 The charity's main annual event, the Grand Finale of the Great Orchestra of Christmas Charity, had been organized by Jerzy Owsiak for twenty-seven years on the second Sunday after Christmas. It consisted of concerts and auctions, and thousands of volunteers went into the streets to raise money for medical equipment for children's hospitals across the country. The Owsiak Foundation's activity had been polluted by PiS, which accused the organization

149

of fraud and unjust enrichment, to the detriment of the foundation's original purpose.

9 See the Executive Board report published on August 16, 2018 (http://n-15-5. dcs.redcdn.pl/file/o2/tvn/web-content/m/p1/f/9a1de01f893e0d2551ecbb7ce4d c963e/f7a7a3dd-3bfe-4887-af6a-da85d3073284.pdf).

References

Alexander, J. C. (2006) *The Civil Sphere*. New York: Oxford University Press.

CBOS. (2016) Program "Rodzina 500 plus" jako element system wsperiania rodzin i dzietności. February. https://www.cbos.pl/SPISKOM.POL/2016/K_025_16. PDF.

CBOS. (2017) O polityce, która nie buduje wspólnoty. November. https://www. cbos.pl/SPISKOM.POL/2017/K_160_17.PDF.

Davies, N. (2001) *Heart of Europe: The Past in Poland's Present*. Oxford: Oxford University Press.

Davies, N. (2005) *God's Playground: A History of Poland*. Oxford: Oxford University Press.

Drzazga-Lech, M. (2011) Mitologizacja Lecha Kaczyńskiego: Obraz prezydenta RP w wybranych dziennikach. In: P. Gliński and J. Wasilewski (eds.) *Katastrofa smoleńska: Reakcje społeczne, polityczne i medialne*. Warsaw: Wydawnictwo IFiS PAN. Polskie Towarzystwo Socjologiczne.

Garton Ash, T. (1983) *The Polish Revolution: Solidarity*. New Haven: Yale University Press.

Gliński, P. and J. Wasilewski. (2011) Przedmowa. In: P. Gliński and J. Wasilewski (eds.) *Katastrofa smoleńska: Reakcje społeczne, polityczne i medialne*. Warsaw: Wydawnictwo IFiS PAN. Polskie Towarzystwo Socjologiczne.

Lis, T. (2019) *Umrzeć za Gdańsk: 12 rozmów o Pawle Adamowiczu, wolności i magii Gdańska*. Warsaw: Wydawnictwo Ringier Axel Springer Polska Sp. z o.o.

Lukowski, J. and H. Zawadzki. (2001) *A Concise History of Poland*. Cambridge: Cambridge University Press.

Michnik, A. (2011) *In Search of Lost Meaning: The New Eastern Europe*. Berkeley: University of California Press.

Mościcka-Bogacz, A. (2011) Antymitologizacja Lecha Kaczyńskiego: Obraz prezydenta RP w wybranych dziennikach. In: P. Gliński and J. Wasilewski (eds.) *Katastrofa smoleńska: Reakcje społeczne, polityczne i medialne*. Warsaw: Wydawnictwo IFiS PAN. Polskie Towarzystwo Socjologiczne.

Porter-Szűcs, B. (2011) *Faith and Fatherland: Catholicism, Modernity, and Poland*. Oxford: Oxford University Press.

Rotfeld, A. D. and A. V. Torkunov (eds.). (2015) *White Spots – Black Spots: Difficult Matters in Polish–Russian Relations, 1918–2008*. Pittsburgh: University of Pittsburgh Press.

Szczerbiak, A. (2016) An anti-establishment backlash that shook up the party system? The October 2015 Polish parliamentary election. *Perspectives on European Politics and Society* 18(4): 404–27.

Zubrzycki, G. (2006) *The Crosses of Auschwitz: Nationalism and Religion in Post-Communist Poland*. Chicago: University of Chicago Press.

Żukowski, T. (2011) Polacy wobec tragedii smoleńskiej: Przegląd wybranych badań demoskopijnych. In: P. Gliński and J. Wasilewski (eds.) *Katastrofa smoleńska: Reakcje społeczne, polityczne i medialne.* Warsaw: Wydawnictwo IFiS PAN. Polskie Towarzystwo Socjologiczne.

6

The "Thirteenth Immigrant"?

Migration and Populism in the
2018 Czech Presidential Election

Bernadette Nadya Jaworsky

Within the past decade, the Czech Republic has succumbed to the populist "specter" haunting Europe (Milačić and Vuković 2018). With the rise of its centrist (or, as some would argue, right-leaning) populism, it has become part of what a senior fellow at the Brookings Institution calls "the most important European political development of the 21st century" (Galston 2018). The 2018 re-election of the first Czech president voted in democratically proved to be a nail-biter but populism prevailed. Incumbent Miloš Zeman, who has variously been called both a left- and right-wing populist,[1] won on a platform largely built on fear of migration and refugees, intertwined with worries about the Islamification of the country. In his increasing securitization of migration, Zeman has treated migrants, refugees, Muslims, and terrorists as interchangeable, stating: "I do not claim that all Muslims are terrorists, I say that all terrorists are Muslims" (Buchert and Hamšíkm 2011; see also Naxera and Krčál 2018). Promising to rescue and protect the people of the Czech Republic from "Prague café society,"[2] which would welcome migrants and refugees, this "lonely wolf" (Stojarová 2018)[3] defeated his challenger, Jiří Drahoš, by a slim margin, just 51.4 to 48.6 percent.

Zeman is hardly "lonely" when it comes to his views on migration. Although the Czech Republic has few migrants – about 5 percent of the 10.6 million population, with nearly half of them other Slavs from Ukraine, Slovakia, and other countries (Czech Statistical Office 2019) – and even fewer Muslims (just 10,000 or 0.1 percent; Pew Research Center 2017), there exist widespread negative attitudes toward newcomers, especially refugees. In 2017, 60 percent of the population mentioned immigrants and foreign workers as a group they would not want to have as neighbors and 57 percent mentioned Muslims (Rabušic and Chromková Manea 2018). A strong majority, 68 percent, are completely against accepting refugees from war-affected countries, 35 percent are willing to accept them if they will return to the country of origin after the conflict is over, and only 3 percent embrace a positive attitude about accepting refugees. Moreover, 68 percent of the population perceive refugees as a threat to security of the Czech Republic, 82 percent to Europe, and 71 percent as a global threat (Červenka 2018). And decisions by those in power reflect such sentiments. In 2015, the European Union mandated that the Czech Republic accept 2,691 refugees relocated from Italy and Greece; by mid-2017, it had hosted just twelve, stoking fears about the potential "thirteenth immigrant" (Junek 2017). The country is being sued by the European Commission for its noncompliance with the quota.[4]

There are several explanations concerning the puzzle of why the Czech Republic appears to be so virulently antimigrant and anti-Islam in the face of such low levels of migration and Muslims. One posits the ethnic homogeneity of the country; most people have little or no actual contact with migrants or Muslims (Bečka et al. 2017). Jan Čulík (2017) suggests that "defensive nationalism" is a "defining feature" of modern Czech history. Some blame the mass media, especially tabloid newspapers and extremist blogs, for riling up people's fears and anxieties (Stojarová 2018). It is no wonder, then, as Strapáčová and Hloušek (2018: 4) suggest, that Czech politicians reach for populist rhetoric concerning migration instead of "an analysis of real challenges, risks, as well as the moral and international obligations stemming from the Czech Republic's membership in the EU." A chicken–egg dilemma emerges: Are populist politicians like Zeman fueling public sentiments on migration or is public opinion driving the political rhetoric? Does it matter? The bottom line is that an increasingly pervasive populism and an atmosphere of fear and xenophobia have brought about serious challenges within the Czech civil sphere, not only with regard to processes of inclusion and exclusion, but also by a "stretching" of the regulative institution of "office."

Alexander (2006: 31) characterizes the civil sphere as "a solidary sphere, in which a certain kind of universalizing community comes to be culturally defined and to some degree institutionally enforced." Exactly who is included in such a community, however, is contested, through a discursive system of binary codes. Exclusion of those considered "polluted" is ongoing: "Just as there is no developed religion that does not divide the world into the saved and the damned, there is no civil discourse that does not conceptualize the world into those who deserve inclusion and those who do not" (Alexander 2006: 55). Exclusionary populists seize upon this dynamic, emphasizing an in-group ("the people") and an out-group or -groups, most commonly "elites," but also immigrants and minorities, whose interests may be fostered by elites (Mudde and Kaltwasser 2013; Müller 2016). In the case of the Czech Republic, historically, there has been an "internal" Other, the Roma ("Gypsy") minority, widely considered unassimilable and "unadaptable." To a degree, some immigrant groups have been marginalized, but mostly there had been a relatively quiet coexistence prior to the migrant/refugee "crisis" of 2015.[5] Since then, an "external" Other has become the main threat to society, represented by the interchangeable categories of migrants, refugees, and Muslims. The boundaries drawn by the populist president against this external Other are strong, and the nation's culture and identity, not to mention its safety, are portrayed as being at stake. Indeed, the country faces an "invasion," according to President Zeman.[6]

Arguably, Zeman's rhetoric contributes to the rising tide of xenophobia and marginalization of the non-European migrants and refugees living in the Czech Republic. What is potentially as dangerous is the populist erosion of the institution of "office." In democratic societies, it is "regulative" civil institutions that offer a control on political power; voting and political parties put representatives into the state, and legal and ethical constraints on corruption and self-interest emerge from their entry into office (Alexander 2006: 132–50). In the Czech case, the institution of office has been turned on its head, threatening the broader solidarity of the national community. President Zeman purports to speak for the "bottom 10 million" in a country of 10.6 million (Eckhardt 2013), excluding the elites of "Prague café society" and, of course, migrants, refugees, and Muslims. The universalistic ambitions of the civil sphere are thwarted. What's more, the communicative institutions of the civil sphere, such as mainstream mass media, don't step up and denounce such exclusion; they are generally in lock-step with the president. In Alexander's (2019) terms, "societalization"[7] of the migration issue does not occur and President Zeman's breach of office is not transformed into a threat to the social whole.

To explore the populism–migration nexus in the Czech Republic, this study asks: How did candidates employ populistic migration discourse in their battle for the Czech presidency? It focuses in particular on the two candidates in the presidential runoff election held on January 26–7, 2018: between incumbent President Miloš Zeman and challenger Jiří Drahoš. I look at interviews with these candidates, their one-on-one debates, and media coverage of their commentary on migration in national daily newspapers, on radio and TV, and in magazines. In addition, I marshal public statements made by President Zeman while in office since 2013. Exploring this meso-level of cultural representations made by the president and a presidential contender is fitting in the Czech case, since the public tends to hold the office of president in very high esteem, even if its power is mainly symbolic (Čulík 2017; Swain 2018). The president of the first Czechoslovak Republic, Tomáš Garrigue Masaryk (1918–35), and Václav Havel, president of Czechoslovakia from 1989 to 1992 and the Czech Republic from 1993 to 2003, are legendary heroes. Moreover, as Naxera and Krčál (2018: 198) point out, "Through his speeches, the President [Zeman] creates certain narratives – in this sense, presidential speeches are understood as an integral part of the public sphere, which is also linked to the construction of the shape of democracy in a given country" (see also Reisigl 2008).

In this chapter, I engage in a cultural sociological reconstruction of the narrative battle concerning migration performed by President Zeman and challenger Drahoš in the 2018 Czech presidential election, offering an alternative to the "thin" conceptions of culture in much of the literature on populism (Gauna 2018: 40–1; cf. Enroth 2019). Such a detailed and in-depth reconstruction of meanings builds upon and offers an alternative to political science accounts of populism, even those which approach the topic culturally, as a performative style (Moffitt 2016) or as a free-floating semiotic code (Laclau 2005). To do so, I follow the structural-hermeneutical method advocated by the Strong Program in cultural sociology, which highlights the relative analytical autonomy of culture. It is an independent variable as important in shaping actions and institutions as more material and instrumental forces (Alexander and Smith 2003: 12; see also Kane 1991). The Czech case of a migrant/refugee "crisis" without actual migrants or refugees, similar to "anti-Semitism without Jews" (Lendvai 1971), reveals the pervasive and autonomous power of cultural meanings. I also utilize "thick description," reconstructing meanings in a rich and persuasive way through an analysis that consists of "sorting out the structures of signification" (Geertz 1973: 9): in other words, bracketing out the pure cultural text.

I find that although their stories may appear divergent, the two candidates' views on migration converge in three important aspects. First, both strongly emphasize that the Czech Republic must refuse EU refugee quotas. Further, they highlight the potential threat to "European culture." Finally, they argue that migrants should be helped in their countries of origin. In the end, it is a matter of content versus style. There is a sense within the discourse of both Zeman and Drahoš that the Czech Republic faces a crisis of sorts, and each presents himself as the most fit for the office of president. But while Zeman unambiguously performs populism and antipluralism, Drahoš presents himself as an alternative to the status quo.

The Populism–Migration Nexus and the Civil Sphere in the Czech Republic

According to Alexander (2006: 49), within the civil sphere, the performance of deep cultural codes sustains its civil community and "normative demands for civility and mutual respect express themselves in figurative images, salty metaphors, hoary myths, and binary oppositions." In particular, binary codes divide members and potential members into pure and impure categories, similar to Durkheim's (1995 [1912]) division of sacred and profane. A culture structure of discourse at the level of motives, relationships, and institutions presents sacred–civil and profane–anticivil codes for defining those who belong (Alexander 2006: 53–67). Indeed, the civil sphere is a space in which the boundaries of belonging, for example, those drawn toward immigrants or other outsiders, are negotiated (Jaworsky 2016). The civil motives most relevant to this analysis reflect active, autonomous, rational, reasonable, and sane individuals, and their relationships are open, truthful, and straightforward. Civil institutions of law and office are rule-regulated and based on equality and inclusiveness.

At the same time that the candidates in the Czech Republic's 2018 presidential election perform civility, they also seek to demonstrate their fitness for office. The institution of "office" curbs political power, preventing elected officials from "simply becoming another cog in the state machine, from becoming the servant of social rather than civil power, and even from acting in a purely self-interested way" (Alexander 2006: 133). It is a moral obligation to faithfully execute the duties of office, and in developed civil spheres, communicative institutions like the media may expose breaches, even creating scandals and leading to the "societalization" of social problems from other spheres. As mentioned above, in the Czech Republic, this process is stalled, with the media generally supporting the exclusionary and often anticivil rhetoric of President Zeman and other politicians (Jelínková 2019). Further, a large number of media outlets had been consolidated between 2013 and 2015 into the hands of oligarchs, including the also-populist prime minister, Andrej Babiš. As Štětka (2016: 4–5, 10) points out, "a handful of the country's richest businessmen have between themselves almost completely divided the news media market" and "it can be argued that, in the Czech Republic, instrumentalization of the media for their proprietors' particularistic goals has become a standard and largely accepted practice, rather than an occasional deviation from what is still being considered a 'normal' role of media in a democratic society." This scenario represents a serious erosion of the media's role as a check on the institution of office.[8] Zeman (2013) sees it differently: he perceives a "significant part" of the Czech media as an "island of negative deviation," the part that he believes "focuses on brainwashing, media hype and the manipulation of the public opinion."

For a long time after 1989, the communicative and regulatory institutions[9] of the Czech civil sphere had represented a beacon to other countries in the postcommunist domain, and the country has been a "frontrunner of democratic transition" in the area, with "a stable polity, firmly rooted in liberal democracy . . . especially notable for the emergence and stability of its party democracy" (Havlík 2019: 369). But, as Havlík argues, that has changed since the rise of the political party ANO 2011 (*Akce nespokojených občanů*, or Action of Dissatisfied Citizens 2011),[10] bringing the country in line with the illiberal tendencies throughout Central and Eastern Europe, especially Poland and Hungary. He further states that the technocratic, "centrist" populism (Pop-Eleches 2010) of ANO 2011 "poses a threat to the foundations of liberal democracy that is much like that posed by the more radical versions of populism" (Havlík 2019: 370). The appeal of centrist populism lies not in radical ideology but in its antipolitical stance, eschewing the established political elite and promising to empower the people. The competence of the leader is demonstrated through "common sense" and, especially in the case of the Czech Republic, a commitment to fight corruption (Havlík and Voda 2018; Naxera and Krčál 2019) and run the country like a "family business" (Babiš 2017, quoted in Havlík 2019: 379). Further, as Havlík (2019: 376) notes, "[T]he almost mythical notion of the Czechs was not defined in ethnic, racial, religious, or class terms. Instead, it depicted a land of ordinary people who are exceptional for their diligence, extraordinary manual skills, brightness, and wit." Unlike its Central European neighbors, Poland, Hungary, and Slovakia, primordial, nationalistic, and/or religious ideology is virtually absent in the Czech Republic, and its populism claims to defend "liberal values" (Slačálek and Svobodová 2018).

Populism is further embroiled in the Czech case through the civil sphere's paradoxical construction. While the civil sphere exhibits utopian aspirations, in its "real" instantiation, some individuals are judged as worthy of inclusion while others are not; such a contradiction is "the price of civil society" (Alexander 2006: 9). As Junker and Chan (2019: 109) argue:

[P]opulism draws its power from the tension in civil spheres between particularistic identity and universal morality. In performing politics, a populist entrepreneur exploits the underlying logical tension of the civil sphere to rally support for his or her cause. He or she will typically

157

diagnos[e] a complex social problem, caused perhaps by structural changes in the economy and unequal access to political power, as the result of the pure will of "the People" being emasculated by liberal constraints and ethnic others.

Such a rhetorical move offers what they call "cultural relief" from the "felt but unrecognized tension between particularistic identity and universalistic morality." More concretely, in its core ideals, the civil sphere is pluralist and populism is antipluralist (Müller 2016). Populism always has an "us" vs. "them" dimension, with "us" as "the people" – even if often ambiguously defined – and "them" as elites and the immigrant or minority Others they advocate for. This construction is evident throughout the discourse of both presidential candidates, albeit less for Drahoš than for Zeman.

For some time now, populism has been argued to be a conceptual catch-all, a perhaps overused and indistinctly theorized term to describe political developments across the globe in the past thirty years. As Moffitt (2016: Chapter 2) elaborates, it has been formulated as ideology (Mudde 2007), strategy (Weyland 2001), discourse (Hawkins 2009), and political logic (Laclau 2005). He further argues that "it is useful to acknowledge that there is no single definition of populism waiting to be 'discovered' if the 'right words' can simply be found to describe it" (Moffitt 2016: 27). Nevertheless, Moffitt (2016: 28–9) offers a definition that suggests conceptualizing populism as "political style," or "the repertoires of embodied, symbolically mediated performance made to audiences that are used to create and navigate the fields of power that comprise the political, stretching from the domain of government through to everyday life." A performative approach that sees all political performances as constructed takes in not only the rhetorical but also the aesthetic dimension. And a focus on cultural performances allows for an in-depth and "thick" (Geertz 1973) reconstruction of meaning (Gauna 2018). Further, as Canovan (1999: 6) points out, populism is not only a style of ordinary, routine politics, but a "characteristic mood" with "the revivalist flavour of a movement, powered by the enthusiasm that draws normally unpolitical people into the political arena." In the Czech case, voter turnout in the 2018 presidential election was the highest since 1998 (Swain 2018). Clearly, the candidates' performances attracted the public in a way that resulted in political action.

For the purposes of this analysis, I largely rely on Moffitt's conceptualization of populism. The three primary features of populism as a political style include (1) an appeal to "the people" versus "the elite"; (2) "bad manners," in the sense of coarse political rhetoric and a disregard for "appropriate" behavior; and (3) the "spectacularization of failure," underlying crisis, breakdown, or threat, which can be resolved by "strong leadership and quick political action" (Moffitt 2016: 29, 44, 114). Instead of crisis as an external trigger for populism, populism is actually a trigger for crisis, the performance of which is an internal feature of populism. As in the case of the Czech Republic and the migrant/refugee "crisis," whether said crisis is real or not is not important. Instead, the performance of crisis is what matters. According to Moffitt (2016: 121–30), such performances encompass six steps:

1. Identify failure.
2. Elevate the failure to the level of crisis by linking it into a wider framework and adding a temporal dimension.
3. Frame "the people" versus those responsible for the crisis.
4. Use media to propagate performance.
5. Present simple solutions and strong leadership.
6. Continue to propagate crisis.

As will become evident from my analysis below, these steps are visible in the discourse of the two presidential candidates on migrants and refugees. They especially highlight step 5, their superior ability to address the migrant/refugee "crisis" facing the Czech Republic. The analysis also points to the insistence of the Strong Program in cultural sociology concerning the relative autonomy of culture structures – the candidates' rhetoric creates the "crisis," not the other way around, as many accounts of populism would purport (cf. Moffitt 2016: 114–19).

Visvizi (2017: 2–3) notes that migration and populism form a complex relationship and that country context is crucial; further, there are "critical junctures" at which "the escalation of that migration–populism nexus can be either lessened or exacerbated." I posit that the 2018 Czech presidential election represents such a juncture of extreme exacerbation. As I will elaborate below, even though both candidates in the final runoff agreed in principle about the most important aspects of migration, the issue escalated into a "crisis mode" in which the incumbent painted his challenger as diametrically opposed to his ideas for resolving the potential threat to the nation.

Czech Presidential Politics as a Narrative (Non)Battle

That fears about migration and Islam fueled the latest Czech presidential election is no surprise. Islamophobia had blossomed in the media already

159

after 9/11 and in response to such incidents as the Danish cartoons affair (Sedláčková 2010, cited in Slačálek and Svobodová 2018: 483). And during the migrant/refugee "crisis" of 2015–16, dehumanization and securitization of the refugee "wave" was dominant (Tkaczyk et al. 2015). In an election that Western observers had dubbed "a battle of ideas between populism and elitism, between authoritarianism and liberal democracy, between east and west" (Cameron 2018), or an "electoral test" between "liberals and populist nationalists" (Bakke and Sitter 2018), the two candidates in the final round hardly differed in their views on migration and Islam. While the narratives in the ideological battle for the presidency appeared to diverge, in reality, the "hero" of the plot that could best lead the country would engage in very similar actions to resolve its impending migration crisis. The ostensible battle is thus tempered, with both contenders calling upon the same civil codes that frame the civil sphere. In the following sections, I first outline the contours of each candidate's migration narrative, and then point to three points of similarity: saying no to EU quotas; preventing European culture from being threatened; and helping migrants in their countries of origin. Following Moffitt (2016), I highlight both candidates' performance of a migrant/refugee "crisis."

Zeman's Story: Millions of Migrants, Three Solutions

Miloš Zeman's narrative begins with the interchangeable categories of migrants, refugees, and Muslims, leaving Africa, the former Ottoman Empire, or other countries of origin. In an interview with the privately owned *TV Barrandov*, Zeman outlined a "realistic" scenario in which a population the size of the entire Czech Republic would very soon arrive in Europe:

> Yesterday I was listening to a study, which I don't believe but I will quote it, that 100 million migrants are ready in Africa who want to get to Europe. Let's split it by ten, Mr. Soukup [the interviewer]. And it can easily be a realistic number. Imagine that another 10 million migrants would come to Europe through Spain, France. It doesn't need to go exclusively through regular routes. I think if the EU finally won't find the courage to fortify its external borders, which it still blabs about but doesn't do anything, in that case we will have those 10 million migrants here after a couple of years. (*TV Barrandov* 2018a)

Through his tempering of the sensationalist, 100-million migrant scenario, Zeman is attempting to demonstrate that he is a rational, realistic, and sane individual, performing the sacred–civil side of the discourse of civil society. Of course, he doesn't believe that 100 million migrants in Africa are coming to Europe. But one-tenth, a "realistic number," will enter after "a couple of years" if the EU's external borders are not "courageously" fortified. He has successfully performed in crisis mode, adding the temporal element that Moffitt (2016: 123) stresses: "This sense of impending doom presents society at a precipice, which if stepped over, cannot be reversed." Moreover, according to Zeman, some of the places of origin are not so dangerous as to require political or humanitarian help.

> For example, Eritrea or Ethiopia are definitely not states where the civil war would rage. Even though there is a pretty cruel regime in Eritrea, civil war hasn't broken out yet. In other words, if migrants come from these and from other countries, they come for economic reasons and not for political or humanitarian ones. (*TV Barrandov* 2018b)

Through this statement, Zeman is espousing a common European discourse about "economic migrants" not deserving of refugee status (Goodman et al. 2017; Crawley and Skleparis 2018). He portrays the relations with such migrants through the anticivil side of the civil sphere binary, as deceitful, calculating, and conspiratorial (Alexander 2006: 58): they are posing as refugees even though they really are not fleeing for political or humanitarian reasons. Migration scholars have complicated the simplistic dichotomy between "forced" and "voluntary" migration, showing how these constructed categories result in consequences for people on the move and the policies affecting them (Crawley and Skleparis 2018).

But as we reach the middle of the migration story put forth by Zeman in the televised interview, the real peril of the "crisis" is revealed. In a civilizationalist (Brubaker 2017) argument, he cites the danger migrants bring:

> *Zeman*: Look, since the beginning I've been arguing that the culture of these migrants is basically incompatible with European culture. And I think that migrants themselves realize it too, and that an increase in crime rates is caused exactly by the fact we've opened space to these migrants, including the attacks against the police.
> *Interviewer*: It [the European Union] perhaps doesn't do anything [to fortify its external borders] because the European commissioner Federica Mogherini said Islam has its place in European space and in European culture.
> *Zeman*: It definitely has its place in European history because Europe fought with Islam, particularly with the Ottoman Empire, for several centuries until we managed to beat Islam. (*TV Barrandov* 2018b)

The implication is that Europe must again fight against and "beat Islam." The migrants' culture is "basically incompatible" with the "European culture" of "the people." But this civilizationalism does not reflect simply a nationalist style of populism. Brubaker (2017) distinguishes between Northern and Western European populisms and Eastern and Central European populisms, arguing that the former are based on a more secularist and liberal conception of civilizationalism, and the latter are more nationalist. However, as Slačálek and Svobodová (2018) argue, Czech national identity is progressive, intellectual, and liberal, in contrast to, say, Poland and Hungary, which are more conservative and nationalist. Thus, the Czech Republic's populism is more like the Northern and Western European civilizationalist variety. Moreover, because the Czech Republic is among the most atheistic countries in the world, the fear of Islam is "*as a religion*, not *as a rival religion*" (Slačálek and Svobodová 2018: 480).

Zeman has consistently maintained this style of "clash of civilizations" (Huntington 1996) argument throughout his political career. Even before becoming president in the country's first democratic presidential election, he often performed his populistic stance (Moffitt 2016): for example, appearing in 2011 on the cover of a prominent national magazine wearing a t-shirt emblazoned with a crossed-out mosque, grabbing widespread headlines with his assertion: "A moderate Muslim is a *contradictio in adjecto*, thus a contradiction, just as a *contradictio in adjecto* is a moderate Nazi" (Buchert and Hamšíkm 2011). And throughout his first term, note Naxera and Krčál (2018: 195, emphasis mine), "the dominant treatment of the phenomenon of security expressed by the President is primarily linked to the creation of the vision of Islam and immigration as the *absolute largest threat* to contemporary Europe."

This portrayal of threat has also been espoused through Zeman's "bad manners" style of populism (Moffitt 2016: 44–5). In explaining to an audience of workers at a butcher's shop in the city of Zlín how the application of sharia law by refugees would look ("unfaithful women will be stoned to death and thieves will have their hand cut off"), Zeman deftly weaves together xenophobia and sexism, commenting: "We will be deprived of the women's beauty since they will be shrouded in burkas from head to toe, including the face. Well, I can imagine women for whom it would mean an improvement, but there are few of them and I cannot see any such here" (ČTK 2015b). Such crass and inappropriate discourse represents one of the hallmarks of Zeman's political style (Noack 2014; Naxera and Krčál 2018; Swain 2018). He is aligning himself with the ways ordinary Czechs in the pub might talk about Muslims (or women), which may have been a factor in his eventual electoral success (Swain

2018). This incident is reminiscent of Trump's defense of his unfortunate "grab them [women] by the pussy" remark: "This was locker-room banter" (Fahrenthold 2016). The level of authenticity is raised because it invokes a familiar genre for the audience, whether in a Czech pub or in a US locker room.[11] The populist power of "bad manners" has yet to be fully unpacked, analytically speaking (Enroth 2019: 5).

As the narrative comes to its end, Zeman positions himself as unwavering in his commitment to address the problem of impending migration into the Czech Republic: "[M]y stance doesn't change" (*TV Barrandov* 2018b). He also asserts a truthful and open relationship with his constituency, which makes him qualified to fulfill the duties of office. In the final presidential debate before the election, he answers the moderator's query about his "recipe for the migration crisis solution" almost impatiently, offering three definitive answers:

> I said it several times but I'll gladly say it again. It means three things: [first] deportation of those who are in the European territories illegally and who didn't get asylum. By the way, that radicalization emerges also among the Czech Muslims, but that's another thing. Secondly, to help those who need this help in the countries of their origin, and it's something, Mr. Drahoš, that I said for the first time in 2015. And it's a long time ago. And, third, protection of external borders, of course, and we've been talking about this already. It means not letting any of the illegal immigrants in here, because this migrant can claim asylum exclusively in the first safe country and it's definitely not the Czech Republic. (*Česká televize* 2018)

His first solution to the potentially millions of arriving migrants is permanent and wide in geographical scope: the deportation of "illegal" migrants from Europe if their asylum claims are not approved. He takes the opportunity to pause and equate migrants and Muslims, implying their "radicalization." Second, he advocates helping "those who need help" in their homelands, inferring that only some people may actually be deserving of help. Finally, he simultaneously invokes the protection of the EU's external borders and the Dublin Agreement, which stipulates that asylum seekers should apply in the first safe country in which they arrive. There is thus no possibility for the land-locked Czech Republic to receive them. Zeman also implies that such a migrant belongs among "illegal immigrants," blurring the line between deserving and undeserving asylum seekers even further. Having a solution to a crisis (even if manufactured) is a crucial step in the performance of populism (Moffitt 2016).

Drahoš's Story: "We're a Society Which is Able to Handle Everything"

For Jiří Drahoš, the narrative begins rather differently: there are in fact migrants who deserve to enter the country. "Real" refugees who leave their homeland for "reasons of war" are clearly distinguished from "economic migrants": "The refugee is somehow defined and there is an international convention for this" (Bohuslavová and Danda 2018). In an interview given in June 2017, Drahoš had stated, "There should be no problem accepting some 2,600[12] screened refugees or migrants from a security perspective. Of course, in the light of past experiences, I wonder how many of them would actually stay here" (*iDNES.cz* 2017).[13] There should be "no problem" accepting refugees and "we do not need to fear," because "we're a society which is able to handle everything" (Kreč and Bartoníček 2018). Drahoš reiterates such a sentiment in an interview given to the newspaper *Právo* shortly before the second round of the election, asserting that the Czech people don't want to be afraid and be "scared by politicians": "They want to hear we have our self-confidence and that we have our national pride and if we want to, we'll overcome everything" (Bohuslavová and Danda 2018). The country is invoked as active, autonomous, and realistic, reflecting the sacred side of the binary of civil motives (Alexander 2006: 57).

The codes of the civil sphere are also invoked with regard to the law of the land, which must be a rule-regulated institution that reflects equality (Alexander 2006: 59). When asked, "To what extent do Islam and migrants threaten Czechia according to you?" Drahoš replies:

> The migration crisis is a big problem and it will be a problem in the coming years too. It's not an issue which could be solved in a heartbeat. Yes, *we* have to make decisions on our own as the Czech Republic, who *we* want on *our* territory and who will live here with *us*. If *someone* wants to live here with *us*, he has to go through the standard asylum process, accept *our* laws and written rules. It's not possible[14] a community will be established *here* which doesn't equate men's and women's rights or one which promotes marriages of thirteen-year-olds. *Here*, *our* laws must be valid for *everyone*. (Bohuslavová and Danda 2018, emphasis mine)

The middle of the narrative is thus about a country that, along with its sovereign right to control who is present on its territory (Dirks 1998), embraces liberal democratic values such as equality and just laws that are universal in their application. And this country is facing a "big problem," or a crisis that cannot be "solved in a heartbeat." As I will further elaborate below, like Zeman, Drahoš is invoking a civilizationalist argument in his performance of the migrant/refugee "crisis." It's simply not acceptable to have a community established in the country that doesn't subscribe to liberal democratic values. And although laws are applicable to "everyone," Drahoš nevertheless separates "us" from a nameless "someone." In "flagging" the nation (Billig 1995),[15] with terms such as "we," "our," and "here," Drahoš is claiming a certain exclusivity. The paradox of the civil sphere with regard to the tension between universalism and particularism is evident.

The end of the Drahoš narrative presents the candidate as someone who has the answers to the "migration crisis" facing the Czech Republic, because he is a "fighter" (Kalan 2018). In fact, he recalls that when confronted with radical budget cuts proposed by the government for the Czech Academy of Sciences when he was in charge, he prevailed: "This would mean the end of this institution. We started to protest and lobby, I met with all the decision makers – and we won. I remember politicians saying I play tough, but fair" (Kalan 2018). In other words, because he embodies the values coded by the civil sphere ("fair"), he is an ideal candidate to fulfill the role of office: "Of course, everyone has egos and personal ambitions, but at the end of the day the only thing that matters is whether you are suitable for the job. Whether you have proper moral and managerial qualities" (Kalan 2018). Drahoš aims to demonstrate that he is the "moral" choice. Further, unlike Zeman, he is a "political blank slate," unsullied by "any scandal whatsoever": "I'm an outsider, and this is my biggest advantage" (Kalan 2018). As an academic and former head of the Czech Academy of Sciences, he is forward-thinking: "I consider myself a representative of the world which is going to come." In short, the performance of his political style offers the Czech public an alternative to Zeman's lack of fitness for office. In offering a solution to a "crisis," he thus attacks the inability of the existing political system and delegitimizes it (Moffitt 2016: 128).

Divergent Narratives, Convergent Solutions: A Tale of Two Populisms?

Although the migration narratives of Zeman and Drahoš may appear quite divergent, and each certainly sought to differentiate himself from his opponent, as noted above, the two presidential contenders actually converged along three important points. First, both are adamant that the country should not adhere to EU quotas set for the country to resettle refugees arriving in Southern Europe.[16] Second, although Zeman talked about it much more explicitly, they both agree that they cannot allow "European culture" to be threatened. Finally, both candidates believe that migrants should be helped in their countries of origin. In this section,

I reconstruct the migration battle between Zeman and Drahoš, revealing the ways in which it was essentially a nonbattle. Indeed, a political scientist specializing in the politics of Central and Eastern Europe asks whether this election was "a tale of two populisms" occurring "between two insiders posing as political outsiders, offering different variants of the populist grand narrative of the people versus the elites" (Hanley 2018).

One of the biggest battles in the contest between Zeman and Drahoš played out on the billboards and press advertisements sponsored by the anonymous "Friends of Miloš Zeman" that read "STOP immigrants, STOP Drahoš, this country is ours!" It takes the words closing Zeman's 2015 Christmas speech literally:

> During preparations for the demonstration in support of migration on November 17, someone had informed our intelligence services that, on a banner at this demonstration, the following sign will be displayed: "This country does not belong to us. Refugees welcome."
>
> Somebody had advised the organizers that this sign is exceptionally stupid, and so they replaced it with a slightly less stupid sign: "This land belongs to all. Refugees welcome."
>
> And to close my Christmas message, I would like to make two clear statements: *This country is ours.* This country is not, and it cannot be, for all. (Western Cannon 2017, emphasis mine)

When asked about the billboard and advertisement, Zeman replied, "Mr. Drahoš is connected to migration, and so it is a true story. I would like to recall his words from last June where he said we'll bear 2,600 migrants. And so, as migration is a sensitive topic, connecting Drahoš to migration is logical and legitimate" (*TV Barrandov* 2018b). Zeman is affirming his motives as a civil sphere actor who is rational and reasonable (Alexander 2006). Drahoš reacted by saying this type of campaign was no surprise, painting his opponent with the opposite civil codes as dishonest and distorted: "I have expected exactly this type of lies and disinformation. This is just slander" (ČTK 2018). He continued by appealing to the prevailing sentiment among the Czech public: "I only agree with the part saying 'Stop Immigrants.' None of us wants *waves* of immigrants here" (emphasis mine). And this statement was not an isolated case among Drahoš's discourse on migrants. In response to the moderator of the final presidential debate, who asked for his solution to the EU quotas, he unequivocally asserted a consistent position:

> In the news, I heard today that even Germany is abandoning this principle [open doors] which I've been criticizing *since the beginning*. In the last debate, I heard from Miloš Zeman a very untrue opinion that I am the only politician promoting illegal migration or something like this. I

strongly object to this. I am a person who has stated *from the beginning*: "Quotas are wrong, we need to protect the EU borders." (*Česká televize* 2018, emphasis mine)

Drahoš is not against the EU as such: "Of course, we won't handle migration ourselves, we can't embed our borders in concrete and wait until it will *flood* us one day. We need to deal with it within Europe" (Bohuslavová and Danda 2018, emphasis mine). But in the end, he, like Zeman, is peddling fear, through his use of water metaphors that portray migrants as a danger to the nation (Santa Ana 1999; Ono and Sloop 2002). He asserts that no one wants "waves of immigrants" to "flood" the country. He is not as explicit as Zeman, who, peddling the crisis-infused language of populism (Moffitt 2016), warned of an imminent "tsunami" in 2016;[17] nevertheless, their discourse has converged. What is crucial is that both claim to have a solution to the "crisis" facing the Czech Republic.

I have already noted that Zeman propagates a "clash of civilizations" rhetoric in which European culture is endangered by the interchangeable trio of migrants, refugees, and Muslims. Admittedly, Drahoš is not nearly as vociferous in his anticivilizational discourse, but he concurs that there is potential danger, stating that "we must defend *our* culture" (Kalan 2018, emphasis mine). He continues in his deictic discourse that "flags" the nation: "*We* should talk about how to preserve *our* identity. *We* know what things look like in France and other countries with danger zones. *We* don't want to have it *here*" (Kalan 2018, emphasis mine). In the final presidential debate, he stresses the responsibility of refugees: "And these people, obviously, have to respect *our* laws, *our* rules and *our* cultural rules" (*Česká televize* 2018, emphasis mine). Arguably, by referring to "these people," he is engaging in a process of Othering. In spite of their apparent agreement, however, Zeman consistently paints Drahoš as a "welcomer" of migrants, seeking to perpetuate a battle:

> *Zeman*: Let me quote one phrase from the petition [referring to a call by scientists Drahoš signed in 2015]. "To Europe, people should arrive in such a way that freedom and dignity is preserved." Isn't this a call for migrants' acceptance?
>
> *Drahoš*: Your interpretations of some phrases are amazing. We have similar opinions on migration at least in some aspects. I've been refusing quotas since the beginning. (*Česká televize 1* 2018)

In an earlier interview, Drahoš had exasperatedly replied to a query about signing the call, "If you knew you'd be labeled as a 'welcomer,' would you sign the document?": "There is not any *if*. The call was prepared and I signed it. There is no word about welcoming or inviting. It even starts with us not wanting to underestimate threats resulting from migration. That's key" (Bohuslavová and Danda 2018). In their final debate, he turns the tables on Zeman: "I just remind you that in '99 the government of Miloš Zeman offered 5,000 Muslim migrants from Kosovo space in the Czech Republic. It was a humanitarian step, I guess. I don't doubt it. I'm just saying." But Zeman fires back with a cultural argument: "Yes, but these were different migrants. These were migrants from the former Yugoslavia and migrants of that time were culturally related to us and I was supporting it, of course" (*Česká televize* 2018).[18] In the end, both men have argued that what is "ours" – culture, laws and rules – must be protected.

The third area of convergence concerns the idea of helping people in their home countries in order to prevent migration. Zeman even goes so far as to indicate that migration is harmful to countries of origin, in a 2017 speech given in front of the UN General Assembly:

> [M]y opposition starts from the fact that the massive migration from African and other countries represents a brain drain. The young, healthy people, mainly men, who leave their countries, represent the weakening of the potential of those countries and everybody who welcomes migrants in Europe agrees to the brain drain and with permanent backwardness of those countries. What we need is to help those countries with electricity, hospitals, schools, water resources and so on in order to stabilize the population in those domestic countries, but not to support the migration. (Zeman 2017)

But Zeman's comment is clearly a double-edged sword. At the same time that he purports to want to help them, he relegates "African and other countries" to a state of "backwardness" in need of "stabilization." Drahoš, when asked by an interviewer for the newspaper *Hospodářské noviny* under what circumstances he would accept refugees, offers a similar solution, entangled with words about "economic migrants":

> I've always been saying that migration quotas are a wrong action from the side of the EU. Since the beginning I've been refusing these quotas. In 2015, it was primarily about real refugees and not economic migrants. But also in their cases, it is possible to help them in countries closer to their country: for example, we support their permanent stay in Turkey. It doesn't mean we need to open the borders. We shouldn't do it in any case. (Kreč and Bartoníček 2018)

Drahoš repeats in the presidential debates that "*these people* have to be helped in *their* countries" (*Česká televise 1* 2018, emphasis mine), calling for a "Europe which helps in countries where migration, where migrants come from, to Europe, safe Europe" (*Česká televize* 2018). He is placing the countries migrants come from in contrast to a "safe Europe"; he is cementing the fact that "the people" exist in contradistinction to outsiders.

In the end, the content of each candidate's discourse hardly differed in substance: it was a narrative (non)battle. What was different, though, was their political style. Zeman performed populism in a more classic sense, for example with his "bad manners," while Drahoš presented himself as the civil choice for the office of president. Zeman has presented simple solutions to the migrant/refugee "crisis" while Drahoš has pointed to its complexity. I would thus contest the characterization of this contest as "a tale of two populisms" (Hanley 2018). However, it is a cautionary tale just the same. The closeness of the race reflects the fact that each candidate had strong public appeal in certain sectors of the population. But while Drahoš came close to victory, prevailing in urban areas among the more educated, Zeman performed particularly well among rural, less educated, and working-class voters, among whom there was an increase in votes (Santora 2018). It seems that Zeman and his supporters prevailed in their depiction of Drahoš as "pro-migrant/refugee," and the latter's protestations were not enough to overcome such a portrayal.

Conclusion: "These Are Good Times for Populism"

In this chapter, I have reconstructed the complex migration–populism nexus in the Czech civil sphere, arguing that the ostensible battle between the two latest presidential contenders on the migration issue and the "crisis" facing the Czech Republic was hardly a clash of opinions. The content of their migration discourse and their performance of crisis (Moffitt 2016) converged, even as their political style of delivery was starkly different. As one astute observer opined, Drahoš potentially made the fatal error of entering the fight from the right: "Instead of highlighting a defense of migrants and refugees as a key point of differentiation, Drahoš chose to fight on Zeman's home territory and lost" (Swain 2018). Regardless of whether such a strategy could have been successful, Drahoš's performance of fitness for the duty of office simply wasn't enough to overcome Zeman's portrayal of himself as protector of the Czech people from "crisis" and the interchangeable and dangerous trio of migrants, refugees, and Muslims. Already as far back as 2015, Zeman had defended "ordinary" Czechs' feelings about migration, saying they "cannot be seen as racist or fascist" (Čulík 2015). Indeed, anti-immigrant and Islamophobic attitudes have largely been legitimized and secured a spot in mainstream Czech society (Čulík 2017; Naxera and Krčál 2018).

What is to be done? The picture for Western liberal democracies seems bleak. For example, Canovan (1999: 3) points to the fact that populism and democracy are inextricably intertwined: "[I]nstead of being a symptom of 'backwardness' that might be outgrown, populism is a shadow cast by democracy itself." The Czech Republic, although still a posttransition bastion of liberal democratic values, is no exception to the fact that, as Moffitt (2016: 159) puts it, "These are good times for populism," especially in Europe. Gardner-Gill (2018) offers a timely warning: "Zeman and other European populists are best analyzed neither as forming a new trend, nor as malformations of traditional politics. They are instead capturing the voices, hearts, and minds of a portion of their respective electorates, and they are doing it with more success than the liberal democratic order would have hoped." But even in the face of what Stojarová (2018: 42) calls the "*zemanisation* of public discourse (mainstreaming of nationalism by populist leaders)" in the Czech Republic, its civil sphere remains a utopian project worth hoping for (Alexander 2006: Chapter 20).

Notes

1 Upon his initial election in 2013, *The Guardian* called Zeman a "center-left" populist, but after his re-election in 2018, it dubbed him "far-right" (Gardner-Gill 2018). In 2016, *The New York Times* referred to him as a "leftist populist" (Bilefsky and Richter 2016). Gardner-Gill (2018) points out that "the standard postwar political spectrum does not easily fit politicians like Zeman. Zeman's populism is his defining characteristic, and he is best analyzed not as being on the left or right."

2 Zeman coined this term in 2014 to refer to a stratum of Czech society that variously includes "journalists, artists, students, pundits, political commentators, NGO activists and citizens who have in one way or another opposed or spoken against the president" (Hornát 2015). He first used "the raging Prague *lumpencafé*," to describe protestors calling for his resignation on the twenty-fifth anniversary of the Velvet Revolution, recalling Karl Marx's *lumpenproletariat*, or those lowest classes of workers without class consciousness. Afterwards, it evolved into *Prazska kavarna* or "Prague café," which stands in contrast to *Ceska hospoda*, or "Czech pub." Hornát beautifully captures the essence of this social group:

> In conjunction, the two words create a pejorative metaphor that aims to form in people's minds a picture of a group of metropolitan-based, elitist (pseudo-)intellectuals, who claim themselves to be the arbiters of conventional wisdom, who are dogmatic in their political and social views, intolerant of the less well-off and who are a priori opposed to dissenting opinions . . . they lack the rational and practical outlook and experience of the hard-working man, who simply does not have the time

to endlessly conspire about social and political ills of the country over a glass of red wine.

In true populist form, Zeman pits Prague café society against "the people"; when queried about the refugee "crisis" potentially dividing Czech society, he answered: "[O]n the one side there is the 'Prague Café', on the other side is ninety to ninety-five percent of the Czech society" (Hornát 2015).

3 Although he has garnered the support of the leading (populist) political party (ANO – Action of Dissatisfied Citizens), Zeman operates largely on his own. The political party he founded (Party of Civic Rights) has virtually no power, with just one seat in the Senate and none in the Chamber of Deputies.

4 The European Court of Justice launched hearings on the cases against the Czech Republic, Poland, and Hungary on May 15, 2019 (McEnchroe 2019). On April 2, 2020, the Court found that the three countries had failed to live up to their obligations; the European Commission must decide on any further action against them, but no sanctions are imminent since the quota system has been discontinued (Stevis-Gridneff and Pronczuk 2020).

5 In fact, Vietnamese immigrants, about 11 percent of the migrant population, could be seen as a "model minority," a term coined in the 1960s in the United States (Petersen 1966).

6 In his Christmas speech of 2015, Zeman stated: "I am profoundly convinced that we are facing an organized invasion, and not a spontaneous movement of refugees" (Western Cannon 2017).

7 "Societalization" can be seen as the process through which problems in noncivil spheres escape their institutional boundaries and become a general concern within the civil sphere. Alexander (2019: 3) describes the process: "It is only when sphere-specific problems become *societalized* that routine strains are carefully scrutinized, once lauded institutions ferociously criticized, elites threatened and punished, and far-reaching institutional reforms launched." I would argue that this process has not occurred in the case of the migrant/refugee "crisis" in the Czech Republic.

8 That is not to say that alternative media are entirely absent; of course, there is space for influential journalistic commentary that is more independent. Moreover, intellectuals and professors maintain a role in providing an alternative reading of contemporary events from a more critical and democratic perspective. However, just as many "alternative news" sites have arisen that sow disinformation allegedly supplied by Russia, such as *Parlamentní listy*, with its 8 million users in a country of 10.5 million, or even more radical sites like *AE News*, *Lajkit.cz*, and *Protiproud* (Schultheis 2017).

9 According to Alexander (2006: Part II), the "communicative institutions" of the civil sphere include the media, public opinion polls, and civil associations, while the "regulatory institutions" consist of voting, political parties, and office.

10 The party, named for *ano*, the word for "yes" in Czech, became "the most successful new political party since the fall of communism (winning 18.7 percent of votes in the 2013 general election and a victory with 29.6 percent in the last general election in October 2017)" (Havlík 2019: 370).

11 I am grateful to my colleague Pavel Pospěch for this insight.

12 Drahoš is referring to the number of refugees who should be accepted by the Czech Republic under the EU quotas.

13 This comment reveals the scope of the analytical puzzle concerning why the civil sphere of the Czech Republic is so filled with antirefugee discourse, in spite of the fact that there are few refugees. For example, of the eighty-nine Iraqi Christian refugees actually resettled in the country in 2016, many have left, moving on to Germany or even back to Iraq (Hejl 2016).

14 In the sense that it's "unacceptable."

15 Billig (1995: 93) argues that in "banal nationalism," deixis performs major interpretive work, through "small words" such as "we," "our," "this," and "here": "Small words, rather than grand memorable phrases, offer constant, but barely conscious, reminders of the homeland, making 'our' national identity unforgettable."

16 Although in 2017, Drahoš did state that the country could handle 2,600 refugees from a "security perspective," by the time the runoff election was underway, he repeatedly expressed his disapproval of the EU quotas.

17 Saying, "I am convinced that next year the migration wave will spill over our territory," Zeman warned: "Some blame me for spreading hatred, fear or panic, but these politicians, on the other hand, remind me of peacefully bathing Czech tourists on Thai beaches at a time when there is a small inconspicuous ripple called a tsunami on the horizon" (Hovorková 2016).

18 The Czech Republic accepted 3,500 refugees from Bosnia and Herzegovina and 1,100 Muslims from Kosovo in the 1990s, and Martin Rozumek, director of the Organization for Aid to Refugees (OPU), recalls: "There was no great debate and no hysteria at all. I do not remember any protests" (ČTK 2015a). Baker (2017) reflects on the reasons Bosnian Muslims (and, to a degree, those from Kosovo) were not subject to the same suspicion as Middle Eastern Muslim refugees today. She argues that these have to do with "how narratives of identity, religion and security inside and outside Bosnia have combined then and now." Whereas in the 1970s and 1980s,

> news images of Palestinian hijackers and Libyan and Iranian state-sponsored terrorists, mediated further by the stereotyped terrorist villains of Reagan- and post-Reagan-era Hollywood, had mapped the security threat of Islam on to brown, male, vigorous bodies of "Middle Eastern" appearance, and more specifically on to "Arabs" (no matter that Iranian ethnic identity is not Arab at all). ... Light-skinned Bosnians wearing Western clothes were not "visibly Muslim" in European symbolic politics.

References

Alexander, J. C. (2006) *The Civil Sphere*. New York: Oxford University Press.

Alexander, J. C. (2019) *What Makes a Social Crisis? The Societalization of Social Problems*. Cambridge: Polity.

Alexander, J. C. and P. Smith. (2003) The strong program in cultural sociology: Elements of a structural hermeneutics. In: J. C. Alexander (ed.) *The Meanings of Social Life*. New York: Oxford University Press.

Babiš, A. (2017) *O čem sním, když náhodou spím*. Prague: Czech Print Center.

Baker, C. (2017) Why were Bosniaks treated more favourably than today's Muslim refugees? On differing narratives of identity, religion and security. London School of Economics and Political Science, March 7. https://blogs.lse.

ac.uk/europpblog/2017/03/07/why-bosniaks-treated-more-favourably-than-to days-refugees/.

Bakke, E. and N. Sitter. (2018) The Czech presidential election and Europe's populism crisis. *TransCrisis*, January 19. https://www.transcrisis.eu/the-czech-presidential-election-and-europes-populism-crisis/.

Bečka, J., B. Doboš, F. Gantner, J. Landovský, L. Pítrová, M. Riegl, and S. Waitzmanová. (2017) Migration as a political and public phenomenon: The case of Czech Republic. In: R. Łoś and A. Kobierecka (eds.) *The V4 Towards Migration Challenges in Europe: An Analysis and Recommendations.* Łódź: Wydawnictwo Uniwersytetu Łódzkiego.

Bilefsky, D. and J. Richter. (2016) Czech man is charged with attempted terrorism. *The New York Times*, August 2. https://www.nytimes.com/2016/08/03/world/europe/czech-man-attempted-terrorism.html?ref=world.

Billig, M. (1995) *Banal Nationalism.* London: Sage Publications.

Bohuslavová, R. and O. Danda. (2018) Drahoš: K migrační krizi se vyslovuji jasně. Vítač nejsem. *Právo*, January 18. https://www.novinky.cz/domaci/460831-drahos-k-migracni-krizi-se-vyslovuji-jasne-vitac-nejsem.html.

Brubaker, R. (2017) Between nationalism and civilizationism: The European populist moment in comparative perspective. *Ethnic and Racial Studies* 40(8): 1191–226.

Buchert, V. and I. Hamšíkm. (2011) Miloš Zeman: Nepřítelem je Islám. *Reflex*, August 4. https://www.reflex.cz/clanek/zpravy/44753/milos-zeman-nepritelem-je-islam.html.

Cameron, R. (2018) Milos Zeman vote settles Czech presidency – or does it? BBC, January 27. https://www.bbc.com/news/world-europe-42848835.

Canovan, M. (1999) Trust the people! Populism and the two faces of democracy. *Political Studies* 47(1): 2–16.

Červenka, J. (2018) Postoj české veřejnosti k přijímání uprchlíků – duben 2018. *Tisková zpráva Centra pro výzkum verejného mínění* (CVVM), June 8. https://cvvm.soc.cas.cz/cz/tiskove-zpravy/politicke/mezinarodni-vztahy/4649-postoj-ceske-verejnosti-k-prijimani-uprchliku-duben-2018.

Česká televize. (2018) Prezidentský duel – Finále. *Česká televize*, January 25. https://www.ceskatelevize.cz/porady/12026078214-volba-prezidenta/2184 11033190125-prezidentsky-duel-finale/.

Česká televize 1. (2018) První prezidentský duel. *Česká televise 1*, January 24.

Crawley, H. and D. Skleparis. (2018) Refugees, migrants, neither, both: Categorical fetishism and the politics of bounding in Europe's "migration crisis." *Journal of Ethnic and Migration Studies* 44(1): 48–64.

ČTK (*Česká tisková kancelář*). (2015a) Proč zrovna teď Čechům vadí uprchlíci? Experti mají odpověď. *Týden.cz*, September 4. https://www.tyden.cz/rubri ky/domaci/proc-zrovna-ted-cechum-vadi-uprchlici-experti-maji-odpoved_35 4675.html.

ČTK (*Česká tisková kancelář*). (2015b) Zeman: Refugees will apply sharia law. *Prague Post*, October 16. https://www.praguepost.com/czech-news/50288-zeman-refugees-will-apply-sharia-law.

ČTK (*Česká tisková kancelář*). (2018) Zeman backs advertisement linking Drahoš with migration. *Prague Daily Monitor*, January 19. http://praguemonitor.com/2018/01/19/zeman-backs-advertisement-linking-draho%C5%A1-migration.

Čulík, J. (2015) Beyond Hungary: How the Czech Republic and Slovakia are responding to refugees. *The Conversation*, September 7. https://theconversation.

com/beyond-hungary-how-the-czech-republic-and-slovakia-are-responding-to-refugees-47122.

Čulík, J. (2017) Why is the Czech Republic so hostile to Muslims and refugees? *Europe Now*, February 9. http://eprints.gla.ac.uk/136656/.

Czech Statistical Office. (2019) Data on number of foreigners. Czech Statistical Office, May 14. https://www.czso.cz/csu/cizinci/number-of-foreigners-data.

Dirks, G. E. (1998) Factors underlying migration and refugee issues: Responses and cooperation among OECD member states. *Citizenship Studies* 2(3): 377–95.

Durkheim, É. (1995 [1912]) *The Elementary Forms of the Religious Life*. London: The Free Press.

Eckhardt, I. (2013) Update: Ex-PM Milos Zeman wins Czech presidential vote. *Actualne.cz*, January 26. https://zpravy.aktualne.cz/update-ex-pm-milos-zeman-wins-czech-presidential-vote/r~i:article:769669/.

Enroth, H. (2019) The return of the repressed: Populism and democracy revisited. *American Journal of Cultural Sociology*. doi: 10.1057/s41290-019-00080-z.

Fahrenthold, D. A. (2016) Trump recorded having extremely lewd conversation about women in 2005. *The Washington Post*, October 8. https://www.washingtonpost.com/politics/trump-recorded-having-extremely-lewd-conversation-about-women-in-2005/2016/10/07/3b9ce776-8cb4-11e6-bf8a-3d26847eeed4_story.html.

Galston, W. A. (2018) Order from chaos: The rise of European populism and the collapse of the center-left. Brookings Institution, March 8. https://www.brookings.edu/blog/order-from-chaos/2018/03/08/the-rise-of-european-populism-and-the-collapse-of-the-center-left/.

Gardner-Gill, B. (2018) The Czech Republic's populist president. *Stanford Politics*, February 20. https://stanfordpolitics.org/2018/02/20/czech-republics-populist-president/.

Gauna, A. F. (2018) Populism, heroism, and revolution: Chávez's cultural performances in Venezuela, 1999–2012. *American Journal of Cultural Sociology* 6(1): 37–59.

Geertz, C. (1973) *The Interpretation of Cultures: Selected Essays*. New York: Basic Books.

Goodman, S., A. Sirriyeh, and S. McMahon. (2017) The evolving (re)categorisations of refugees throughout the "refugee/migrant crisis." *Journal of Community & Applied Social Psychology* 27(2): 105–14.

Hanley, S. (2018) The Czech presidential elections: A tale of two populisms? *In the Long Run*, March 6. http://www.inthelongrun.org/articles/article/the-czech-presidential-elections-a-tale-of-two-populisms/.

Havlík, V. (2019) Technocratic populism and political illiberalism in Central Europe. *Problems of Post-Communism* 66(6): 369–84.

Havlík, V. and P. Voda. (2018) Cleavages, protest or voting for hope? The rise of centrist populist parties in the Czech Republic. *Swiss Political Science Review* 24(2): 161–86.

Hawkins, K. A. (2009) Is Chávez populist? Measuring populist discourse in comparative perspective. *Comparative Political Studies* 42(8): 1040–67.

Hejl, J. (2016) Iráčtí křesťané odjeli do Německa. Nadace přesto zvažuje, že do Česka přivede další uprchlíky. *Aktuálně.cz*, July 6. https://zpravy.aktualne.cz/domaci/nevydavat-krestane-odjeli-do-nemecka-nadace-presto-zvazuje-z/r~bd4616d83f8b11e6a3e5002590604f2e/.

Hornát, J. (2015) The Prague Café: A brief incursion into Czech presidential discourse. *openDemocracy*, November 11. https://www.opendemocracy.net/en/can-europe-make-it/prague-caf-brief-incursion-into-czech-presidential-discourse/.

Hovorková, J. (2016) Zeman: Příští rok se migrační vlna přelije přes naše území. *Forum 24*, January 25. https://forum24.cz/zeman-pristi-rok-se-migracni-vlna-prelije-pres-nase-uzemi/.

Huntington, S. P. (1996) *The Clash of Civilizations and the Remaking of World Order*. New York: Simon & Schuster.

iDNES.cz. (2017) Drahoš by nejmenoval vládu závislou na KSČM. 2600 migrantů není problém, řekl. *iDNES.cz*, June 29. https://www.idnes.cz/zpravy/domaci/diskuse-s-prezidentskym-kandidatem-jiri-drahosem.A170629_175731_domaci_kop.

Jaworsky, B. N. (2016) *The Boundaries of Belonging: Online Work of Immigration-Related Social Movement Organizations*. Cham: Palgrave Macmillan.

Jelínková, M. (2019) A refugee crisis without refugees: Policy and media discourse on refugees in the Czech Republic and its implications. *Central European Journal of Public Policy* 13(1): 33–45.

Junek, A. (2017) Výzva: Tyto volby rozhodne imaginární 13. imigrant, tvrdí ekonom Tomáš Sedláček. *Seznam Zpravy*, September 25. https://www.seznamzpravy.cz/clanek/tyto-volby-rozhodne-imaginarni-13-imigrant-tvrdi-ekonom-tomas-sedlacek-37366.

Junker, A. and C. Chan. (2019) Fault line in the civil sphere: Explaining new divisions in Hong Kong's opposition movement. In: J. C. Alexander, D. A. Palmer, S. Park, and A. S.-M. Ku (eds.) *The Civil Sphere in East Asia*. New York: Cambridge University Press.

Kalan, D. (2018) Exclusive: Jiri Drahos – the dark horse in the Czech presidential elections. *Euronews*, June 8. https://www.euronews.com/2018/01/12/jiri-drahos-the-dark-horse-in-the-czech-presidential-elections.

Kane, A. (1991) Cultural analysis in historical sociology: The analytic and concrete forms of the autonomy of culture. *Sociological Theory* 9(1): 53–69.

Kreč, L. and R. Bartoníček. (2018) Drahoš: Lidé si myslí, že k nim má Zeman blízko. Je to ale výsostný intelektuál, který v životě nepřeřízl prkno a neví, co je fyzická práce. *Hospodářské noviny*, January 16. https://archiv.ihned.cz/c1-66018150-drahos-jsem-lidem-bliz-nez-milos-zeman-a-chci-jim-vysvetlit-ze-dovedu-jejich-zajmy-zastavat-stejne-jako-on.

Laclau, E. (2005) *On Populist Reason*. London: Verso.

Lendvai, P. (1971) *Antisemitism without Jews: Communist Eastern Europe*. Garden City, NY: Doubleday.

McEnchroe, T. (2019) ECJ launches hearings into migration quota case against Czech Republic, Hungary and Poland. *Radio Praha*, May 15. https://www.radio.cz/en/section/news/ecj-lauches-hearings-into-migration-quota-case-against-czech-republic-hungary-and-poland.

Milačić, F. and I. Vuković. (2018) The rise of the politics of national identity: New evidence from Western Europe. *Ethnopolitics* 17(5): 443–60.

Moffitt, B. (2016) *The Global Rise of Populism: Performance, Political Style, and Representation*. Stanford: Stanford University Press.

Mudde, C. (2007) *Populist Radical Right Parties in Europe*. Cambridge: Cambridge University Press.

Mudde, C. and C. R. Kaltwasser. (2013) Exclusionary vs. inclusionary populism:

Comparing Contemporary Europe and Latin America. *Government and Opposition* 48(2): 147–74.

Müller, J.-W. (2016) *What Is Populism?* Philadelphia: University of Pennsylvania Press.

Naxera, V. and P. Krčál. (2018) "This is a controlled invasion": The Czech president Miloš Zeman's populist perception of Islam and immigration as security threats. *Journal of Nationalism, Memory & Language Politics* 12(2): 192–215.

Naxera, V. and P. Krčál. (2019) "You can't corrupt eight million voters": Corruption as a topic in Miloš Zeman's populist strategy. *Studies of Transition States and Societies* 11(1): 3–18.

Noack, R. (2014) The expletive-filled presidential interview that has all of the Czech Republic embarrassed. *The Washington Post*, November 4. https://www.washingtonpost.com/news/worldviews/wp/2014/11/04/the-expletive-filled-presidential-interview-that-has-all-of-the-czech-republic-embarrassed/?utm_term=.ff79d1b66222.

Ono, K. A. and J. M. Sloop. (2002) *Shifting Borders: Rhetoric, Immigration, and California's Proposition 187.* Philadelphia: Temple University Press.

Petersen, W. (1966) Success story, Japanese American style. *The New York Times*, January 9. https://timesmachine.nytimes.com/timesmachine/1966/01/09/356013502.html?pageNumber=180.

Pew Research Center. (2017) Europe's growing Muslim population. Pew Research Center, November 29. http://www.pewforum.org/2017/11/29/europes-growing-muslim-population/.

Pop-Eleches, G. (2010) Throwing out the bums: Protest voting and unorthodox parties after communism. *World Politics* 62(2): 221–60.

Rabušic, S. L. and B-E. Chromková Manea. (2018) *Hodnoty a postoje v České republice 1991–2017 (Pramenná publikace European Values Study).* Brno: Masarykova univerzita (Muni Press).

Reisigl, M. J. (2008) Rhetoric of political speeches. In: K. Knapp and G. Antos (eds.) *Handbook of Communication in the Public Sphere*, Vol. 4. Berlin and New York: Mouton de Gruyter.

Santa Ana, O. (1999) *Brown Tide Rising: Metaphors of Latinos in Contemporary American Public Discourse.* Austin: University of Texas Press.

Santora, M. (2018) Czech Republic re-elects Milos Zeman, populist leader and foe of migrants. *The New York Times*, January 27. https://www.nytimes.com/2018/01/27/world/europe/czech-election-milos-zeman.html.

Schultheis, E. (2017) The Czech Republic's fake news problem. *The Atlantic*, October 21. https://www.theatlantic.com/international/archive/2017/10/fake-news-in-the-czech-republic/543591/.

Sedláčková, L. (2010) *Islám v médiích.* Liberec: Nakladatelství Bor.

Slačálek, O. and E. Svobodová. (2018) The Czech Islamophobic movement: Beyond "populism?" *Patterns of Prejudice* 52(5): 479–95.

Štětka, V. (2016) Between instrumentalization and para-journalism: Current challenges to democratic roles of the media in the Czech Republic. Frontiers of Democracy Working Papers. https://publications.ceu.edu/node/44975.

Stevis-Gridneff, M. and M. Pronczuk. (2020) EU Court rules 3 countries violated deal on refugee quotas. *The New York Times*, April 2. https://www.nytimes.com/2020/04/02/world/europe/european-court-refugees-hungary-poland-czech-republic.html.

Stojarová, V. (2018) Populist, radical and extremist political parties in Visegrad countries vis à vis the migration crisis: In the name of the people and the nation in Central Europe. *Open Political Science* 1(1): 32–45.
Strapáčová, M. and V. Hloušek. (2018) Anti-Islamism without Moslems: Cognitive frames of Czech antimigrant politics. *Journal of Nationalism, Memory & Language Politics* 12(1): 1–30.
Swain, D. (2018) Zeman, again. *Jacobin Magazine*, November 2. https://www.jacobinmag.com/2018/02/czech-republic-milos-zeman-presidential-elections.
Tkaczyk, M., P. Pospěch, and J. Macek. (2015) *Analýza mediálního pokrytí uprchlické krize (výzkumná zpráva).* Brno: Masarykova univerzita (Muni Press).
TV Barrandov. (2018a) Rozhovor s Milošem Zemanem, Prezidentem České Republiky. *TV Barrandov*, January 1.
TV Barrandov. (2018b) Rozhovor s Milošem Zemanem, Prezidentem České Republiky. *TV Barrandov*, January 18.
Visvizi, A. (2017) Querying the migration–populism nexus: Poland and Greece in focus. Institute of European Democrats (IED), June 8. https://www.iedonline.eu/download/2017/IED-Budapest-Visvizi.pdf?m=1500636444&.
Western Cannon. (2017) Czech president: "Trojan Horse" migrant wave an "organised invasion" of Europe. YouTube, December 19. https://www.youtube.com/watch?v=mYKJlc2CLJE.
Weyland, K. (2001) Clarifying a contested concept: Populism in the study of Latin American politics. *Comparative Politics* 34(1): 1–22.
Zeman, M. (2013) Inauguration Speech of Miloš Zeman. Prague Castle, President of the CR, March 8. https://www.hrad.cz/en/president-of-the-cr/current-president-of-the-cr/selected-speeches-and-interviews/inauguration-speech-of-milos-zeman-11885.
Zeman, M. (2017) Speech of the president of the Czech Republic at the 72nd session of UN General Assembly. Prague Castle, President of the CR, September 19. https://www.hrad.cz/en/president-of-the-cr/current-president-of-the-cr/selected-speeches-and-interviews/speech-of-the-president-of-the-czech-republic-at-the-72nd-session-of-un-general-assembly-13609.

7

Memory Culture, the Civil Sphere, and Right-Wing Populism in Germany

The Resistible Rise of the *Alternative für Deutschland* (AfD)
Werner Binder

Until recently, Germany considered itself immune from the siren calls of right-wing populism to which other societies have succumbed. The historical experience of Nazi rule and the collective memory of the Holocaust were often thought of as vaccinations against the allures of nationalism, racism, and petty resentment, which therefore were presumably not able to gain a foothold in German society at large. This alleged immunity has been put into question by the astonishing rise of the AfD (*Alternative für Deutschland*/Alternative for Germany), which started in 2013 as a "party of professors" (mainly in economics) unsatisfied with the political management of the Greek debt crisis but quickly transformed into an Islamophobic anti-immigration party, which is currently the biggest opposition party in the German parliament. The AfD not only changed the party landscape in Germany, being the first successful party right of the Christian Democrats (CDU/CSU), but also had a tremendous impact on the German civil discourse in "trying to expand the limits of what is sayable."[1] Most notably, the party introduced a "folkish" vocabulary into political discourse that was not just reminiscent of but often directly borrowed from Nazi speak while attacking the memory culture and "Holocaust identity" of contemporary Germany. Since its inception, the party has been working ceaselessly toward a narrowing down of the boundaries of solidarity in German society and toward a closing of the German mind.

This chapter analyzes the rise of right-wing populism in Germany empirically while exploring the link between memory cultures and civil solidarity theoretically. In Jeffrey C. Alexander's theory of the civil sphere (2006), universal solidarity is conceived as a utopian idea, constantly, albeit distortedly, being realized in real civil societies suffering from social strains and tensions. According to Alexander, space and time, being mere "vagaries" (2006: 460) and "contingencies" (2006: 571), lead to contradictions in the institutionalization of the universal values of the civil sphere and consequently limit the expansion of solidarity. While it is certainly true that nation-states and their foundational "myths of origin" define a civil core group vis-à-vis uncivil outsiders (Alexander 2006: 196–202), the German case suggests that national memory cultures may even facilitate the incorporation of outsiders and strangers into civil society. Consequently, collective memory may be as important for the progressive movements of the civil sphere as it is for their reactionary counterparts. It is the canonization of the Holocaust as the foundational myth of an open German society that has recently come under attack by right-wing populists in Germany. Thus, this chapter contributes not only to the further development of civil sphere theory (CST), highlighting the role of collective memory and accounting for populist movements within the framework, but also to the study of collective memory and populism in general, extending the theoretical framework of CST to relatively uncharted territories, which so far have not been adequately mapped by the binary code of the civil sphere.

In the first section, I introduce the theoretical concepts of the civil sphere, collective memory, and memory culture, arguing that not only anticivil discursive formations but also the universalizing discourse of civil society reference history in nostalgic or traumatic ways. Elaborating the concept of memory culture, I demonstrate how collective memory as a system of collective representations, not only structured by the binary code of the civil sphere but itself structuring the discourse of civil society, fits into the CST framework. The second section discusses how West German postwar society and its civil sphere were shaped by three consecutive memory cultures, while the East German state propagated a distinct socialist memory culture. After the war, West Germany was still dominated by a folkish memory culture, mourning the defeat of the Germans in World War II while quickly aligning itself with "the West" against the "communist threat." In the 1950s and 1960s, this primordial conception of identity was replaced by the heroic "*Wirtschaftswunder*" identity, referencing the hyperinflation and economic crisis of the 1920s as cultural trauma. In the 1970s and 1980s, a new "Holocaust" identity emerged with the collective guilt of the Germans in World War II as its traumatic core. After reunification, German identity became once more a contested ground, even though the Holocaust identity was further institutionalized in the 1990s and early 2000s. The third section will account for the rise of the AfD and its rapid transformation from an ordoliberal immigration-friendly, Euroskeptic party to an anti-immigration, right-wing populist party.

In doing so, this study solves two puzzles: Why is the AfD more successful in Eastern Germany? And why do its representatives attack Germany's official memory culture, despite questionable political gains and backlash from civil society? In the wake of the "refugee crisis," it became clear that the ethics of solidarity implied by (or blamed on) Germany's Holocaust identity, which is more strongly rooted in Western Germany, are incompatible with the political aims of the right-wing populists, who reject both postwar Germanys in favor of a racially and culturally homogenized imagination of a "pre-postwar" Germany. Thus, this study demonstrates how the concept of memory culture may aid our understanding of real civil societies and their struggles with populism.

The Civil Sphere, Collective Memory, and Memory Culture

Heir to the Parsonian conception of a "societal community," the "civil sphere" is a social system that facilitates communal feelings of belonging and solidarity in modern society. Alexander (2006), who coined the term, emphasizes the autonomy of the civil sphere vis-à-vis other social spheres – for example, the state or the market – by virtue of a cultural code used to draw symbolic boundaries between those who deserve solidarity and inclusion and those who do not. Drawing on Durkheim and the structuralist tradition, Alexander conceptualizes the code of civil society as a binary between "sacred" and "profane," respectively "democratic" and "repressive." This binary provides a classificatory grid for (Durkheimian) collective representations, shared social meanings that allow a society to make sense of itself.

Collective memory can be conceived as a set of collective representations of a society's past, structured by the cultural grid and symbolic binaries of civil society. Rather than being a disengaged representation of history, collective memory is a selective representation of events with emotional and moral significance for a society, which aligns with the intuitions of CST (cf. Alexander 2006). Furthermore, I regard collective memory as formative, not just culturally structured but structuring the discourse of civil society. While symbolic binaries provide a grid for mapping the discourse of civil society, its particular "landscape of meaning" (Reed 2011) is shaped by sedimented layers of remembered history, with significant historical events and epochs in the role of landmarks providing a moral compass and orientation. Collective memories are able to form cultural systems in the Geertzian sense (cf. Schwartz 1996), being at the same time models of history and models for (civil) society. Drawing on Aleida Assmann (2013), I will use the term "memory culture" to refer to a cultural system of collective representations and social practices organized around the collective memory of certain formative historical events and epochs.

It is as "memory culture" that collective memory becomes an integral part of the civil sphere, produced and reproduced by educational and communicative institutions, and often protected by law and other regulative institutions.[2] In contrast to political memory cultures imposed by authoritarian and totalitarian states, civil memory cultures typically emerge from below, initially promoted by social movements and other nonstate actors. A crucial carrier group for collective memories are generations, with generational shifts often paving the way for the emergence of new memory cultures (cf. Eyerman 2004: 69ff.; Giesen 2004: 127ff.). While it is often possible to discern a hegemonic memory culture, there are always side- and undercurrents to the mainstream. Real civil societies harbor a plurality of memory cultures, including remnants from former hegemonic memory cultures as well as subaltern countermemories.[3] Memory cultures matter in the context of the ongoing struggles of the civil sphere, as each memory culture allows for (or at least favors) different modes of incorporation as well as different forms of social solidarity.

The link between collective memory and social solidarity can be found in Alexander's *The Civil Sphere* (2006: 199–202), although it is underdeveloped and mostly confined to the distortive effects of foundational myths narrowing the scope of social solidarity. In search of a more appreciative view on collective memory as a facilitator of solidarity, we can turn toward Alexander's works on cultural trauma: in "constructing cultural traumas," identifying with "the suffering of others," Alexander (2004: 1) writes, "societies expand the circle of the we." Nonetheless, it should be noted that Alexander's constructivist theory of cultural trauma avoids any reference to "collective memory," steering clear of "lay theories" of cultural trauma, which treat it as analogous to individual traumas rooted in experience and memory. While a clear distinction between collective memory and cultural trauma (and, consequently, social solidarity) may have a certain intellectual appeal, there is an argument to be made about a less constructivist – but no less cultural – understanding of how societies deal with their past.

In the collaborative book *Cultural Trauma and Collective Identity* (Alexander et al. 2004), "the line between constructivist and realist or naturalistic notions of trauma was not easily maintained," one of Alexander's collaborators, Ron Eyerman (2019: 4), retrospectively admits. In order to retain the link between collective memory, cultural trauma, and social solidarity, respectively, I follow the example of Eyerman (2004) and Giesen (2004), who both (in their own way)

181

advocate a moderate constructivism that leaves room for collective memories as well as traumatic experiences. I believe that the notion of collective memory, understood as "memory culture" (Assmann 2013), can be integrated seamlessly into Alexander's general theoretical framework (2006), which would in turn allow us to investigate the links between specific collective memories and social solidarity empirically. Despite the inherent universalism of the civil sphere, the particular history of a (civil) society, not simply constructed but rather reconstructed as collective memory, does not need to be an obstacle to the expansion of social solidarity but may instead become the driving force behind its universalizing discourse. Contemporary German memory culture, as discussed by Assmann (2013), is a paradigmatic example of collective memory in service of – and formative of – a civil sphere.

Memory cultures do not have to revolve around the suffering of others but may instead be organized around primordial "myths of origin," traumatic suffering of one's own group or the nostalgic remembrance of past triumphs and achievements – often resulting in a shrinking "circle of the we." This is particularly salient in the case of (radical right) populist memory cultures, which frequently impose nativist limitations on solidarity and belonging, often combining the nostalgic longing for a glorious past with apocalyptic visions and excessive self-victimization: the innocent "people" suffering at the hand of corrupt elites and immoral minorities can only be saved by the populist hero. The narrow moralistic imagination of "the people" in the populist discourse excludes a large number of citizens from the societal community (liberals, minorities etc.), while its political antipluralism threatens to undermine the foundations of an autonomous civil sphere, which thrives on pluralism beyond the populist "common sense" and "will of the people" (cf. Müller 2016). While the polarizing logic of populism ostensibly exemplifies the general logic of the discourse of civil society (Alexander 2019a: 5), populist discourses in fact twist this logic in uncivil ways, limiting the free play of signifiers, reducing social meanings to primordial facts, and trying to monopolize the symbolic means of discursive production.

Facing the populist backlash, civil society must rely on civil memory cultures shaped by collective representations of historical injustices and struggles. The subjugation of women and the feminist struggle, slavery and the civil rights movement, anti-Semitism and the quest for Jewish emancipation are not only historical cases of uncivil exclusion and "civil repair" (see Alexander 2006) but have also become an integral part of the discourse of American civil society. Recognizing collective memory at the heart of civil society, we are able to understand why populists engage in acts of historic revisionism despite their modest impact on day-to-day politics. Controversies over the history and memory of a society – for example, about Confederate flags in the United States (Talbert 2017) – are not minor skirmishes in the struggle over the civil sphere but concerted efforts to limit or expand circles of belonging and solidarity. Paraphrasing Orwell, we can say: whoever controls the meanings of the past and is able to mobilize them effectively in the struggles over the civil sphere controls the direction in which society is heading.

Memory Culture, the Civil Sphere, and National Identity in Postwar Germany

In the 1930s, the Weimar Republic's fledgling civil sphere was obliterated by Nazi totalitarianism. A German civil sphere re-emerged after World War II, albeit with limited autonomy, in a now-divided country. In Soviet-occupied East Germany, the communist DDR (German Democratic Republic) effectively abolished the civil sphere, cracking down on social movements, censuring the media, and controlling the courts. It "denazified" its elites and propagated a top-down *socialist memory culture*, casting itself as antifascist Germany, while the Western BRD (Federal Republic of Germany) became the legal successor of Nazi Germany. The West German civil sphere, despite formal autonomy and democratic re-education, was initially stagnant and depoliticized, only gaining political momentum and autonomy from the 1960s onward. With the reunification of Germany in 1990, the West German civil discourse and memory culture spread to the East, creating once more a unified German civil sphere. Nevertheless, even today, there are marked cultural-political differences between Western and Eastern Germany, the populist AfD getting twice as many votes in the "new" federal states. I will now briefly sketch the postwar developments regarding the civil sphere and memory culture in the BRD, still dominant in the reunified Germany, as well as some characteristics of the DDR memory culture, which are necessary to account for the specific appeal of populism in Eastern Germany.

Primordial Identity and Folkish Memory Culture

After World War II, East Germany's state propaganda celebrated the victory of the Allies as a liberation from fascism, while at the same time symbolically excluding its citizens from the group of perpetrators. In contrast, most West Germans regarded the outcome of the war as a defeat, although they did not see themselves as perpetrators either, balancing German war atrocities with war crimes committed against

Germans, such as mass bombings and violent expulsions. West German postwar discourses on national identity hardly mentioned the failed Weimar Republic or polluted Nazi Germany but instead appealed to primordial qualities, "timeless German virtues" (Giesen 2004: 125), and classic German culture. Grounding national unity in ethnicity, language, and culture (which entailed the call for reunification with East Germany), this folkish memory culture maintained certain continuities with Nazi ideology, including a contempt for pluralism, while departing in other ways: for example, no longer conceiving primordialism primarily in biological or racial terms. By aligning itself quickly with "Western civilization" against the "Eastern Bloc," the postwar BRD overcame its narrow-minded nationalism, embracing the spirit of trans-Atlanticism instead. Moving forward, both Germanys decided to leave the burden of their past behind.

After the war, both German states, but particularly the West, had to deal with the influx of millions of refugees (about 10 to 12 million), mostly German-speakers expelled from former German or occupied territories, which raised questions of solidarity and belonging. Notwithstanding commonalities in language and culture, the incorporation of (largely unwelcome) masses of refugees into both new German societies was a difficult and astounding feat. Despite its narrow breadth, the primordial collective identity and folkish memory culture of West Germany allowed for the incorporation of large numbers of ethnic Germans (*Volksdeutsche*) who had not been citizens of the German empire (*Reichsdeutsche*). In West Germany, these ethnic Germans, who often had been living abroad for centuries, were granted a status (*Aussiedler*) different from foreigners (*Ausländer*), which allowed for their immediate naturalization. In accordance with the Stalinist doctrine of "socialism in one country," the "peasant and worker state" of the DDR had a similar mode of incorporation, based not only on a commitment to socialism, but also on ethnicity and culture. This primordial mode of incorporation remained important until after reunification, when more than a million "ethnic" Germans from former communist countries resettled in Germany as citizens. As in the case of the "new" citizens from the former DDR, the political-cultural integration of these newcomers into the reunified BRD is often questioned by liberals, as they disproportionally vote for the populist AfD.

Wirtschaftswunder *Identity and Ordoliberal Memory Culture*

In order to understand the political culture of contemporary Germany, we must examine the transformation of memory culture in the old BRD.

A new form of German national identity emerged in the 1950s and 1960s in West Germany, accompanying the miraculous economic recovery dubbed the *Wirtschaftswunder* (Giesen 2004: 125f.; Tognato 2012: 41–53). The heroic narrative of the *Wirtschaftswunder* is still today an important strand of German memory culture and has played a crucial role in the emergence of right-wing populism in Germany. In order to understand the peculiar combination of neoliberal economic policies and illiberal conservative authoritarianism characteristic of large parts of the German conservative discourse and the early AfD, it is necessary to discuss the economic doctrine of ordoliberalism, which emerged during the economic crisis in the 1920s and became hugely influential in postwar Germany. This specific German brand of economic liberalism, named after the journal *ORDO*, established in 1948, "sits midway between Keynesian interventionism and neoliberalism" (Grimm 2015: 266), advocating a strong state and a proper legal-political framework for a functioning market society.

Ordoliberalism has been less a reaction to the excesses of state control during Nazism and World War II, which Foucault claimed in his lectures on biopolitics (2008: 322f.), than a response to the perceived failure of liberalism in the 1920s. The early proponents of ordoliberalism not only opposed the democratic pluralism of the Weimar Republic but also were initially supporters of the Nazi government takeover and turned only at the end of the 1930s into critics of national socialism (Manow 2001: 181f.). Ordoliberalism, as Philip Manow (2001: 185–8) has shown, has an elective affinity with political illiberalism, conceptualizing the market as a disciplinary tool for the moral betterment of society, informed by a "Protestant deep grammar." Critical of the modern welfare state, ordoliberals argued that the state must use work and discipline to deter its citizens from living "in sin." A social and economic order based on market principles must be established and maintained by a strong state with a legal framework encouraging and regulating economic behavior. Rule of law, rather than justice, is a central tenet of ordoliberalism, later echoed in the ordoliberal critique of the political management of the Greek debt crisis (and the AfD's critique of the "refugee crisis").

After World War II, the ordoliberals – supported by the myth that they had always opposed the Nazis – shaped the postwar economic order of West Germany.[4] Ordoliberalism and the heroic narrative of the economic miracle became a central part of West German collective memory and identity, symbolized by the former currency the *Deutsche Mark* and the *Deutsche Bundesbank* as the leading institution (cf. Tognato 2012: 41–53). The *Wirtschaftswunder* identity gave (West) Germans a positive self-representation, untarnished by the defeat and the war crimes of

World War II. In comparison to the ethno-cultural conception of German identity, the ordoliberal *Wirtschaftswunder* identity expanded inclusion into West German society on the basis of "civic-economic participation" (cf. Jaworsky 2015). Only by participating in the economic reconstruction of West Germany did the postwar German refugees truly become citizens, and there was even a (limited) incorporation of millions of labor migrants (the so-called "*Gastarbeiter*"), mostly from Southern Europe and Turkey, into West German society. While the DDR also hosted workers from socialist "brother" states such as Cuba or Vietnam, these workers were strongly segregated and usually not allowed to stay for longer periods of time, which left East Germany much more ethnically homogeneous than the West.

Although West Germany's economic miracle ended with the oil crisis in 1973, it has an afterlife in the nostalgic ordoliberal memory culture, which shapes German conservative policies even today. In the introduction to his book on societalization, Alexander (2019b: 1f.) observes that the German economist Hans-Werner Sinn, who happens to be an exemplary ordoliberal thinker, fails to take into account the role of the "civil sphere" when rejecting Angela Merkel's rescue policy in the Greek debt crisis as economically unfeasible and – if one looks closer – morally wrong. Indeed, one can even argue that ordoliberal thinking has no place for a civil sphere independent of the state and the market. The rules of the game are set by a political and economic elite to ensure the functioning of the market and promote the virtue of citizens, who are reduced to atomistic economic actors. Being highly skeptical toward an autonomous civil sphere capable of changing the rules of the game, ordoliberal governance can in principle dispense with public discourse and democracy, aiming instead for output legitimacy: economic freedom, prosperity, and moral virtue.

Holocaust Identity and Postheroic Memory Culture

During the *Wirtschaftswunder* years, West Germany, despite a free press and democratic elections, was not yet fully democratized owing to the limited autonomy of its commercialized and de-politicized civil sphere (accurately described by Habermas 1989 [1962]). The conservative party (along with former Nazis) dominated the political landscape well into the 1960s, a decade of cultural and political turmoil also in West Germany. Only in the 1970s and 1980s did German civil society start to face the dark sides of recent German history, giving rise to a postheroic identity and memory culture centered on the Holocaust. Immediately following the war, Karl Jaspers (2000 [1947]: 65) spoke of the "metaphysical guilt" of the Germans, resulting from "the lack of absolute solidarity with the human being as such"– albeit with little public resonance. It needed a new generation of Germans, often critical of capitalism, to confront their parents and political elites about their involvement in Nazi crimes and to discredit the heroic narrative of the economic miracle as the foundation of German identity. This call for a new German identity is probably best captured by Adorno's (1998: 191) famous line from a radio speech broadcast in 1966, which summarizes the single most important ideal of democratic education as follows: "never again Auschwitz."

The student movement in the 1960s played a crucial role for German civil society coming to terms with its polluted past (*Vergangenheitsbewältigung*), although the memory politics of the student activists were still subordinated to a broader antifascist and anticapitalist agenda. This started to change with the election of Willy Brandt, who spent the Nazi years in exile, as German chancellor in 1969. In his election campaign, the leader of the Social Democrats (SPD) successfully called upon the German people "to dare more democracy." It was Brandt's iconic knee fall at the Warsaw memorial in 1970 (cf. Rauer 2006) that moved the question of German guilt into the center of public debate. Nevertheless, in the 1970s and 1980s, this postheroic memory culture based on Germany's "trauma of perpetrators" (Giesen 2004) was still a grassroots phenomenon, largely independent of state and mainstream culture, its generational carrier group consisting mainly of aged members of the former counterculture (Assmann 2013).[5]

In the 1980s, Germany's memory culture was still hotly debated, as the infamous *Historikerstreit* attests, in which Jürgen Habermas and other intellectuals criticized conservative historians for engaging in – what they viewed as – historical revisionism. In this context, Habermas coined the term "constitutional patriotism" (*Verfassungspatriotismus*), calling for a German identity based on the Holocaust and the universalist values of the constitution. The conservative chancellor Helmut Kohl was clearly not a proponent of this new memory culture, stirring controversy in 1985 when visiting a German military cemetery with Ronald Reagan, where SS soldiers had also been buried, in contrast to his fellow party member and president Richard von Weizsäcker, who, commemorating the fortieth anniversary of the end of the war in 1985, called Germany's capitulation a "day of liberation" – without denying the collective responsibility for the atrocities of the war.

In East Germany, the formation of collective identity vis-à-vis the Nazi atrocities was decidedly different. Here, antifascism was not the hard-fought accomplishment of a grassroots movement but, from the beginning, official state doctrine, a top-down imposition that never

187

became an integral part of DDR culture. The Holocaust could not become a perpetrator trauma, because it was perpetrated by the fascist "other," the DDR seeing itself in continuity with the communist resistance against Nazi Germany. Ironically, the official memory culture of the DDR allowed for the emergence of a neo-Nazi counterculture in East Germany as early as the 1980s. With the reunification of Germany in 1990, nativist conceptions of national identity gained salience in broader parts of the population, especially in the former East. An alternative memory culture emerged, with neo-Nazis gathering at the Kyffhäuser memorial (to await the return of Kaiser Barbarossa) or marching through Dresden (to commemorate the Allied bombing of the city). Even today, despite the lower number of immigrants, the "new" federal states in the East have a higher rate of right-extremist attacks than the "old" federal states – and the anti-immigrant AfD receives more than double the percentage of votes compared to the West.[6]

In the 1990s and 2000s, at the same time as nativist identities and revisionist countermemories consolidated themselves in subcultures, the traumatic memory of the Holocaust became the official memory culture of reunified Germany, embodied by the Memorial to the Murdered Jews of Europe in the center of the new capital, and a point of reference in various political debates. Wreaking havoc on the continent in the past, Germany felt obliged to overcome its national egotism and work toward a peaceful, prosperous, and ever closer European Union – with the Holocaust identity replacing the nationalist *Wirtschaftswunder* identity just as the Euro succeeded the *Deutsche Mark* in 2000 as the official currency (cf. Tognato 2012). Joschka Fischer, foreign minister of the center-left government elected in 1998, justified the German military intervention in the Kosovo conflict, citing Adorno, "I have not only learned: never again war. I have also learned: never again Auschwitz." While such appropriations of the Holocaust memory by the state and institutions triggered criticisms by former activists and left-wing intellectuals (cf. Assmann 2013), it nevertheless remained central to the German civil sphere. Now, the rise of Nazism was primarily remembered as a failure of civil society, and not as a failure of liberalism, and as a total breakdown of solidarity to be avoided at all costs in the future. Being much more than shared history, Germany's memory culture entails an "ethical framework," which "ties remembering to the universal value of human rights" (Assmann 2013: 207), thus fusing past, present, and future in the context of civic action.

With regard to social inclusion, German Holocaust identity promotes multiculturalism and cross-group solidarity, which has been of particular importance for the incorporation of refugees and asylum seekers into

German society. From 1991 to 2005, Germany admitted more than 200,000 Jews as "refugees" (*Kontingentflüchtlinge*) from former Soviet territories, vastly outnumbering the existing Jewish population, in a conscious effort to revive Jewish life in Germany. Inclusion, however, always entails an exclusion of sorts: the German civil sphere, rooted in its postheroic memory culture, excludes all those not willing to live up to its moral standard, which applies not only to domestic nationalists and racists but also to intolerant or even anti-Semitic newcomers – an issue that is often debated in relation to Muslim immigration. When it comes to Germany's Holocaust identity, allegiance to its memory culture, constitutional patriotism, and solidarity with vulnerable minorities are non-negotiable criteria of belonging. Nevertheless, the public consensus emerging in the two decades following reunification was soon to be questioned by the ordoliberals of the early AfD as well as the right-wing radicals who later hijacked the party.

The Resistible Rise of the AfD

The unexpected success of the AfD, which was founded in 2013 as an ordoliberal Euroskeptic party but quickly turned into an anti-immigration populist party, was a political earthquake that shook not only the German party system but also civil society to its core. Failing to enter the parliament in 2013, the party gained a foothold in several regional parliaments and finally garnered 12.6 percent in the federal elections in 2017, emerging as the biggest opposition party in the German parliament after the coalition of the two "people's parties" (CDU/CSU and SPD). In the following section, I account for the rise and transformation of the AfD in the context of the memory cultures that define the landscape of meaning of the German civil sphere.

Setting the Stage: The Sarrazin Controversy (2009–2010)

In order to understand the rise of the AfD, we must examine the controversy surrounding public statements by Berlin's former finance senator Thilo Sarrazin, still today a member of the center-left SPD, and the subsequent publication of his book *Germany Abolishes Itself* (2010). Sarrazin argued that the demographic decline in Germany had led to a relative growth of the German lower classes and certain "unproductive" immigrant groups (mainly Turks and Arabs), which posed a threat to the genetic make-up and consequently to the prosperity of Germany. Rooted in an ordoliberal worldview with nostalgic references to the time

189

of the economic miracle, Sarrazin's intervention nevertheless opened a Pandora's box which allowed racism and eugenics to enter German civil discourse.

It all started in 2009, when the respectable Berlin-based cultural magazine *Lettre International* published an interview with Sarrazin, who had just become a member of the executive board of the *Deutsche Bundesbank*. In the interview, Sarrazin discusses the economic and social problems of the German capital (highlighting the difficult heritage of the former socialist East Berlin and the heavily subsidized West Berlin) as obstacles to its competitiveness and future as an elitist city – in itself not a very populist or even popular notion. The interview mainly received publicity for Sarrazin's claim that "70 percent of the Turkish and 90 percent of the Arab population in Berlin" were unwilling to integrate into German society: "I do not have to acknowledge anyone who lives by welfare, denies the legitimacy of the very state that provides that welfare, refuses to care for the education of his children, and constantly produces new little headscarf-girls" (Berberich and Sarrazin 2009).[7] Sarrazin combines the ordoliberal critique of the welfare state with demographic concerns about German society, widespread in German conservatism (usually with regard to the lower classes) and on the far right (mostly concerning immigrants). Although his statement about Turks and Arabs received most of the attention, Sarrazin conceptualizes inclusion not on the basis of ethno-cultural belonging but as civic-economic participation, rooted in ordoliberal memory culture. This is evident from the fact that he criticizes Germans living on social welfare while praising the successful integration of Vietnamese and Eastern European immigrants.

In the book that followed a year later, Sarrazin (2010) applies this reasoning to the whole of Germany, theoretically underpinned by a crude biological and cultural determinism – and, yes, racism. According to Sarrazin, the German welfare state and immigration policy create false incentives, which lead to a relative decline of the productive parts of the population. In the context of Germany's civil memory culture, his claims regarding the heredity of intelligence and the IQ differentials between different ethnic groups, reminiscent of Nazi race theory and eugenics, caused a public scandal which eventually cost him his position at the *Deutsche Bank*. Although Sarrazin explicitly distanced himself from Nazi Germany, bemoaning the loss of Jewish bankers and intelligentsia while pronouncing the new Jewish immigrants a positive influence on German society, his remarks met fierce resistance from civil society and civic associations.[8] Furthermore, his critique of the "Nazi dictatorship" did not prevent him from questioning the official memory culture, identifying the German "Nazi trauma" (2010: 263) as one of the reasons Germany has not been able to take decisive steps to save itself.

At its core, Sarrazin's argument is an ordoliberal critique accusing German political elites of having failed to secure the competitiveness of German society with an adequate legal-political framework, which should include selective immigration policies as well as eugenic family policies: for example, financial incentives for educated women to have children. The (ordoliberal) state has the obligation to protect Germany's economic competitiveness and prosperity, thus saving its civil society, deluded by multiculturalism and political correctness, from itself. From an ordoliberal perspective, there is little need for an autonomous civil sphere because citizens are primarily incorporated into society through their economic activity. Despite these qualifications, Sarrazin's book is clearly racist in identifying the threats to German prosperity and society as follows: (1) the disproportionate growth of the lower classes and migrant groups with an inferior genetic make-up; (2) the spread of cultural patterns undermining the work ethic and civility in German society; and (3) religious doctrines like Islam, supposedly incompatible with German society and economy.

Sarrazin advocates a biological, cultural, and religious racism, portraying specific groups as inherently uncivil, which not only is incompatible with the values of German civil society, shaped by the memory of Holocaust, but also undermines the very conception of an autonomous civil sphere. Once objectified and inherited traits have become decisive for inclusion and exclusion, the civil struggle over meaning ends. Fortunately, Sarrazin's attack against civil society is still part of its discourse; his attempt to reduce the meaning of civility to "hard" biological and cultural facts is just another move in the language game of civil society. In the discourse of German civil society, it was Sarrazin who was portrayed as uncivil and as a threat to the country's multicultural society, although there were prominent conservatives and ordoliberals defending him, usually sharing his concerns while disagreeing with his more provocative statements. The leadership of the center-left Social Democrats tried to exclude Sarrazin from the party – without success. Formally still a member of the SPD, Sarrazin never joined or even publicly endorsed the AfD. Nonetheless, his ordoliberal and racist discourse created a political climate in which the right-wing populism of the AfD could rise and prosper. Interestingly, Sarrazin's argument, setting out from the economy-centric perspective of ordoliberalism but venturing deep into the racist territories of biological and cultural determinism, prefigures the subsequent transformation of the AfD.

191

First Act: The Euro Crisis and Lucke's AfD (2013–2015)

After the success of his first book, which sold over a million copies, Sarrazin published a second on the European debt crisis titled *Europe Does Not Need the Euro* (2012). Sarrazin was one of many German (ordoliberal) economists who opposed Merkel's rescue policy toward Greece. In 2013, the AfD was founded by an economics professor, Bernd Lucke, who left Merkel's CDU over the handling of the Euro crisis. Like Sarrazin, Lucke is a staunch proponent of an ordoliberal worldview upholding competitiveness as a moral principle. Lucke and other ordoliberal critics feared that the political management of the debt crisis and the continued existence of an unreformed monetary union, which ordoliberal economists have been criticizing since the 1990s, could have a negative impact on Germany's as well as Europe's competitiveness. The AfD argued that the loans to Greece and the expansive fiscal policy of the European Central Bank not only violated the moral principle of competitiveness but were also a clear violation of European law (*"Rechtsbruch"*). Warning of the "moral hazards" of Merkel's rescue policy, which threatened to undermine incentives for fiscal responsibility, especially for the states affectionately nicknamed PIIGS (Portugal, Ireland, Italy, Greece, Spain), the party called for disciplinary action and reform: Greece should leave the eurozone, also for its own good; or a "strong" Northern Euro, modeled after Germany's former currency, should be separated from a "weak" Southern Euro; or Germany itself should leave the Euro and reintroduce the *Deutsche Mark* once again as the national currency.

The original AfD was a Euroskeptic party, grounded in an ordoliberal memory culture centered on Germany's economic miracle in the 1950s and 1960s, that mobilized populist resentments against the European Union in the name of national sovereignty (Bebnowski 2015; Grimm 2015). For many in the party, the EU and the Euro were a plot to weaken Germany. In the ordoliberal discourse of the AfD, the EU became a polluted symbol, best captured by the expression "EUdSSR" (alluding to the Soviet Union). Furthermore, the populist anger of the AfD was directed at the established parties in the German parliament, none of which opposed Merkel's rescue policy, ridiculing them as *"Blockparteien"* ("fake" parties of the socialist DDR), or even *"Systemparteien"* ("system parties," a term originally employed by the Nazis). A radical invective language, often drawing inappropriate historical comparisons, which became the trademark of the AfD, was already present at its ordoliberal inception.

In the beginning, the AfD was not yet an anti-immigration party but advocated an active immigration policy attracting qualified immigrants. After narrowly failing to enter the federal parliament in 2013, the party won a few seats in the European elections in 2014. Interestingly, it turned out to be more successful in Eastern Germany, where it campaigned on an anti-immigration ticket. In the "new" federal states, where the *Wirtschaftswunder* identity as well as the Holocaust identity of the old BRD were less anchored in memory culture, the party was also less economically liberal: Eastern party leaders like Björn Höcke defended the welfare state, at least for ethnic Germans, advocating a more "socialist" form of nationalism. Tolerated by the party leadership, the right wing, in which Nazi vocabulary and racist slurs were common, grew increasingly powerful. Flourishing on the fertile ground prepared by Sarrazin, although omitting his critique of the German lower classes, the AfD far right propagated a Nazi-esque *Lebensraumpolitik* in reverse, calling for a defense of the homeland against invasive immigrants while stoking fears about demographic decline and population transfer (using the Nazi term *Umvolkung*).[9]

The (limited) success of Pegida (cf. Heins and Unrau 2020), a Sarrazin-inspired anti-Islam movement founded in 2014 in Dresden, played a crucial role in the radicalization of the AfD. It is no accident that Pegida originated in a city whose local memory culture revolves around its mass bombing by Allied forces in World War II – a striking example of self-victimization resulting in a narrowing of solidarity. Since the 1990s, neo-Nazis and other far-right groups have gathered annually in Dresden on the anniversary of the bombing, February 13 – including future AfD politicians like Höcke, who participated in the sixty-fifth anniversary march in 2010. The emergence of Pegida sparked a debate within the AfD concerning how to position oneself with regard to the Islamophobic message of the movement; this was eventually won by the right wing of the party, which regarded "the protestors as natural allies" (Gauland, quoted in Eppelsheim 2018). While the party leadership around Lucke distanced itself from Pegida, in March 2015, far-right members of the AfD signed a declaration in Erfurt out of solidarity with Pegida and in protest against their own party's ordoliberal leadership. After Höcke, one of the signatories of the declaration, refused to distance himself from the NPD, Germany's (traditional) right-wing extremist party, AfD leader Lucke finally tried to rally the moderates and exclude him from the party, but it was already too late. On July 4, 2015, Frauke Petry, who defended Höcke, the poster boy of the far right, against the party leadership, won a vote against Lucke to succeed him as party leader. Lucke left the party with many of his ordoliberal supporters, proclaiming it had "fallen irretrievably into the wrong hands."

Second Act: Petry's AfD and the "Refugee Crisis" (2015–2017)

Under the new leadership of Petry, the AfD reinvented itself as an Islamophobic anti-immigration party – initially with limited success. In the summer of 2015, when hundreds of thousands of Syrian refugees were already on their way over the Mediterranean and Aegean Sea and on the so-called "Balkan route," the polls for the AfD were still below the threshold of 5 percent. On September 4, 2015, Angela Merkel decided to open the German borders to refugees stranded in Hungary to avoid a humanitarian disaster, temporarily suspending the Dublin Agreement, which mandated that refugees must apply for asylum in the state in which they had entered the European Union.

According to the AfD, Merkel's decision was a clear violation of European law (like her rescue policy in the debt crisis), which entailed a moral hazard by encouraging even more refugees to come. Furthermore, it framed the opening of the borders as a loss of state control. Merkel responded to the critics of her refugee policy, also within her own party, by promoting a "welcome culture" (*Willkommenskultur*),[10] appealing to the moral responsibility of Germans (derived from Germany's Holocaust identity) as well as to the potential benefits of immigration for Germany's booming economy and declining demography (resonating with its *Wirtschaftswunder* identity). While many conservative critics agreed with Merkel's judgment of the situation as a humanitarian crisis, they were nevertheless worried about the message she was sending with her iconic selfies with refugees, her ostentatious optimism, captured by her claim "*Wir schaffen das*" ("We can do it"), and her propagation of a "welcome culture," which was more popular among leftist liberals than in her own party. In the fall of 2015, support for the AfD almost doubled but stayed well below 10 percent. Merkel's refugee policy enjoyed a broad support in German politics and media, strongly resonating among those who shared the country's Holocaust identity and regarded the crisis as an opportunity for redemption.

In her New Year's address broadcast on December 31, 2015, Merkel again defended her refugee policy against critics and repeated her mantra "We can do it." That fateful night, however, events took place that had a huge impact on the German political landscape and Merkel's refugee policy: groups of young men, predominantly from Maghreb countries, sexually molested and robbed several (German) women in the center of Cologne. To make matters worse, the police as well as the media did not report on these incidents immediately and were later accused of covering the events up – lending credibility to denunciations of the media in AfD and Pegida circles, who had been using the term "*Lügenpresse*" ("lying press," also originally coined by the Nazis). After being publicized and scandalized, the uncivil behavior of young men with Arab and Muslim background led to a backlash in the public discourse on refugees, despite the fact that almost no Syrian nationals were among the perpetrators. Even the conservative *Frankfurter Allgemeine Zeitung*, which supported Merkel's refugee policy in 2015, turned into a fierce critic (while maintaining distance from the AfD). The polls for the AfD quickly rose above 10 percent and have since then remained in the double digits.

The "refugee crisis" left German society polarized and had a profound impact on immigration policies and discourses. Not only in AfD circles but also among more mainstream conservatives, the memory of the "refugee crisis" became imbued with traumatic qualities. Notwithstanding the fact that Merkel remained "enemy number one" for the AfD and Pegida, she initiated a U-turn in immigration policy as well as rhetoric. In early 2016, she struck a deal with the Turkish president Recep Erdoğan, which almost stopped the flow of Syrian refugees into Europe. A year after the opening of Germany's borders to hundreds of thousands of refugees, there was little talk of – and even less enthusiasm for – the "welcome culture" once promoted by Merkel. The program of her party, the CDU, for the federal elections in 2017 stated explicitly that "a situation like in the year 2015 should and must not repeat itself as all participants have learned from this situation. We want the number of refugees coming to us to stay permanently low" (CDU/CSU 2017: 63). The year "2015," initially coded as Germany's finest hour, became a traumatic reference in the public discourse. A commentary in the *Frankfurter Allgemeine Zeitung* entitled "Never again 2015" (Bananas 2017) evoked Adorno's famous dictum "never again Auschwitz." The strength of the formula lies in its ambiguity: it leaves open whether Merkel made the right choice in a catastrophic situation, which needs to be avoided in the future, or if she was wrong all along. While not a full-blown cultural trauma, "2015" has undoubtedly become a polluted symbol in the center-right discourse. It is telling that Annegret Kramp-Karrenbauer, who succeeded Merkel with her support in a close race for the party leadership, immediately organized a workshop revisiting the refugee crisis and migration policy. In the end, all participants agreed that they had to make sure "that something like 2015 is not going to happen again" (Gathmann 2019).

Petry was undoubtedly successful as a party leader, more than doubling the percentage of votes for the AfD. Nevertheless, she, too, struggled to keep the right wing of her party in line, which felt emboldened by the general shift in the political climate. On January 17, 2017, Höcke spoke to an audience in Dresden decrying Berlin's Holocaust memorial as reprehensible: Germans are "the only people in the world to plant a memorial of shame in the heart of its capital" (Taub and Fisher 2017). Among German neo-Nazis, the word "shame" has a specific ring to it, as they also refer to the German capitulation in World War II as the "day of shame." What Höcke promises has become a staple in populist rhetoric, namely "freedom from shame" (Berlant 2016), which, in this context, refers first of all to the "collective guilt" of Germans. But there is more. In the same speech, Höcke compared the bombing of Dresden to Hiroshima and Nagasaki and called the landmark speech of former president Weizsäcker, who called the capitulation a "day of liberation," "a speech against his own people." The literary scholar Heinrich Detering (2019: 29–36) has shown in his analysis of Höcke's Dresden speech that the day of capitulation is the traumatic reference of the text, signifying Germany's defeat, occupation, and re-education by the Allies and thus the beginning of the German shame. We can glimpse here a radical memory culture, in which May 8, 1945, separates a sacred Germany (including Nazi Germany!) from the polluted postwar Germany. Unsurprisingly, Höcke's full-blown attack on Germany's memory culture characterized by the Holocaust as a "trauma of perpetrators" caused public outrage. Petry, trying to moderate the party for a government coalition with the conservatives in 2017, initiated a procedure to exclude Höcke from the party – and failed, like her predecessor.

Third Act: Gauland's AfD and Its War Against German Memory Culture (2017–present)

Shortly before the elections in 2017, Petry lost a decisive vote on the party program. As a consequence, and in spite of the electoral success of her party, winning 12.6 percent of the votes, she stepped down as a party leader after the elections and was followed by a dual leadership, economics professor Jörg Meuthen, representing the economic liberalism of the West, and Peter Gauland, former CDU member, representative of the nationalist right in the East.

Gauland exhibited a great talent for provoking scandals: for example, symbolically excluding ethnic minorities; stating that not every holder of a German passport is in fact a German; or insulting public figures with a migration background, including German national football player Jérôme Boateng. Furthermore, Gauland frequently attacks German memory culture, among other things, claiming that Germans should be proud of what their soldiers achieved in the two world wars. On June 2, 2018, he made a particularly scandalous statement at a congress of the party youth: "Hitler and the Nazis are just bird shit in more than 1,000 years of successful German history" (DW 2018), downplaying the role of Nazi Germany for German identity while at the same time alluding to Nazi speak (the "thousand-year kingdom" was an important trope for the Third Reich). Gauland, a self-proclaimed admirer of authoritarian Prussia, does not deny, much less endorse, the crimes of Nazi Germany – he even compared Merkel in her destructiveness to Hitler – but challenges the overarching importance of the Nazi period for German identity. Statements like this reliably cause public outrage, but they don't seem to hurt the AfD in the polls. A large proportion of its voters clearly do not share Germany's civil memory culture but indulge nostalgically in "fake" memories of a powerful Germany which was ethnically and culturally homogeneous, such as the BRD of the economic miracle or, even better, good old Prussia. Displacing the *Wirtschaftswunder* identity centered on the success story of postwar West Germany in favor of an imaginary pre-postwar Germany characterized by a shared primordial identity, not only in cultural but also in biological terms, the AfD increased its appeal among Eastern German voters, cutting itself loose from its original ordo-liberal roots.

While previous attempts to curb the radical right wing of the AfD have all failed, usually ending with moderates leaving the party, recent attempts of the party leadership to draw a red line on their right – despite being ridiculed by Höcke as "political bed-wetting" – have been more successful. To avoid observation by Germany's domestic security agency, an internal paper of the party advises its members to avoid vocabulary polluted through Nazi usage, such as *Systemparteien* (system parties) or *Umvolkung* (population transfer). At the beginning of 2019, André Poggenburg, a far-right leader from an Eastern federal state, who appeared publicly with a blue garden cornflower, a symbol used by the Nazi underground movement in Austria in the 1930s, was forced to resign and left the AfD.

The dividing line is again memory culture: publicly showing sympathy for Nazi Germany, as well as any attempt to re-sacralize this polluted period of German history, is taboo, while its relativization in service of a more positive German identity is the official party position. In this regard, Höcke, the unofficial leader of the AfD far right, walks a fine line: he cultivates an "unapologetically provocative language, packed with echoes from the 1930s," as *The New York Times* (Bennhold and Eddy 2019) observes, and espouses political views that mirror the antiparliamentarism and the "Führer"-principle of National Socialism, evoking the "longing of the German people for a historical figure [suggesting himself] who will heal the wounds in the Volk, overcome division and bring back order." At the same time, he refrains from defending German war crimes – and prefers to talk about the "war crimes" of the Allies. Instead

197

of purifying Nazi Germany, he tries to create ambiguity about powerful symbols such as Adolf Hitler, claiming that he was not "absolutely evil": "The world has – man has – shades of gray. . . . Even the worst severe criminal perhaps has something good, something worth loving, but he is still a severe criminal" (quoted in Troianovski 2017). In the discourse of German civil society, in which Hitler functions as a polluted symbol of absolute evil, an embodiment of all uncivil qualities, such a statement is simply unacceptable – but apparently not enough to force Höcke out of the party.

How can we explain the obsession of prominent AfD figures with German memory culture despite the civil backlash they face? The Holocaust identity is central to the universalizing discourse of the German civil sphere, polluting any preferential treatment of ethnic Germans while promoting solidarity with minorities in need – which stands in stark contrast to the nativist agenda of the populists. The AfD neither denies nor defends the Holocaust publicly (despite a few anti-Semites in its ranks), but it interprets it in a rather narrow way, calling for solidarity with Israel and the Jews against the Muslim threat.

Conclusion

In his piece "On the Concept of History," Walter Benjamin famously draws on Paul Klee's painting *Angelus Novus*, interpreting it as "the angel of history," who faces a catastrophic past as the storm "we call progress" drives "him irresistibly into the future" (2006 [1940]: 392). I am suggesting that civil societies, just like Benjamin's angel, do not simply march toward a bright utopian future, but move forward facing the failures of solidarity in the past. This orientation toward the past is characteristic not only of anticivil backlash movements, but also of progressive civil movements, as the German case shows. The paradox of the civil sphere, being a particular instantiation of universal principles, cannot be dissolved into the neat binary of polluted particularism and sacred universalism, reducing space and time to "vagaries" and "contingencies" (Alexander 2006). In contemporary German memory culture, the Holocaust is never a purely universal symbol (Alexander 2002) but also a national symbol imposing particular ethical obligations and civic duties on Germans as Germans (Giesen 2004; Assmann 2013).

Furthermore, the process of working through the past for the sake of the future transcends the notion of "civil repair" found in *The Civil Sphere* (Alexander 2006), which is primarily about providing a remedy for historical injustices: for example, the incorporation of Jews in postwar Germany. In contrast, the ethical responsibility implied by Germany's Holocaust identity extends into the far future toward groups yet unknown; it is particular in its origin but universal in its outreach. As civil memory culture, it informs the incorporation and inclusion of all kinds of newcomers, including Muslim refugees from Syria. It is for this reason that the AfD has identified German memory culture as an obstacle which stands in its way of redrawing the boundaries of belonging and solidarity in German society. In fighting the German exceptionalism of a postheroic memory culture, the AfD aims to turn Germany into a "normal country," proud of itself and largely ignorant of the dark parts of its history – and, most importantly, cold-hearted and ignorant of the suffering of others. Despite these efforts, Germany's civil memory culture remains strong and vital, not only in public discourses but also in popular culture.[11]

While it is certainly justifiable to speak of a German exceptionalism in terms of memory culture, I nevertheless claim that the nexus between particular history and universal values can also be observed in other civil spheres and discourses. The discourses of Western civil societies are often shaped by traumatic references to historical (i.e., spatially and temporally situated) failures of solidarity, such as colonization, slavery, or genocide. Memory cultures are a driving force behind the universalizing discourses of civil society, which turns them into attractive targets for populist movements, which have their own form of memory politics characterized by nostalgia (Karakaya 2018) and self-victimization. Historical revisionism, often successful, can be observed in many authoritarian and populist contexts, for example in Hungary, where Viktor Orbán rehabilitated the anti-Semitic Horthy regime, or in Vladimir Putin's Russia, where Joseph Stalin has been reinstated as a heroic figure.

In Germany, with its institutionalized memory culture vigilantly guarded by its civil society, historical revisionists have a harder time. Although not everything is well in the state of Germany, it seems that the AfD reached a plateau with its 2017 results. Support for the party remained at best stagnant in the European elections in 2019. On the federal level and in Western Germany, the party has no option for governance, while in Eastern Germany coalitions with a strong AfD presence (over 20 percent) are more likely, though currently ruled out by all other parties, possibly transforming the AfD into an Eastern German protest party. This difference between Western and Eastern Germany, as I have argued, can be accounted for in terms of differences in memory culture, which have their roots in the divided history of Germany.

While the resistible rise of the AfD is certainly a success story, it is also a cautionary tale about the failures of ambitious politicians (Lucke, Petry) stirring populist resentments and entering into a devilish pact with a radical right they were no longer able to control. The ordoliberal memory culture, with its illiberal and anticivil tendencies, has not only been crucial for the initial success of the party but also engendered its ideological transformation. Although the AfD may not be in its entirety a racist neo-Nazi party, the remaining conservatives evoke memories of the conservative politicians who were instrumental for Hitler's resistible rise to power in 1933. However, the undeniable success of the AfD has its limits. While the party undoubtedly had an impact on mainstream politics, driving centrist parties and public discourses to the right, it failed to initiate a "conservative revolution." To the contrary: the voters left behind by the rightward shift of the other parties flocked to the Green Party (the only established party that positioned itself consistently anti-AfD), which became the second biggest party in the recent European elections in Germany, with 20.5 percent compared to the 11 percent of the AfD – a damning verdict for a populist party. Thus, I am inclined to describe the AfD as a case of "successful failure" (similar to Pegida; cf. Heins and Unrau 2020).

The history of civil society is not only a history of struggles over inclusion and exclusion, but also a battle to preserve and cultivate the collective memory of failures of solidarity in the past. Western civil discourses are driven by redemptive processes beyond "civil repair," which are fueled by memory cultures remembering the victims of colonialism, slavery, and genocide. It is a battle that civil society cannot afford to lose. As Benjamin reminds us, "*even the dead* will not be safe from the enemy if he is victorious" (2006 [1940]: 391), and neither will civil society.

Notes

1 Alexander Gauland, one of the two AfD party leaders, in an interview with the *Frankfurter Allgemeine Zeitung* (Eppelsheim 2018).
2 In Germany and many other, mostly European, countries, the denial of the Holocaust is not warranted by the right of free speech but persecuted as crime.
3 The fact that Holocaust denial is prohibited by law in many countries suggests that there are indeed groups and subcultures espousing such views, if not publicly. In Germany, alternative radical-right memory cultures thrived in neo-Nazi subcultures before they entered the public discourse with the rise of the AfD. An example of countermemories persisting under the political censorship of a totalitarian state can be found in Bartmanski and Eyerman's study of the Katyń massacre in Polish memory (2019; see also Chapter 5 in the present volume).
4 The economic thought of ordoliberalism's founder, the Freiburg economist Walter Eucken, had a strong influence on the economic policies of Ludwig

Erhard, West Germany's iconic minister of economic affairs (1949–63), the most salient example being the 1957 antitrust law.

5 The most striking material representation of this grassroots movement are *"Stolpersteine"* ("stumbling blocks"), privately funded miniature memorials commemorating victims of Nazi rule, which have spread since 1992 throughout many cities in Germany and beyond. Recently, the symbol has been appropriated by right-wing radicals, rendering the murders of German nationals by refugees as "Merkel's stumbling blocks" (cf. Mounk 2019).

6 A similar observation can be made about Austria, whose official memory culture – well into the 1990s – painted it as the first victim of Nazi Germany (and of Austrian-born Hitler), oblivious to the enthusiasm with which the "take-over" of 1938 (*Anschluss*) was met by large parts of the Austrian population. In 2017, the Austrian right-wing populist party FPÖ peaked with more than 25 percent of the electoral votes (comparable to the AfD in Eastern Germany). The cases of the DDR and Austria suggest that official memory cultures dissociating themselves from Nazi crimes, if unchecked by a critical civil society, may create conditions under which right-wing countercultures thrive and prosper.

7 Criticized for his unsubstantiated numbers, Sarrazin stated in a later interview that if one lacks a figure, one must "create one pointing in the right direction, and if nobody can refute it, I have asserted my estimation" (Klein 2010). This "liberal" use of empirical evidence and abuse of statistics is also characteristic of his book. Despite his warnings about mass immigration from Turkey, at the time of its publication in 2010, Germany had for the fifth year in a row a negative net immigration from that country.

8 The general secretary of the Central Council of Jews in Germany, Stephan Kramer, was not flattered by Sarrazin's (2010: 93–7) assertion that Jews had attained an average IQ of 115 through centuries of biological-cultural selection, comparing Sarrazin's racial conception of Jewishness ("All Jews share a specific gene") to Nazi ideology (dpa 2010).

9 While the Nazis used the term approvingly and in an active sense, envisioning the Aryanization and Germanization of Eastern Europe, the AfD uses the term critically and defensively, warning of the Islamization and de-Germanization of Germany. Nevertheless, the racial-demographic logic behind these opposing uses of the word is fundamentally the same.

10 A "welcome culture" has been long called for by immigrant associations in Germany and is criticized in Sarrazin's book (2010: 307, 326f.).

11 Consider, for example, Rammstein's recent music video, "Deutschland" (2019), which has more than 100 million views (see https://www.youtube.com/watch?v=NeQM1c-XCDc&has_verified=1 (accessed April 16, 2020).

References

Adorno, T. W. (1998) *Education after Auschwitz. Critical Models: Interventions and Catchwords*. New York: Columbia University Press.

Alexander, J. C. (2002) On the social construction of moral universals: The "Holocaust" from war crime to trauma drama. *European Journal of Social Theory* 5(1): 5–85.

Alexander, J. C. (2004) Toward a theory of cultural trauma. In: J. C. Alexander, R. Eyerman, B. Giesen, N. J. Smelser, and P. Sztompka (eds.) *Cultural Trauma and Collective Identity*. Berkeley: University of California Press.

Alexander, J. C. (2006) *The Civil Sphere*. New York: Oxford University Press.

Alexander, J. C. (2019a) Frontlash/backlash: The crisis of solidarity and the threat to civil institutions. *Contemporary Sociology* 48(1): 5–11.

Alexander, J. C. (2019b) *What Makes a Social Crisis? The Societalization of Social Problems*. Cambridge: Polity.

Alexander, J. C., R. Eyerman, B. Giesen, N. J. Smelser, and P. Sztompka (eds.). (2004) *Cultural Trauma and Collective Identity*. Berkeley: University of California Press.

Assmann, A. (2013) *Das neue Unbehagen an der Erinnerungskultur: Eine Intervention*. Munich: Beck.

Bananas, G. (2017) Hauptsache, nie wieder 2015. *Frankfurter Allgemeine Zeitung*, July 3. http://www.faz.net/aktuell/politik/bundestagswahl/wahlpro gramm-von-cdu-und-csu-hauptsache-nie-wieder-2015-15089223.html.

Bartmanski, D. and R. Eyerman. (2019) The worst was the silence: The unfinished drama of the Katyń massacre. In: R. Eyerman (ed.) *Memory, Trauma, and Identity*. New York: Palgrave.

Bebnowski, D. (2015) *Die Alternative für Deutschland: Aufstieg und gesellschaftliche Repräsentanz einer rechten populistischen Partei*. Wiesbaden: Springer.

Benjamin, W. (2006 [1940]) On the concept of history. In: W. Benjamin, *Selected Writings. Volume 4, 1938–1940*. Cambridge, MA: Harvard University Press.

Bennhold, K. and M. Eddy. (2019) "Hitler or Höcke?" Germany's far-right party radicalizes. *The New York Times*, October 26. https://www.nytimes.com/2019/10/26/world/europe/afd-election-east-germany-hoecke.html.

Berberich, F. and T. Sarrazin. (2009) Klasse statt Masse. Von der Hauptstadt der Transferleistung zur Metropole der Eliten. Thilo Sarrazin im Gespräch. *Lettre International* 86: 199.

Berlant, L. (2016) Trump, or political emotions. *The New Inquiry*, August 5. https://thenewinquiry.com/trump-or-political-emotions/.

CDU/CSU. (2017) *Für ein Deutschland, in dem wir gut und gerne leben. Regierungsprogramm 2017 – 2021*. https://www.cdu.de/system/tdf/media/dok umente/170703regierungsprogramm2017.pdf?file=1.

Detering, H. (2019) *Was heißt hier "wir"? Zur Rhetorik der parlamentarischen Rechten*. Stuttgart: Reclam.

dpa. (2010) Alle Juden teilen ein bestimmtes Gen. *Die Zeit*, August 28. https://www.zeit.de/gesellschaft/zeitgeschehen/2010-08/sarrazin-juden-gene-migration.

DW. (2018) AfD's Gauland plays down Nazi era as a "bird shit" in German history. *DW*, June 2. https://www.dw.com/en/afds-gauland-plays-down-nazi-era-as-a-bird-shit-in-german-history/a-44055213.

Eppelsheim, V. P. (2018) Wir versuchen, die Grenzen des Sagbaren auszuweiten. *Frankfurter Allgemeine Zeitung*, June 7. http://www.faz.net/aktuell/politik/inland/gauland-interview-afd-will-grenzen-des-sagbaren-aus-weiten-15627982.html.

Eyerman, R. (2004) Cultural trauma: Slavery and the formation of African-American identity. In: J. C. Alexander, R. Eyerman, B. Giesen, N. J. Smelser, and P. Sztompka (eds.) *Cultural Trauma and Collective Identity*. Berkeley: University of California Press.

Eyerman, R. (2019) Introduction: Identity, memory, and trauma. In: R. Eyerman (ed.) *Memory, Trauma, and Identity*. Cham: Palgrave Macmillan.

Foucault, M. (2008) *The Birth of Biopolitics: Lectures at the Collège de France 1978–79*. Houndmills: Palgrave Macmillan.

Gathmann, F. (2019) Dass sich so etwas wie 2015 nicht wiederholt. *Spiegel Online*, February 11. https://www.spiegel.de/politik/deutschland/cdu-was-annegret-kramp-karrenbauer-in-der-migrationspolitik-will-a-1252702.html.

Giesen, B. (2004) The trauma of perpetrators: The Holocaust as the traumatic reference of German national identity. In: J. C. Alexander, R. Eyerman, B. Giesen, N. J. Smelser, and P. Sztompka (eds.) *Cultural Trauma and Collective Identity*. Berkeley: University of California Press.

Grimm, R. (2015) The rise of the German Eurosceptic party Alternative für Deutschland, between ordoliberal critique and popular anxiety. *International Political Science Review* 36(3): 264–78.

Habermas, J. (1989 [1962]) *The Structural Transformation of the Public Sphere: An Inquiry into a Category of Bourgeois Society*. Cambridge, MA: MIT Press.

Heins, V. and C. Unrau. (2020) Anti-immigrant movements and the self-poisoning of the civil sphere: The case of Germany. In: J. C. Alexander, T. Stack, and F. Khosrokhavar (eds.) *Breaching the Civil Order: Radicalism and the Civil Sphere*. New York: Cambridge University Press.

Jaspers, K. (2000 [1947]) *The Question of German Guilt*. New York: Fordham University Press.

Jaworsky, B. N. (2015) Mobilising for immigrant rights online: Performing "American" national identity through symbols of civic-economic participation. *Journal of Intercultural Studies* 36(5): 579–99.

Karakaya, Y. (2018) The conquest of hearts: The central role of Ottoman nostalgia within contemporary Turkish populism. *American Journal of Cultural Sociology*. doi:10.1057/s41290-018-0065-y.

Klein, S. (2010) Zartbitter. *Süddeutsche Zeitung*, March 1.

Manow, P. (2001) Ordoliberalismus als ökonomische Ordnungstheologie. *Leviathan* 29(2): 179–98.

Mounk, Y. (2019) How a teen's death has become a political weapon. *The New Yorker*, January 28. https://www.newyorker.com/magazine/2019/01/28/how-a-teens-death-has-become-a-political-weapon.

Müller, J.-W. (2016) *What is Populism?* Philadelphia: University of Pennsylvania Press.

Rauer, V. (2006) Willy Brandt's kneefall at the Warsaw Memorial. In: J. C. Alexander, B. Giesen, and J. L. Mast (eds.) *Social Performance: Symbolic Action, Cultural Pragmatics, and Ritual*. Cambridge: Cambridge University Press.

Reed, I. (2011) *Interpretation and Social Knowledge: On the Use of Theory in the Human Sciences*. Chicago: University of Chicago Press.

Sarrazin, T. (2010) *Deutschland schafft sich ab: Wie wir unser Land aufs Spiel setzen*. Munich: Deutsche Verlags-Anstalt.

Sarrazin, T. (2012) *Europa braucht den Euro nicht: Wie uns politisches Wunschdenken in die Krise geführt hat*. Munich: Deutsche Verlags-Anstalt.

Schwartz, B. (1996) Memory as a cultural system: Abraham Lincoln in World War II. *American Sociological Review* 61(5): 908–27.

Talbert, R. D. (2017) Culture and the Confederate flag: Attitudes toward a divisive symbol. *Sociology Compass* 11(2). doi.org/10.1111/soc4.12454.

Taub, A. and M. Fisher. (2017) Germany's extreme right challenges guilt over Nazi past. *The New York Times*, January 18. https://www.nytimes.com/2017/01/18/world/europe/germany-afd-alternative-bjorn-hocke.html.

Tognato, C. (2012) *Central Bank Independence: Cultural Codes and Symbolic Performance*. Houndmills: Palgrave Macmillan.

Troianovski, A. (2017) German politician's comments about Hitler stoke debate. *Wall Street Journal*, March 7. https://www.wsj.com/articles/german-politicians-comments-about-hitler-stoke-debate-1488912569.

8

Populism and the Particularization of Solidarity

On the Sweden Democrats
Henrik Enroth

The broad outlines of the story are by now well known. In democratic societies on both sides of the Atlantic, we have seen the rise and electoral success of political parties and leaders – often misleadingly characterized as being to the "right" rather than to the "left" – challenging the political mainstream in the name of "the people" or "the nation," against "the elite" or "the establishment," typically with an anti-immigration agenda. When the word "populism" is currently used, this tends to be what it refers to.[1]

It is often noted that consensus is hard to come by on the subject of populism and its role in political life (Mudde and Kaltwasser 2017). Lately, however, as parties and leaders variously fitting this description have gained political power, a consensus has in fact formed as to the threat to democracy posed by these developments. Political scientists studying populists in power have concluded not only that many populist parties and leaders have successfully made the transition from voicing anti-establishment protest to governing (Albertazzi and McDonnell 2015). Moreover, once in power, populists have flouted the norms of democratic governance, subverted the autonomy of democratic institutions, and compromised the integrity of the processes on which representative democracy rests. The threat to democracy posed by populism would thus be the threat posed by any political party or leader rising to power by way of the ballot box, and then proceeding to dismantle the institutions of democracy. The message of the moment has been that democracies die not only by coups d'état and other dramatic seizures of power; democracies also, and more frequently, die a more or less slow and gruesome death at the hands of elected autocrats (Levitsky and Ziblatt 2018).

It may be a sign of the times that this has been presented as the main cause for alarm not only by political scientists but also by cultural sociologists. The scenario is familiar: "the populist demagogue" not only "monopolizes the power of symbolic representation," but also "destroys the organizational autonomy of regulative institutions. Populists cannot tolerate independent courts," nor "other powerful media elites" than the ones they control themselves. "As the regulation of impersonal office is destroyed, power becomes personal and familial, and corruption reigns." And with "office and journalism destroyed, elections become empty showcases for staging dramaturgic demagoguery" (Alexander 2019: 8).

This is, of course, no mere scenario. At the time of writing, the ailment is real and pervasive. Nor can there be any doubt that the diagnosis is correct: institutional autonomy is literally vital in a modern democracy; without it, democracies die. But the diagnosis is also incomplete: institutional destruction by autocrats dressed up as populists for election season is not the only way the condition of democracy can worsen under the influence of populist parties and leaders. A consequence of the above scenario, Jeffrey Alexander (2019: 8) concludes, is that "the presuppositions of a universalizing solidarity become severely constrained." This conclusion is premised on an understanding of democracy not only as a set of institutions and procedures to secure the ordered succession of leadership by giving all citizens an equal say in electing their leaders. Democracy, from this point of view, is also and no less a symbolic code structuring the historically variable senses of community of situated agents.

One of the contributions of civil sphere theory to the study of political life is the observation that democracy depends not only on autonomous institutions and fair and transparent processes, but also on "the existence of solidary bonds that extend beyond political arrangements" (Alexander 2006a: 38), bonds formed and transformed in civil discourse. Democracy has always rested on the possibility of extending senses of solidarity in a universalizing direction (Derrida 2005; Alexander 2006a; Enroth and Henriksson 2019). The culture of democracy projects "a wider and more inclusive sphere of solidarity," an aspirational community always imperfectly instantiated in political institutions and processes (Alexander 2006a: 193).

This chapter illustrates how the conditions for universalizing solidarity can become severely constrained also where there is no institutional encroachment, where regulative and communicative institutions are intact, and where populists are not even in a position to exert much political power, electoral success notwithstanding. To appreciate this kind of situation, we must look at what populists are doing not only when they are in power, but also on their way there. In general terms, as we might expect, what populists are doing on their way to power is no different from what other parties and leaders do: putting forth their messages and policies in relation to the symbolic codes that structure political life. What is different is *how* populists are doing so, and the result of their efforts. Unlike most protest movements in the history of democracy, populism of the kind discussed in this chapter is not emancipatory; the grievances articulated by populist parties and leaders typically do not amount to a case for broadened civil inclusion. On the contrary, such grievances amount to a particularization of civil solidarity: a case for exclusion of the designated others – elites and immigrants – on whom populists like to pin their misfortunes.

I consider how this has been done in one specific context, Sweden, by one specific party: the Sweden Democrats, a self-described "national-ist" and "social conservative" party with an anti-immigration agenda and a neo-Nazi background. In the 2010 national election, the Sweden Democrats received 5.7 percent of the vote, more than enough for rep-resentation in parliament. In the 2014 election, it was 12.86 percent, making the Sweden Democrats the third largest party in the Riksdag. In 2018, it was 17.53 percent, at which the party remained the third largest in the Riksdag, having hoped for – indeed expected – more (*DN* 2018a; *Valmyndigheten* 2018). Recent polls have the party as the second largest, closely tied with the Social Democratic Party (*DN* 2019b; *Novus* 2019, 2020).

The most obvious way in which the Sweden Democrats have disrupted Swedish political life is by simply being where they have now been for a decade: at a pivotal yet isolated position in parliament, hedged in, so far, by an electorally ineffective *cordon sanitaire* of the established parties.[2] More specifically, and actively, what the party has achieved during its decade on the national political scene is to engage with the civil code in three distinct ways: (1) *inverting*: reconceptualizing what has been deemed civil as uncivil; (2) *appealing* to the civil code: laying claim to established civil ideals; and (3) *appropriating*: adopting and adapting elements of the civil code. None of these moves are uniquely populist or inherently detrimental to democracy. However, in this case, the provi-sional result has been not only a particularization of solidarity, but also what looks like a fracturing and polarization of the civil sphere.

Inverting the Civil Code

Populism of the kind that we have seen in recent years is largely predi-cated on a reversal of civil and uncivil in the culture of democracy (Enroth 2019). We can expect the form and content of such reversal to vary, within as well as between cases and contexts. In the case at hand, this is what the Sweden Democrats have done with what the party itself refers to as a Swedish "culture of consensus." This is something that both natives and observers often point out as an essential, even defining, character trait: to be Swedish is, allegedly, to seek consensus.

The ideal of "incorporating voices into a harmonious community discussion" is often mentioned as characteristic of political institutions and processes in Sweden, as well as of social life at large (Katzenstein 1985; Jepperson 2002: 74; Rothstein and Trägårdh 2007: 235). The Swedish political system has long been regarded as exemplary of what political scientists have called a "consensus model" of democracy (Lijphart 1977). During the postwar period, political institutions have supposedly been characterized by "a low intensity of conflict, together with a highly effective machinery for conflict resolution. The predominant style of policy-making is seen as concertative and deliberative, and the level of inter-elite agreement is high" (Elder et al. 1988: 182; cf. 465–7). "Seen as" is key here, more so than has been realized by political scientists. These are civil ideals as much as they are – or were – factual descriptions of the social and political life of the country. And as civil ideals go, it may be noted that references to the "concertative and deliberative" are more or less generic in a comparative perspective, likely to be found not only in a purportedly consensual democracy such as Sweden, but also in markedly different and more conflictual political systems such as the United States (Alexander 2006a: 57–8).

As political scientists have also found, while the consensus model may indeed have depicted the institutional realities in Sweden during the postwar period, at least since the 1980s, these civil ideals have increasingly become just that: ideals, not so much reflecting the actual political process as providing a structure of meaning within which that process unfolds. In the parliamentary context, past decades have seen inter-party conflict on the rise, power-sharing diminished, and negotiations in decline (Loxbo and Sjölin 2017; Enroth and Sjölin 2018: 197–9). And in Sweden as elsewhere, division and polarization have been on the rise in public discourse, a tendency exacerbated by the explosion of social media, and by the kind of political parties and leaders discussed in this book (Enroth and Sjölin 2018: 201).

None of this is to say that consensus has vanished as a civil ideal. On the contrary, this ideal has remained very much present in Swedish political life, but, interestingly, less explicitly so among its erstwhile friends than among its newfound enemies. The Sweden Democrats pay homage to consensus, but they also revaluate it from civil to uncivil, from virtue to vice. In a book published in the run-up to the 2018 national election, the leader of the party, Jimmie Åkesson (2018: 91–2), lists some of the ideals to which any newcomer to Sweden needs to subscribe: "In our country we respect each other, strive towards equality between men and women [*jämställdhet mellan könen*], seek shared understanding [*samförstånd*] over conflict, resolve oppositions [*motsättningar*] through dialogue and democracy." He adds, "Modesty is a virtue. Team spirit and collective striving have served our little nation well" (Åkesson 2018: 57).

But these virtues "can also be a weakness," Åkesson (2018: 22–3) cautions, at least, it seems, for the native population: "Swedes in general are sensible, but unfortunately not seldom caught in the fine-meshed web of the culture of consensus." Here "the culture of consensus" designates oppression rather than civil inclusion. As described, the phenomenon is ubiquitous, framed in terms not just political but characterological, a precarious blend of the psychological and the cultural, the personal and the political, that is integral to the party's mode of communication. In part, it manifests as a psychological condition. Aside from being generally sensible, Swedes are also beset by "an almost pathological self-contempt" (Åkesson 2018: 39). This is presented as internalized, an affliction imposed from without, apparently by the "despotic [*maktfull-komligt*] machinery," the "hegemonic power apparatus," into which the Social Democratic Party is said to have metamorphosed at some point during the postwar period (Åkesson 2018: 24).

As a political condition, the culture of consensus has left democracy "weakened" by "taboos" and "oppression of opinion [*åsiktsförtryck*]" (Åkesson 2018: 37). One such presumed taboo, one purportedly oppressed opinion, to which the party keeps returning is the notion that "it is only in Sweden that it is bad to be a nationalist. . . . At least that is how it is in the eyes of the dominant social-liberal establishment" (Åkesson 2018: 22). The culture of consensus is also invoked as an explanation for the alleged policy failure around which the discourse of the party revolves: immigration and integration. "It is the distinctive timidity – the self-contempt – which has so strongly contributed to the enormous and growing integration problems that we are living with today" (Åkesson 2018: 68).

If timidity and self-contempt – the uncivil obverse of the culture of consensus – make for failed integration, what is needed to replace "the extreme, reckless immigration policy" pursued by the Social Democratic Party and the social-liberal establishment are their binary opposites. On the matter of "how you hold a society together," Åkesson (2018: 92) describes "the biggest difference between us and the other parties" like this: "Lack of demands [*kravlöshet*] and self-contempt stand against a sense of duty and pride." This is how virtues conventionally associated with the culture of consensus become vices: modesty and team spirit, shared understanding and dialogue, become timidity and self-contempt, that is, "weakness," in the area of immigration policy. In lieu of weakness, we need strength, that is, "we need to raise demands. Demands that those who come to our country and want to build a future here must adapt to what our society looks like and how it works. You cannot expect to be able to live just like you did in your home country" (Åkesson 2018: 66).

In view of the forceful binary construct through which the party is pitted against its others, the demands cited seem underwhelming, in that they are demands not only with which all established parties could and do agree, but also by which all current and prospective citizens are legally obliged to abide: "In Sweden no courts of law shall adjudicate based on Muslim sharia law. In Sweden we shall not allow polygamy. In Sweden we shall never accept or legitimize child marriage. Nor shall we ever allow young girls to be forced to marry against their will" (Åkesson 2018: 66–7). In the same spirit, it is explained that in the ideal Sweden toward which the Sweden Democrats strive, "serious criminals [*grovt kriminella*] – murderers, rapists, pedophiles – are locked up instead of well-behaved [*skötsamma*] law-abiding citizens having to lock themselves up," and "the interests of the crime victim are placed ahead of those of the criminal" (Åkesson 2018: 58). "If you are prepared to accept this, if you are prepared to adapt, then you are welcome to be a part of our modern *folkhem* [people's home]. If you are not prepared to accept the demands we raise, then you will have to live somewhere else" (Åkesson 2018: 62).

If these populist-conservative *idées fixes* seem less than forbidding as demands on those who migrate to the country, they nevertheless serve their purpose in the binary construction of the party and its opponents. It may be noted that the inversion of the civil code is achieved by explicit reference to what is to be inverted, rhetorically reinforcing the culture of consensus so as to reinforce its reversal, making the revaluation of civil values seem all the more dramatic and bold. Talk of "taboos" and "oppression of opinion" makes the civil code look like an overpowering imposition by "the social-liberal establishment." In semiotic terms, this is how the protagonists and the antagonists of the populist narrative are constructed in one stroke.

In political terms, this is why such simplistic constructs have proved so difficult to challenge (cf. Enroth 2019): the key to the populist inversion of the civil code is not only to devalue what others value, but also to devalue what others value by presenting your own values as devalued by others, those others being cast as hegemonic elites. The Swedish culture of consensus is inverted not simply by declaring the civil to be uncivil, by redescribing the virtuous as weak, but also by making clear, one, that the Social Democratic Party and the dominant social-liberal establishment have imposed upon us civil ideals that become weakness – timidity and self-contempt – in the area of immigration and integration policy; and, two, that they also devalue the nationalism that, if allowed to flourish, would turn timidity and self-contempt into a sense of duty and pride.

Appealing to the Civil Code

The party's enthusiasm for presenting itself and its constituents as victimized opens not only for inversion but also for appeal to the established civil code. This is often delivered as an accusation of undue, undemocratic, solitary confinement by the other parties in the Riksdag, and of unfair, politically motivated, scrutiny by "the large media houses" and "the left-liberal establishment" (Åkesson 2018: 9, 12–13). Unsurprisingly, this appeal has fallen on deaf ears among political opponents and in the national media. All the while, the wisdom of the established parties' *cordon sanitaire* has been intensely and extensively debated in Swedish public life, albeit typically in narrow cost–benefit terms: whether this strategy has served to reduce or boost the party's electoral performance.

Extraparliamentary Activism

What makes the Sweden Democrats' appeal to the civil code instructive is not least the extent to which it has formed a response to perceived grievances suffered by the party itself. One such response occurred in October 2015, when it was announced that the party's political agenda would henceforth be pursued outside parliament, in various forms of activism apparently – and ironically, although nobody in the party leadership seemed to see the irony – to be funded out of the Sweden Democrats' share of state subsidies to political parties in parliament. This was delivered matter-of-factly as an inevitable consequence of the party's growing frustration with parliamentary work, a frustration itself presented as an inevitable consequence of the strategy of isolation to which the party was subjected in the Riksdag. At a press conference, the party leadership declared that it was "putting the party in campaign mode," so as to get "all members and supporters to do what they can to spread this message to the Swedish people," the message being that "the entire Swedish welfare state is facing total wreckage" under the weight of immigration. The aim of the campaign, it was made clear, was to "create such pressure that the other parties will simply have to stop and listen" (*DN* 2015a, 2015b).

211

This was immediately after the party had proposed, and the other parties in the Riksdag had unanimously rejected, a national referendum on immigration. This was also during a period of intense influx into Southern Europe of refugees out of Syria. Around the same time, Swedish newspapers and broadcast media reported that party activists had placed themselves in various locations on the Mediterranean, on and around the borders of the European Union, ostensibly with the aim of distributing flyers (*DN* 2015a, 2015b; *SvD* 2015). The flyers were to make clear to any would-be refugees to Sweden that the country held no future for them. In fact, the flyers suggested that Sweden did not at the time hold much of a future for anyone. "NO MONEY, NO JOBS, NO HOMES," the flyers said, in large block letters, reflecting the mood and creed on which the party has built much of its electoral appeal. The flyers were signed "Sweden Democrats," "SD-Women," and "The People of Sweden" (*DN* 2015b).[3]

This was a carefully, if not exactly adroitly, staged performance. The message, the mode of delivery, and the undertaking of distributing this message *in situ* in the midst of an unfolding refugee crisis might suggest a less than perfect pitch for the concerns, and indeed the comprehension, of people who have just put their lives at stake being smuggled across the Mediterranean. But this would be to miss the point, since the performance was not intended for those who happened to be onstage but for a specific domestic audience. While the scene was international, urgently of the moment, and imbued with human tragedy, the performance was in this respect out of sync with the moment, addressing as it did not the plight of the Syrian refugees but the perceived plight of those members of the audience whose own future would supposedly be in jeopardy should these refugees reach Sweden.

What is striking about this episode is the apparent inability of the party leadership to see how such a performance could be legitimately perceived as anything but a forceful reaction to uncivil exclusion from parliamentary politics and public life, and as doing what needs to be done to save the welfare state from total wreckage. It should be noted, however, that this was not, in the history of the party, the extraordinary event it seemed to observers in 2015. Indeed, for the Sweden Democrats this episode was a retreat to the party's default position. As the current leader of the party has recalled, when he joined in 1995, "the Sweden Democrats was mostly an extraparliamentary protest movement, albeit with parliamentary ambitions" (Åkesson 2018: 14). In recent years, the details about this extraparliamentary protest movement and its legacy have been left mainly to "the large media houses" and "the left-liberal establishment" to explore. While most of it has long been known, much of it had been forgotten when the party entered the Riksdag in 2010.

Whitewashing Nazism

One detail of which we have been reminded was a march held, to public dismay, in Stockholm on November 30, 1992, in honor of Sweden's last imperial king, Karl XII. The march was organized by the Sweden Democrats, at that time one of a number of neo-Nazi groups that had taken to celebrate, yearly, the day of the king's death in a ceremony to be concluded by placing a wreath at his monument. Like the year before, the main participants in the march were neo-Nazi skinheads, who, as it turned out, never got near the monument to the king because at that point the police had lost control of the riots that had erupted between the skinheads and the antiracist activists protesting the march (*DN* 1991, 1992). Two decades later, in October 2012, in an internal memo circulated in the party organization, it was categorically declared that the Sweden Democrats had no room for "extremists" or "racists" (*DN* 2012), and that the party would henceforth adopt a "zero-tolerance" policy (Åkesson 2012). The party now describes itself as "nonracist" (SD 2014: 13).

Whitewashing the extraparliamentary protest movement of its racist and neo-Nazi history has been the Sweden Democrats' most troubled and troubling appeal to the civil code. Several aspects of the effort are noteworthy. For one, the model has been the clean slate, the fresh start; a restless attempt to distance oneself from what must be considered, in a political organization, a quite recent past. Asked by a reporter in 2018 what he found most disturbing in the party's history, Jimmie Åkesson replied: "[T]hat people don't give up, that people don't stop nagging [*tjata*]" (*DN* 2018a), that is, a reference not to the party's history but to getting questions about the party's history. For another, the approach to publicized misdeeds has been to regard them as the isolated acts of "individual fools and extremists, who have not been members of the party for 25–30 years" (Åkesson 2018: 12–13). This effortlessly segues into the party's other appeal to the civil code, that of unfair treatment: "[W]e are still being held responsible for what individual people did in the beginning of the 1990s" (Åkesson 2018: 13).

For yet another, neither before nor since the zero-tolerance policy was announced has there been any shortage of fools and extremists who are still members of the party, many of whom, in fact, have had or still have key positions in the party organization. For reasons of space, if nothing else, this is not the place to detail the racist, anti-Semitic, homophobic, and sexist slurs, the photographs of party functionaries wearing swastika armbands, the street fights involving members of the party leadership, and the public accusations of sexual assault in the party. Those who have

213

compiled such details have found that, on average, one such incident per week had been reported during the four-year period 2014–18, that is, well after the introduction of the zero-tolerance policy (*DN* 2014; *Expo* 2016, 2018).

Nor, it must be noted, is this just any whitewash. As Philippe Lacoue-Labarthe (1990 [1988]: 77) has suggested, Nazism may be exactly what cannot – and should not – be whitewashed, what "never ceases to haunt modern consciousness as a sort of endlessly latent 'potentiality', both stored away and yet constantly at hand within our societies." This "endlessly latent potentiality" is what so spectacularly, and ironically, eludes the Sweden Democrats' zero-tolerance policy. Ironically, since the potentiality has been and still is so frequently actualized in the party's ranks, it can hardly be described as stored away. By dismissing rather than engaging with this inextricable part of the party, the zero-tolerance policy – whether genuinely felt or believed expedient – not only evades but also effectively invalidates what has become the moral lesson of the Holocaust: that "evil is inside all of us, and in every society," and, therefore, that "there is no audience that can legitimately distance itself from collective suffering, either from its victims or its perpetrators" (Alexander 2003: 55). As illustrated by the adventure in the Mediterranean in 2015, and by the weekly parade of individual fools and extremists, this is a party that has predicated its rise to power on distancing itself from both.

The moral lesson of the Holocaust was in fact repeatedly and insistently inculcated in the run-up to the 2018 election. The immediate occasion was not so much the Sweden Democrats themselves as a number of demonstrations by neo-Nazi groups, with counterdemonstrations. One of the people to show up in the counterdemonstrations was Hédi Fried, a Swedish Holocaust survivor, writer, and activist in her nineties. Her presence underscored, and encouraged, comparisons between the current situation in Sweden and the situation in interwar Europe. Fried was shown in print and broadcast media receiving prominent representatives of the established political parties in her home. "Her message to the politicians: she has experienced the displacement of norms before, in Germany in the 1930s," read a caption in Sweden's largest daily newspaper, *Dagens Nyheter*. "We must understand that democracy is threatened," Fried said in the article, and when asked how democracy is threatened, she replied: "[B]ecause the Sweden Democrats are even in the Riksdag. That was how it happened in Germany, there were small steps, you didn't see it coming" (*DN* 2018b).

As an appeal to the civil code, as an attempt by the party leadership to turn the Sweden Democrats from uncivil to civil, the whitewashing effort has, so far, been less than successful. This social performance has not come across as authentic (cf. Alexander 2006b), at least not to those whose opinions are voiced in the political mainstream and in the national media. Established agents of the civil sphere have called the party's bluff: the dressing up of the uncivil in the trappings of civil discourse. "I don't believe you one bit," Hédi Fried imagined herself responding to the Sweden Democrats' insistence that the party has come a long way since the 1990s (*DN* 2018b). The perceived inauthenticity has much to do with the specious idea of the clean slate, and with the ties that demonstrably still bind the present to the past.

Consider the "nationalism" on which the party prides itself. "Since my early teens I have called myself a nationalist," Åkesson mentions in his book. "At that time, in the early 1990s, that was common among young people in my generation. It was completely normal to express senses of patriotism [*fosterlandskänslor*], affirm the cultural heritage, learn about our history, feel proud of what Swedes through the centuries have succeeded in accomplishing" (Åkesson 2018: 22). "Completely normal" is a key phrase with the Sweden Democrats, the whole point of the whitewashing effort being to turn the party from an extraparliamentary protest movement to "a party by and for completely ordinary people" (Åkesson 2018: 17). What "completely normal" and "completely ordinary" can be taken to mean is of course a matter of context. A journalist at *Dagens Nyheter* was able to fill in, first-hand, the context and details missing in Åkesson's account of his youth. The current party leadership, the journalist recalled, "during their student days in Lund around the turn of the millennium used to celebrate Karl XII on the day of his death each 30 November, with a torch-light procession, placing a wreath, and reading [Esaias] Tegnér's heroic poem 'Karl XII'" (*DN* 2018c).

"It may seem surprising that the man who lost the empire should be a national hero," Gayatri Chakravorty Spivak remarked in Sweden in the early 1990s, on the subject of the neo-Nazi celebrations of Karl XII, which were then on everybody's mind. But, she added, "an object lost can produce much more politico-ideological momentum" (Spivak 1995: 27; cf. Enroth 2015; Spivak 2015). Implicit in Spivak's remark is a warning, unheeded at the time, and unheeded still: this sense of loss, with the politico-ideological momentum it can be made to generate, is generic; its subjects and objects are contingent, accidentally rather than essentially associated with the skinheads and their passionate attachment to the empire and the man who lost it. As psychoanalysts know, attachments get recathected (Freud 1955 [1920–2]). In retrospect, reclaiming an object lost, and the idea that reclaiming the lost object amounts to a cultural restitution, a purification of what has been polluted, turns out to be a constant – perhaps the indispensable constant – on the Sweden

215

Democrats' march from neo-Nazi riots to a pivotal position in parliament. What has most notably changed on this two-decade march is not the dynamic behind the protest movement-turned-party, but the lost object on which its energies are expended.

Appropriating the Civil Code

A decade or so after the skinhead riots in Stockholm, the seventeenth-century empire had been replaced in the party's political cosmology by the twentieth-century welfare state. Karl XII, the man who lost the empire, had been replaced by Per Albin Hansson, legendary leader of the Social Democratic Party and popularly known as the man who gave us the *folkhem*. "An important goal for the Sweden Democrats is the recreation of the *folkhem*," it is declared in the party program from 2003, revised in 2005 (SD 2005: 9). The title of Jimmie Åkesson's (2018) book is *Det moderna folkhemmet* – the modern *folkhem*.

Particularizing the folkhem

This metaphor – the people's home – has been a key element of the Swedish civil code in the postwar period. The *folkhem* is an integral part of a symbolic structure still largely centered on the ambitions and achievements of the Social Democratic Party, and on the kind of welfare state model that evolved under its reign. In the Swedish context, political innovation and ideological reinvention tend to proceed, on left and right alike, by rhetorical moves making reference or laying claim to this legacy (Skinner 2001; cf. Alexander 2006b). The Social Democrats made the notion of the *folkhem* their own and built their vision of the welfare state around it, but as the Sweden Democrats point out in their program, the metaphor had been around before Per Albin Hansson picked it up and put it to use in a famous speech in 1928 (SD 2014: 11). While enthusiastically paying due to Hansson and waxing lyrical over the welfare state he envisioned, the Sweden Democrats also seek to wrench the *folkhem* from the Social Democrats and retrace it to what they see as its true origin in what the party calls "social conservatism," describing themselves as the "natural heirs" to this legacy (Åkesson 2018: 35). "Had Per Albin Hansson lived today," Åkesson has ventured, "he would in all likelihood have called himself social conservative and nationalist." And: "Had Per Albin also been a Sweden Democrat? That is my firm conviction" (Åkesson 2018: 40, 42).

The turn to the welfare state is something of a trend among nominally right-wing populist parties, and it has been observed and analyzed as such by political scientists (Oskarson and Demker 2015; Fenger 2018; Krause and Giebler 2019). Yet the meaning of this turn remains to be explored. Parties such as the Sweden Democrats turning to the welfare state is neither simply a strategic reach for votes, nor solely a shift in policy, let alone ideology. Most conspicuously and consequentially, this is an appropriation and reinterpretation of a key element in the symbolic code that structures political life in many democracies. The Swedish case illustrates this with perfect clarity.

When the metaphor of the *folkhem* was first adopted by Per Albin Hansson in the 1920s, it became enlisted in an ongoing expansion of civil solidarity that involved progressive liberals as well as Social Democrats. From the turn of the century, and in the idiom of the day, the nation was invoked as the overarching sphere of solidarity within which the plight of the rural poor and the working class could be addressed. Such evolving and expanding senses of solidarity underpinned the introduction of universal franchise in 1919, once the poor and the working class had been incorporated within a sphere of solidarity in which the threat of social upheaval could be averted, initially in the name of the nation, later in the name of the *folkhem* (Enroth and Henriksson 2019; cf. Karlsson 1993; Levin 1997; Linderborg 2001; Björck 2008).

Appeals to the nation among early twentieth-century liberals and Social Democrats thus paved the way for the progressive appropriation of the older conservative notion of the *folkhem*: in the progressive usage both nation and *folkhem* served to subsume – and transcend – the particularities of class within a universalizing vision of civil solidarity (Linderborg 2001: 252, 377; Hellström 2010: 97). For progressive liberals and the Social Democrats of the day, this was a move from the particular in the direction of the universal, from the local and municipal to the national, from the past with its oppressive feudal ties, to a future of emancipation and progress achieved through reform. This is a contextually specific illustration of what Reinhart Koselleck (2004 [1979]) has identified as a general tendency in modernity: an existential shift from a locally circumscribed and historically determined "space of experience" to an always open "horizon of expectation."

Against this backdrop, the Sweden Democrats' appropriation of the *folkhem* is not so much a return to an idea "which the Social Democrats have long rejected" (Åkesson 2018: 35) as it is a return to older particularizing rather than universalizing visions of solidarity. While the party makes much of the generic references to the nation in the 1920s, the universalizing ideals on the basis of which the Swedish welfare state was constructed are carefully ignored (cf. Rothstein 1998; Kildal and Kuhnle 2007; Enroth and Henriksson 2019). "Sweden is built on nationalism,"

Åkesson (2018: 46) explains, "the same sort of nationalism that the Sweden Democrats carry on." This sort of nationalism, we learn in the party program, is "open and nonracist," since "we define the nation in terms of culture, language, identity and loyalty" (SD 2014: 13).

Nationalism, defined in terms of culture, creates "the fundamental conditions for everything that sustains the *folkhem*" (Åkesson 2018: 45). "Culture," in turn, "could be defined as the way of life that unites a society or a certain group of people," a way of life illustrated in the party program by a picture of a dish of crayfish with crown dill, a Swedish specialty traditionally enjoyed in August (SD 2014: 18). And with the nation defined in terms of culture, culture is then defined, in a circular fashion, in terms of the nation: "In its broadest meaning the Swedish culture could be defined as the sum of everything that has ever been thought, written, said, created or done by persons who belong to the Swedish nation." But what the party is mainly interested in preserving is "what we think of as the kernel of the Swedish culture," what has "left its mark on the development of our society, is deeply embedded in Swedish history, is widespread among previously and/or now living Swedes, has a strong symbolic significance for Swedish identity or is in some way unique for the Swedish nation or a certain part of the Swedish nation" (SD 2014: 19).

Aestheticizing the Nation

The substance of this culture on which the past and future of the country and its welfare state are believed to rest is predictably elusive in the written material produced by the party. Ruminations by members of the party leadership prove more instructive. In 2019, Swedish National Television aired a documentary about Mattias Karlsson, former leader of the Sweden Democrats' party group in the Riksdag and often referred to as the party ideologist. In one scene in the documentary, Karlsson is driving from his mother's house in the rural Småland region of the country to a local event at which he is to give a speech. The speech is going to be about how his "mental map" of this part of the country has changed. "Mariannelund, for instance. My entire life, until a few years ago, I thought about Emil" – this is a reference to "Emil in Lönneberga," the fictional farm boy made iconic by Astrid Lindgren, celebrated author of children's books – "when he got his head stuck in the soup tureen, and went to the doctor in Mariannelund. Now I think about Sweden's most brutal gang rape, and that there was an honor killing there. That illustrates a bit what all this is about for me" (SVT 2019: 04:45–05:30; cf. Lindgren 1963).

What all this is about is what the parable does not, and does not need to, explicitly say: that the perpetrators of the gang rape and the honor killing in Mariannelund were not Swedish, that this was inflicted on the community by influences foreign to the place. The contrast between the literary Mariannelund to which Emil in Lönneberga goes to the doctor at some point in the early twentieth century and the actual Mariannelund of the brutal gang rape and the honor killing a century or so later is meant to tell us something about how Sweden has changed in the interim, with the fictional turned into the measure of the factual.

What all this is about is also what the parable is explicitly offered to illustrate: how "the mental map" relied upon by certain people to get their bearings has changed as the country has changed. It is suggested that "until a few years ago" such a map could, for the people in question, be drawn based on the stories we were told as children. Whether genuinely entertained or offered in a political speech to give local color to the doctrinal point about immigration, the notion that what is properly and desirably Swedish – the way of life that unites the society – can be found in children's books about peasant life in Småland in the first decade of the twentieth century is revealing in more ways than one.

Upon closer inspection, the culture to which the party and its supporters so frequently and insistently refer not only appears to be fictional in the aesthetic sense of having been imaginatively brought into existence, but is actually understood by members of the party leadership to be fictional also in the ontological sense of having no obvious or tangible existence outside the symbolic realm. Over footage of himself mowing grass with a scythe – less than nimbly, it would seem – Mattias Karlsson speaks pensively in the documentary of his "dreams and ideals about the perfect way of life [tillvaron]. I'm a romantic at heart, you know. I want some kind of Carl Larsson way of life which of course does not exist. But it is still hard to free yourself of those visions" (SVT 2019: 53:10–53:27).

Carl Larsson was a fin-de-siècle Swedish painter famous for his idyllic watercolors of family life in rural settings.[4] Larsson's art and name are as iconic in context as Astrid Lindgren's Emil in Lönneberga, and as intensely associated with an agricultural way of life that dominated the country well into the twentieth century. His work is in the spirit of what is known in Sweden as "National Romanticism," an aesthetic movement sharing with the nationalist political movements of the day, and with the Sweden Democrats today, the conviction "that the indigenous arts, history, music and folk traditions of a nation contributed to the spiritual and political survival of its people" (Berman 2003). With their picturesque portrayal of domestic life, the watercolors – reproduced by Larsson himself and extensively circulated in a book called *A Home*

(Larsson 1920 [1899]) – spawned a popular aesthetic ideal in architecture and interior decoration, celebrating the rural as "the untouched and the genuine" (Eriksson 1998: 20; cf. Lengefeld 1997).

It may be noted that Mattias Karlsson speaks of himself when he admits to wanting some kind of Carl Larsson way of life, expressing what would appear to be a matter of taste, a personal preference rather than a political statement. But this is a finer, and in fact misleading, point in a mode of discourse that relies entirely on synecdoche, constantly, almost imperceptibly, moving from the personal to the political, from the party to the people, from the local to the national, and back. "Many Sweden Democrats, myself included, feel that as a people, we're under extreme pressure," Karlsson says in the documentary, "we" being presumably we "as a people," the people of Sweden. "And for many years we were pushed aside, bullied, run over [undanskuffade, utmobbade, överkörda]" (SVT 2019: 1:10:23–1:10:43). This makes it less clear exactly who "we" are, but the experiences, as described, and the idiom of victimization in which they are described, suggest the party as much as the people. "I feel some kind of sorrow about that, actually. It's like you don't really belong anywhere," Karlsson says about the strain between his political career and his rural working-class background. "I will never feel at home with the elite in Stockholm," a personal grievance that swiftly morphs into a cultural misery: "To feel at home, to feel safe, to feel that you are a part of a community, that this is disappearing. There is an enormous sorrow in that. And when you feel that somebody is about to destroy or take your home, as you have understood it, away from you . . . that creates strong feelings of sorrow and frustration" (SVT 2019: 49:27–50:29).

Picturing the home that is being destroyed or taken away from you in the image of Carl Larsson's quixotically bucolic A Home would seem a standing invitation to sorrow and frustration, but then picturing your home in this fashion makes it all the more easy to think of it as being destroyed or taken away from you. From its prominent place in the cultural mainstream, this aesthetic vision – the untouched and the genuine – is fused with the political vision of restoring a national culture once untouched but recently violated by forces alien to it, which in turn is fused with the vision of restoring the folkhem in the same terms.

National Romanticism staked its claim around the turn of the nineteenth century by way of the same figure, then, as now, serving as comfort and contrast in troubled times (Stråth 2012: 657). The notion of a national culture being violated is what lends the gang rape and the honor killing in Mariannelund their carefully calculated symbolic weight: women's bodies being the favored ground where certain men's battle for the nation is waged (Theweleit 1987 [1977]; Pitkin 1999; Landes 2001). At issue is not only or primarily the literal violation of another human being, but the metaphorical violation of a nation rendered in watercolor and in storybook prose, an imaginary home so delicately drawn as to require constant and vigilant protection; so delicately drawn, in fact, that even its self-appointed guardians recognize that the image dissolves if examined.

That the national culture in whose name the *folkhem* is to be reclaimed by its true heirs turns out to be not only an imagined but also an imaginary community, a heavily edited, ideologically and aesthetically corrected tourist brochure of selected parts of the country, in no way diminishes the rhetorical and affective force of this construct. On the contrary, by reference to this national culture, civil solidarity can be particularized by marking off both "the elite in Stockholm" – the people with whom Mattias Karlsson will never feel at home, people who may be suspected of a lack of commitment to or feeling for this version of Sweden – and those who migrate to the country as a priori threats against the same culture.

This culture is also what enables the concomitant construction of the party itself and its supporters as the last bulwark standing between the nation and its enemies. "Our opponents have forced us for real into an existential struggle [*kamp*] for the survival of our culture and our nation," Mattias Karlsson wrote on Facebook on election night 2018 (*DN* 2018c), an instant flashback, in the heat of the moment, to the 1990s and the yearly celebrations of the man who lost the empire. Insofar as the national culture appears elusive or even illusory, examination of this construct can be evaded by drawing attention to the threat of violation, or annihilation, rather than dwelling on the specifics of what is being violated or annihilated.

Primordializing Gender Equality

This is how the party has appropriated one of the most incontrovertible elements of the civil code in this country, what is described in a motion to the Riksdag as "Sweden's long and progressive tradition of equality," a tradition which the party "wants to build on, develop, and adapt to the new circumstances and challenges of modern society" (SD 2017: 2). "We should be proud," it is declared in the opening pages of the motion, "that Sweden historically has a long tradition of protecting women's safety and integrity. Already 800 years ago Birger Jarl is believed to have instituted one of the world's oldest laws banning violence and threats against women" (SD 2017: 2).

For the Sweden Democrats, building on, developing, and adapting the long tradition of gender equality in Sweden has most notably meant framing the subject politically as a single-front battle to combat "violence and threats against women." This, in turn, has meant cautioning against "people with a completely different cultural view of women than the Swedish, who cannot respect women's physical integrity. This view of women can result in everything from sexual harassment to assault rape" (SD 2017: 15). It is further noted in the motion that "immigrants [*invandrare*] are five times as often suspected of rape as Swedes. . . . And it is obviously not immigrant Norwegians or other similar people who are behind this new view of women and this terrible violence against women" (SD 2017: 15).

This is a particularly lucid illustration of how the Sweden Democrats' appropriation of the civil code amounts to a primordialization of civil qualities: making gender equality specific to a national culture, and therefore unavailable to groups marked off as uncivil, especially – although in this instance implicitly – Muslims (cf. Alexander 2016: 78). The same divide between a civil core group nationally defined and an uncivil out-group culturally defined is conspicuous in another policy area historically at the heart of the universalizing ambitions of the Swedish welfare state: childcare. In this area, what is and has been since the 1970s a right for all families is implicitly redefined as a right for the native population but an obligation for the immigrant population.

Political ambitions in the area of childcare, it is declared as a matter of principle in the party program, should "support families without interfering with their agency [*handlingsfrihet*]" (SD 2014: 24). "The Sweden Democrats want to give families more possibilities to choose the way of life that is best suited for them and their children" (SD 2016: 41). Presumably in response to "the new circumstances and challenges of modern society," this liberal core principle turns out to be applicable only to the national core group. In a notable exception to the principle, the party has proposed "compulsive preschool for children in disadvantaged areas [*utsatta områden*]." "Many children with a foreign background [*av utländsk härkomst*] grow up in our disadvantaged areas without partaking of the Swedish culture, our Swedish values and our way of life. Maybe they grow up with honor-culture and other values we do not accept in our country" (SD 2018a: 4). Therefore, "children who grow up in disadvantaged areas with two foreign parents should from three years of age attend compulsory preschool" (SD 2018a: 4). For a party eager to paint itself as the true heir to the *folkhem*, this is a striking departure from the kind of universal policies introduced in the formative era of the welfare state (Rothstein 1998), a particularization of universalizing elements of the civil code. The code is rewritten by essentializing out-group attributes as uncivil, which are then politicized by making the out-groups in question the targets of specific rather than universal policies.

At the same time, and no less striking, forms of gender inequality widely deemed uncivil by established parties have been reinterpreted in civil terms by the Sweden Democrats, again by the attribution of essences, in this case biological rather than cultural (cf. Mulinari and Neergaard 2017). In the area of labor market policy – another key area in the postwar *folkhem* – the party proposes that "all forms of quota and preferential treatment [*positiv särbehandling*] based on gender [*kön*] are to be abolished" (SD 2018b: 35). The party program explains that there are "biological differences" between "most women and most men, beyond what can be observed with the naked eye. In a society where people are free to shape their lives themselves these differences will in all likelihood lead to differences in preferences, behavior, and life choices" (SD 2014: 8). What are referred to in the party program as unspecified "differences in how most men and most women choose to live their lives do not therefore have to be a problem, a sign of discrimination, or the result of an oppressive gender system [*könsmaktsordning*]" (SD 2014: 8–9).

The threat being targeted here is not the immigrant population but the enemy within, the left-liberal establishment, the elite in Stockholm who may be suspected not only of a lack of commitment to or feeling for Swedish culture, but also of subscribing to academic theories positing the existence of a gender system. This is yet another illustration of the peculiar time-travel aspect to the party's redrawing of civil boundaries: contingent uncivil exclusions from the past being turned into civil ideals in the present. In this case, the time warp brings us back to the 1950s, prior to the political reforms that would make Sweden a beacon in the area of gender equality (Östberg and Andersson 2013: 182), to a time when even progressive members of the women's movement took for granted the political relevance of biological differences between women and men (Hirdman et al. 2012: 581–2). In defense of latter-day civil emancipation in this area, the Riksdag's Committee on the Labor Market, in which the party has presented its case against all forms of quota and preferential treatment, has remarked on this time warp that if the party got its way, "the clock would be turned back for what has been achieved in Sweden in the area of equality" (Swedish Riksdag 2018: 9).

As a derogatory figure of speech, "turning back the clock" presumes the onward march of history construed as progress, a modernist notion that once inspired the building of the *folkhem* and remains the default position in Swedish political life. This is also a notion squarely at odds with the worldview of the Sweden Democrats. Sweden has been "torn apart," Åkesson (2018: 38) notes in a speech reprinted in his book, "as a consequence of a distinctive politics of disintegration [*utpräglad splittringspolitik*]." "We must get away from all these constructed conflicts that the left-liberal establishment wants to force upon us." What is ailing Swedish society, Åkesson (2018: 57–8) explains,

> is not about class, about how much you make. It is not about gender [*kön*] or sexual orientation. It is not about skin color, about where you are born or where your parents are born. The major conflict in society today, that is about the constructive against the destructive. It is about those who want to contribute to the communal [*det gemensamma*] against those who want to destroy the communal. It is about those who build the cars against those who burn the cars.

For someone watching rather than playing this language game, symbolically rendering the fault line in Swedish society as a tension between those who build the cars and those who burn the cars would not seem a less constructed conflict than what the left-liberal establishment has presumably forced upon us. But this construct captures the very quintessence of the party, the dynamic behind its march from street to parliament: the narrative of loss and decline, and the summoning of the good old times, most recently the era of the *folkhem* and the welfare state, the boom years after World War II when the nation had room not only for one, but two, car manufacturers. In other words, what this construct illuminates is the element of melancholia in betting your fortunes politically on reclaiming – and symbolically retaining – a lost object (Freud 1957 [1914–16]; Lepenies 1992 [1969]).[5]

Fracturing the Civil Sphere

"Insofar as the founding cultural myths and constitutional documents of democratic societies are universalistic," Alexander has remarked (2006a: 61), "they implicitly stipulate that the discourse can always be further extended, and that it eventually must be." This is exactly what is denied by the Sweden Democrats' variety of populism; this is an aspect of the founding cultural-political myths of the country that the party does not accept. As we have seen, the point of the party's tinkering with the civil code has been to rewrite that code in a particularizing language, thus betraying not only the spirit of the political legacy that the party seeks to appropriate, but also the spirit of democracy as such, the notion that universality "can always be further extended, and that it eventually must be."

The narrowing of civil solidarity is all the more insidious when it is done not only by inverting, but also by appealing to and appropriating, the civil code, and when the uncivil is inscribed into a familiar symbolic universe which is seemingly safe, widely cherished, and prima facie apolitical. Hence Emil in Lönneberga and Carl Larsson, and the crayfish with crown dill, and hence Hédi Fried's response to the question of what she found most worrisome in the 2018 electoral season: not the neo-Nazis of the moment but yesterday's neo-Nazis, the protest movement whose parliamentary ambitions came true, the narrowing of civil solidarity by increments, manifested culturally as much as politically.

There is also what might appear at first glance to be a somewhat more upbeat moral of the story: the apparent failure of the party to reinvent itself, to shed its neo-Nazi past and convincingly pass itself off as civil. Not only are regulative and communicative institutions essentially intact after a decade with the Sweden Democrats on the national political scene, albeit not exactly in power. The symbolic boundaries of the civil sphere seem to be holding up as well. Hence the parliamentary isolation in which the party has so far found itself, even though this situation may be changing (*DN* 2019a). And hence the scrutiny in broadcast and print media of past and present deeds and misdeeds. But a disquieting question remains, namely whether and to what extent, and to whom, all this matters; for whom, exactly, does the party's performance come across, or fail to come across, as convincing?

What seems to have happened in Sweden is what has also happened in many other places where populism has risen and spread in recent years. While the insistent drawing of symbolic boundaries around the Sweden Democrats has minimized the party's political influence, three consecutive national elections strongly suggest that marking off the party as uncivil has had no adverse electoral effects for the party itself. And then there has been the suspicion that the parliamentary containment policy might in fact have had the perverse effect of increasing rather than diminishing the party's electoral appeal.

From the point of view of the civil sphere, the predicament is that the drawing of symbolic boundaries around the Sweden Democrats has itself been particularized as an elitist ruse, yet another way in which the left-liberal establishment imposes its worldview on "ordinary people." Whether the target of such boundary work has been the recurrent lapses in the party organization into racism, anti-Semitism, homophobia, and sexism, the party functionaries wearing swastikas, or the street fights involving members of the party leadership, the effect of declaring this uncivil seems to have been to reinforce the party line; insofar as there is an ethical or moral issue here it is not the behavior reported but the reporting of the behavior, the fact that people don't stop nagging. Criticizing the party for failing to take responsibility for its Nazism becomes another way in which the elusive "we" are being pushed aside, bullied, run over.

Placed alongside the party's electoral track record, what this suggests is anything but upbeat: that the received civil code has lost its power to compel a sizeable portion of the population; that the modern consciousness which Nazism will never cease to haunt may have been a more sectional construct than many of us who share that consciousness have wanted to believe. As parties in what used to be a conservative mainstream now seem willing to break the parliamentary isolation of the Sweden Democrats (*DN* 2019a), just how long and how far we can expect this code to be upheld by the agents and institutions that have so far upheld it, such as the Riksdag, is an open question.

The situation with the party and its supporters seems the exact opposite of what is treated at length in the American context in the third and fourth parts of *The Civil Sphere*: excluded or marginalized groups seeking inclusion by contesting entrenched cultural representations of their members as uncivil, not seldom by appeal to the same ideals in the name of which the groups in question were excluded (Alexander 2006a). What we are now seeing in Sweden and in other places where populism has recently risen and spread are people nominally on the inside opting out of the civil sphere; not contesting the ways in which civil ideals are applied by elites, but contesting the universal status of the same ideals, thus delegitimizing not only the elites and institutions purporting to uphold civil ideals, but those ideals as such. The discourse of civil inclusion consists, from this point of view, not of shared ideals imperfectly instantiated in political life, but of imposed "taboos," the "oppression of opinion."

This notion, so successfully implanted and exploited by the Sweden Democrats, is, I suggest, a threat to democracy whether or not populist parties and leaders impinge on institutional autonomy. The threat lies not only in the particularization of solidarity in and of itself, although this is certainly harmful if we wish to address "the broader problem of a democratic social life" (Alexander 2006a: 37). The threat lies above all in the fracturing and polarization of the civil sphere, in the rift between those who do and do not recognize this aspirational community, the very idea of which is that it "transcends particular commitments, narrow loyalties, and sectional interests" (Alexander 2006a: 43). In the case at hand, as in many other cases where populists of the same ilk have burst on the scene, such a rift is already manifest.

To be sure, this is a plight that cannot be attributed solely to populist parties and leaders. In context, the rise and electoral success of the Sweden

Democrats are as much a symptom as a cause of a more complex and protracted retreat of civil ideals in political life (Enroth and Henriksson 2019). But we should make no mistake: a democratic society in which the idea of universalizing solidarity is getting lost on a significant section of the citizenry – and on an apparently growing number of its representatives – is a society that is losing touch with its founding cultural myths.

Acknowledgments

I want to thank the editors as well as the participants in the conference "The Civil Sphere and Populism," held at Yale University on June 14–15, 2019, for stimulating discussions and helpful comments on an earlier version of this chapter.

Notes

1 When I use the term "populism" in this chapter, this is the kind of populism I have in mind, well aware of the fact that this is not a universally applicable definition. For a general consideration, in philosophical and historical terms, of populism and its troubled relationship to democracy, see Enroth (2019).
2 This containment policy may be loosening, as the leaders of the conservative Moderates and Christian Democratic parties have opened for parliamentary collaboration with the Sweden Democrats (*DN* 2019a).
3 In March 2020, the party re-enacted the same drama in Turkey, on the border to Greece, where Jimmie Åkesson distributed flyers with the message "Sweden is full. Don't come to us!," signed "The people of Sweden, Sweden Democrats" (*DN* 2020).
4 See http://www.carllarsson.se/en/.
5 I am grateful to Marcus Morgan, whose perceptive comments on a draft version of this chapter made the melancholy element in the party's discourse clear to me.

References

Åkesson, J. (2012) DN Debatt: "Politiska skandaler drabbar alla svenska riksdagspartier." *Dagens Nyheter*, December 2.
Åkesson, J. (2018) *Det moderna folkhemmet: En Sverigevänlig vision*. Sölvesborg: Asp & Lycke.
Albertazzi, D. and D. McDonnell. (2015) *Populists in Power*. Abingdon and New York: Routledge.
Alexander, J. C. (2003) *The Meanings of Social Life: A Cultural Sociology*. Oxford: Oxford University Press.
Alexander, J. C. (2006a) *The Civil Sphere*. New York: Oxford University Press.

Alexander, J. C. (2006b) Cultural pragmatics: Social performance between ritual and strategy. In: J. C. Alexander, B. Giesen, and J. L. Mast (eds.) *Social Performance: Symbolic Action, Cultural Pragmatics, and Ritual*. Cambridge: Cambridge University Press.

Alexander, J. C. (2016) Progress and disillusion: Civil repair and its discontents. *Thesis Eleven* 137(1): 72–82.

Alexander, J. C. (2019) Frontlash/backlash: The crisis of solidarity and the threat to civil institutions. *Contemporary Sociology* 48(1): 5–11.

Berman, P. G. (2003) National Romanticism. In: *Oxford Art Online*. https://doi.org/10.1093/gao/9781884446054.article.T061109.

Björck, H. (2008) *Folkhemsbyggare*. Stockholm: Atlantis.

Derrida, J. (2005) *Rogues: Two Essays on Reason*. Stanford: Stanford University Press.

DN. (1991) Sverigedemokraterna hotar med vapenvåld: "Det är en allvarlig signal till samhället." *Dagens Nyheter*, December 3.

DN. (1992) Demonstration urartade igen. *Dagens Nyheter*, December 1.

DN. (2012) Åkesson städar upp i SD. *Dagens Nyheter*, October 12.

DN. (2014) SD:s tid i riksdagen kantas av skandaler. *Dagens Nyheter*, September 5.

DN. (2015a) Sverigedemokraterna anser sig ha nått vägs ände i försöken att påverka övriga partier i invandringsfrågan. *Dagens Nyheter*, October 15.

DN. (2015b) SD delar ut flygblad på 20-tal platser vid EU:s gräns. *Dagens Nyheter*, November 9.

DN. (2018a) Jimmie Åkesson: Vi är inte längre något katten släpat in. *Dagens Nyheter*, February 10.

DN. (2018b) Hédi Fried: Vi måste förstå att demokratin är hotad. *Dagens Nyheter*, September 7.

DN. (2018c) Niklas Orrenius: "Fläskig krigsretorik visar SD:s nationalistiska kärna." *Dagens Nyheter*, September 12.

DN. (2019a) Ewa Stenberg: Den politiska gemenskapen mellan KD, M och SD blir allt tydligare. *Dagens Nyheter*, October 16.

DN. (2019b) Rekordstöd för SD – knappar in på S. *Dagens Nyheter*, October 18.

DN. (2020) Ministern om Åkessons flygbladsutdelning: "Helt oseriöst." *Dagens Nyheter*, March 4.

Elder, N., A. H. Thomas, and D. Arter. (1988) *The Consensual Democracies? The Government and Politics of the Scandinavian States*. Oxford: Basil Blackwell.

Enroth, H. (2015) Community? In: H. Enroth and D. Brommesson (eds.) *Global Community? Transnational and Transdisciplinary Exchanges*. London and New York: Rowman & Littlefield.

Enroth, H. (2019) The return of the repressed: Populism and democracy revisited. *American Journal of Cultural Sociology*. https://doi.org/10.1057/s41290-019-00080-z.

Enroth, H. and M. Henriksson. (2019) The civil sphere and the welfare state. In: J. C. Alexander, A. Lund, and A. Voyer (eds.) *The Nordic Civil Sphere*. Cambridge: Polity.

Enroth, H. and M. Sjölin. (2018) Democracy and the cartel party. In: H. Enroth and M. Hagevi (eds.) *Cartelization, Convergence, or Increasing Similarities? Lessons from Parties in Parliament*. London and New York: Rowman & Littlefield/ECPR Press.

Eriksson, E. (1998) Internationella impulser och nationell tradition 1900–1915. In: C. Caldenby (ed.) *Att bygga ett land*. Stockholm: Arkitekturmuseum and Byggforskningsrådet.

Expo. (2016) Här är 9 SD-företrädare som blev kvar i partiet trots antisemitiska uttalanden. *Expo*, December 5.

Expo. (2018) Så gick det med Åkessons nolltolerans – en skandal i veckan. *Expo*, September 3.

Fenger, M. (2018) The social policy agendas of populist radical right parties in a comparative perspective. *Journal of International and Comparative Social Policy* 34(3): 188–209.

Freud, S. (1955 [1920–2]) *Beyond the Pleasure Principle, Group Psychology and Other Works*. London: The Hogarth Press.

Freud, S. (1957 [1914–16]) *On the History of the Psycho-Analytic Movement, Papers on Metapsychology and Other Works*. London: The Hogarth Press.

Hellström, A. (2010) *Vi är de goda: Den offentliga debatten om Sverigedemokraterna och deras politik*. Hägersten: Tankekraft förlag.

Hirdman, Y., U. Lundberg, and J. Björkman. (2012) *Sveriges historia: 1920–1965*. Stockholm: Norstedts.

Jepperson, R. L. (2002) Political modernities: Disentangling two underlying dimensions of institutional differentiation. *Sociological Theory* 20(1): 61–85.

Karlsson, S. O. (1993) *Arbetarfamiljen och det nya hemmet: Om bostadshygienism och klasskultur i mellankrigstidens Göteborg*. Stockholm, Stehag: Symposion.

Katzenstein, P. (1985) *Small States in World Markets*. Ithaca, NY: Cornell University Press.

Kildal, N. and S. Kuhnle. (2007) *Normative Foundations of the Welfare State: The Nordic Experience*. New York: Routledge.

Koselleck, R. (2004 [1979]) *Futures Past: On the Semantics of Historical Time*. New York: Columbia University Press.

Krause, W. and H. Giebler. (2019) Shifting welfare policy positions: The impact of radical right populist party success beyond migration policy. *Representation*. https://doi.org/10.1080/00344893.2019.1661871.

Lacoue-Labarthe, P. (1990 [1988]) *Heidegger, Art and Politics: The Fiction of the Political*. Oxford: Basil Blackwell.

Landes, J. B. (2001) *Visualizing the Nation: Gender, Representation, and Revolution in Eighteenth-Century France*. Ithaca, NY: Cornell University Press.

Larsson, C. (1920 [1899]) *Ett hem: Tjugufyra målningar med text*. Stockholm: Bonnier.

Lengefeld, C. (1997) Den svenske och den tyske Carl Larsson. In: B. Henningsen, J. Klein, H. Müssener, and S. Söderlind (eds.) *Skandinavien och Tyskland 1800–1914: Möten och vänskapsband*. Stockholm: Nationalmuseum.

Lepenies, W. (1992 [1969]) *Melancholy and Society*. Cambridge, MA: Harvard University Press.

Levin, H. (1997) *Kvinnorna på barrikaden: Sexualpolitik och sociala frågor, 1923–1936*. Stockholm: Carlssons.

Levitsky, S. and D. Ziblatt. (2018) *How Democracies Die: What History Reveals About Our Future*. London: Viking.

Lijphart, A. (1977) *Democracy in Plural Societies: A Comparative Perspective*. New Haven: Yale University Press.

Linderborg, Å. (2001) *Socialdemokraterna skriver historia: Historieskrivning som ideologisk maktresurs, 1892–2000.* Stockholm: Atlas.

Lindgren, A. (1963) *Emil and the Great Escape.* Oxford: Oxford University Press.

Loxbo, K. and M. Sjölin. (2017) Parliamentary opposition on the wane? The case of Sweden, 1970–2014. *Government and Opposition* 52(4): 587–613.

Mudde, C. and C. R. Kaltwasser. (2017) *Populism: A Very Short Introduction.* Oxford: Oxford University Press.

Mulinari, D. and A. Neergard. (2017) Doing racism, performing femininity: Women in the Sweden Democrats. In: M. Köttig, R. Bitzan, and A. Petö (eds.) *Gender and Far Right Politics in Europe.* New York: Palgrave Macmillan.

Novus. (2019) Novus/SVT oktober 2019: Väljarna är avvaktande. https://novus. se/valjaropinionen/svtnovus-valjarbarometer/2019-2/novus-svt-oktober-2019-valjarna-ar-avvaktande/.

Novus. (2020) Novus/SVT Senaste väljarbarometer. https://novus.se/valjaropin ionen/.

Oskarson, M. and M. Demker. (2015) Room for realignment: The working-class sympathy for the Sweden Democrats. *Government and Opposition* 50(4): 629–51.

Östberg, K. and J. Andersson. (2013) *Sveriges historia: 1965–2012.* Stockholm: Norstedts.

Pitkin, H. F. (1999) *Fortune Is a Woman: Gender and Politics in the Thought of Niccolò Machiavelli.* Chicago: University of Chicago Press.

Rothstein, B. (1998) *Just Institutions Matter: The Moral and Political Logic of the Universal Welfare State.* Cambridge: Cambridge University Press.

Rothstein, B. and L. Trägårdh. (2007) The state and civil society in a historical perspective: The case of Sweden. In: L. Trägårdh (ed.) *State and Civil Society in Northern Europe: The Swedish Model Reconsidered.* New York, Oxford: Berghahn Books.

SD. (2005) *Sverigedemokraternas principprogram 2003.*

SD. (2014) *Sverigedemokraternas principprogram 2011.*

SD. (2016) Inriktning och mål för jämställdhetspolitiken m.m., punkt 1. Minority Reservation in Labor Market Committee Report 2016/17:AU5, the Swedish Riksdag.

SD. (2017) Åtgärdsprogram för kvinnor i vardagen. Motion 2017/18:3060, the Swedish Riksdag.

SD. (2018a) En förskola i världsklass. Motion 2018/19:380, the Swedish Riksdag.

SD. (2018b) Jämställdhetspolitikens mål och jämställdhetsintegrering, punkt 1. Minority Reservation in Labor Market Committee Report 2018/19:AU8, the Swedish Riksdag.

Skinner, Q. (2001) *Visions of Politics, Vol I: Regarding Method.* Cambridge: Cambridge University Press.

Spivak, G. C. (1995) Love, cruelty, and cultural talks in the hot peace. *Parallax* 1: 1–31.

Spivak, G. C. (2015) Global? In: H. Enroth and D. Brommesson (eds.) *Global Community? Transnational and Transdisciplinary Exchanges.* London and New York: Rowman & Littlefield.

Stråth, B. (2012) *Sveriges historia: 1830–1920.* Stockholm: Norstedts.

SvD. (2015) SD:s kampanj mot flyktingar döms ut. *Svenska Dagbladet,* November 10.

SVT. (2019) Mattias Karlsson: Året fram till valet. Swedish National Television SVT1, March 19.

Swedish Riksdag. (2018) Jämställdhet och åtgärder mot diskriminering. Labor Market Committee Report 2018/19:AU8.

Theweleit, K. (1987 [1977]) *Male Fantasies I: Women, Floods, Bodies, History.* Cambridge: Polity.

Valmyndigheten. (2018) Valresultat 2018. https://www.val.se/valresultat/riks dag-landsting-och-kommun/2018/valresultat.html.

9

Left Populism in a Communist Civil Sphere

The Lesson of Bo Xilai

Andrew Junker

In September 2013, one of the most powerful figures in Chinese politics, Bo Xilai, was sentenced to life imprisonment for corruption. At the time of his downfall, he was the Chinese Communist Party (CCP) secretary of Chongqing, a landlocked western municipality encompassing 30 million residents. As party secretary since 2007, Bo Xilai was the most powerful figure in Chongqing. He also fashioned himself as a populist reformer, emphasizing policies to reverse economic inequality, to privilege the majority over elites, to stamp out corruption, and to revive Chinese socialist morality and "red culture." Under Bo's leadership, Chongqing increased its welfare spending, built affordable housing, enacted *hukou* household registration reform, required party cadres to visit with and learn directly from the poor, spent millions of dollars planting trees to beautify the industrial city, arrested thousands of people for corruption and organized crime, and de-commercialized the city's satellite television station to make public television emphasizing red culture and "shared prosperity" through equitable development. His governance approach became known as the "Chongqing model," frequently contrasted against the neoliberal-friendly and hegemonic "Guangdong model." Breaking from CCP norms for national politicians, Bo welcomed media attention. When he was mayor of Dalian, he was known as "Mr. Fashion" and "the most debonair Chinese official" (Yu 2010: 181). Bo cultivated a charismatic and appealing public style, smiling and joking at news conferences and presenting himself as affable and authentic while speaking frankly about doing good public service. In Chongqing, his speeches emphasized "the people," livelihood issues, shared prosperity, punishing corrupt elites, and stopping the polarization of society into haves and have-nots. His model attracted support from many people who saw market-led reforms as favoring elites and dealing regular working people an unfair hand. As a leader, Bo was popular; as a politician, he was *populist*.

We have here what appears to be, prima facie, a case of populism in a nondemocratic society. I have chosen to explore this case within the context of a volume on populism and the civil sphere because I am interested in the extent to which populism is specific to democracy and the civil sphere. Using a case of Chinese populism, or something as close to populism as I could find in the contemporary People's Republic of China, I aim to shed some new light on the extent to which populism is specific to democracy and the civil sphere.

By looking at populism in an authoritarian context, I am swimming against the current. In recent decades, there have been many scholars calling for us to see populism as intrinsic to democracy and, especially, the cultural organization of democracy. For example, an influential essay by Canovan (1999: 3) argues that populism comes from "tensions at the heart of democracy" and its appearance in politics follows democracy "like a shadow." Arditi (2004: 141) embraced her position, exploring populism as "a possibility embedded in the very practice of democracy itself." Riedel (2017) says populism is a feature of democracy's genetic DNA. Brubaker (2017: 362) sees it as "chronically available in contemporary democratic contexts." Mudde, Kaltwasser, and others have taken up similar positions. Seeing populism as intrinsic to democracy has the merit of turning our attention away from the social grievances that fuel populist movements, which are important but relatively well recognized, and instead focuses on the internal dynamics, especially the cultural meanings, that are central to populist movements in democracies. In short, attention has now turned to the cultural sociology of democracy. How is populism embedded in, or a product of, the cultural organization of democracy and the civil sphere?

If populism really is intrinsic to democracy, then populism in non-democracies should either not exist or be different in ways that help us understand how democracy and populism interact. With this logical implication in mind, I take up the Chinese case in order to help specify the scope of populism's contingency, as well as its universality. By turning to China, the world's largest, most powerful, and best-organized authoritarian regime, I explore how a case of populism unfolded there and what elements of Chinese political culture made such populism possible. These observations are then used to reflect on the relationship of populism to the civil sphere and democracy. I conclude that, in this instance, Bo Xilai did not exploit contradictions in the political culture, as proposed by culturalist theories of populism in democracy. Nevertheless, Bo found in the PRC's leftist political culture useful ingredients for mounting

233

populist discourse. This observation challenges theories emphasizing the specific cultural foundations of populism in democracy and suggests instead that perhaps populism's most elemental cultural organization is to be found in the constitution of modern political legitimacy itself. In addition, the Bo Xilai case suggests that different outcomes for populism in democracies and authoritarian regimes may be ultimately determined by the lack of freedoms in authoritarian regimes rather than by cultural differences.

Defining the Key Term "Populism"

I disaggregate the term "populism" into three distinct phenomena. First, I follow Brubaker (2017: 360) in seeing populism as a "discursive and stylistic repertoire." This discourse approach is quite similar to those who see populism as "thin ideology" (e.g., Mudde 2004; Stanley 2008; Elchardus and Spruyt 2016). The contents of the populist discursive repertoire are somewhat fluid, but a discourse is recognizably populist when actors emphasize the idea of a pure and homogeneous people against corrupt and evil elites (e.g., Mudde 2004; Rooduijn 2014). Populist discourse emphasizes a romanticized solidarity of "the people." Populists like to speak in the name of "the people" to foment "some kind of revolt against the established structure of power" (Canovan 1999: 3). The trope of "people versus the elite" is especially important for outsider politicians and political entrepreneurs, who try to use populism to gain power at the center of established institutions. If we see populism as "only" discursive repertoire rather than an essentialized phenomenon, then we can see populism being used widely by different political actors, not just those typically seen as populist. As Brubaker (2017) notes, populist rhetoric is available to any public speaker in democratic contexts, some of whom may just dabble with populist rhetoric to spice up a speech while others may go full throttle to build a populist movement based on the discursive and stylistic repertoire.

When populism as repertoire is used to mobilize resources and people (Jansen 2011), then I speak of populist movements, which involve, for example, special-purpose associations and campaigns targeting populist goals. These are empirically distinct from the simple deployment of populist cultural repertoire. Finally, in addition to populist repertoires and populist movements, we might also venture to speak of populist solidarity communities. Somewhat more late Durkheimian and less instrumental than a populist movement, a populist solidarity community (or "society" or "sphere") may form when the populist movement community becomes an end in itself, a community with its own intrinsically rewarding shared identity, morality, logic, social practices, and sense of belonging, all of which are derived from the shared imagery of homogeneous, everyday people in revolt against a corrupt elite.

Is Populism Intrinsic to Democracy? If So, How?

Historically, social scientists have explained populism using a materialist framework based on grievances, such as economic inequality creating anger at elites and leading to populist movements. More recently, however, a trend in the literature on populism has emerged to complement this materialist view with cultural arguments. Rather than only see populism as a product of social grievances and social conditions, many have come to see it also as a product of the specific cultural organization of democracy – claiming, in effect, that the political culture of democracy contains within it a contradiction in meanings that creates the conditions for populism to emerge.

There are different views on what the specific contradiction is that facilitates the rise of populism. Perhaps the most common version of this formulation is that liberal democracy puts into tension the ideals of majority rule and of protecting minority rights, and that populist movements erupt as a breach in the perennial balance between the two. As Mudde and Kaltwasser state, populism and liberal democracy have an "ambivalent" relationship, which is due to the

> internal contradiction of liberal democracy, that is, the tension between the democratic promise of majority rule and the reality of constitutional protection of minority rights... In this struggle, populism is clearly on the side of majority rule. Moreover, as an essentially monist ideology that believes in the existence of a "general will of the people," populism is hostile towards pluralism and the protection of minorities. (Mudde and Kaltwasser 2012: 17; for similar positions, also see Beetham 1992; Mudde 2004; Pappas 2014)

There are other candidates that attempt to account for how populism is generated out of cultural contradictions within liberal democracy. Canovan, drawing on Oakeshott, argues that populism is spurred by a contradiction between pragmatic and redemptive political "faces" or "styles" that coexist within democracy. These two faces are "opposed" but "also interdependent," while "between them lies a gap in which populism is liable to appear." In her view, the pragmatic political style views democracy as an unenchanted institutional mechanism for resolving conflicts among competing interest groups without violence or repression, whereas the redemptive political style views democracy as a means for collective salvation, emphasizing the enchanted, redemptive possibilities of democratic community. She holds that it is the tensions between the two "that provide the stimulus to populist mobilization" (Canovan 1999: 9, 10).

Still another variant on the theme of internal contradictions within democracy comes from my work with Chan on the civil sphere (Junker and Chan 2019), which proposed that the key contradiction that spurs populism is the tension between particularistic, national identity and democracy's universalistic idealism. Using civil sphere theory (CST), we argue that democratic solidarity is anchored at two different spots in the hearts of its polity members. At one place, it is tethered to deeply felt sentiments of ethno-nationalist belonging, of the particularistic self-identity of being, for example, American, French, or Korean. And in another spot of the heart, democratic solidarity is tethered to the noble, universalistic ideals of democracy, like human rights and political equality. These two moral commitments, made primarily through socialization, inadvertently produce a structure of meaning cleaved by their mutual contradiction. Moreover, this contradiction can be exploited by right-wing populist entrepreneurs to attack liberal elites for "selling out the people" in the name of universal values. Like Mudde, Canovan, and others above, Chan and I see a contradiction in the cultural meanings that organize democracy, and the civil sphere in particular, as facilitating the emergence of populism.

All of these approaches share the perspective that something specific to the cultural organization of democracy and/or the civil sphere facilitates the rise of populism. They imply that in real existing civil spheres, the democratic civil sphere's cultural organization of affect and meanings within political culture make populism both possible and endemic. Running in tension with this line of reasoning is the fact that populism does not occur only in modern liberal democracies. Consider, for example, the decade of the Cultural Revolution in China, which was populist in rhetoric, mobilization, and even in Durkheimian social formation. Does the possibility of populism occurring in a communist state system undercut the proposition that populism is inherent in democracy? Or does such populism suggest that underneath the different political cultures and institutions of democracy and authoritarianism, there is a common modernist code of political legitimacy that makes populism possible in both? Do both cases involve the same codes of the civil sphere, even if the civil sphere in China is buried to the point of near invisibility? How does CST explain and interpret populism in China?

China and Civil Sphere Theory

Approaching these questions requires that we conceptualize China's political culture within the framework of CST. Following Alexander (2006), the modern civil sphere, when fully developed, is a form of universalistic political solidarity based on shared morals and logical principles, and that is institutionally supported through formal regulative and communicative institutions. The combined effect of these different elements gives the civil sphere some autonomy from the state and some capacity to curtail state action. Whether or not China has any degree of a civil sphere is debatable.

Perhaps the obvious position is to argue that China does not have a civil sphere because it has neither liberal democratic political institutions nor any universalistic solidarity sphere that is meaningfully autonomous from the state. Moreover, China has its own cultural traditions that shape and maintain social and political solidarity. These traditions come both from its own traditional history and from modern communism (Palmer 2019). Given the alignments of forces, both institutional and cultural, against the democratic civil sphere, some will find it logically forced to argue that China has some kind of latent or limited civil sphere, in the sense used by Alexander.

Nevertheless, there are strong arguments suggesting that the universal reach of CST applies even to Communist Party-led China in some limited form (e.g., Khosrokhavar 2015, 2019; Kivisto and Sciortino 2019: 294). In favor of that position, we can note that the Chinese communist revolution certainly aspired to create social solidarity based on modern and universalistic ideals of liberation, freedom, equality, creative autonomy, and dignity. In the CCP's seventy-plus years in power, the party has repeatedly attempted to lead society to overcome various forms of economic and social inequality, including those based on class, gender, and ethnicity, at times through revolutionary mobilizations but more typically in the last four decades through policy reforms. Some of these efforts have been tremendously successful, such as bringing over 850 million people out of extreme poverty since the 1970s. Like any civil sphere in any real society, many attempts at civil repair in China have not been successful, and some of the failures have been spectacularly devastating, as in the Great Leap Forward and the Cultural Revolution. But we can still identify in those projects the modernist ambitions of social solidarity, equality, autonomy, and freedom from oppression that are all associated with the civil sphere.

Khosrokhavar (2015, 2019) argues that even in authoritarian societies civil spheres can exist in immanent and suppressed ways. We see empirical validation of this assertion when protest uprisings occur in authoritarian contexts but still mobilize under the banners of civil sphere morality, as occurred in the Arab Spring movements of 2011 (Alexander 2011). Key to Khosrokhavar's formulation is that he distinguishes between a subjective civil sphere and an institutionalized one, meaning that people might hold or learn the values and principles of an autonomous civil society even when living in authoritarian settings. This distinction between subjective and institutionalized civil spheres allows Khosrokhavar to explore how the cultural elements of a civil sphere can circulate and trigger social movements, even in places where civil spheres are not politically institutionalized and where states are hostile to autonomous civil society. Khosrokhavar's theorization emphasizes the role of the Internet and social media in creating this subjective "world civil society" or "virtual civil sphere." Websites like Facebook and Twitter effectively circulate notions of "self-determination, individual freedom, and the dignity of the individual," reinforcing subjective moral and logical commitments to an ideal civil sphere (Khosrokhavar 2015: 148, 155). At the same time, Khosrokhavar (2019) also notes that countervailing social forces can undermine civil spheres, transforming nascent civil solidarities within authoritarian regimes into "ambivalent" or "uncivil" spheres.

Since the election of President Trump, the rise of "fake news" has shifted how many see the progressive potentiality of the Internet in democratic societies. In China over the past decade, state control over the Internet has become so thorough that it effectively prevents the diffusion mechanism proposed in Khosrokhavar's 2015 analysis. Fictional media, like Hollywood movies, and capitalist retail advertising still enter China from overseas, and may have some similar effects to those Khosrokhavar attributed to social media, but these effects are less politically direct or articulate. At the same time, Chinese education, propaganda, and party-supervised organizational life are incessantly at work reinforcing collectivist and patriotic belief in the paternalistic state. Much of that effort appears today to be quite successful in achieving its aims.

From these different theoretical threads – namely populism, democracy, China, and CST – we can synthesize two conclusions relevant to studying Bo Xilai's case. First, populism in China, whether as a cultural repertoire or as social mobilization, is inherently threatening to the regime. This is because populism, which implicitly favors some kind of civil autonomy, challenges the paternalistic domination of society by the state. Given how threatening populist challenges are for authoritarian systems, we can expect that any leader using populism would seek some balance that harnesses popular frustrations against elites without also alienating the rulers themselves. In the analysis of Bo Xilai below, we see that he attempted that delicate compromise.

Second, the uncertainty of how to classify China vis-à-vis CST suggests that we need more empirical understanding of what moral codes and cultural elements are involved in the constitution of contemporary China's political culture. Bo Xilai's populism provides us with a useful case study, because we can look for what moral appeals and what contradictions, if any, he exploited to create a message that resonated with the general public. In the analysis below, I conclude that the political culture of CCP-led China, similar to democracies, contains within it symbolic resources that make populist insurgency possible, at least discursively. The big difference between populism in democratic and China's communist civil spheres, then, is found not so much in their respective cultural organizations as in the capacity and readiness of the CCP to use repression and propaganda to eliminate populist challenges. Thus, formal political institutions and social control, rather than ideal culture, is the more decisive factor.

Bo Xilai's Populism

China does not usually feature in the news about populism because there isn't much to see. Populism is associated with opposition movements targeting the structure of power. Without elections or the autonomous space for opposition movements, the Chinese public sphere does not provide much structural opportunity for populism. Nevertheless, there are exceptions to the rule, one of which was Bo Xilai, who, as party secretary of Chongqing, was the most powerful leader in the huge municipality of 30 million mostly rural residents from 2007 until 2012.

The Bo case has a few advantages for our purposes. First, Bo has been widely described, by both supporters and detractors, as "populist." Some speculate that his populist style made him considered dangerous by the central leadership and that contributed to his downfall. Second, Bo and the Chongqing model he led were well liked by pro-Mao, leftist populists in the general public, as seen, for example, on the leftist website Utopia (*wuyou zhi xiang*).

Finally, a third advantage of the Bo Xilai case is its importance to contemporary China. Bo's leadership was nationally recognized and by many measures quite successful (Huang 2011; Szelenyi 2011; Lu 2012). As the party secretary of Chongqing, Bo developed and championed China's most prominent alternative urban development model. Commentators on the left, who criticize pro-market reforms for going too far, see the fall of Bo as primarily about neutralizing the ideological threat he posed to the neoliberal-friendly development model exemplified by the cities of Guangzhou and Shenzhen and embraced by Beijing (Zhao 2012; Meng 2016). When viewed from this perspective, Bo's sudden fall from power – including removal from his post, being expelled from the party, trial, and life imprisonment – was not just about a corrupt official or elite factional competition. It was also about subduing a major ideological challenge to the Beijing consensus for its model of economic development. For this reason, Bo's political demise has been viewed as comparable to "the downfall of Mao's designated heir Lin Biao in 1971 or the crackdown in 1989" (Zhao 2012: 1).

Born in the momentous year of 1949, Bo Xilai, like China's President Xi Jinping, is a "princeling," meaning a child of a famous CCP leader from the revolutionary era. Bo's career depended in part on the behind-the-scenes support of his father, Bo Xibo, who was a key ally of former President Jiang Zemin. Bo Xilai was mayor of Dalian from 1993 to 2003, then governor of Liaoning Province, then China's minister of commerce from 2004 to 2007, and finally became Chongqing's Communist Party secretary in 2007, where he remained until his fall. Bo accumulated many feathers in his cap during his career, including being widely credited for transforming the Dalian economy, where property values increased tenfold in ten years, and for greatly improving the city's living conditions; being a successful trade negotiator in the Ministry of Commerce, including during China's ascension to the World Trade Organization; and turning around the economic fortunes of Chongqing's economy. In addition to being ambitious and effective, he was also widely disliked and even feared by many with whom he worked. In public, he was charismatic and flashy, but "back stage" he was known for despotism and even brutality (Wines 2012). At several points in his career, he was denied positions or honors he coveted owing to dislike of him by colleagues and superiors. In 2007, when hoping for a vice-premiership and a spot on the Politburo Standing Committee of the CCP, he was instead shunted to the relative periphery, namely Chongqing. Assignment to the post of party secretary of Chongqing, an industrial western city beset with seemingly intractable problems like a criminalized local economy, a majority rural population, and severe pollution, was widely viewed as being banished to the political periphery. Bo is reported to have opposed the appointment because he, like many others, saw it as an attempt to definitively sideline him at fifty-eight years old from the central corridors of power.

Instead, however, Bo used his position in Chongqing as a kind of de facto campaign platform to get himself catapulted back to the center of power (Lam 2010; Yu 2010; Johnson 2012). This is where populism enters the Bo Xilai story. It was in Chongqing that Bo embraced a populist discourse emphasizing regular people over elites. By making bold policy choices, he succeeded in changing the city's apparently dismal fate, bringing economic growth and investment. During the 2008 global financial crisis, for example, Chongqing reported a remarkable annual growth of 14.3 percent as other cities in China were slowing down (Yu 2010: 152). Chongqing's success gave it the luster of an alternative development model emphasizing balance between economic growth and economic equality. Bo called this *gongtong fuyu*, which means "equitable prosperity" or "getting rich together." Economists have considered the Chongqing model a serious and largely successful alternative to the neoliberal-friendly model of Guangdong and Shenzhen. Under Bo's leadership, Chongqing reduced social and economic inequality while increasing economic production. The Chongqing model involved technocratic institutional mechanisms that stopped real estate speculation, created affordable housing, expanded urban residency rights to rural residents, and aimed to increase the annual income of all poor residents (Huang 2011; Yuan 2011; Lu 2012; Zhao 2012). Bo successfully blended policies that favored state-led development with increasing foreign direct investment.

Another side of the Chongqing model was not about technocratic policy choices but about performativity and mobilization through nostalgia for the days of Mao. In 2008, Bo effectively invented a new electronic text genre called the "red text." His first text, which shared a quotation from Chairman Mao, was re-texted 16 million times. Red texts became a new genre of social messaging associated with Bo (Yu 2010: 195). He also organized and frequently led gatherings to sing Mao-era songs, which came to be known as *changhong*, or "singing red." Official statistics reported that in the eighteen months between June 2008 and November 2010, Chongqing hosted 226,100 singing red events (Tong 2012). Bo personally led the singing of "The East is Red" at some of these concerts, which included thousands or even tens of thousands of people (Yu 2010).

Bo also pursued other policies to promote left populism. For example, he required Chongqing officials to spend time each week listening in person to complaints from the rural poor. Officials were each to "adopt" a poor citizen and visit the family twice a year "as one might with a relative" (Zhao 2012: 8). In 2011, Bo took the controversial step of de-commercializing Chongqing satellite television. The broadcaster was turned into an instrument for revitalizing red culture and offering television programs about social inequality and equitable development (Lu 2011). But the leftist campaign also had risks. Eventually, just before

Bo was dismissed, Premier Wen Jiabao criticized these red culture initiatives as a return to the forbidden ultra-leftist tactics of the Cultural Revolution, essentially using Bo's red populism as the cudgel with which to strike him down.

In June 2009, after the singing red campaign was established, Bo initiated the second campaign that defined his era as Chongqing chief, which was an aggressive war on organized crime and official corruption, called the "strike black" (*dahei*) campaign. The campaign involved arrests of over 5,000 gangsters, wealthy business owners, and government officials (Wang 2013). Bo's strike black campaign seized national media attention by immediately targeting the former chief of police for Chongqing, who was eventually tried and executed in 2010 for his collusion with organized crime. Bo's anticorruption campaign created huge publicity and drama in national and international media, increasing his local popularity and broadening his national appeal. The campaign, we can also speculate, may have started as a convenient distraction: shortly before it was launched, photos had been circulating online in China showing Bo's high-school-age son, Bo Guagua, partying and leading a debauched lifestyle in an expensive British private school (Yu 2010: 207).

Since the arrest of Bo, the strike black campaign has often been criticized for being ruthless and trampling on the rule of law, including arbitrary arrests, degrading rights and due process, using torture to gain confessions, expropriating private wealth to fund expensive public works projects, and targeting political and economic enemies. Perhaps less than an exercise in the rule of law, the campaign was a performance of populist power. Even while it was ongoing, efforts were underway to turn the campaign into a movie and television series (Wines 2012). Bo's key subordinate, vice-mayor and police chief Wang Lijun, implied the performative dimension of strike black when he said that it appealed to the popular ideal of "stealing from the rich to give to the poor." But Wang also said that his political model was not Robin Hood but Vladimir Putin. According to Wang (quoted in Tong 2012), "Out of ten people, Putin would destroy two of the rich people, and the other two rich people, seeing this, would willingly give away what they have in order to preserve themselves. The remaining six poor people would say 'well done.'" The strike black campaign, as a performative project, communicated Bo's willingness and ability to bring down elites and champion the ordinary people.

Throughout these campaigns, Bo promoted himself with a populist style, emphasizing down-to-earth leadership, while still being charismatic, media-savvy, handsome, and charming to the media (Lam 2010; Yu 2010; Johnson 2012). In 2011, his Chongqing comeback strategy appeared to be working and he was widely considered a promising candidate for membership on China's most powerful leadership body, the Politburo Standing Committee, which was to be chosen at the Eighteenth Party Congress in 2012. His anticipated portfolio would have been to oversee all of China's domestic security.

We might call all of this policy reform and cultural innovation the substantive project of Bo's Chongqing model. The model emphasized equitable development, a massive crackdown on official collusion with organized crime, and the promotion of pre-reform-era socialist values. There remains another side to the Bo Xilai story, however, which concerns the scandals that triggered his fall: in February 2012, his long-time ally Wang Lijun feared that Bo had turned against him and so attempted, unsuccessfully, to defect through the US consulate in Chengdu. The event led to Wang's arrest by the national police. It also triggered the exposure of Bo's wife, Gu Kailai, on suspicion of the murder of her British business associate, Neil Heywood. For that crime, she was eventually charged and sentenced to death (commuted to life imprisonment). On the final day of Bo's trial in 2013, he accused Wang and his wife of having an affair, adding more fodder for perception of a soap-opera-like scandal (Li 2013). When the scandal of Wang Lijun's attempted defection happened, it triggered the pretext for Bo's dismissal and incarceration. Within days, Beijing became "awash" with rumors of an attempted but failed national coup (Aderlini 2012), allegedly organized by Bo's ally Zhou Yongkang to overthrow China's top leaders, Hu Jintao and Wen Jiabao. If those rumors were true, then Bo's arrest precipitated a major crisis in Chinese politics. Although we cannot know for certain what occurred, the entirety of the picture suggests that Bo used populism to propel himself back to the center of power and that populism also made him a target for those who did not want him there.

Was Bo Xilai a Populist Leader?

Bo Xilai's career situation when he arrived in Chongqing helps to explain why he took the risky path of embracing a populist discursive and stylistic repertoire. His appointment had sidelined him and he needed extraordinary measures to propel himself back into the center of power. Putting aside the question of motivation, let's look at how much and in what ways Bo actually adopted a populist discourse. Recall that populism is a discursive repertoire that romanticizes a homogeneous "people" and vilifies elites and elite values. Was Bo's discourse populist in this sense? How did he speak of the people and elites?

Bo's speeches certainly emphasized "the people" and corrupt elites. Nevertheless, his populist discourse was leftist and thus different from the right-wing populism that prevails today in democracies. As a left-wing populist, Bo spoke of "the people" in class terms and scarcely emphasized their particularistic attributes as ethnic Chinese. For example, in a February 2012 speech (Bo 2012), he spoke of "the people" with terms that connoted ordinary folks, the working class, or the masses. These terms all carry the meanings of people as the regular folks and as the unified majority, which is a standard populist trope. Bo's depiction of the people primarily referred to economic class. Of his many terms for "the people" in the materials I examined, he did not refer to people as "citizens" (*gongmin*) and infrequently to people as an ethnic kin group (*zu*). His version of "the people" is fundamentally about economic rather than political or ethnic standing. This statement from a 2011 speech (Bo 2011) captures well this emphasis: "[We must] really fix the actual problems of ordinary people (*laobaiing*) having clothes, food, housing, work, and the like. [We need to] ensure the low- and middle-income masses (*zhong di shouru qunzhong*) have enough to eat, enough to wear, good homes to live in, and let them get by in comfort."

His portrayal of "the people" also fits the homogenized and at times romanticized ideal as identified in our working definition of populism. In the materials I examined, Bo did not spend much time presenting an enchanted or romanticized view of the people, but that does not mean it is not there. The masses of workers and peasants are the symbolic heart of the image of society that was propagated in Chongqing through the red culture campaign and television broadcasting. Bo's own public statements also occasionally romanticized "the people." For example, in a 2009 press conference about the strike black campaign, he legitimized the campaign by saying it was a response to "the strong voice of the people calling for the crackdown."[1] In another statement expressing an enchanted representation of the people, Bo (2012) criticized party cadres who are lazy and isolate themselves from the people. In contrast to cadres, he said "the masses of the people are the most pure and honest 'materialists.'" In Chinese socialism, of course, to be a materialist (*weiwu zhuyi zhe*) is a noble thing. In these examples, Bo invoked an enchanted and homogenized representation of the people that fits our definition of the populist discursive repertoire. Perhaps because his version of the people is left-wing, his representations of the people did not emphasize the kind of ethnic "heartland" rhetoric that Taggart (2000) made so central to his definition of populism.

Following our definition above, populist discourse should also involve portraying elites as villains and rejecting elite values. Bo's portrayals of elites are quite ambivalent. In the materials I examined, the only elites he portrays as villains are corrupt or lazy officials. Corrupt officials, Bo frequently stated, were the CCP's biggest existential threat (Bo 2011, 2012). Bo also severely criticized lazy party officials, who might not break the law but were in danger of "slowly killing" the party through waste and neglect. Here, for example, is a colorful excoriation of what he portrayed in 2012 as the nine types of bad officials:

> First, there are those who talk, make reports, and write essays all without using their brains. They talk big, but it's all bluster. They just string together a bunch of nonsense, continually making up impressive-sounding things to say without any idea of what it actually means. Second, there are those who hang around without doing anything, just shuffle work this way and that, pass the buck to others, sit around and debate what to do without ever actually getting up to do anything. Third, there are those who have meetings to decide about more meetings and create new documents to implement old documents, just working to look busy and important. Fourth, there are those who never go into the field, don't do any research, don't understand what their superiors are saying, and don't understand what those below them need. These guys are what we call the "officials with three moves" – thump, point, spin. They thump their chests when making a decision, point to their brains as they make hasty and thoughtless choices, and then, when things go wrong, they turn, spin ass around, and disappear without a trace. Fifth, there are those officials who only report good news, not bad news, pass on things people want to hear, exaggerate any accomplishments, and skip over any problems. Then, sixth, there are those who are lazy and undisciplined. They get to the office, drink a cup of tea, smoke a cigarette, and spend half the day on a single phone call. Seventh, there are those who don't read books and don't study. They just play video games, speculate on stocks, and play poker and mahjong. Eighth are those who live extravagantly and wastefully. Constantly pleasure-seeking, refurbishing the office to be more and more luxurious, upgrading the office car to be more and more fancy. Ninth are those who are slick and tactful in their dealings and like to be "nice" in everyone's eyes. They equivocate and never take a strong public stance. They are like bricklayers who only smooth out the wet concrete or like carpenters who, when measuring, squint through just one eye to avoid seeing everything around them. The only thing these guys don't want to be are blacksmiths, who face the real problems directly, like iron against iron! (Bo 2012)

These criticisms of corrupt and irresponsible officials are not fully in line with the populist analytical type because Bo does not excoriate the elites as a class for exploiting the political system for personal gain at the expense of the ordinary people. But his criticisms fall neatly within what we might call communist populism, which, like Mao, attacks bureaucrats for furtively usurping the revolution. Bo only dared to explicitly criticize the bad apples of the party; elsewhere he strongly defended its values and leaders. He did not suggest that bad officials are the result of a systematic deficiency in party institutions or ideology. Instead he vigorously and unequivocally praised the party and its leadership. Naturally, we should put his rhetorical stance in context: Bo was the CCP secretary for Chongqing, he was vying for a top spot in the central power structure, and this was not a democracy in which regular people might vote for him in opposition to the wishes of those at the political center. Rational incentives precluded Bo from engaging in a more populist attack on political leaders at the center, as expected within a democratic system. Here, we see him striking a balance between harnessing anger at those in power and not challenging the legitimacy of the central leadership or the party.

Bo also did not use his speeches to attack the emergent capitalist classes. Criticizing owners of capital for exploiting labor could have been a regular theme for him, especially given that his central ideological position was to criticize the way society had become polarized into haves and have-nots (*liangji fenhua*) and to advocate for a strong interventionist government to promote "equitable prosperity." He criticized the system that allowed inequalities to form and become reinforced, but he did not attack the wealthy as a class, or owners of factories or titans of industry per se. In fact, much like during his tenure as mayor of Dalian, he was exceptionally successful at recruiting global manufacturers to set up factories in Chongqing (Huang 2011). For example, he persuaded the infamous Taiwanese firm Foxconn, known for high suicide rates among its workers in Shenzhen, to move 200,000 jobs from Shenzhen to Chongqing. At the same time, he prevented the company from replicating in Chongqing its manipulative workplace housing model (Zhao 2012: 6). In summary, when it came to vilifying elites and elite values, Bo deployed the populist discursive repertoire in a muted way. He used the populist repertoire to gain popular support but always within what he probably imagined were safe enough boundaries.

Conclusion: Cultural Resources for Populism

I return now to the theoretical considerations that prompted this inquiry. A number of scholars have argued for ways in which the cultural organization of democracy, and especially some kind of contradiction in "the heart of democracy," facilitates populism such that it follows democracy "like a shadow." But if populism is tied to the symbolic structure of democracy, then how do we understand populism in authoritarian settings? How universal are its cultural dynamics? How do these dynamics relate to the civil sphere?

Bo Xilai, like populist politicians in democracies, found cultural resources within his own context, namely the CCP-dominated political culture of China, to make compelling populist claims. This finding raises questions for those who emphasize cultural mechanisms for explaining a robust relationship between democratic culture and populism, like populism being derived from the tension between majority rule and minority rights or between the pragmatic and redemptive democratic "styles." In particular, Bo's populism conjured up a kind of epic narrative of Chinese unity and modernization through the singing red campaign and other activities that harnessed nostalgia for the Maoist era of collective campaigns. At the same time, he also emphasized economic equality through a discourse of "getting rich together" and robust policy reforms to more equally distribute the benefits of economic growth. The strike black campaign was dramatic and powerful in this regard as well, as many common people yearned for corruption to be stopped and relished the idea of punishing crooked officials, crime bosses, and crony capitalists, all of whom were thought to enjoy abundance when ordinary people could not get ahead.

What does the Bo Xilai case of populism say about our governing question: to what extent is populism specific to democracy and the civil sphere? It suggests both challenges to the theoretical framework I outlined above and some promising new directions. Bo found cultural resources within the communist political culture to make compelling populist claims, meaning that although populism differs by context, it is widely available. This suggests that the cultural fundamentals of populism go beyond the particular cultural organization of liberal democracy. Perhaps populism's most basic cultural requirement is the anchoring of political legitimacy in "the people," which means it would be an endemic possibility not just in democracy, but for any modern nation.

Modern civil spheres, whether democratic or communist (if we dare posit such a possibility), have in common the foundational notion that political legitimacy ultimately comes from "the people," who are imagined in secular and egalitarian terms. Political challengers can harness this ideal and oppose the government by claiming elites are failing to act in the genuine interests of the people. Thus, populist criticism should, in principle, be culturally available to anyone motivated to use it, whether in democratic or authoritarian settings. Populism may be intrinsic to modern political culture, rather than democratic culture in particular.

247

The most striking difference between Bo Xilai's populism and populism in democracies is not found in its symbolic organization. Instead, the difference lies in the capacity for people to mobilize in opposition. In a democracy, the communicative and regulative institutions of the civil sphere create the freedom for populist discourse to breathe, grow, and become social movements and electoral campaigns. Bo Xilai was an extraordinary figure because his powerful position as Chongqing party secretary allowed him to assert a populist project which implicitly criticized the prevailing authorities and amplified his political influence in national politics. After he consolidated thoroughgoing control over Chongqing, dramatized by the execution of the former chief of police for corruption, he had enormous freedom to pursue his ambitious political quest under a populist flag. As he succeeded in raising his profile nationally, he became more of a threat to his intra-party factional competitors and to the hegemonic consensus for a neoliberal-friendly development model. Without the institutions that protect the autonomy of opposition forces in society, Bo's project was swiftly brought to a halt when central authorities arrested him on charges of corruption. We can conclude from this outcome that the difference between populism in democracies and in China is decisively found in the capacity and readiness of the CCP-led state to use repression and propaganda to eliminate insurgent challenges. Thus, civil sphere institutions rather than subjective symbolic culture ultimately bear most consequentially on political outcomes.

Acknowledgments

Sincere thanks are due to Yunyi Chen, former Teaching Assistant, Centre for China Studies, Chinese University of Hong Kong, for suggesting this topic, identifying and translating key research materials, and providing valuable comments.

Note

1 "Ting dao minzhong dui dahei chu e qianglie de hushing" (https://www.youtube.com/watch?v=_EuNGqxTr3w).

References

Aderlini, J. (2012) Beijing on edge amid coup rumors. *Financial Times*, March 21.

Alexander, J. C. (2006) *The Civil Sphere*. New York: Oxford University Press.

Alexander, J. C. (2011) *Performative Revolution in Egypt: An Essay in Cultural Power*. London and New York: Bloomsbury Academic.

Arditi, B. (2004) Populism as a spectre of democracy: A response to Canovan. *Political Studies* 52(1): 135–43.

Beetham, D. (1992) Liberal democracy and the limits of democratization. *Political Studies* 40(1): 40–53.

Bo, X. (2011) Bo Xilai: Suoxiao san ge chaju cujin gongtong fuyu – Bo Xilai zai Chongqing shiwei sai jie jiu ci quanhui shang jianghua zhaiyao. Aisixiang. m.aisixiang.com/data/43980.html.

Bo, X. (2012) Bo Xilai 2012 nian 2 yue 2 ri jianghua. China Institute for Reform and Development. http://www.chinareform.org.cn/Explore/saying/201203/t20120324_137601.htm.

Brubaker, R. (2017) Why populism? *Theory and Society* 46(5): 357–85.

Canovan, M. (1999) Trust the people! Populism and the two faces of democracy. *Political Studies* 47(1): 2–16.

Elchardus, M. and B. Spruyt. (2016) Populism, persistent republicanism and declinism: An empirical analysis of populism as a thin ideology. *Government and Opposition* 51(1): 111–33.

Huang, P. C. C. (2011) Chongqing: Equitable development driven by a "third hand"? *Modern China* 37(6): 569–622.

Jansen, R. S. (2011) Populist mobilization: A new theoretical approach to populism. *Sociological Theory* 29(2): 75–96.

Johnson, I. (2012) China's falling star. *The New York Review of Books*, March 19. https://www.nybooks.com/daily/2012/03/19/chinas-falling-star-bo-xilai/.

Junker, A. and C. S. Chan. (2019) Fault line in the civil sphere: Explaining new divisions in Hong Kong's opposition movement. In: J. C. Alexander, D. A. Palmer, S. Park, and A. S.-M. Ku (eds.) *The Civil Sphere in East Asia*. New York: Cambridge University Press.

Khosrokhavar, F. (2015) The civil sphere and the Arab Spring: On the universality of civil society. In: P. Kivisto and G. Sciortino (eds.) *Solidarity, Justice, and Incorporation: Thinking through The Civil Sphere*. Oxford: Oxford University Press.

Khosrokhavar, F. (2019) The civil sphere and its variants in light of the Arab Revolutions and jihadism in Europe. In: J. C. Alexander, T. Stack, and F. Khosrokhavar (eds.) *Breaching the Civil Order: Radicalism and the Civil Sphere*. New York: Cambridge University Press.

Kivisto, P. and G. Sciortino. (2019) Conclusion. In: J. C. Alexander, D. A. Palmer, S. Park, and A. S.-M. Ku (eds.) *The Civil Sphere in East Asia*. New York: Cambridge University Press.

Lam, W. (2010) Xi Jinping's Chongqing tour: Gang of princelings gains clout. *China Digital Times*, December 19. https://chinadigitaltimes.net/2010/12/xi-jinpings-chongqing-tour-gang-of-princelings-gains-clout/.

Li, J. (2013) Bo Xilai tells of Wang Lijun's secret "love affair" with his wife Gu Kailai. *South China Morning Post*, August 27.

Lu, K. (2012) The Chongqing model worked. *Foreign Policy*, August 8. https://foreignpolicy.com/2012/08/08/the-chongqing-model-worked/.

Lu, X. (2011) Government subsidies, market socialism, and the "public" character of Chinese television: The transformation of Chongqing satellite TV. *Modern China* 37(6): 661–71.

249

Meng, B. (2016) Political scandal at the end of ideology? The mediatized politics of the Bo Xilai case. *Media, Culture & Society* 38(6): 811–26.

Mudde, C. (2004) The populist zeitgeist. *Government and Opposition* 39(3): 541–63.

Mudde, C. and C. R. Kaltwasser. (2012) *Populism in Europe and the Americas: Threat or Corrective for Democracy?* Cambridge: Cambridge University Press.

Palmer, D. A. (2019) Three moral codes and microcivil spheres in China. In: J. C. Alexander, D. A. Palmer, S. Park, and A. S.-M. Ku (eds.) *The Civil Sphere in East Asia.* New York: Cambridge University Press.

Pappas, T. S. (2014) Populist democracies: Post-authoritarian Greece and post-communist Hungary. *Government and Opposition* 49(1): 1–23.

Riedel, R. (2017) Populism and its democratic, non-democratic, and anti-democratic potential. *Polish Sociological Review* 3(199): 287–98.

Rooduijn, M. (2014) The nucleus of populism: In search of the lowest common denominator. *Government and Opposition* 49(4): 573–99.

Stanley, B. (2008) The thin ideology of populism. *Journal of Political Ideologies* 13(1): 95–110.

Szelenyi, I. (2011) Third ways. *Modern China* 37(6): 672–83.

Taggart, P. (2000) *Populism.* Buckingham: Open University Press.

Tong, Z. (2012) Quanmian fansi Bo Xilai shi mincui zhuyi, Fenghuang wang pinglun, Tong Zhiwei. News.iFeng.com. http://news.ifeng.com/mainland/special/chungking/content-2/detail_2012_12/24/20481387_0.shtml.

Wang, P. (2013) The rise of the Red Mafia in China: A case study of organized crime and corruption in Chongqing. *Trends in Organized Crime* 16(1): 49–73.

Wines, M. (2012) In rise and fall of China's Bo Xilai, an arc of ruthlessness. *The New York Times*, May 6. https://www.nytimes.com/2012/05/07/world/asia/in-rise-and-fall-of-chinas-bo-xilai-a-ruthless-arc.html.

Yu, S. (2010) *Xin Taizidang.* Hong Kong: Mirror Books.

Yuan, G. (2011) Rural development in Chongqing: The "Every Peasant Household's Income to Grow by 10,000 Yuan" project. *Modern China* 37(6): 623–45.

Zhao, Y. (2012) The struggle for socialism in China: The Bo Xilai saga and beyond. *Monthly Review* 64(5): 1–17.

10

A Civil Sphere Theory of Populism

American Forms and Templates, from the Red Scare to Donald Trump

Jason L. Mast

In this chapter, I discuss how contemporary approaches to populism conceptualize language, and examine how they connect this source of meaning to the processes of emergence and consolidation of populist social relations. Next, I describe how civil sphere theory (CST) conceptualizes language, and I suggest how the framework, in the way that it connects the symbolic order to the social arena of civil and non-civil spheres, creates theoretical spaces for the emergence of populism. Focusing on those spaces, I propose civil sphere definitions, forms, and causes of populism. Finally, I apply these formulations to US civil sphere processes and presidential campaigns, from the 1950s to the present, and suggest how the civil sphere approach opens up new understandings of the processes by which populist social relations emerge and take root in the American community.

Language and Emergence in the Populism Literature

One of the defining features of populism is the development of a starkly drawn, antagonistic division between the "people" and the governing establishment or social elite (Urbinati 2019). The most promising approaches conceive of populism as an understanding or subjective orientation that becomes widely shared across substantial portions of a collectivity. It is a collective representation of the social whole, a cosmology of its internal differences; populism reduces social distinctions to a small number, and charges them with moral significance. The archetypical populist narrative holds that a corrupt and morally compromised elite monopolizes institutions of power and lords them over a people, who are conceived of as the true bearers of civic virtue, moral rectitude, and authentic national identity. The plot is one of restoration: the people will act collectively to reclaim authority over the key public institutions of civil society and the state, and purge these arenas of corrupt elites, impure agents, and, in the US case, counterdemocratic structural forces.

Populism is a meaningful orientation toward the social world. It is organized by language and cultivated through communication. Activists and aspiring candidates explain the social world through its genre conventions, and citizens reproduce its logic and invoke its signs when they tell each other stories about the public state of affairs, and discuss what they plan to do about its ills. These meanings shape people's actions in direct and indirect ways. Kazin's (2017) magisterial look at populism in American history represents it as such. In his analysis, we see that populist narratives are an endemic if not constitutive feature of American political discourse and civic understandings. Kazin (2017: 1) defines populism in light terms, describing it as "a language whose speakers conceive of ordinary people as a noble assemblage not bounded narrowly by class, view their elite opponents as self-serving and undemocratic, and seek to mobilize the former against the latter." In this approach, populist language can be evident in or even pervade public discourse without a populist "revivalist" mood emerging (Canovan 1999) or its simplified group formations taking shape.

How we conceptualize language has considerable implications for how we conceive of populism, where we look for it in the social world, and how we explain both its purchase for those who embrace it, and its consequences. We can see this in the literature on populism. For instance, Mudde (2017) points out that increasingly studies of populism train their focus on language and shared, collective understandings of social divisions, which he calls the ideational approach. An exemplar of the framework, Mudde represents the cultural form that precipitates the populist understanding as a "thin ideology." He emphasizes that he means ideology in the broadest of terms, or, to paraphrase, as a body of normative ideas about the nature of people and society that create a shared mapping of the social and political landscapes for members of a community. Populist ideologies are thin, he explains, in the sense that they are not elaborate and extensive mappings of political principles, values, means, and aims.

Mudde's framework is simultaneously too broad and too narrow. As an interpretive framework through which people come to make sense of their worlds, in his version, populism lies somewhere between understandings about the nature of existence, on the one hand, and general advice and a few specifics about policy orientations, on the other. Language is mainly conceptualized as a tool for describing things. The only guide

Mudde gives us for why people may come to interpret their worlds in populist ways is a reference to political preferences and interests.

Another approach emphasizes the strategic aspects of populism (Weyland 2017). It turns our focus toward figures who talk in populist-discursive ways because they think that they will gain from engaging in this practice. Aslanidis (2016), for instance, turns to Erving Goffman and the social movements literature to explain how populist understandings are the product of exposure to discursive frames. A "populist frame," he argues, can be "perceived as the systematic dissemination of a frame that diagnoses reality as problematic because 'corrupt elites' have unjustly usurped the sovereign authority of the 'noble People' and maintains that the solution to the problem resides in the righteous political mobilization of the latter in order to regain power" (Aslanidis 2016: 99). Aslanidis further argues that framing improves our understanding of the phenomenon because it connects populist discourse to cognition. Once we make the cognitive turn, he claims we are able to apprehend populism for what it really is, namely "deliberate activity" (Aslanidis 2016: 99–100).

This illuminates why candidates may employ populist tropes, and draws our attention to how they make such calculations. It struggles, however, to tell us much about how or why citizens may be drawn to such frames, or how the frames might cultivate among citizens strong feelings of antagonism toward the elite. Are audiences not capable of seeing the instrumentality motivating the populist speaker? If they are as rational and strategic as the candidate, then one would think so. If this is the case, then populism is, in effect, merely transactional. Why go through the populist drama, then? On the other hand, if the audiences are not able to accurately detect the "deliberate activity" behind the populist presentation, then why not? Is it due to false consciousness? To address this issue, Aslanidis (2016: 100) argues that the frames affect audiences because they resonate with the latter's "cultural toolkits." This concept was introduced (Swidler 1986), however, to demonstrate that people are strategic in their use of cultural symbols (Vaisey 2009; Mast 2020). To invoke it to explain frames' purchase is simply to reiterate the logic of deliberate activity.

Another version of the political-strategy approach, which also conceives of discourse as practice, emphasizes the pragmatic dimensions of populism. Bonikowski and Gidron (2016), for instance, represent populism as the product of aspiring political actors who strategically cultivate this subjective mapping amongst their constituencies in order to accumulate capital and gain advantage vis-à-vis their competitors in the relational field of politics and state administration. The authors conduct automated text analyses for these populist-discursive phrases in

JASON L. MAST

US presidential campaign speeches from 1952 to 1996. Two surprises in their findings are relevant to our purpose. The authors find that in terms of the frequency of saying populist phrases, the former army general and Republican president (from 1953 to 1961) Dwight Eisenhower and longtime senator and Republican presidential candidate (in 1996) Bob Dole were two of the most aggressively populist campaigners in postwar America (Bonikowski and Gidron 2016: 1606). By conventional standards,[1] neither of these lifelong public servants approximates the populist form either in campaign style or as administrators or leaders. These findings indicate that focusing just on talk and strategy, and bracketing the structural dimensions of discourse and the nonrational dimensions of action, as in the framing approach, leads us to miss some key features of the populist phenomenon. Only by connecting populist talk to a more complex theory of meaning will we be able to unpack how populist genre features provoke identification and sentiments of solidarity among citizen publics.

The Civil Sphere Theory of Language, and Its Relation to the Social

The civil sphere theory of populism I develop below is predicated on the notion that language, and therefore meaning, is multilayered (Alexander 2006: 53–61). Some of its elements are foundational, in the sense of being enduring and structuring. Others are more flexible, context-sensitive, adaptable, and ephemeral. The civil sphere theory of populism posits that the phenomenon develops out of the interplay of these levels of meaning. While the meaning structures are collective and extra-individual in nature, they are also unequally distributed across groups and individuals. A person's location in the social arena will influence which levels of these symbolic structures they are exposed to, and shape the range of meanings they will become familiar with within any particular level. The organization of this symbolic universe is related to the organization of the social world. The nature of this relationship is key: while it is theoretically contingent and variable, the orders are nonetheless connected and share points in common, ones that remain much more stable and durable than others. The relationship grants both orders dimensions of autonomy. The symbolic order patterns experience, but actors have the capacity to act back on and manipulate it.

The discourse of civil society, structured by its binary codes, creates a variably thin and thick cosmology of the social arena. The complex, highly differentiated social order is symbolically patterned. The symbolic order bends at the boundaries of noncivil spheres, and it bends differently for different types of people. This rule of variability is true of symbolic patterns within noncivil spheres, as well. The civil sphere is an anchoring node in this universe of meanings, and it contributes significantly to the constitution of collective identity. It can act as a counterforce to the splintering effects of noncivil sphere processes, and may serve as a trusted source of critique and interpretation. Citizens' identities are cobbled-together constellations of meanings drawn from the multiple social spheres they are embedded in and interact with. Populism plays on the tensions between these spheres. It excites and exploits their differences, on the one hand, or critiques and seeks to reform them, on the other.

Toward a Civil Sphere Theory of Populism

In civil sphere terms, populism is a discourse that constructs the civil sphere as profoundly compromised. The populist "mapping of the social" insists that the social center, the civil sphere, is broken and must be fixed. Populism, therefore, is a project of repair and restoration. Being compromised means that the civil sphere's boundaries need attention. They need to be strengthened because in their current form they have allowed undesirable, undeserving, counterdemocratic, and ultimately dangerous persons or structural forces into this powerful but also vulnerable space. Populism simplifies the cosmology of the civil sphere, reducing it to its putative true and authentic representatives, on the one hand, and to those persons or forces that threaten and distort it, on the other. The former are core groups and in-groups. The latter are the undesirables, the undeserving, the counterdemocratic, and the dangerous. All of these representations of purity and danger are to be found in noncivil spheres.

Regarding the latter category, particular ethnicities may be constituted as undeserving, certain sexualities and genders as undesirable, specific religions as dangerous, and members of a race as incapable of embodying the community's standards of the ideal citizen, for example. Returning to the former, core groups are typically successful at claiming to be authentic representatives, in part, because their primordial noncivil characteristics, such as race, ethnicity, and religion, have signified the civil sphere's founders and protectors from its origins, through its vicissitudes, to the present. These are the archetypical signs of "full civilship" (Mast 2019). Founding myths, and narratives of having cultivated and defended the civil sphere, fuse particular noncivil characteristics with civilness, and lend them outsized power, which can have the effect of making them sources of distortion within the civil sphere (see Alexander 2006: Chapter

16). Theoretically, these features represent the noncivil intruding into the civil, or the particular asserting dominance not only over other identity groups but over the collective representations of the universal, as well. Alexander's theory of the civil sphere helps explain this.

The Civil Sphere, Democratic Elections, and the State

What exactly is the civil sphere, and why are citizens who embrace populist narratives so concerned about its status? Democratic elections serve as a gateway between the civil sphere and the state. The state is one of the most powerful tools for affecting changes back on the civil sphere, and on noncivil spheres, as well. Campaigns take place in the civil sphere, and move the victors into the state.

In democratic elections, candidates talk in symbolically coded registers of the broader community's civil discourse. They narrate versions of the ideal civil community, emphasizing that it is constituted by freedom, for instance, or dedicated to justice, or that fairness and equality are its sacred values. At campaign rallies, during televised debates, and in interviews with the press, candidates specify how the civil sphere is presently compromised. They name forces that are distorting it, and they suggest which kinds of people are preventing it from becoming the ideal version of itself. When candidates propose policy plans, they are telling citizen audiences how they will use the power of the office and the mechanisms of the state to act back on the civil sphere, and how they will improve conditions in and between noncivil spheres. On Election Day, citizens vote for the candidate who performed the ideal vision of the community that best approximates their own senses of national identity. They vote for the figure who they believe will use the power of the state effectively to move the national community closer to a particular civil ideal. In this way, democratic elections move people and particular cultural understandings – discourses and narratives of the ideal community – from the civil sphere into the state.

Once in office, a candidate-turned-politician uses the powers of office to act back on the civil and noncivil spheres through rational bureaucratic as well as still more discursive and performative means. In contentious democratic politics, the opposition is always cast as standing in the way and preventing the ideal from being brought to fruition. Here we turn to Alexander's (2006) theory of the civil sphere, which I present briefly and in abstract terms, in order to establish a model for discussing how populism in the late-modern United States is precipitated by boundary shifts and intrusions between and amongst its civil and noncivil spheres.

Noncivil Spheres

The United States is a social arena comprised of multiple social spheres, most of which are noncivil spheres, and one of which is the civil sphere. Noncivil spheres are institutional arenas like the state, economy, family, religion, or political party. Communities formed of shared identities, which are organized around meaningful characteristics and practices such as those associated with gender, race, ethnicity, or sexuality, also constitute noncivil spheres. Noncivil spheres have their own *particular* criteria for inclusion. They have their own norms and rules that guide participation, and their own symbolic means for determining what distinguishes an ideal member from a bad one. Noncivil spheres produce their own forms of power and dimensions of stratification, and they have their own bases of legitimacy for justifying their unequal distributions of resources. Noncivil spheres' boundaries are found where their media of exchange, interests and means of pursuing them, distributions of power, and their bases of authority to command are no longer recognized as legitimate. Noncivil spheres do not differ from one another entirely, however; some evaluative criteria are shared by a great number of noncivil spheres. Yet the spheres do have boundaries, and cross-boundary intrusions produce agitation. Populism arises out of an accumulation of unwanted intrusions.

All of these spheres, noncivil and civil alike, are in motion. Their boundaries are always shifting and the relations between them are variable. Spheres may peacefully coexist adjacent to one another, or their boundaries may become sites of intense conflict. For instance, a noncivil sphere may find itself critiqued according to the evaluative codes of another sphere. When the evaluative criteria of a noncivil sphere like religion is brought to bear on another noncivil sphere like sexuality to judge if its practices are moral, for example, the backlash is likely to be intense. Classification changes within one sphere may lead to conflict with a seemingly unrelated sphere. For instance, processes of resignification in a gender sphere, like the increasing prevalence of trans- or nonbinary gender, may lead to conflict over the norms governing the shared use of public spaces such as bathrooms. Those who do not recognize the justification claims of nonbinary genders may engage in backlash practices.

Social actors are embedded in multiple noncivil spheres at the same time. Their identities are composites of their noncivil sphere associations. They feel dimensions of solidarity with others who signal that they, too, identify with particular noncivil spheres. Contemporary actors are members of the *civil sphere*, as well, though to varying degrees, depending on the composition of their noncivil identities and memberships.

JASON L. MAST

The Civil Sphere

The civil sphere is one independent sphere within this greater arena of spheres. It differs from the noncivil spheres in that its criteria for inclusion are not based on ascribed characteristics such as race or gender, or on achieved statuses such as professional titles or accumulated resources like wealth. Instead, the civil sphere is structured by collective representations of abstract, universalistic civil characteristics and capacities, ones that roughly two millennia of political and normative discourse has specified as representing the constituent elements of the ideal democratic citizen. Alexander (2006: Chapter 4) calls this culture structure the binary code of civil society.

The civil sphere is a structure of understanding and feeling. A binary cultural code is the bedrock of the former. It structures understanding by distinguishing democratic traits, actions, and motives from undesirable, counterdemocratic ones. People are allowed in and made full members of the civil community to the extent that they demonstrate that they embody the positive, democratic side of the code. They are excluded from the civil sphere if they are deemed incapable of embodying the civil capacities, or unwilling to participate accordingly. These figures are interpreted as constituted by the characteristics specified by the negative, counterdemocratic side of the code. This code's substantive dimensions, both positive and negative, are not derivative of noncivil sphere identities or interests. They are in theory characteristics any human, regardless of gender, race, ethnicity, religion, and so on, is capable of embodying. Good democratic citizens are rational, active, reasonable, calm and controlled, realistic and sane. Excluded are those who embody the opposite side of the code. They are held to be irrational and prone to succumbing to their emotions, or they are dependent on other people's interpretations, and overly deferential to others' judgment. They are passionate, even mad. Populism suppresses the civil code. Populist narratives emphasize noncivil characteristics instead, and argue that they are more pertinent criteria for determining who may be a member of the "people," and who should be allowed to enter and participate in the civil sphere.

The civil sphere is also a structure of feeling. Having an intuitive understanding of critical, evaluative criteria that dictate membership and guide participation in the civil sphere, and feeling like one embodies the positive aspects of this code in an absolute way, represents the feeling of possessing full civilship (Mast 2019). It means feeling like one has free and unencumbered access to its social spaces and public arenas, or as if one could show up and participate in public discussions and debates at one of the coffeehouses in Habermas's public sphere. Being included means having a voice. It means feeling confident in sharing one's opinions on matters of public concern, and being uninhibited by anxieties over potential sanctioning or exclusionary reactions for having spoken.

Metaphorically, the civil sphere is the "center" of American civic and political culture (Alexander 2006: 61–2). In a healthy and vibrant "arena of spheres," as I put it above, the binary code of civil society is akin to being the hegemonic discourse of the broader, imagined community. Real civil societies are complicated, however. The civil sphere is populated by core groups and in-groups, who act within it with a strong sense of full civilship. Out-groups, on the other hand, have only limited access to it, or no access at all. They are out-groups, after all, because they are interpreted as embodying the negative characteristics of the civil code. The populist narratives of the 2016 US presidential election were not describing a healthy and vibrant arena of spheres but instead a damaged and endangered civil sphere.

Populism in Civil Sphere Terms

In this section, I translate the features of populism discussed in the first section into CST terms. As mentioned above, in civil sphere theoretical terms, populism is a discourse that constructs the civil sphere as compromised, and in dire need of repair. Populism aims at the restoration of the civil sphere. Its boundaries need attention. They must be strengthened and, in a conceptual sense, moved in social space. Bolstering its boundaries will produce the effect of limiting the flow of out-groups who aim to make their way in and gain inclusion. Moving the boundary, or shortening the civil sphere's diameter, will result in reducing the number and kinds of noncivil sphere identities in the civil sphere by expelling those who only recently gained access, or by making their presence feel encumbered, monitored, and rescindable. Populist narratives assert that the civil sphere is in danger now, however. They do not propose long-term reform projects. Action must be taken; the next election is critical.

Populism builds a plot by asserting that current circumstances require that the "people's" noncivil sphere identity traits represent the most important and determinative criteria on which citizens must base their interpretations and actions. This symbolic inflation displaces the binary codes of civil society and obscures their performative power, or their ability to shape people's interpretations of the present. For instance, political parties and electoral coalitions are noncivil solidarity spheres. Populism inflates the degrees of antagonism between the parties, or between these opposing solidarity spheres. It insists that party identification should determine one's vote regardless of which candidate appears to better embody the positive, democratic codes of civil society.

Translating populism's features into CST terms enables us to identify a couple of basic forms that populist restoration movements may take. One form aims to re-establish the hegemony of core groups' primordial, non-civil identities within the civil sphere. It consists of core groups claiming providence based on primordial criteria, and asserting dominion over the symbolic civil center. This version focuses attention on a small number of noncivil spheres and reduces their symbolic complexity. Elevating some of their structural features, it argues that these essential traits are the most important criteria for determining action, on the one hand, and that they are either morally superior or dangerous, on the other. Turning to the practice of campaigns and elections, populist narratives tell citizens that they should focus on these noncivil criteria and use them to determine how to vote. In addition to elevating core-group identities, this version of populism also proposes purifying the civil sphere through strengthening barriers to entry and expelling illegitimate interlopers. It argues that it will restore horizontal relations within the civil sphere, but only once it has been purged according to the vertical logics of the pertinent ethnic, racial, religious, or other noncivil criteria. This represents a rationale for authoritarianism: the only way the true community's horizontal relations can be restored is by going through an intense period of internal policing that sorts people in terms of a strict verticality.

While the first CST form of populism is based on core-group primordialism, the second is based on structural intrusion. This second form of CST populism aims to re-establish a civil sphere that is undistorted by organizations and actors who have gained excessive power in noncivil spheres, and then exercised this power within the civil sphere itself, through dominating communicative institutions and eroding their autonomy, for instance, and through exercising disproportionate influence over the sphere's regulative institutions. In the primordialist form, we see a populist movement channeling a kind of affirmative energy into symbols of core-group essence, and a negative energy into those of out-groups deemed to be polluting. In the structural-forces form, by contrast, we see the movement channeling negative energy at symbols of social structural forces and actors who have outsized power over and within them, and positive energy toward representations of a civil sphere in which the people pursue community through practices of cooperation and deliberation that are undistorted by noncivil sphere powers, resources, and interests. This form of populism seeks to cleanse the civil sphere of noncivil intrusions that are structural in nature, and whose resources have accumulated in the hands of a few powerful actors.

The first form approximates the conventions of right-wing populism, and the second form resembles what is conventionally called left-wing populism. In the 2016 US presidential election campaigns, Republican candidate Donald Trump structured his campaign around the first form, and Democratic candidate Bernie Sanders around the second. These forms are not mutually exclusive, however. A candidate may make one form the dominant theme in his or her campaign narrative, and then complement it with features from the second form. As we will see, George Wallace engaged in this strategy in 1968, for instance. Different combinations can yield different forms of populist fronts. Combining a critique of structural forces with a championing of core-group identities makes for a powerful blend, which is suggestive of a workers' populism that also invokes ethno-national, noncivil sphere traits in an effort to push the state administration to reform not only the economic sphere but also the state itself so that it will rewrite its immigration regulations.

Candidate Sanders maintained strict boundaries on his populist narrative. He limited it to critiquing market incursions into the state, a development that, he argued, had enabled the market to then invade and distort the civil sphere through both direct financial as well as state-regulatory means (through the Citizens United ruling, for instance). Candidate Trump combined the two forms. On the one hand, he emphasized the purity of primordial core groups, and cast particular religious, racial, and ethnic noncivil sphere identities as profoundly dangerous, and as having invaded the civil sphere. On the other, he plagiarized candidate Sanders's critique of a corrupted state elite and a compromised market. Sanders's oft-repeated phrase of staging a "political revolution" was populist in its revolutionary imagery while it simultaneously remained rooted in the civil by the qualifier "political." In contrast, Trump marshaled civil codes to achieve anticivil and counterdemocratic ends. He argued that the political elite must be uprooted and its leaders imprisoned. While he incorporated themes of market forces causing distortions within the civil and noncivil spheres, he maintained that he could take care of these personally through phone calls to his business associates, and thus a revolution of the Sanders variety would not be necessary.

With these formulations in hand, we can move toward identifying some of the sources and causes of populism that the civil sphere framework brings to light. The first CST form of populism outlined above represents core-group, primordial noncivil traits asserting dominance over the civil sphere. One way this is precipitated, however, is through an accumulation of instances in which the civil code has crossed boundaries into noncivil spheres and forced changes within them so that their internal power and resource distributions, and their norms and hierarchies of relations, conform more closely to the civil ideal. This is a form of "frontlash" (Alexander 2019). Through such processes, gender relations within the family may come under scrutiny, for instance, or business owners may be pressured to provide their goods and services to customers whom they would have declined to serve prior to the civil intervention. For instance, prior to the civil intrusion into the noncivil, a baker may have declined to prepare a cake for a gay couple planning their wedding. Frustrations accumulate within noncivil spheres as agents continue to deploy the civil code within them and insist on compliance with it. Populist sentiments form and consolidate as a surplus of resentments accumulate from such experiences. A form of backlash populism may arise that seeks to re-establish former vertical relations within and across noncivil spheres, and to reduce the influence of the civil and the frequency with which it is invoked. In this scenario, a populist people's "demands" are the surplus of resentments born of civil intrusions on the noncivil sphere identities, resources, and vertical relations with which members of the "people" strongly identify and feel solidarity.

Successful civil repair movements also represent frontlash. These movements aim to expand the civil sphere in order to include those who have been excluded owing to unjust terms. Strings of successful civil repair movements precipitate backlash. For those who propel the backlash, the civil code is experienced as intrusive. It represents simultaneously cultural condescension and oppression. It is, after all, a code of critique. It dictates how real social conditions fall far short of the democratic ideal. Criticism causes embarrassment and cultivates resentment. Citizens will make demands for autonomy from the code, or the freedom to harbor their own sentiments and beliefs, free of criticism. These demands accumulate over time. Agents in communicative institutions, such as talk radio hosts, for instance, identify the structure of sentiments taking root across publics. They specify, refine, and crystallize these sentiments and frustrations into narratives that have a strong intuitive appeal to their audiences. This dynamic seeds populism, but is insufficient in itself to precipitate a robust populist movement. These dynamics are ongoing. They vary in terms of intensity. Multiple collective resentment formations develop, peak, and dissolve all the time, and each according to its own timeline.

A CST Analysis of Right-Wing American Populism: From the Red Scare to Donald Trump

A particular form of right-wing populism burst into the American civil sphere in 2016 and laid claim to the center. Its narratives outlined what we can call Trumpist civilship. It articulated a vision of strengthening the civil sphere's boundaries in order to severely restrict access to it; of contracting its boundaries in order to expel or unsettle groups who recently gained access to it; and of reconstituting vertical relations within the civil sphere and across spheres in a way that privileges core-group primordial characteristics.

Trumpist civilship was not entirely new. Rather it was the reanimation of one of the two right-wing populist forms that began to emerge in the 1950s and hardened into archetypes in the early 1960s. The style of politics Trump pursued had not strutted the national stage (with a few exceptions) and gained such audience approval since George Wallace consolidated its tropes into a coherent form during his gubernatorial and presidential campaigns some fifty years earlier. The form envisioned a restricted civil sphere structured by primordial hierarchies, and non-civil spheres free of civil intrusion. It was open and explicit about its certitude regarding racial and ethnic fitness for civil participation, and brusque in its expression of masculinity's lead role in gender relations. It championed blue-collar laborers, and denigrated intellectuals, policy experts, and cultural and media elites. Wallace performed as a single "strongman" standing up to the system. He had no need for strategists or a team of stage and costume managers. It was him, on stage, speaking forcefully to supporters, mainly white men who worked with their hands.

Richard Nixon fashioned the second form. Formally, this version rejected the *explicitness* of the first form's particularism and its open embrace of primordial hierarchies. It did not entirely reject the substance of the form's cultural predilections, however. Instead, it recoded these sentiments into more normatively acceptable, less exclusionary signs, like "the great silent majority," and "law and order," for instance. This version translated the first form's sentiments into signifiers with two meanings, a signified for each of two audiences: one for those who leaned toward the inclusive and universalist, and one for the exclusionary and particular. The Nixon form would follow in the wake of the Wallace form, and alternately court and condemn the latter's adherents. Naming its supporters the silent majority, and identifying its enemies as the press, the administrative establishment, and movement activists of all stripes, the Nixon form was designed with the ambitions of seizing the middle as well as the right flank of the electorate. It aimed to retake the social center.

The Nixon template dominated the ascendance and maturation of the New Right. Its dominance within the Republican Party, however, produced internal backlash movements in which the Wallace form would thrust itself back onto the stage. In the 1990s, after twelve

years of Ronald Reagan and George H. W. Bush playing "conservative president" in the Nixon mode, Patrick Buchanan found that the
Wallace character could still generate considerable support. In the
2010s, after eight years of President Barack Obama's performance of
an inclusive universalism, and of frontlash victories (Alexander 2019),
Donald Trump tried on the Wallace costume yet again. In 2016, the
Wallace-like populist defeated Democratic candidate Hillary Clinton, an
Obama-esque, inclusive, "stronger together," multiculturalist woman,
to win the presidency.

The rise and success of Trumpist civilship shocked the network of
agents who had dominated the civil sphere's communicative institutions,
and who had narrated the ascendance and expansion of a national and
civil identity rooted in the inclusive ethos of multiculturalism. Suddenly,
in 2016, these opinion-makers and journalists were narrating the arrival
of something that appeared entirely foreign, as if they were witnessing
an alien invasion of the civil sphere. The entry of Trumpist civilship
onto the national stage was, rather, the spectacular if contingent and
improbable crystallization of backlash (Alexander 2019) processes a
half-century in the making. If journalists at the leading legacy press
organizations had peered through the multicultural discourse to the
periphery, they would have noticed that they had a network of far-right
colleagues constructing radically different narratives of the American
civil sphere and distributing them through the latest online platforms, as
well as over the airwaves.

Many of the most anticivil and antipluralist elements of Trumpist
civilship have circulated within segments of the American right since the
United States' triumphant expansion in the wake of the Great Depression
and World War II. Franklin D. Roosevelt's Democratic Party was the
Big Bang of the twenty-first-century American cultural and political
order. Led by Roosevelt, expansionist Democrats threaded public state
institutions into a multitude of noncivil spheres, most prominently the
economic but also the civil, domestic, and intimate spheres. Roosevelt's
New Deal interventionism dominated mid-twentieth-century America's
narratives of desirable governance. Throughout much of the 1950s,
President Truman and his Republican successor, Dwight Eisenhower,
perpetuated this cultural order, and supplemented it with a robust inter-
nationalist component.

The right in the late- and post-Roosevelt years experienced an identity
crisis. The party's branding – its signs of economic excess and cultural
refinement, its insistence on the virtues of laissez-faire capitalism, and its
warnings about the dangers of coddling the needy with support programs
– fit poorly with the post-Depression recovery period. Ultimately, the

party's inflation of the Red Scare narrative, and this effort's dramatic implosion, would push conservatism further to the margins. Yet it was in this context, one marked by a sense of impending collapse crosscut by fits of missionary zeal against the left and communism, that the right began to assemble its new dramatic and discursive form.

In Kazin's (2017) representation of mid-twentieth-century anticommunist populism, we can see the right discovering the characters and basic plotlines around which it would eventually develop its narratives for reclaiming the civil center. Intellectuals, liberal professors, and the media and cultural elite were weakening the civil sphere's boundaries and ushering in godless communists, they argued. These figures would play the role of the enemy establishment. The right still needed to cast itself as an agent in the drama, however, and identify a virtuous people it could champion and claim to protect. For the latter, it introduced the "middle American," a figure who through hard work and self-discipline had saved up and bought a home of his or her own. The right folded this character into narratives of government and civil intrusion, on the one hand, and religious revival, on the other. For instance, taxes and integrationist policies aimed at desegregation represented the civil imposing itself illegitimately within domestic, intimate, and local community noncivil spheres, it would argue. The intellectual elite's disregard for religion, and its alternately curious and tepidly antagonistic responses to communism, signaled its godlessness. The right would represent and protect "average Joes" against these forces. Eventually, this dramatic arrangement would produce, for "the first time in United States history," a movement of activists and politicians that mobilized "a populist vocabulary to *oppose* social reform instead of support it" (Kazin 2017: 167).

Yet the right also had to represent itself as a character in the drama. It retired its costume, the Monopoly game's Rich Uncle Pennybags, along with props that had signified privilege. Into this role stepped figures like Eugene McCarthy and Robert Welch of the John Birch Society, who, through impassioned and exaggerated performances of international threats and domestic infiltration, and this narrative's erosion, delayed for years the enactment of this new framework of discursive populism. These dramatic elements would have to mature. In the meantime, as historian Lisa McGirr (2001) describes it, mid-century conservatism morphed into an obscure and marginalized social sphere, a site of ridicule, populated by leaders and supporters whom opinion-makers and academics were describing as irrational, "paranoid radicals." The far right not only grew marginalized in the broader public sphere, but also found that those within its own party, the Republicans, ignored or distanced themselves from it.

The New Right and Its Populisms

World War II had drawn to the fore the contradictions of fighting to liberate peoples abroad while Jim Crow laws were perpetuating institutionalized racism at home. While developments like the 1954 *Brown v. Board of Education* Supreme Court ruling formalized the civil-coded ethos of overturning unjust hierarchies rooted in primordial constructions of race in noncivil spheres, the ruling itself had little impact on racist institutions that were essentially routinized in the patterns of everyday life across the United States. The civil rights movement, a series of dramatic protests by black activists and citizen supporters staged throughout the subsequent ten years and into the mid-1960s, sought to translate African American identity into the positive codes of the civil sphere that signify the capacities of ideal democratic citizenship. While parts of the movement pursued inclusion and others sought separation, combined, the movement forced a range of noncivil spheres to confront the calls for civil recoding and to reinterpret their norms, resource distributions, and hierarchies, accordingly. These efforts were only partially successful, of course. They contribute, however, to the context – antiwar protests, student activism, urban uprisings for racial justice, police violence at the Democratic National Convention in Chicago, for instance – that helped birth and begin to consolidate the US grassroots far-right movement in the early 1960s.

With the electoral campaign narratives of political liberalism and internationalism dominant in the civil sphere, and social movements calling for justice in noncivil spheres and inclusion in the civil, conservatives increasingly experienced the American civil sphere as if they were outsiders in their home cultural landscape. Additionally, many of the citizens whom the right was naming "middle Americans" no longer felt that their "cultural status [was] secure in a society that seemed to be unravelling," as Kazin put it. To these people, "No one in power . . . realized that *they* were the real, the indispensable America" (Kazin 2017: 223). Kazin is describing how some core groups experience frontlash processes. These expressions capture well the sentiments that precipitate the populist forms I outlined above. The civil sphere's boundaries were in flux. Noncivil sphere identities that had felt as if they embodied the civil criteria for democratic citizenship in seamless fashion now found their senses of civilship weakened. The sense of civil authority they had experienced as natural now seemed constructed and contingent, if not contested. Richard Nixon's symbol of the silent majority would spark recognition among many of these citizens, and facilitate their identification with the Republican Party.

It was in this context that two templates of late-twentieth-century right-wing populism and Trumpist civilship formed. Networks of anticommunists, pro-business libertarians, and exclusionary social conservatives began to consolidate into a movement around the fringes of the Republican Party. McGirr (2001) describes how the Republican senator from Arizona Barry Goldwater became the totem of this embryonic but energetic grassroots movement. Goldwater's nomination in 1964 split the Republican Party. Its establishment distanced itself from the "extremist" candidate and his supporters in a move that foreshadowed the flight of neoconservatives and core-party Republicans from candidate Trump in 2016. Goldwater consolidated the party's marginalized factions, however. This included gaining the support of the John Birch Society, whose "ideas lay outside the bounds of respectable political discourse" (McGirr 2001: 128), a feature that describes the 2016 election, as well.

Goldwater faced the Democratic incumbent, Lyndon B. Johnson, who had become president in the wake of John F. Kennedy's assassination. For Goldwater supporters, Johnson represented the epitome of liberal excess: he was politically profligate and morally permissive, which combined to blind people to the value of freedom, and erode their commitment to the value of self-responsibility, they argued. During his campaign, Goldwater decried the expanding liberal state and warned that its growth and penetration into ever more spaces of the economic sphere, at both the national and local levels, threatened core American freedoms. The state was also intruding into too many areas of citizens' private lives, which was why, he explained, he had to vote against the Civil Rights Act of 1964, five months before the election.

Johnson knew that in signing the Civil Rights Act he risked hastening the trend of Southern Democrats departing for the emerging New Right. Yet he also understood that doing so would present to the electorate a more inclusive vision of the national community, one grounded on civil codes and not on noncivil, core-group primordialist justifications. It is not that he was simply virtuous or idealistic; rather, he strategized (within this morally coded context) that this particular vision of the civil ideal would resonate with more voters than it would alienate. Goldwater, on the other hand, understood that his opposition to the Act would harm his campaign, and associate it with race-based rationales for exclusion. Nonetheless, he had organized his campaign vision around the narrative of protecting personal freedoms from government intrusion, and he acted performatively to signal that message. Goldwater lost to Johnson by record numbers. He failed to win California, which, in addition to Arizona, was the base of his support owing to his libertarianism and strong stance against communism. He won five states in the Deep South, however, where arguably his refusal to sign the Act was interpreted in specific, race-based terms, inasmuch as in the abstract terms of protecting the civil and noncivil spheres from boundary intrusions and reformist projects. The election set in motion the redrawing of the national electoral map.

The Wallace and Nixon Templates of Right-Wing Populism

I have described how new dramatic elements and narratives emerged on the right in the context of liberal political domination. The 1968 election consolidated and crystallized these features into two fleshed-out, iconic representations of right-wing populism, forms that have continued to animate right-wing politics and the civil sphere to this day. George Wallace entered the race with a hard right, populist dramatic assemblage formed through his prior campaigns for office. "Segregation now! Segregation tomorrow! Segregation forever!" sticks with a candidate, even if he performed it half a decade prior and in a state gubernatorial campaign. Wallace primarily performed the core-group, primordialist populist form I outlined above. He constituted a people by elevating blue-collar workers and white men who worked with their hands. He juxtaposed this constellation of noncivil spheres with black identity, on the one hand, and, on the other, with soft-handed bureaucrats, policy experts, and professors, or figures who he argued pushed programs that intruded into the average Joe's noncivil spheres of employment, domesticity, and racial superiority. He also performed variations of the second, structural-forces form of populism. He fused the primordial-identities form to the latter through critiques less of structural forces themselves than of the figures who monopolized their resources, such as "limousine liberals," or, in the administrative sphere, appointed judges. He cast himself as a fighter. He projected confidence, adroitness, and pugnaciousness.

Wallace had a talent for breaching norms and then narrating the breach in positive, civil terms. For instance, he simultaneously championed segregation and the maintenance of race-based, primordial hierarchies in the civil sphere and in public spaces, while also insisting that his stance preserved freedoms for all races by, for instance, protecting African Americans from domineering policies such as the "senseless, asinine busing of little children" (quoted in Kazin 2017: 254). This practice would appear again in 2016, during instances in which candidate Trump would describe crime in black neighborhoods as evidence that African Americans are incapable of embodying the civil democratic codes, only to claim in the next moment that he would welcome nothing more than to have African Americans join him in support of his campaign.

Nixon was not a populist. His campaign for office in 1968, however, established the second iconic representation of late-modern, right-wing American populism, which is a populism that only signifies itself periodically, and in coded ways. Nixon was an establishment figure, a career politician, and a stiff one at that. Yet through coordinating with advertisers, the media expert Roger Ailes, and a political strategist and demographics whiz kid named Kevin Phillips, the Nixon campaign wrote the script for right-wing politicians on how to gain and exercise considerable power over the social center.

Nixon's campaign distracted from the candidate's establishment past by constructing another establishment, principally the press and the Democratic Party, the latter of which had controlled both houses of Congress for all but a few years since the start of the Great Depression. Along with intellectuals, opinion-makers, and academics, for the right, these groups constituted the liberal elite, which the Nixon campaign cast as the people's enemies from above. The campaign constructed its base in broadly inclusive terms by claiming to represent the civil sphere's principal core groups, the national community's dominant identity noncivil spheres, and lumping them together into the category of the silent majority. They further bolstered this solidarity sphere, or growing constituency of Nixon supporters, by signifying enemies and dangers from below. As mentioned above, they constituted these out-groups with signs that connote two meanings. Regarding the first meaning: in the context of antiwar and racial justice protests, the Nixon campaign's claim of representing those who value "law and order" signified that its supporters were good democratic citizens who, in contrast to protestors, were grateful for the blessings their country afforded them. They would be thankful for the chance to get a college education, for instance, and not use the opportunity to criticize and denigrate the American system. If these types of folks felt change was needed, they would lobby for it only through institutionalized, peaceful, and legal means. The campaign sign worked by suggesting that to oppose the candidate is to oppose law and order. It suggested that those who oppose law and order are constituted by counterdemocratic characteristics, and either unwilling or unable to act according to the positive, democratic codes that sustain the civil sphere. This is standard institutionalized democratic coding, and, given the events of the time, a reasonably predictable strategy.

This coding's felicity, however, is not simply due to the reality of events, or the confrontational, frequently violent clashes that were occurring between activists and protestors and the armed authorities in urban spaces. Regarding the sign's second meaning: it was felicitous because it connoted what was being denoted by the Wallace campaign, but in a more civil, less explicit, and less inflammatory way. The Nixon template of populism is parasitic on its far-right, Wallace-populist cousin. It requires that the Wallace template of populism denigrate particular noncivil sphere identity groups through justification narratives rooted in primordialist or similar criteria. The Nixon template sustains itself, and makes inroads into controlling the middle, by alternately embracing the Wallace form, and denigrating and distancing itself from it, in accordance with fluctuations in the sentiments of the civil sphere's broad coalition of core groups. In less abstract terms, the Nixon campaign won by representing the antiwar movement as irrational, irresponsible, and disloyal, and combining this with its Southern Strategy, or its tactic of appealing to whites in the South by coding African Americans in counterdemocratic ways and championing policies that would inhibit desegregation.

These are the populisms of cultural backlash. Ronald Reagan, who won the presidency in 1980, performed the Nixon script and elevated it as only a seasoned actor could. The subsequent twelve years of Republican control of the executive branch, during the combined three terms of Reagan and George H. W. Bush (Bush Sr. hereafter), signified the right's full return to the center of the civil sphere, and its capacity to exercise considerable power within it. It also illustrates the dynamics of interdependency between the Nixon and Wallace templates of populism. For this we turn to the presidential campaigns of 1992. That year, the Democratic candidate, Bill Clinton, dislodged incumbent Bush Sr. from the presidency. To do so, Clinton fashioned himself a New Democrat, or as part of the "Third Way" iteration of neoliberal politics. This signaled that he would be more ideologically flexible and open to compromise with the center right, which is a testament to the extent to which the right had moved the electorate's sentiments closer to its cultural and political preferences over the prior decade. Two populist candidates competed in the 1992 election. Rather than the curious case of Ross Perot, our interest here lies in Patrick Buchanan's challenge for the Republican nomination.

Buchanan challenged Bush Sr. because of the Republican establishment's reliance on the Nixon-populism template, which had dominated conservative strategizing and governance since both populist templates formed in the 1960s. In practice, the Republican establishment would mobilize the far right for electoral gain only to then suppress and distance itself from it. Except for in moments of need, the establishment would support the far right neither legislatively nor performatively. Yet moments of need did arise. For instance, in the run-up to the 1988 election, the Bush Sr. campaign activated primordial, racist criteria by invoking the "Willie Horton case,"[2] a tactic designed to encourage portions of the far right to support the Republican candidate. Three years later, Bush Sr. publicly disavowed the support of David Duke, a former leader of the Ku Klux Klan, and spoke out against Duke's gubernatorial campaign. "I don't want to tell the voters of Louisiana how to cast their ballot," Bush Sr. said, but "I don't believe that person ever deserves one iota of public trust. . . . [I]t is inconceivable that someone [like Duke] can reasonably aspire to a leadership role in a free society" (Suro 1991). In these examples, we see the Bush Sr. campaigns alternately embracing and then distancing themselves from the far right.

Buchanan had worked with Republican presidents Nixon, Ford, and Reagan as a speechwriter and strategist. In fact, he had penned the phrase "the great silent majority" for Nixon. In 1992, Buchanan attacked Bush Sr. from the far right: through his passivity, the president was complicit in the moral decay of the social center, and in the spread of lawlessness in its urban centers. He was a "globalist" who was ceding US sovereignty to international organizations, Buchanan claimed. Buchanan's campaign performances were generating great enthusiasm amongst his supporters, and his events were exciting affairs, journalists reported. Owing to his impressive showing in the primaries, the Bush Sr. camp offered Buchanan a speaking slot at the Republican National Convention. Buchanan used the event to declare that the United States was in a "culture war," and that the left was suppressing Christianity while at the same time flooding the civil sphere with radical feminists and homosexuals. On race, he invoked the Los Angeles urban uprisings of earlier that same year to paint a vision of civil society under siege by irrational and violent mobs, understood to be black, and protected only by armed young men, understood to be white. Buchanan conjured this image of their operations in the city: "And as those boys took back the streets of Los Angeles, block by block, my friends, we must take back our cities, and take back our culture, and take back our country. God bless you, and God bless America." These troops' actions were "rooted in justice, and backed by moral courage," Buchanan declared (Federal News Service Transcript 1992).

This is a clear representation of right-wing populism in the Wallace mode. It also demonstrates how the CST of populism explains the phenomenon in a radically new way. Buchanan is invoking particular racial identity noncivil spheres, and arguing that those spheres' criteria for inclusion should shape people's understandings of who is fit to participate in the civil sphere. White people are just and moral, in Buchanan's narrative, while black people are irrational and violent. He is arguing that these race-based criteria are more important than the democratic codes of civil society. Buchanan is warning his audience that if it interprets the social world through the abstract, universalist codes and not through primordial, race-based ones, the civil sphere will be destroyed. In his call

271

to "take back our country," he is encouraging particular core groups to claim dominion over the civil sphere. In 2012, while covering the Republican National Convention in Tampa, Florida, a *New York Times* reporter recalled Buchanan's 1992 convention speech. Nagourney (2012) observed that, "Republicans gathered here to nominate Mitt Romney suggest that... speeches [such as Buchanan's] would hardly give them pause today. What many viewed as the fringes of the Republican Party 20 years ago have moved closer to the mainstream." This is the civil sphere dynamic of frontlash and backlash.

On Policies and Practices: Right-Wing Populism Today

It is a short leap from Buchanan's 1992 speech at the Republican National Convention to the performances candidate Donald Trump delivered in 2015 and 2016. In fact, candidate Trump borrowed liberally from Buchanan's two campaigns in the 1990s.[3] Identifying what connects Trumpist populism to its antecedents while also specifying what makes it particularly representative of its time, we need to return to earlier in the analysis, or to the 1960s and 1970s, and add another dimension to the civil sources of populism.

In her history of the rise of the New Right, McGirr argues that particular liberal policies were flashpoints for right-wing backlash. She notes that "it was not only the federal government's actions to end racial discrimination that many conservatives opposed. Much closer to home was the enactment of legislation at the state level to put an end to racial discrimination in housing" (McGirr 2001: 185). As I mentioned at the outset, in democratic elections, campaigns present ideal visions of the civil community. Candidates promise that, if elected, they will institute policies that will make the real world more closely approximate their supporters' civil ideal. Operationalizing ideal visions into policies is complex. Distortions are introduced. The practices of enacting and enforcing policies are complex, as well. Points of contact are often contentious.

McGirr (2001: 185) continues:

> After the Civil Rights Act was signed into law in 1964, the Right's hostility toward federal government remedies for racial discrimination focused on attacks against state fair housing legislation, affirmative action, and, in the late 1960s and 1970s, busing. As the locus of civil rights struggles shifted from the South to the North, white resistance to these demands broadened, providing the Right with new adherents.

These processes concretize, in a literal way, civil ideals intruding into noncivil sphere spaces, relations, and institutions. They represent the left's ideals being converted into policies, which will ultimately be enforced in real, physical spaces – in neighborhoods – by representatives of the state. McGirr argues that such processes created resistance, which hardened into backlash, and culminated in the birth of populist conservatism.

In August 2015, Barack Obama was halfway through the penultimate year of his presidency. Seventeen figures entered the race for the Republican nomination, giving the party's base a wide range of candidates from which to choose. Jeb Bush offered another round of big-tent compassionate conservatism. Ted Cruz promised a strict social and fiscal conservatism, one guided by a Christian compass. Marco Rubio, John Kasich, Chris Christie: with many options, primary-goers would be able to vote for a candidate who represented their sentiments closely. In his outsider status, and through his norm-breaching discourse, in terms of both substance and delivery, candidate Trump resurrected the Wallace and Buchanan populist template, updated and stylized it with his idiosyncrasies, and performed the character on the national stage.

The candidate's attacks on domestic political, media, and cultural elites, and on international partners, commitments, and trade agreements, contributed to his populist persona. His direct and detailed discursive attacks on groups around the periphery of the civil sphere, however, distinguished him from the other candidates, who performed according to the Nixonian script of right-wing constituency building. Through introducing the sign "political correctness" into the election drama, candidate Trump established a foundation upon which he could attack noncivil identity out-groups, both domestic and foreign, and on which he could cast himself as an agent for reclaiming, cleansing, and restoring the civil sphere to prior, more restrictive boundaries. In practice, it thrilled significant portions of the conservative base.

Trump introduced the issue when he declared his candidacy in summer 2015, and both he and the topic were received as outliers. The first televised Republican debate in August, however, demonstrated that the candidate and his pet issue of PC culture were finding a core constituency within the conservative right. In the opening minutes of the event, Fox News moderator Megyn Kelly engaged in the following exchange with candidate Trump:

> *Kelly*: Mr. Trump, one of the things people love about you is you speak your mind and you don't use a politician's filter. However, that is not without its downsides, in particular, when it comes to women. You've called women you don't like "fat pigs, dogs, slobs, and disgusting animals." [*Laughter*]
> *Trump*: Only Rosie O'Donnell. [*Laughter*] ...

Kelly: Your Twitter account has several disparaging comments about women's looks. You once told a contestant on *Celebrity Apprentice* it would be a pretty picture to see her on her knees. Does that sound to you like the temperament of a man we should elect as president . . . ?

Trump: I think the big problem this country has is being politically correct. [*Applause*] I've been challenged by so many people and I don't, frankly, have time for total political correctness. And to be honest with you, this country doesn't have time, either. This country is in big trouble. We don't win anymore. We lose to China. We lose to Mexico both in trade and at the border. We lose to everybody.

The policies of school busing, the enforcement of fair housing practices, and affirmative action exemplify civil repair projects entering into people's domestic lives. In 2016, candidate Trump generated identification and solidarity through narrating the civil sphere in two ways. First, he would strengthen and constrict its boundaries at the nation's borders by building a wall and forestalling immigration from Muslim countries. Second, he insisted that he would stop the civil code from continuing to intrude into the *capillaries* of noncivil spaces and relations. The capillaries are intimate spaces and practices between friends, family members, and small- to medium-sized networks of familiar relations. They are the noncivil areas in which jokes are told, preferences in music, film, and television are expressed, and allegiances to sports teams are shared or contested in friendly ways, for instance. Candidate Trump battled civil repair not in neighborhoods and schools. He opposed it, rather, at sites within and proximate to intimate relations.

Political correctness is an assemblage of discourses and strategies designed to identify and critique entrenched, unjust hierarchies in other discourses, hierarchies that are typically rooted in primordial assumptions about racial, gender, sexual, and ethnic differences. Being politically correct means being mindful to not invoke these hierarchies, on the one hand, and it means speaking up when one encounters someone else repeating them, on the other: in a joke, for instance. The term proliferated in the 1990s, and over the next two decades, its practices became institutionalized in much of the American left, and in its center, as well. As a symbol, its trajectory into the American center followed the institutionalization of multiculturalism. Backlash to these phenomena alternately percolated and raged within the right during Obama's presidency, which we can see in the classification system of politically correct types that emerged. Those who engaged in politically correct practices were "social justice warriors" or "white knights," for instance. They "virtue signaled," declared they were "woke," and joined in "call-out culture."

Candidate Trump maintained the Wallace populist persona, and stuck to his script as condemnation poured in from establishment Republicans and the left. Republican candidate Ted Cruz adopted the path Nixon charted in relation to Wallace in 1968. Cruz coasted in Trump's wake, assuming and hoping that eventually either the Republican establishment or the civil sphere would declare that Trump had breached one too many norms. Populist fronts require symbols of the establishment against which to perform. Who better to signify the establishment than Jeb Bush in the primaries? Could a stage director cast a more suitable person in the role of the establishment for the general election than Hillary Clinton? The stage was set. The "deplorables" turned out on Election Day. In 2016, the Wallace and Buchanan populist Donald Trump won the presidency.

Conclusion

Civil repair projects may translate democratic, universalist ideals into policies, or they may be circulated through personal interactions and become norms. Civil repair projects that are formalized into policies, such as school busing or fair housing regulations, or border walls and immigration restrictions, are enforced by the state. Civil repair projects of the interactional variety, such as political correctness, on the other hand, are regulated by discursive practices, in which one person draws on the democratic code of the civil sphere to name and critique an unjust hierarchy that someone else invokes in interaction. These repair sites are regulated by emotions as well. McGirr (2001) describes right-wing backlash being propelled by liberal "disdain" and "ridicule"; Massey (2005) points to the left's "self-righteousness" and "arrogance"; Kazin (2017) remarks on its "condescension." These are not characteristics of just the left, of course.

The civil ideal guiding the policy examples of civil repair was that race should not be part of the criteria by which people choose where to live, or to whom to buy or sell their houses, for instance. Similarly, in the political correctness example, the civil repair project is aimed at getting people to stop degrading others through either lazy or intentional recourse to unjust, particularistic cultural tropes. One could argue that these projects represent a kind of force, a civil force, perhaps, one that is rooted in justice, and backed by moral courage. But then, you see, I just quoted Pat Buchanan to you. Therein lie the frontlash and backlash sources of populism.

Notes

1 Jack Kemp challenged Dole for the Republican nomination. He described Dole's as "a pain, sacrifice, and bitter medicine" campaign.
2 The case refers to a series of three commercials the Bush Sr. campaign allowed to be aired in the support of the candidate in 1988. William R. Horton, an African American who had been convicted of murder, raped a woman, and stabbed her fiancé while on prison furlough. Bush Sr. also invoked the Horton case in his campaign speeches.
3 Pat Buchanan ran for president again in 1996 with the campaign theme "Make America First Again." He promised to focus on "'forgotten Americans' left behind by bad trade deals, open-border immigration policies and foreign adventurism" (Alberta 2017).

References

Alberta, T. (2017) The ideas made it, but I didn't. *Politico Magazine*, May/June. https://www.politico.com/magazine/story/2017/04/22/pat-buchanan-trump-president-history-profile-215042.

Alexander, J. C. (2006) *The Civil Sphere*. New York: Oxford University Press.

Alexander, J. C. (2019) Frontlash/backlash: The crisis of solidarity and the threat to civil institutions. *Contemporary Sociology* 48(1): 5–11.

Aslanidis, P. (2016) Is populism an ideology? A refutation and a new perspective. *Political Studies* 64(SI): 88–104.

Bonikowski, B. and N. Gidron. (2016) The populist style in American politics: Presidential campaign discourse, 1952–1996. *Social Forces* 94(4): 1593–621.

Canovan, M. (1999) Trust the people! Populism and the two faces of democracy. *Political Studies* 47(1): 2–16.

Federal News Service Transcript. (1992) Pat Buchanan 1992 Republican Convention Address. C-Span.org, August 17. https://www.c-span.org/video/?31255-1/pat-buchanan-1992-republican-convention-address.

Kazin, M. (2017) *The Populist Persuasion: An American History*, revised edition. Ithaca, NY: Cornell University Press.

Massey, D. (2005) *Return of the "L" Word: A Liberal Vision for the New Century*. Princeton: Princeton University Press.

Mast, J. L. (2019) Introduction: Fragments, ruptures, and resurgent structures: The civil sphere and the fate of "civilship" in the era of Trumpism. In: J. L. Mast and J. C. Alexander (eds.) *Politics of Meaning/Meaning of Politics: Cultural Sociology of the 2016 US Presidential Election*. Cham: Palgrave Macmillan.

Mast, J. L. (2020) Representationalism and cognitive culturalism: Riders on elephants on turtles all the way down. *American Journal of Cultural Sociology* 8(1): 90–123.

McGirr, L. (2001) *Suburban Warriors: The Origins of the New American Right*. Princeton: Princeton University Press.

Mouffe, C. (2000) *The Democratic Paradox*. London: Verso.

Mudde, C. (2017) Populism: An ideational approach. In: C. R. Kaltwasser, P. Taggart, P. O. Espejo, and P. Ostiguy (eds.) *The Oxford Handbook of Populism*. Oxford: Oxford University Press.

Nagourney, A. (2012) "Culture war" of 1992 moves in from the fringe. *The New York Times*, August 29. https://nyti.ms/QTuxaq.

Suro, R. (1991) The 1991 election: Louisiana; Bush denounces Duke as racist and charlatan. *The New York Times*, November 7. https://nyti.ms/29wbpmD.

Swidler, A. (1986) Culture in action: Symbols and strategies. *American Sociological Review* 51(2): 273–86.

Urbinati, N. (2019) Political theory of populism. *Annual Review of Political Science* 22: 111–27.

Vaisey, S. (2009) Motivation and justification: A dual-process model of culture in action. *American Journal of Sociology* 114(6): 1675–715.

Weyland, K. (2017) Populism: A political-strategic approach. In: C. R. Kaltwasser, P. Taggart, P. O. Espejo, and P. Ostiguy (eds.) *The Oxford Handbook of Populism*. Oxford: Oxford University Press.

Commentary

Demarcating Constructive from Destructive Populisms: Civil Translation vs. Civil Mimicry

Carlo Tognato

Over the past decade, the surge of populism in the West and beyond has not only drawn attention to the variety of ways in which populists have gone about distorting the functioning of liberal democracy by politicizing the civil service, the military, domestic security agencies, and law enforcement, by undermining the independence of the judiciary branch, by discrediting democratic elections, and by reducing liberal media to mere organs of propaganda (Walt 2017). It has also brought into focus the fact that populists go after fundamental normative standards in public discourse such as truth, rationality, reasonableness, trustworthiness, transparency, good faith, and accountability, with potentially dramatic consequences on civil interactions. To understand the stakes, it is necessary to unpack what the erosion of such standards actually brings about.

Whenever such standards come under attack, the authenticity tests that civil actors and civil institutions are expected to pass in order to maintain their civil credentials become less and less stringent. As a result, performative anomalies start to accumulate in civil practices and are progressively normalized. Most importantly, though, populists gain a freer hand at diluting civil interactions by injecting them with noncivil elements. And the more they receive a pass at smuggling the latter into the former, the more blurred the civil character of such performances will become in the eyes of their audiences. At some point, an increasing number of observers will start to be persuaded that there is little difference between civil and noncivil performances and will be tempted to think that civil translation[1] might no longer be that necessary for the purpose of gaining support for their own causes from other members of society. This, in turn, will curtail their ability to sustain generalized solidarity and trust across society and will make it even harder to uphold truth, rationality, reasonableness, trustworthiness, transparency, good faith, and accountability as civil normative standards in public discourse. In the end, civil interactions will plunge into a perilous vicious circle that will lead to further degradation of authenticity standards in civil performances and to an even more dramatic erosion of those normative standards in public discourse.

To break that circle, it is necessary to ensure a careful and systematic monitoring of civil dynamics for the purpose of calling out the injection of destructive noncivil logics into civil life whenever it has the potential to void it from the inside out. On this front, this volume provides a particularly useful resource.

Populisms may play a role in such perilous injection, but they are not bound to. To understand why and when they do so, a suitable analytical framework is necessary for the purpose of distinguishing between some forms of populism that play into civil life either by participating in the broadening of the horizon of civil solidarity and inclusion within society or by consolidating prior expansions from other forms of populism that work as Trojan horses and help smuggle pernicious, noncivil logics within the walls of civil communities. The former do not threaten civil life but rather contribute to support it, while the latter are detrimental to it. To prevent the civil fabric of society from degrading, it is therefore necessary to recognize the former as potential instruments of civil repair and consolidation that need to be productively channeled and reveal the latter as threats to civil life that beg for prompt and vigorous responses.

One might be tempted to think that productive forms of populism may be distinguished from destructive ones based on whether they engage in civil translation. Accordingly, they might pass as productive for civil life if they play the civil game by recasting their particularistic claims in universalistic terms and by tapping into civil discourse to that end. And they might be dismissed as destructive if they fall short of it. The reality of populism, however, is much more complex than that, and this volume may help to understand why.

As its contributors show, there are important continuities between populist politics and institutional democratic politics, to the point that populism might be regarded, to quote Marcus Morgan (Chapter 1), "as an intensification of routine political dynamics." Populists of all types, both constructive and destructive, after all, regularly appear to translate their noncivil claims into civil terms for the purpose of pushing their agendas across society and, as a result of that, to paraphrase Jason Mast (Chapter 10), the noncivil ends up intruding into the civil and "the particular assert[s] dominance over not only other identity groups but over the collective representations of the universal, as well." This is apparent in Mast's chapter (10) on Donald Trump's populism during

279

the 2016 US presidential election; in María Luengo and Małgorzata Kolankowska's chapter (5) on Polish populists and their attempts to root the universalizing elements of the civil within particular national civil ideals; in Bernadette Nadya Jaworsky's chapter (6) on Czech populists' discourse on migration during the 2018 presidential election and the fabrication of "a migrant/refugee 'crisis' without actual migrants or refugees"; and in Celso Villegas's chapter (2) on civil responses to populism in the Philippines.

If, however, all types of populists appear to engage in some civil translation by seeking to particularize the universalist ideals of the civil sphere, such engagement is per se not useful to demarcate productive from destructive forms of populism. To find an adequate criterion of demarcation, we must therefore dig under the surface of civil translation and try to complexify this category.

In this volume, contributors distinguish between a form of populism that "can be a 'societalizing' form of 'frontlash' that overcomes marginalization" and one that constitutes "a reactive 'backlash' that (1) amplifies polarization and (2) attacks the autonomy of the civil sphere's communicative and regulative institutions" (Villegas, Chapter 2). One seeks to re-establish the autonomy of the civil sphere after the perceived colonization on the part of actors or organizations with a powerful foothold in noncivil spheres and the other "aims to re-establish the hegemony of core groups' primordial, noncivil identities within the civil sphere. . . . [P]opulist narratives tell citizens that they should focus on these noncivil criteria and use them to determine how to vote" (Mast, Chapter 10). One is both agonistic and pluralistic and "holds the potential to act as an agent of civil repair" and the other wages "a direct assault upon civil institutions" and upon the autonomy of the civil sphere (Morgan, Chapter 1).

Bearing such distinctions in mind, one might be tempted to conclude that, to demarcate destructive forms of populism from productive ones, one should look at whether or not their engagement on the front of civil translation results in the demise of the autonomy of the civil sphere or whether or not populists' intention behind it is to produce such a demise. Such a criterion of differentiation, though, is analytically much less sharp than it might appear at first sight. The end impact of an exercise of civil translation, after all, might be hijacked by a multiplicity of factors. So, if that were the criterion, populists who seek to undermine the autonomy of the civil sphere and yet fail at it would end up being classified on the side of the productive forms of populism. On the other hand, if we took their intention behind their engagement on the front of civil translation as our criterion of demarcation, we would end up with a yardstick that would also be hardly applicable. To defend themselves, after all, and to confuse their audience, populists who are after the demise of an autonomous civil sphere might still argue that their very engagement in civil translation should indicate their intention to play according to the rules of the civil game, and thus it should be taken to reaffirm their commitment to the autonomy of the civil sphere. At that point, populists who sought to bring down the autonomy of the civil sphere and those who were committed to uphold it would become practically indistinguishable.

If the engagement per se in civil translation may not serve as a criterion of demarcation or its impact, or the intention behind it, because of this observational equivalence, then we need to zoom in for the purpose of identifying how different types of populists – both productive and destructive – might differently engage in civil translation. Our criterion of demarcation, in other words, might have to hinge upon process.

In his chapter about the Sweden Democrats, Henrik Enroth (Chapter 8) would seem to assume that certain forms of populism may attempt to rewrite the code that structures our sense and sensibility of solidarity while adopting the conventional terms of civil discourse. For example, he shows that the Sweden Democrats did so through inversion, that is, by "reconceptualizing what has been deemed civil as uncivil," through appropriation, that is, by appealing to the civil code and laying claim to civil ideals, and then through "adopting and adapting elements of the civil code."

Such inversions, appropriations, adoptions, and adaptations surely lay out a relevant repertoire of strategies that populists of both types – destructive and constructive – may adopt for the purpose of civil translation. The fact that both do, however, also implies that such strategies may not be used as cues to distinguish each from the other.

In his chapter about the AfD, Werner Binder (Chapter 7) observes that the German right-wing populist party had a "tremendous impact" on German civil discourse as it managed "to expand the limits of what is sayable" and succeeded in introducing "a folkish vocabulary into political discourse that was not just reminiscent but often directly borrowed from Nazi speak while attacking the memory culture and 'Holocaust identity' of contemporary Germany." The introduction of alternative political vocabularies in public discourse that are not born out of standard strategies in civil translation might actually provide a cue to more destructive forms of populism that could undermine civil life. Still, this begs the question of what might qualify such vocabularies as such. I believe that in his Introduction Alexander sets us on a fruitful track on this front.

According to Alexander, authoritarian conservatives and antidemocratic populists on the left understand conflict as a form of antagonism among enemies, thereby necessarily falling short of the civil commitment to solidarity that binds the members of a civil community together irrespective of their position along the political spectrum. Civil conservatives and civil progressives, on the other hand, take conflict as a mere confrontation among adversaries who still share a common commitment to the civil community of which they mutually recognize each other as legitimate members. This would appear to imply that the former continue to uphold certain noncivil logics that ground their antagonistic understanding of conflict, irrespective of their participation in the civil process and of their engagement on the front of civil translation, while the latter come out of the process of civil translation adopting the cultural logic of the civil sphere as a shared cultural structure with other members of society, which in turn cements their solidarity with them and enables them to understand conflict in agonistic and pluralistic terms.

In the former case, civil translation would seem to boil down to a Goffmanian operation of face presentation whereby destructive populists merely put on a civil face as they engage in it. In the latter case, by contrast, civil translation works as a fused civil performance and manages to establish a common horizon of meaning and affect between those who fully engage in civil translation and the rest of the civil community. In the former case, in other words, civil translation is degraded to a mere exercise of civil mimicry in which civil understandings of social life are systematically used by populists as ad hoc appendages on their prior noncivil understandings of motives, social relations, and institutions. In the latter case, however, civil translation has a transformational impact on those who engage in it.

When civil translation boils down to an exercise of mere civil mimicry, noncivil cultural structures find a path to interject into civil discourse, thereby recombining in pragmatic settings the cultural DNA of civil life. At that point, different forms of "simplistic yet inveterate binarism," to put it in Alexander's terms (Introduction), may appear on the horizon of social life and may establish new conditions of "discursive constriction and institutional fusion" that ultimately undermine the autonomy of civil institutions, erode the very idea of universalizing solidarity, and concentrate all communicative power of symbolic representations on populist leaders while doing away with the autonomy of the regulative institutions of the civil sphere.

By providing a processual criterion of demarcation between civil-oriented forms of populism and destructive forms, a focus on civil mimicry may also help sharpen Luengo and Kolankowska's (Chapter 5) idea of a pseudocivil sphere. The fact, after all, that the PiS movement equates itself with the "will of the Polish people" according to a nativist perception of Polish society would not be per se sufficient to make it pseudocivil. As a matter of fact, the instantiation of the universalistic ideals of the civil sphere in particularistic understandings of time and place is a characteristic feature of the civil sphere. What might make it pseudocivil, instead, might be the patterned ad hoc way in which populists attach civil categories to noncivil understandings of motives, social relations, and institutions, thereby falling short of engaging in an actual and coherent process of civil translation. Such a pernicious recombination of noncivil cultural structures with civil ones is what might warrant the attribute of pseudocivil.

This turns civil mimicry into a characteristic site for the poisonous injection of noncivil conceptions of solidarity and community into the civil sphere. And as such, it also comes to constitute an ideal site for the observation of dynamics of civil degradation that are associated with destructive forms of populism.

As civil mimicry is constantly on the verge of being detected, denounced, and debunked, authoritarian conservatives and antidemocratic populists have a particular interest in exacerbating the deep sociopolitical divisions that fracture society in an effort at eroding the social base that grounds the normative standards of truth, rationality, reasonableness, trustworthiness, transparency, good faith, and accountability in public discourse. As I pointed out earlier, doing so allows them to relax the authenticity tests that civil interactions are permanently subjected to, thereby making it more difficult to differentiate civil mimicry from transformational civil translation. This, in turn, allows populists to degrade civil performances via the injection of noncivil elements into civil interactions and progressively blurs the line that separates the civil from the noncivil within them. At that point, members of society might increasingly consider that civil translation has become less useful to weave solidarity ties across society, thereby weakening their chances of upholding civil solidarity and generalized trust among them. This will further erode the above-mentioned civil normative standards in public discourse, thereby paving the way to an even more extensive, and poisonous, injection of noncivil logics into civil life, allowing populists to hijack the function of the communicative and regulative institutions of the civil sphere, and paving the way to the demise of an autonomous civil sphere.

Differentiating between genuinely transformative practices of civil translation and mere exercises of civil mimicry is the task of a civil cultural critique of populism. And the target of such critique lies in the patterned syntactical and performative inconsistencies and asymmetries that betray civil mimicry and that expose the ad hoc juxtapositions in discourse and performance between civil and noncivil conceptions of social life on the part of destructive forms of populism.

In his chapter about leftist populism over the transition of Andrés Manuel López-Obrador's presidency in Mexico, Nelson Arteaga Botello (Chapter 4) appears to contribute to such a critique as he detects a problematic patrimonialist underbelly in what some observers might otherwise regard as López Obrador's seemingly civil-minded, left-wing populism. And in his chapter about Recep Tayyip Erdoğan's populism in Turkey, Ateş Altınordu (Chapter 3) sets the stage for a civil cultural critique of it as he pinpoints the presence of noncivil Islamist themes in his discourse.

At the beginning of this chapter, I argued that, to understand how populism may weaken civil life, it is crucial to distinguish between its constructive and destructive forms. In my discussion, I have touched upon the contributions in this book for the purpose of identifying one process – civil mimicry – that may serve as a criterion of demarcation between different populisms. That said, in his chapter about populism in nondemocratic China, Andrew Junker (Chapter 9) reminds us that populism may also surface within noncivil contexts. This begs the question whether within the latter, as well, one might also need to distinguish between constructive and destructive forms of populism. I believe that this is the case and that, indeed, mimicry may also serve as a processual criterion of demarcation between such forms of populism and may thus usefully complement Junker's successful attempt to generalize the theory of populism that this book has laid out.

I will conclude with a brief mention of a series of recent contributions to the analysis of civil dynamics that may enter into a fruitful conversation with this book and that set the stage for my argument in this chapter about the distinction between civil translation and civil mimicry and the demarcation between constructive and destructive forms of populism. As the injection of noncivil logics into civil life constitutes a particular form of discursive competition between civil and noncivil discourses, recent work on such processes of competition in Mexico, Venezuela, Colombia, and China is relevant at this time (Arteaga Botello and Arzuaga Magnoni 2018; Tognato 2018; Villegas 2018; Palmer 2019). Similarly, given that the injection of noncivil logics into civil interactions entails a process of discursive diffusion, Martínez Pérez (2018) and my own recent work (Tognato 2019) may also help unpack the complexity of diffusion both in discourse and performance with their case studies on Cuba and Colombia, respectively. Furthermore, destructive forms of populism often resort to civil mimicry as a tactic for injection. Heins and Unrau (2019) and I (Tognato 2018) have recently touched to different degrees upon such a phenomenon in relation to a German right-wing movement and Colombian revolutionary militants on a university campus. Finally, the weakening of normative standards in public discourse such as truth, reasonableness, good faith, and accountability and the subsequent relaxation of authenticity standards in civil performances may feed into the destabilization of the civil terrain and into an increased porosity of civil dynamics vis-à-vis the intrusion of noncivil logics. I addressed this point in a paper about the erosion of the civil fabric in a Colombian public university (Tognato 2018).

To recapitulate, populisms may plunge social interactions into a perilous vicious circle of degradation by eroding the normative standards in public discourse that keep social life firmly on civil ground. The way they do so is by smuggling noncivil logics into the interactional fabric of civil life, thereby impairing solidarity formation within civil communities. I have referred to such a process as civil mimicry. Bringing civil mimicry into focus may not only provide a criterion of demarcation between destructive and constructive forms of populism. It also identifies one fundamental target onto which a civil cultural critique of populism will need to direct its arrows.

Note

1 In Alexander's civil sphere theory, civil translation is the process by which members of society seek to recast their particularistic interests in general terms for the purpose of eliciting the solidarity of their fellow members. To that end, they tap into the civil codes of liberty and repression that make up civil discourse by attaching to their own motives, relations, and institutions the positive attributes of the civil and by bestowing upon those of their adversaries the attributes of the anticivil. Such binaries work as the structuring cultural metric of legitimacy within the civil sphere. Alexander refers to social movements as primary agents of civil translation (Alexander 2006: 229–34).

References

Alexander, J. C. (2006) *The Civil Sphere*. New York: Oxford University Press.
Arteaga Botello, N. and J. Arzuaga Magnoni. (2018) The civil sphere in Mexico: Between democracy and authoritarianism. In: J. C. Alexander and C. Tognato (eds.) *The Civil Sphere in Latin America*. Cambridge: Cambridge University Press.
Heins, V. and C. Unrau. (2019) Anti-immigrant movements and the self-poisoning of the civil sphere. In: J. C. Alexander, T. Stack, and F. Khosrokhavar (eds.) *Breaching the Civil Order: Radicalism and the Civil Sphere*. New York: Cambridge University Press.

Martínez Pérez, L. (2018) *La Joven Cuba*: Confrontation, conciliation, and the quest for the civil through blogging. In: J. C. Alexander and C. Tognato (eds.) *The Civil Sphere in Latin America*. Cambridge: Cambridge University Press.

Palmer, D. A. (2019) Three moral codes and microcivil spheres in China. In: J. C. Alexander, D. A. Palmer, S. Park, and A. S-M. Ku (eds.) *The Civil Sphere in East Asia*. New York: Cambridge University Press.

Tognato, C. (2018) The civil life of the university: Enacting dissent and resistance on a Colombian campus. In: J. C. Alexander and C. Tognato (eds.) *The Civil Sphere in Latin America*. Cambridge: Cambridge University Press.

Tognato, C. (2019) Conversaciones de paz en las universidades: Performances de la transición en Colombia. In: N. Arteaga Botello and C. Tognato (eds.) *Sociedad, cultura y esfera civil: Una agenda de sociología cultural*. Mexico City: Editorial FLACSO-Mexico.

Villegas, C. M. (2018) *¿La clase media en positivo?* The civil and uncivil uses of "the middle class" in Venezuela, 1958–2016. In: J. C. Alexander and C. Tognato (eds.) *The Civil Sphere in Latin America*. Cambridge: Cambridge University Press.

Walt, S. M. (2017) Top 10 signs of creeping authoritarianism, revisited. *Foreign Policy*, July 27. https://foreignpolicy.com/2017/07/27/top-10-signs-of-creeping-authoritarianism-revisited/.

Conclusion

Is Populism the Shadow of the Civil?
Peter Kivisto and Giuseppe Sciortino

In a relatively short span of time – and a few drawbacks notwithstanding – the vast and motley set of political actors usually labeled "populist" has proven itself highly successful. Populists have been able to challenge, and sometimes utterly undermine, the post-Cold War liberal order. For most academics, it has created something of a cultural shock. A whole generation of political and social theorists had grown up identifying their own Darth Vader with the neoliberal Leviathan, the multidimensional "Empire" described, just two decades ago, by Hardt and Negri (2001). Now, they discover that what they have depicted for years as a pervasive and powerful adversary is actually quite fragile, if not evanescent. It used to be an object of scorn; today, it's becoming a matter of nostalgic longings.

In social and political theory, a whole new set of questions has become pressing. Is an illiberal democracy really possible? Is the language of spite and polarization the only one able to deliver electoral victories? Is the systematic practice of bad manners against marginalized minorities the only social performance that makes actors appear authentic in the eyes of their audiences? Are democracy and liberalism bound to part ways soon? Will a new conservative, Russian-led holy alliance bring about the international stability that has eluded the winners of the Cold War? Where have all the antisystemic, hybrid, decentralized, multicultural, "new social movements" gone?

Unsurprisingly, civil sphere theory (CST) scholars have been intrigued, if not utterly fascinated, by the current populist "zeitgeist" (Mudde 2004) or "moment" (Brubaker 2017b). The populists' ability to evoke a horizontal community of belonging that re-fuses masses, community, nation, and *demos* is, in fact, clearly significant for any theory of democratic solidarity. Populism is, indeed, "good to think with" for anyone interested in the civil sphere (Kivisto 2017).

Does the current, and somewhat unexpected, success of populist movements imply a pressing need to restructure, if not even discard, the CST framework? Elaborated during the 1990s, and achieving its fullest and most mature articulation in 2006, CST could easily appear as just another product of the "globalization" years, one of the many delusions incurred by the period's progressive thinkers (Alexander 2016). We believe, perhaps unsurprisingly, that this is not the case. On the contrary, we believe this volume shows that the CST aspiration to consistently address solidarity, membership, democracy, and inclusion (as well as polarization, segmentation, authoritarianism, and exclusion) is capable, in principle, of providing an original – and definitely much-needed – understanding of the populist currents that seem to define the contemporary social world. At the same time, the exploration of populist actions may help us to revise and improve CST.

It should not be forgotten that CST is an evolving body of sociological interests – an ongoing and collaborative project. Even if rooted in the *fin de siècle*, it has matured with the times. Before the ink on its original 2006 formulation had dried, a small community of scholars, including the original proponent and the authors of the present conclusions, had already started to revise, expand, criticize, and amend it (Kivisto and Sciortino 2015). Further developments have taken place in recent years, when a series of conferences-cum-volumes have allowed the development of CST from the bottom up, through the detailed analysis of a rich variety of cases drawn from very different regions of the world (Alexander and Tognato 2018; Alexander, Lund, and Voyer 2019; Alexander, Palmer, Park, and Ku 2019). The present volume, like the parallel edited volume on radical collective action (Alexander et al. 2020), continues the same journey, bringing the theory to bear on the functioning of allegedly "uncivil" realms.

As in the conclusions to the previous volumes, we will not summarize the findings presented in the previous pages. Nor will we act as guardians of CST orthodoxy, chastising the numerous – indeed sometimes slightly injudicious – terminological and conceptual changes introduced in the framework by some contributors. We will, rather, mine their work for elements and critiques that we find useful for advancing the boundaries of CST research. We will proceed by borrowing from threads of the arguments advanced by the contributors (our differences with some will become evident), weaving them into a more sustained brief on behalf of a CST approach to populism. In so proceeding, we will also locate this brief in relation to similar efforts that have been long underway.

CONCLUSION

CST Is a Theory of Democracy

In a central passage in *The Civil Sphere*, Jeffrey Alexander introduces the idea of civil power. The claim is that societies are not fully democratic when social and economic power are translated, directly or indirectly, into political power, resulting in a merging of the hierarchies of different social spheres. Democracy is only possible when that translation is blocked, when the ruled have the capacity to rule. The following passage is worth quoting at length:

> The ability to effect such blockage, indeed, to institutionalize it in a systematic manner, is how democracy should be defined. Democracy rests on the independent production of a new kind of power, which I will call "civil power." In a democracy, the civil sphere, not social power, decides who will sit at the state's non-bureaucratic top. Civil power is solidarity translated into government control. How does this happen? To the degree that there is an independent civil sphere, the people "speak," not only through the *communicative* institutions that provide cultural authority, but through *regulative* institutions as well. The civil community regulates access to state power. To do so, it constitutes a new and different kind of power of its own. (Alexander 2006: 109–10)

CST is an attempt to provide a realistic account of the civil sphere and democracy. The "people" who speak include both civil and uncivil actors, the liberal and illiberal, the public-spirited and those who are not (Alexander 2013a: 123–39). The civil sphere is consequently an arena of potentially endless, and not necessarily pretty, contentions (Kivisto and Sciortino 2020). Analyzing such contentions, CST reveals that inclusion and exclusion, boundary-making and boundary-blurring processes, backlash and frontlash movements, civil repair and civil stigmatization are driven and made possible by the same set of symbolic codes (Sciortino 2012). In other words, membership in the civil sphere implies the use of similar semiotic structures to elaborate often sharply divergent discourses (Kivisto 2007).

Though reason is not absent from civil contestation, neither is it the whole story; indeed, CST recognizes the role of emotions in shaping beliefs and actions. The term "civil sphere" can be read as a critique of Habermas's public sphere, shaped by his ideal of undistorted communication. In the ideal public sphere, democratic decisions are arrived at dialogically in situations where citizens are prepared to freely and rationally embrace the better argument (Habermas 1996). In the actual civil sphere, the passions also have their say.

The analysis of democracy from the point of view of CST is rooted in the functioning of a multilayered sphere, defined by three interlocked internal tensions. As will be seen, each of these tensions provides fertile ground for the development of one or more dimensions of the populist repertoire. The first is the tension between a set of deeply seated cultural codes establishing the existence of a horizontal solidarity cutting across particularistic loyalties and sectoral interests *and* the actual existence of such solidarity only as a set of processes and practices defined by the particularistic understanding of its most established groups. Marginalized groups may frame their grievances and claims as justified in terms of these codes, thus appealing in symbolic and emotional terms well beyond the numbers of those who are directly affected. At the same time, other members may use the same codes to stigmatize the "excludable" (whoever they may be) as unfit, unprepared, or unwilling to become full societal members. As Talcott Parsons already stressed in the 1960s, any inclusion process triggers among the already included widespread fears that the new members will cause a fundamental devaluation of the original membership category (Parsons 1965). The result is a constant and never-ending struggle between the frontlash universalistic aspirations of some actors and the backlash objectives of others (Alexander 2013b). It is precisely such endemic tension that provides the ground for the politics of exclusion – a twofold opposition, at once vertical and horizontal, against a conflation of those at "the top," at "the bottom," and "outside" – that drives the success of most populist mobilization (Brubaker 2017a).

The second is the tension between such universalistic discourse of civil solidarity *and* the actually existing institutions that incarnate and express such discourse. While all concrete democratic institutions draw their legitimacy from their symbolic connection to civil discourse, they inevitably always fall short of the normative standards and symbolic promises promoted and codified by the very same discourse. No minimally effective polity can ever guarantee a substantial involvement of all its members in the governing of all their lives. Specific institutions may consequently always be accused of betraying their connection to civil power, of having become "owned" by self-serving groups that obfuscate the issues at hand for corrupt reasons.[1] This is the tension that undergirds the populist claim to represent "the people" against "both the established structure of power and the dominant ideas and values of society" (Canovan 1999: 3).

The third structural tension is among the institutional girders of democracy themselves. Alexander, in Part II of *The Civil Sphere* (2006: 51–209), classified civil institutions into two broad categories: communicative institutions (public opinion, mass media, polls, and civic organizations) and regulatory institutions (elections, parties, office, and the legal system). Analyzing institutions, in its original 2006 formulation, Alexander's analysis was meant primarily to stress that civil institutions could prosper only if they could legitimate themselves not only legally, but also in terms of a broader civil discourse.[2] This concern is still an important focus for CST (Alexander 2018, 2019a, 2019b). The new climate, however, also brings to the fore a very different concern. There is an existing tension *among* civil institutions. Within each civil sphere, there is an inevitable tension between constitutionalism and democracy, between the institutions designed to ensure the possibility that the popular will can be translated into civil power and those designed to *protect* individuals, minorities, and noncivil interests precisely *from* the will of the majority. Here, we find the other two elements key to any populist repertoire: majoritarianism (the defense of the people, the ordinary, authentic people, against minorities both at the top and at the bottom) and what may be called anticonstitutionalism, the diffidence regarding any mechanism of checks-and-balances that may constrain the immediate, transparent, and direct expression of the popular will (Mudde 2013a: 17; Brubaker 2020).

These three structural tensions that define the civil sphere also constitute the background that creates the possibility to initiate populist performances. Margaret Canovan, in her classic essay, has described populism as "a shadow cast by democracy itself" (Canovan 1999: 2). She has argued that populism makes sense only against the background of a democratic system.[3] She suggests that modern democracy implies a constant tension between its two different "faces": the redemptive and the pragmatic. It is precisely the endemic gaps between these two faces of democratic politics that make possible the growth of populist actors, claims, and performances. Canovan traces the structural conditions for populism to a single political gap. CST, as discussed above, may better acknowledge the multilayered nature of the populist repertoire, as it connects its various elements to a plurality of structural tensions operating in the civil sphere. Paying more attention to its cultural dimension, CST sees populism as a shadow cast by the civil itself.

Populist Promises, Populist Dangers

Linking the populist repertoire to the structural tensions of the civil sphere helps in understanding why populist performances are somewhat easy to identify impressionistically, but nearly impossible to define satisfactorily in analytic terms. Populist actors are not barbarians clamoring at the gates of the civil sphere, alien to what transpires within it. Rather, the populist discourses they articulate are more easily recognized as a set of discourses combining a wide variety of symbolic materials employed by many types of contentious actors. Many of populism's claims, frames, topoi, jingles, and slogans are individually shared with other types and categories of actors and discourses, making it often difficult to distinguish what is populist and what is not.

What defines populism, in other words, is not a single binary. Peter Wiles (1969) saw it as a syndrome rather than an ideology. It is a broad repertoire of social mobilization tools (Jansen 2011), defined by the combination of many styles (Moffitt 2016, 2017), strategies of political communication (Aalberg et al. 2016) and moods (Berezin 2007). It is a politics of authenticity (Hahl et al. 2018) and sincerity (Garrido 2017) meant to voice important grievances (Ivarsflaten 2008) and express resentment (Bonikowski 2017) as well as redemption (da Silva and Vieira 2018). None of these elements is exclusively populist. Even its proverbial bad manners have often been used by other types of opposition movements as a performative tool.[4]

Defining populism as something rooted inside the civil sphere, however, does not mean that populist actions are just "politics as usual." The "normality" of radical challenges to the established civil institutions needs to be framed in part with an awareness that citizens vary greatly in their levels of political knowledge and engagement (Kivisto and Sciortino 2020). Regarding knowledge, research at the University of Michigan's Institute for Social Research initially conducted in the 1960s offered evidence, subsequently reaffirmed, that most citizens know little about relevant political actors, key issues of the moment, and how the political system works (Campbell et al. 1960). T. H. Marshall presumed a relatively inactive and inattentive citizenry during normal times, in contrast to rare periods of collective efflorescence, which he dubbed "the Dunkirk spirit" (Marshall and Bottomore 1992 [1950]: 46). Recently, Ari Adut (2018) has made the case that most people in civil society are spectators, and that they are comfortable in this role. In contrast to critics such as Robert Putnam, Adut contends that spectatorship is motivated by curiosity. While some with a more republican view of politics might bemoan this reality, from the perspective of CST it is to be expected. Indeed, the very idea of the "performance of politics" recognizes the existence and importance of spectators (Alexander 2004; Alexander and Jaworsky 2014), calling attention to the need to explore actors and audiences in relational terms.

The populist exploitation of the above-mentioned gaps in the structural realities of the civil sphere may have very different consequences according to the robustness of the very same sphere: that is, the extent to which people in different locales at different times are attentive, curious, and committed to the democratic prospect. A second element that can prove to be dangerous is the systematically polarizing "heat" produced by populist contenders. True, the civil sphere fosters a politics in which factions must compete across wide audiences to win over supporters. As Alexander (2006: 123) writes, "Those who wish to assume state power must persuade their fellow members of civil society that they are deserving of their votes, that they will represent their values and interests, in other words, exercise state power in their name."

Left unsaid in this statement is that there are normative democratic boundaries that determine acceptable rules of contestation, central to which is the commitment to the idea that one's opponents are legitimate. And as legitimate, they have the right to engage in ongoing competition for support, the result being a circulation of those temporarily granted state power. This is civil power in action. In CST, partisanship is not uncivil. It is an intrinsic feature of democratic politics, where "normative demands for civility and mutual respect express themselves in figurative images, salty metaphors, hoary myths, and binary oppositions" (Alexander 2006: 49). Contestation – at even its most heated – works in the interest of democracy when all parties maintain a shared commitment to the principles of constitutional democracy. If, instead, opponents are condemned as enemies in the Schmittian sense in an effort to delegitimize them, democracy is at risk (Schmitt 1996 [1932]). When the codification of adversaries as enemies becomes systematic, matched by outspoken hostility toward the civil institutions designed to protect them, populism can shift from a radical – no matter how unpleasant – contender within the civil sphere to a radical challenge to the civil sphere itself.[5]

Are these dangers inevitably embedded in any populist project? Is all populism a threat to democracy, or only some forms of populism but not others? Are there some types of populisms that can expand and strengthen the civil sphere rather than weakening and fracturing it? Most political scientists are adamant that populism is antipluralist by definition (e.g., Galston 2018; Urbinati 2019). Being based, in all its variations, on the assertion that "we (and only we) represent the people," populism inevitably erodes the possibility of negotiated conflict resolution and fosters crisis as the new normal (Müller 2016). Some political theorists, including Marcus Morgan in this volume (Chapter 1), celebrate, on the contrary, the possibility of a potentially positive, plebeian, inclusionary populism with the potential to expand and upgrade the existing civil sphere. If so, how to tell them apart? Is it the left–right divide, or are there other salient differences? Can CST contribute by adding clarity to the issue?

Mapping Populism

A promising starting point for discussing the frequent association of populism with reactionary politics and the possible existence (and social attractiveness) of a progressive populism is looking at the cultural pragmatics underpinning a populist performance of politics. To explore these possibilities, we borrow from Pierre Ostiguy's (2017) socio-cultural typology and adopt it for CST purposes.

Ostiguy presents two axes – high–low and left–right – and brings them together in what he calls a "wheel of axes" intended to illustrate the various combinations and permutations of populism and nonpopulism that can result. The first axis is germane to various strains of populist studies, distinguishing two polarities regarding manners, demeanors, ways of speaking and dressing, vocabulary, and tastes displayed in public. The key feature on this axis is that populism is "the flaunting of the low" (Ostiguy 2017: 73). High antipopulism embraces institutionally mediated authority, proceduralism, and legalism in politics and a cultural valorization of good behavior that is rational, tempered, knowledgeable, and cosmopolitan. In contrast, populism is low, emphasizing a culture that promotes coarse and uninhibited behavior. It embraces parochialism. Its political culture emphasizes personalism, seeking a strong leader with affectual connections to the people (Ostiguy 2017: 79).

In constructing his left–right axis, Ostiguy notes that he is building on a long tradition in political science that sees this axis as a universal feature of democratic societies. The socio-economic cleavage revolves around differing positions regarding egalitarianism. Whereas the left supports greater levels of equality, including but not limited to economic redistribution, the right seeks to legitimize inequality. Linked to this is the politico-cultural dimension. The left advocates for a reduction in power hierarchies and critiques traditional bases of authority. In contrast, the right defends existing authority and hierarchy as essential to the integrity of the social structure, viewing the left's political projects as "threats that erode or destroy" the social order (Ostiguy 2017: 86).

CST's emphasis on modes of incorporation reveals that a critical aspect of defending traditional authority calls for an exclusionary view of who is to be accorded full citizenship rights. Challenges to that authority open up the possibility of an expansive horizon of incorporation of heretofore excluded minorities residing on the periphery into the societal center. And here multiculturalism properly understood locates left–right in terms of the struggles in the civil sphere over inclusion versus exclusion (Kivisto 2012; Alexander 2013b). In so doing, it also speaks to the struggle between those seeking a broader and deeper democracy and those desirous of a more restricted and shallower democracy. Those in the latter category can be either populists or nonpopulists, both working the binary between civic versus ethnic versions of peoplehood (Sciortino 1999).

Radical Right-Wing Populism

As right-wing populist parties have grown in number, gained electoral traction, and in several countries either assumed the reins of power or joined with mainstream parties in coalitions, considerable attention has been focused on what these developments portend for democracy (Kivisto 2017, 2019; Mast and Alexander 2019). One would be hard-pressed to find in the sociological or political science literature an assessment concluding that these developments are salutary, with most offering quite the opposite view. The general consensus is that this type of populism is at its root antidemocratic (e.g., Eatwell and Goodwin 2018). Where observers differ is whether or not they see right-wing populism as being sufficiently robust to constitute an actual threat to democracy (Mudde 2007, 2013b; Müller 2018, 2019).[6]

The distinguishing feature of radical right populism (RRP) is a combination of opposition to some key features of liberal democracy, most notably political pluralism and the constitutional protection of minorities, and a belief in some presumed self-evident inequalities among groups (Rydgren 2007; Müller 2019). This is expressed both as a fear about the future of a restrictive, reactionary version of national identity and as an angry assertion, "you will not replace us." In this regard, culture looms larger as a motivating factor than economic considerations (Hawley 2017). Hostility to "alien" groups is linked to a condemnation of elites who are accused of being responsible for the undermining of national identity.

The exclusionary character of RRP is consequently threefold. The fictive people of RRP is arrived at by subtraction, for not all of the polity's citizens are deemed to be part of the authentic people. First, as noted above, a multiplicity of Others is extracted from the authentic people. The solidarity envisioned by RRP is often primordial, a backlash repudiation of the universalizing aspirations of a relatively autonomous civil sphere. Second, political competitors – depicted as nefarious elites detached from the people and unconcerned about their needs – are likewise removed. If RRP leaders claim that they alone represent the true interests of the people, competitors are not recognized as legitimate opponents with a rightful place in the political process – a fact that often is only clearly evident once an RRP party is in power (Müller 2016). Third, the knowledge elite, socialized in what Alvin Gouldner (1979) called a "culture of critical discourse," is condemned as falling outside of the boundaries of genuine peoplehood. Moving from these premises, it is not surprising that RRP is often characterized by the systematic undermining of the soft norms that differentiate acceptable from unacceptable behavior in the civil sphere (Levitsky and Ziblatt 2018). Systematically preaching uncivil behavior as "authentic," RRP may actually cast a long shadow over what is feared might be the twilight of democracy (Runciman 2018).

Left Populism

In contrast to RRP, which has acquired some analytic clarity on account of research by the people opposed to it, left-wing populism has been primarily explicated by the committed. We refer here to works such as Ernesto Laclau's *On Populist Reason* (2005) and Chantal Mouffe's *For a Left Populism* (2018). Here the interest in populism is clearly oriented by the ambition to find a post-Marxist "royal road to understanding something about the ontological constitution of the political as such," competing with other "ways of constructing the political bond" (Laclau 2005: 67, 63). Laclau is interested in the process by which "a people" is constructed, defined more or less openly with "the central historical actor" (Laclau 2005: ix, 239). Rather than concluding that there, in fact, is no central historical actor to fill the void left by Marx's proletariat after its failure to embrace its world historic mission, Laclau's "people" – an admittedly more heterogeneous amalgam of new social movement actors in need of coalescence into a "people" – are called upon to take up the call.[7]

Building on Laclau's work, *For a Left Populism* sees in populism the potential for "radical democracy." Mouffe (2018: 16) explains the populist moment precisely as a consequence of having entered a world of "post-democracy," in which the core democratic values of equality and popular sovereignty have disappeared, and economic liberalism has largely replaced political liberalism. She writes that the objective "is not the establishment of a 'populist regime' but the construction of a collective subject apt to launch a political offensive in order to establish a new hegemonic formation within the liberal democratic framework" (Mouffe 2018: 80). Podemos and Syriza (with their leadership directly influenced by Laclau and Mouffe) are examples of what she has in mind (Judis 2016). Nevertheless, her relationship to democracy – call it liberal, constitutional, or pluralist – remains ambiguous. Is she attempting to bolster and deepen such democracy, or transcend it by instantiating a novel radical democracy? Is her populism a shadow of democracy or something trying to "wedge out" the civil sphere from the outside (Kivisto and Sciortino 2020)? In both cases, it is clear that this mode of political philosophy does not take us far in providing tools of sociological analysis.[8] Laclau's and Mouffe's suggestions are clearly incompatible with CST, as they rely on a rather underdeveloped understanding of civil society, somewhat derived from Gramsci. Their reference is an "integral state" including both political *and* civil society, blurring the boundaries between the civil and the political spheres (Mouffe 2018: 47).

A different perspective is provided by those empirical studies of really existing leftist populist regimes, generally associated with Latin America (Alexander and Tognato 2018). From a CST perspective, a main difference with RRP is that such regimes are often inclusionary (at least as far as indigeneity, gender, and class are concerned). Leftist movement leaders parallel those on the right insofar as they differ in the extent to which they employ low manners. What is clear is that once in power, there has been, from Perón to the present, a decided tendency for them to undermine political pluralism, doing so in various ways. These include remaking constitutions in their own interests, impeding the functioning of an independent judiciary and other regulatory state institutions, eroding the integrity of the electoral process, attacking the media, undermining traditional political parties, and "using the state to colonize the public sphere and civil society" (de la Torre and Peruzzotti 2018: 44). In short, the historical record does not suggest that these experiences amount to laboratories for democracy, radical or otherwise.

Populism, Nonpopulism, and CST

As the preceding pages indicate, what makes the populist repertoire so powerful is the fact that it can be accessed by many different kinds of contentious actors, radical or even mainstream (remember the "going low" strategy of George H.W. Bush?). Even taken as a full or preponderant package, the populist repertoire is employed by, and in fact characterizes, many different types of populist actors. Unsurprisingly, this makes it quite difficult to define what a populist actually is using a single criterion. At the same time, the use of one or more populist markers does not define an actor as populist. As Ostiguy's (2017) fusing of high–low manners and left–right ideologies makes clear, there are those on the left and the right who are not populists.

We have stressed that contemporary populists are far from being a *tertium genus* beyond right and left. Although many populist actors claim they are external to the classical left–right continuum born out of the French Revolution, we believe it is difficult to deny the wide and substantial differences between the many, successful, right-wing populist movements and the fewer, mostly unsuccessful, left-wing ones. In fact, the main difference between them is precisely the attitude toward the modes of incorporation, the willingness to employ civil codes to expand, rather than defend or contract, the boundaries of solidary membership. Needless to say, such difference is key for CST.

For the purpose of CST work, the most parsimonious definition of populism to arise from our review is that it is *a form of the political characterized by low manners, suspicion toward minorities, and opposition to political pluralism, often matched by distrust of (or even outright opposition toward) the division of power and the rule of law.* All these elements originate in structural tensions typical of all existing modern civil spheres. The populist exploitation of such tensions and gaps implies the risk – but surely not the certainty – of weakening democratic arrangements. In particular, low manners may contribute by advancing a polarizing uncivility and by promoting autocratic strongman leadership. Antipluralism may delegitimize opponents, making them enemies rather than adversaries. Although left and right populism differ regarding the inclusionary/exclusionary binary, they share the basic features of antidemocracy.

This definitional precision is intended to address the concerns raised at the outset of this chapter. It makes clear that there are reactionaries, racists, sexists, and nationalists who are not populists. These political actors may be hostile to democracy without being populist, or they may harbor a restrictive, exclusionary tribal form of democracy. Moreover, this understanding stands in full agreement with Jan-Werner Müller (2016) that being anti-establishment or critical of elites is not necessarily the same as being a populist. One example will suffice to make the point. Bernie Sanders is frequently described as a populist because he calls himself a democratic socialist and is a persistent critic of the economic establishment. His own account of what he means by democratic socialism, however, locates him squarely in the legacy of New Deal liberalism, his goal being the expansion of the welfare state and policies aimed at facilitating a more egalitarian society. And he seeks a politics of inclusion. His manners are high. He embraces political pluralism. In short, he is not a populist, but rather a person of the responsible democratic left.

The account we have offered seeks to spell out the implications of seeing populism as a shadow of the civil, drawing on various currents of recent scholarship and locating them within the broader framework of CST. The civil sphere is the space in social life where democracy becomes a possibility, and to the extent that it is achieved, it needs to be endlessly reconstituted. When civil power is sufficient, it is capable of providing the civil sphere with the autonomy necessary to advance the democratic project. However, CST is far from Panglossian, recognizing that dark, uncivil forces are ever-present in the civil sphere, and there are no guarantees – no evolutionary universals determining – that the forces of light will in the end get the upper hand and the shadows will disappear under the brightness of the noonday sun. CST cannot predict the future. However, as a late-modern expression of the Enlightenment project, it is committed to deploying reason in the service of the democratic imaginary.

Notes

1 The opposite case is also sometimes voiced, usually in support of more "technocratic" institutions. Strong levels of civil participation, so the argument goes, can, through the invocation of the ideal of horizontal solidarity, place unreasonable demands on civil institutions, thus weakening their capacity to operate in an effective and sustainable manner (Crozier et al. 1975; Zakaria 2003).
2 Drawing upon Dewey (1966 [1916]) and Shils (1991), Alexander argued that democracy can only succeed to the extent that it socializes citizens to a moral commitment to democracy as a way of life.
3 Andrew Junker, in his contribution to the present volume (Chapter 9), seems to think otherwise.
4 After all, Joschka Fischer, now a most distinguished European politician of impeccable liberal credentials, started his political career in 1984 adopting an utterly confrontational style, for example addressing the then vice-president of the German parliament with the following opening words: "If I may say so, Mr. President, you are an asshole." Nobody we are aware of has ever called Joschka Fischer a populist.
5 Ateş Altınordu's analysis of the trajectory of Erdoğan in Turkey (Chapter 3) is a particularly interesting example of this shift from radical challenger within the civil sphere to autocratic challenger of the civil sphere itself.
6 Among the most pessimistic are those who draw parallels to 1930s fascism. In her defense of a "liberalism of fear," Judith Shklar (1989: 151) – writing before right-wing populism had gained traction – warned, "Anyone who thinks fascism in one guise or another is dead and gone ought to think again." Is today's right-wing populism one of fascism's guises, or is it different, though bearing a family resemblance? Jason Stanley (2018), concentrating on fascist rhetoric based on the construction of a friend/enemy binary, argues that the term retains its currency. In contrast, Federico Finchelstein (2019: 12) resists conflating fascism and populism, regarding them, instead, as "different chapters in the same transnational history of illiberal resistance to modern

constitutional democracy." He describes populism as an effort "to reform and retune the fascist legacy to a democratic key" (Finchelstein 2019: xiv).

7 While Laclau makes some effort to distinguish himself from both Slavoj Žižek and Michael Hardt and Antonio Negri, from an outside perspective, this might appear to be an expression of Freud's narcissism of small differences.

8 Indeed, that this is not the intention of this project was evident when Laclau (2005: 247–8) contended that he was not dealing with "sociological descriptions," going on to chastise Jacques Rancière for making "certain sociological concessions" (*sic!*).

References

Aalberg, T., F. Esser, C. Reinemann, J. Strömbäck, and C. H. de Vreese. (2016) *Populist Political Communication in Europe*. London: Routledge.

Adut, A. (2018) *Reign of Appearances: The Misery and Splendor of the Public Sphere*. New York: Cambridge University Press.

Alexander, J. C. (2004) Cultural pragmatics: Social performance between ritual and strategy. *Sociological Theory* 22(4): 527–73.

Alexander, J. C. (2006) *The Civil Sphere*. New York: Oxford University Press.

Alexander, J. C. (2013a) *The Dark Side of Modernity*. Cambridge: Polity.

Alexander, J. C. (2013b) Struggling over the mode of incorporation: Backlash against multiculturalism in Europe. *Ethnic and Racial Studies* 36(4): 531–56.

Alexander, J. C. (2016) Progress and disillusion: Civil repair and its discontents. *Thesis Eleven* 137(1): 72–82.

Alexander, J. C. (2018) The societalization of social problems: Church pedophilia, phone hacking, and the financial crisis. *American Sociological Review* 83(6): 1049–78.

Alexander, J. C. (2019a) Frontlash/backlash: The crisis of solidarity and the threat to civil institutions. *Contemporary Sociology* 48(1): 5–11.

Alexander, J. C. (2019b) *What Makes a Social Crisis? The Societalization of Social Problems*. Cambridge: Polity.

Alexander, J. C. and B. N. Jaworsky. (2014) *Obama Power*. Cambridge: Polity.

Alexander, J. C. and C. Tognato (eds.). (2018) *The Civil Sphere in Latin America*. Cambridge: Cambridge University Press.

Alexander, J. C., A. Lund, and A. Voyer (eds.). (2019) *The Nordic Civil Sphere*. Cambridge: Polity.

Alexander, J. C., D. A. Palmer, S. Park, and A. S.-M. Ku (eds.). (2019) *The Civil Sphere in East Asia*. Cambridge: Cambridge University Press.

Alexander, J. C., T. Stack, and F. Khosrokhavar (eds.). (2020) *Breaching the Civil Order: Radicalism and the Civil Sphere*. Cambridge: Cambridge University Press.

Berezin, M. (2007) Revisiting the French National Front: The ontology of a political mood. *Journal of Contemporary Ethnography* 36(2): 129–46.

Bonikowski, B. (2017) Ethno-nationalist populism and the mobilization of collective resentment. *The British Journal of Sociology* 68(SI): S181–213.

Brubaker, R. (2017a) Why populism? *Theory and Society* 46(5): 357–85.

Brubaker, R. (2017b) Between nationalism and civilizationism: The European populist moment in comparative perspective. *Ethnic and Racial Studies* 40(8): 1191–226.

Brubaker, R. (2020) Populism and nationalism. *Nations and Nationalism* 26(1): 44–66.

Campbell, A., P. E. Converse, W. E. Miller, and D. E. Stokes. (1960) *The American Voter*. New York: John Wiley & Sons.

Canovan, M. (1999) Trust the people! Populism and the two faces of democracy. *Political Studies* 47(1): 2–16.

Crozier, M., S. P. Huntington, and J. Watanuki. (1975) *The Crisis of Democracy*. New York: New York University Press.

da Silva, F. C. and M. B. Vieira. (2018) Populism and the politics of redemption. *Thesis Eleven* 149(1): 10–30.

de la Torre, C. and E. Peruzzotti. (2018) Populism in power: Between inclusion and autocracy. *Populism* 1(1): 38–58.

Dewey, J. (1966 [1916]) *Democracy and Education*. New York: Free Press.

Eatwell, R. and M. Goodwin. (2018) *National Populism: The Revolt against Liberal Democracy*. London: Penguin Random House.

Finchelstein, F. (2019) *From Fascism to Populism in History*. Oakland: University of California Press.

Galston, W. A. (2018) *Anti-Pluralism: The Populist Threat to Liberal Democracy*. New Haven: Yale University Press.

Garrido, M. (2017) Why the poor support populism: The politics of sincerity in Metro Manila. *American Journal of Sociology* 123(3): 647–85.

Gouldner, A. (1979) *The Future of Intellectuals and the Rise of a New Class*. New York: Seabury Press.

Habermas, J. (1996) *Between Facts and Norms: Contributions to a Discourse Theory*. Cambridge, MA: MIT Press.

Hahl, O., M. Kim, and E. W. Zuckerman Sivan. (2018) The authentic appeal of the lying demagogue: Proclaiming the deeper truth about political illegitimacy. *American Sociological Review* 83(1): 1–33.

Hardt, M. and A. Negri. (2001) *Empire*. Cambridge, MA: Harvard University Press.

Hawley, G. (2017) *Making Sense of the Alt-Right*. New York: Columbia University Press.

Ivarsflaten, E. (2008) What unites right-wing populists in Western Europe? Re-examining grievance mobilization models in seven successful cases. *Comparative Political Studies* 41(3): 3–23.

Jansen, R. S. (2011) Populist mobilization: A new theoretical approach to populism. *Sociological Theory* 29(2): 75–96.

Judis, J. B. (2016) *The Populist Explosion: How the Great Recession Transformed American and European Politics*. New York: Columbia Global Reports.

Kivisto, P. (2007) In search of the social space for solidarity and justice. *Thesis Eleven* 91(1): 110–27.

Kivisto, P. (2012) We *really* are all multiculturalists now. *The Sociological Quarterly* 53(1): 1–24.

Kivisto, P. (2017) *The Trump Phenomenon: How the Politics of Populism Won in 2016*. Bingley: Emerald Publishing.

Kivisto, P. (2019) Populism's efforts to de-legitimize the vital center and the implications for liberal democracy. In: J. L. Mast and J. C. Alexander (eds.) *Politics of Meaning/Meaning of Politics: Cultural Sociology of the 2016 US Presidential Election*. London: Palgrave Macmillan.

Kivisto, P. and G. Sciortino (eds.). (2015) *Solidarity, Justice, and Incorporation: Thinking through The Civil Sphere*. New York: Oxford University Press.
Kivisto, P. and G. Sciortino. (2020) Reflections on radicalism and the civil sphere. In: J. C. Alexander, T. Stack, and F. Khosrokhavar (eds.) *Breaching the Civil Order: Radicalism and the Civil Sphere*. New York: Cambridge University Press.
Laclau, E. (2005) *On Populist Reason*. London: Verso.
Levitsky, S. and D. Ziblatt. (2018) *How Democracies Die*. New York: Crown.
Marshall, T. H. and T. Bottomore. (1992 [1950]) *Citizenship and Social Class*. London: Pluto Press.
Mast, J. L. and J. C. Alexander (eds.). (2019) *Politics of Meaning/Meaning of Politics: Cultural Sociology of the 2016 US Presidential Election*. Basingstoke: Palgrave Macmillan.
Moffitt, B. (2016) *The Global Rise of Populism: Performance, Political Style, and Representation*. Stanford: Stanford University Press.
Moffitt, B. (2017) Liberal illiberalism? The reshaping of the contemporary populist right in Northern Europe. *Politics and Governance* 5(4): 112–22.
Mouffe, C. (2018) *For a Left Populism*. London: Verso.
Mudde, C. (2004) The populist zeitgeist. *Government and Opposition* 39(4): 541–63.
Mudde, C. (2007) *Populist Radical Right Parties in Europe*. Cambridge: Cambridge University Press.
Mudde, C. (2013a) Three decades of populist radical right parties in Western Europe: So what? *European Journal of Political Research* 52(1): 1–19.
Mudde, C. (2013b) *Are Populists Friends or Foes of Constitutionalism?* Oxford: The Foundation for Law, Justice, and Society.
Müller, J.-W. (2016) *What Is Populism?* Philadelphia: University of Pennsylvania Press.
Müller, J.-W. (2018) The rise and rise of populism? In *The Age of Perplexity: Rethinking the World We Knew*. Madrid: BBVA, OpenMind, Penguin Random House Grupo Editorial. https://www.bbvaopenmind.com/en/books/the-age-of-perplexity/.
Müller, J.-W. (2019) False flags: The myth of the nationalist resurgence. *Foreign Affairs*, March/April. https://www.foreignaffairs.com/articles/2019-02-12/false-flags.
Ostiguy, P. (2017) Populism: A socio-cultural approach. In: C. R. Kaltwasser, P. Taggart, P. O. Espejo, and P. Ostiguy (eds.) *The Oxford Handbook of Populism*. Oxford: Oxford University Press.
Parsons, T. (1965) Full citizenship for the Negro American? A sociological problem. *Daedalus* 94(4): 1009–54.
Runciman, D. (2018) *How Democracy Ends*. New York: Basic Books.
Rydgren, J. (2007) The sociology of the radical right. *Annual Review of Sociology* 33: 241–62.
Schmitt, C. (1996 [1932]) *The Concept of the Political*. Chicago: University of Chicago Press.
Sciortino, G. (1999) "Just before the fall": The Northern League and the cultural construction of a secessionist claim. *International Sociology* 14(3): 321–36.
Sciortino, G. (2012) Ethnicity, race, nationhood, foreignness, and many other things: Prolegomena to a cultural sociology of difference-based interactions. In: J. C. Alexander, R. Jacobs, and P. Smith (eds.) *Oxford Handbook of Cultural Sociology*. New York: Oxford University Press.

Shils, E. (1991) The virtue of civil society. *Government and Opposition* 26(1): 3–20.

Shklar, J. N. (1989) The liberalism of fear. In: N. L. Rosenblum (ed.) *Liberalism and the Moral Life*. Cambridge, MA: Harvard University Press.

Stanley, J. (2018) *How Fascism Works*. New York: Random House.

Urbinati, N. (2019) *Me the People: How Populism Transforms Democracy*. Cambridge, MA: Harvard University Press.

Wiles, P. (1969) A syndrome, not a doctrine: Some elementary theses on populism. In: G. Ionescu and E. Gellner (eds.) *Populism: Its Meanings and National Characteristics*. London: Weidenfeld and Nicolson.

Zakaria, F. (2003) *The Future of Freedom: Illiberal Democracy at Home and Abroad*. New York: Norton.

303

Index

INDEX

SLD (*Sojusz Lewicy Demokratycznej/*
    Democratic Left Alliance) 126
Slovakia 152, 157
Smolar, Pitor, 139–40
Smolensk air crash 125, 130–40, 147
Smolensk Cross 130–1, 136–8
Social Democratic Party (Sweden) 207
Social Democrats (SPD) 187, 189, 191
social drama 50
socialism 21, 145–6, 179, 183–4, 193,
    232, 243–4, 298
    democratic 22
societal community 180, 182
societalization 45–6, 48, 154, 156,
    186, 280
solidarity 8, 29, 53, 68, 116, 127–49,
    237, 257, 274, 278, 281–5,
    289–90
    civil 2–6, 9, 31–7, 76, 78, 178–200,
        279, 283
    democratic 6, 236, 287
    moral 5
    particularization of 205–27
    populist 234–5
    primordial 6, 8, 86
Solidarity Movement 9, 11, 126–7,
    141, 147
solidary spheres 259–60, 269
Soviet Union 11–12, 130, 192
Spaeth, Anthony 51–2, 67
Spain 23, 34, 115, 160, 192
Spivak, Gayatri Chakravorty 215
SRP (*Samoobrona Rzeczpospolitej
    Polskiej/*Self–Defense of the
    Republic of Poland) 126
Stalin, Joseph 130, 184, 199
Stankiewicz, Andrzej 137
Stavrakakis, Yannis 25–6
Štětka, Václav 156
Stojarová, Věra 170
Strapáčová, Michaela 153
strike black campaign 242, 244, 247
Svobodová, Eva 162
Sweden 205–27
Sweden Democrats 205–27, 281
symbolic boundaries 134, 180, 225
symbolism 24, 29, 33, 133, 143, 147
Syria 199, 212
Syriza 21, 296–7
Szułdrzyński, Michał 144

Taggart, Paul 244
Tahrir Square 45–6
Taksim Mosque 84
Team Populism 89
Teehankee, Julio 65
Telewizja Polska (TVP) 125, 129
Terlikowski, Tomasz P. 134
terrorism 87, 152
Thatcher, Margaret 28, 33
thick description 155, 158
Tokarska-Bakir, Joanna 135
trauma work 11
Truman, Harry 264
Trump, Donald 7, 21, 32, 46, 61,
    64, 67–8, 74, 89, 163, 238,
    261–75, 279–80
Turkey 7, 74–90, 168, 186, 284
Turner, Bryan 28
Turner, Victor 135
Tusk, Donald 127, 131–2, 138,
    141–2, 143
tutelary regime 81–3, 89
TV Barrandov 160
Twitter 62, 144, 238, 274

United Kingdom, 12, 20, 27–8
United States 12, 19, 68, 183, 208,
    251–75
Unrau, Christine 284–5
UN Security Council 88
US People's Party 19, 90n.1
Uson, Mocha 62
UW (*Unia Wolności/*Freedom Union)
    126
Uy-Tioco, Cecilia, 55

Velarde, Mike 52
Venezuela 90n.4, 284
Virtue Party 80–1
Visvizi, Anna 159

Wajda, Andrzej 139–40
Wałęsa, Lech 126–7, 141, 145
Wallace, George, 261, 262–4, 268–71,
    275
Wang Lijun 242–3
Warsaw Cathedral 144
Wasilewski, Jacek 131
Wawel Cathedral 131, 136, 139–40
Weizsäcker, Richard von 187, 196